WHILE THE EYES
OF THE GREAT
ARE ELSEWHERE

WHILE THE EYES OF THE GREAT ARE ELSEWHERE

THOUGHTS ON BEING A ROMAN CATHOLIC AT THE DAWN OF THE TWENTY-FIRST CENTURY

BY

WILLIAM L. BIERSACH

TUMBLAR HOUSE
'Bona Tempora Volvant'

**Arcadia
MMVI**

Nihil Obstat: Huh?

✠   *Imprimatur:*   Are you kidding!?!?

Cover art by B. G. Callahan

Tumblar House
PMB 376
411 E. Huntington Drive, #107
Arcadia, CA 91006
www.tumblarhouse.com

AS WITH ALL THAT I DO, THIS EFFORT IS DEDICATED TO THE

BLESSED VIRGIN MARY:

MOST HOLY MOTHER OF GOD
MOTHER OF DIVINE GRACE
VIRGIN MOST MERCIFUL
ARK OF THE COVENANT
REFUGE OF SINNERS
GATE OF HEAVEN
MYSTICAL ROSE
HOUSE OF GOLD
MORNING STAR
SEAT OF WISDOM
HELP OF CHRISTIANS
QUEEN OF ALL SAINTS
DISPENSER OF ALL GRACES
AND
EMPRESS OF ALL THE AMERICAS

Other books by

William L. Biersach

∞

Published by Tumblar House

The Endless Knot
The Darkness Did Not
The Search for Saint Valeria

∞

Published by Catholic Treasures

Of Mary There Is Never Enough

"At least for a while,"
said Elrond.
"The road must be trod,
but it will be very hard.
And neither strength nor wisdom
will carry us far upon it.
This quest may be attempted by the weak
with as much hope as the strong.
Yet such is oft the course of deeds
that move the wheels of the world:
small hands do them because they must,
while the eyes of the great are elsewhere."

—J.R.R.Tolkein
The Lord of the Rings

TABLE OF CONTENTS

Better is a little with the fear of the Lord, than great
treasures without content .

—Proverbs XV:16

∞ ∞ ∞

∞ ∞ ∞

∞   ∞   ∞

INTRODUCTION

BY

CHARLES A. COULOMBE

Therefore there was a remnant left to the earth,
when the flood came.
— Ecclesiasticus XLIV:18

∞ ∞ ∞

SO FAR, THE FIRST DECADE of the 21st century has not been kind to the United States of America, or to the world at large. Opening with a bang on 11 September 2001, it has so far given us war, terrorism, and, as I write these lines, the biggest domestic natural disaster since the 1906 San Francisco earthquake.[*] But these interesting times (in the sense of the Chinese curse), while depressing for all and horrific for those actually living the headlines, will have two results upon those of us who live through them. For the unbelieving, they are random events marking our inexorable march to the grave—and occasionally propelling us there. For the believing, they are highlights on the path to Heaven or Hell—the choice of which destination our behavior during these events will affect. Simply put, they are part of the drama of our individual Salvation or Damnation.

This reality is one that the World, the Flesh, and the Devil constantly work to obscure from our eyes, the better to secure our eternal ruin. But in this hard-hitting work, *While the Eyes of the Great Were Elsewhere*, the distinguished novelist Wil-

---

[*] The destruction of New Orleans by Hurricane Katrina.

liam L. Biersach reminds us of reality. In one sense, Mr. Biersach's opus is an intensely contemporary work; the title is a reference to J. R. R. Tolkien's *Lord of the Rings*, and the noted Rock historian (Biersach's other hat) has his sensibilities planted firmly in this time, speaking to people of today. But what he speaks of are eternal truths, which we ignore only at our eternal peril—despite the best efforts of government, judiciary, media, and the culture at large to sweep them out of sight.

For the actuality of our situation is that human nature, regardless of our technology, wealth, and fashion, is unchanging in all its beauty and depravity—as the disruption of electricity and communications in New Orleans has shown us. How much more unchanging is the Divine Nature, before which each of us must one day stand; every "day of wrath" and "day of mourning" which we must endure in life pales before that general, irrevocable, and final judgment awaiting us. Our fate on that day begins with our reply to that question asked of His disciples by Jesus Christ and continually referred to by Mr. Biersach in this book: "Who do *you* say that I am?" Mr. Biersach not only shows us in many ways *how* we must answer that question, but *why* we must. Moreover, he does so joyfully. The message he brings us is good news; there is a way out of this world of sin and shadows, and our eternity *can* be unparalleled bliss. That being so, Mr. Biersach bids us, as would his patron St. Phillip Neri, to begin the quest for Paradise with hope, with happiness, and with humor. Never, in this writer's admittedly short experience (a mere four decades), has his message been so timely and so needed.

—Charles A. Coulombe
Arcadia, California
1 September 2005
The Feast of St. Giles

AUTHOR'S PREFACE, 1994

THE ONLY SANITY

The Church is a ship, and even if the ship is in dif-
ficulty, it is necessary that we at least be in it.
— Saint Augustine
The Divine Remedy

∞ ∞ ∞

WHEN SOMEONE ASKS ME, "What do you do, Bill?" my
usual prepared answer is, "I teach full time at a university, and
I work part time at a Catholic bookstore." This answer is
somewhat misleading because lately I've been putting in more
hours at the store than in the classroom. In a greater sense, it
misses the mark entirely, for in truth what I am "doing"
every minute of every hour of every day of my life is working
out my Salvation in fear and trembling.

This little tome—or collection thereof—is intended as a
word of encouragement for those Catholics who, against all
odds, are attempting to hold on to their Faith for dear life, or
perhaps trying to rediscover it in the midst of the rumbling
chaos. No one knows better than I how hard that can be in a
world gone mad. It's an arduous and often lonely task.
There are moments between classes on campus when I stop
and look at the students and faculty milling around, absorbed
in their socio-political causes, flaunting their provocative
fashions, expounding on their romanticized pantheism, mesmerized by the undulating cacophony pouring into their ears
through those little doodad headphones, oblivious to their
peril; and I pause to think, "One of us is insane—and by
Heaven, it's not me!"

The Catholic Faith is indeed the only sanity, for it is the sole road to Heaven. All else leads to damnation and is therefore unequivocally insane. Only a madman would desire to go to Hell, yet that is where the world is going in a hand basket. If sanity requires standing alone, so be it. The necessity is not novel to this century.

But the Catholic Church is also in peril, a condition familiar to Her from the beginning. The present hazard is more precarious than in any previous age. Never was the Barque of Peter assailed on so many fronts, both within and without, with such cunning and ferocity. *Leaks are sprouting on all decks, and most of the crew seems to be maniacally attempting to alleviate the situation by drilling more holes!*

What folly it must seem to board a sinking ship and lash ourselves to the masts. But this, too, has been the faithful sailor's song from the outset:

> But we preach Christ crucified, unto the Jews indeed a stumblingblock, and unto Gentiles foolishness:
>
> But unto them that are called, both Jews and Greeks, Christ the power of God, and the wisdom of God.
>
> For the foolishness of God is wiser than men; and the weakness of God is stronger than men.
>
> —I Corinthians I:23-25

To unite ourselves to Christ is to take up our crosses and follow Him to Calvary. This was always the message of the Church until the modernists infiltrated Her universities and seminaries and convinced several generations that life in the tangible, edible, perishable here and now is more important than Eternity in the intangible, indelible, infinite hereafter.

> If you assault the teachings of God's Church, you assault God. And the wages of that sin are certainly death. What is truly inexplicable is why people would reject the filet mignon of Catholicism for the Big Mac of pseudo-Catholicism. Yet this is what a large part of the generation of Catholics who preceded us have done. Still, what is one to expect from the generation who brought us Mood Rings and Pet Rocks?
>
> —Charles A. Coulombe
> *Everyman Today Call Rome*

Our plight today, then, is essentially the same as it has been for all Catholics down through the centuries. We must follow Christ into the thick of battle, until His words resound in our ears more clearly and piercingly than the clatter of swords around us:

> Blessed are ye when they shall revile you, and persecute you,
> and speak all that is evil against you, untruly, for my sake:
> Be glad and rejoice, for your reward is very great in heaven.
> For so they persecuted the prophets that were before you.
> —St. Matthew V:11-12

If we look for the approval and comfort of our fellow men, we will not get it. They will denigrate and denounce us. See, even people who call themselves Catholics—those who have ransacked our churches, wrecked our Mass, and diluted the Faith with their syrupy "dialogue" and insincere "fellowship"—have no tolerance for the likes of us.

And yet, faithful Catholics we are, and faithful Catholics we must remain. Like Simon Peter we can only say:

> Lord, to whom shall we go? thou hast the words of eternal
> life.
> —St. John VI:69

Jesus alone is the Way, and He established His Church as the means. Be it folly or despair, there is no other path to God. But as a very wise character by the name of Gandalf once said:

> "Despair, or folly? It is not despair, for despair is only for
> those who see the end beyond all doubt. We do not. It is wis-
> dom to recognize necessity, when all other courses have been
> weighed, though as folly it may appear to those who cling to
> false hope. Well, let folly be our cloak, a veil before the eyes
> of the Enemy!"
> —J.R.R.Tolkien
> *The Lord of the Rings*

As I said at the beginning, I hope this book will provide encouragement to all the faithful as well as the new seeker of Truth. The teacher in me, however, has not been sleeping. Education has been my profession for going on nineteen years. To educate does not just mean to instruct, but to "lead forth," to develop mentally, morally, and aesthetically—to challenge.

Much of this book is the result of working my way back to the Faith from a position of ardent atheism. There were many hurdles to overcome, doubts to address, concepts to learn, errors to unlearn, and hardest of all, injustices to forgive. Perhaps some of the books I read, the approaches I took, and the solutions I found will be of help to others who are also trying to climb aboard the boat but keep falling back into the sea.

Nothing makes that climb more difficult than open wounds—those gaping, bloody gashes we didn't deserve and don't know how to heal. And each time we approach the boat a wave comes along and hurls us headlong into the bow, pounding the point home again and again that it was aboard this same boat we were injured in the first place. The heart cries, "Flee!" but the soul whispers, "Stay!" And the mind, yes the mind: amidst these anguished and stormy feelings, it is imperative that we understand there were reasons why things went haywire. Knowing what went wrong puts a sword in our hand, for understanding is often the first stroke against hatred.

My reader will come to realize that I, too, have been wounded in the foray. Like everyone else, I have my horror stories. But the very fact that I returned to the Church after a twelve-year hiatus is proof of God's mercy:

> I was found by them that did not seek me: I appeared openly
> to them that asked not after me.
> —Romans X:20

If I could find my way back, blind and bitter as I was, then there is hope for many a traveler on this road to Damascus.

Finally, may I meld myself with a great Saint in his superbly-worded request:

> Devout reader, should this work, as I trust it will, prove acceptable to you, I beg that you will recommend me to the Blessed Virgin, that she may give me great confidence in her protection. Ask this grace for me; and I promise you, whoever you may be, that I will ask the same for you who do me this

charity. O blessed are they who bind themselves with love and
confidence to these two anchors of salvation, Jesus and Mary.
Certainly, they will not be lost.

—Saint Alphonsus Liguori
The Glories of Mary

May Jesus and Mary keep you.

—William L. Biersach
Rock Haven
Init: December 30, 1993; Saint Sanibus (303 AD)
Finis: March 30, 1994; Saint John Climacus (605 AD)

N.B.: Familiarity with *The Hobbit* and *The Lord of the Rings*
by J. R. R. Tolkien is not a prerequisite for the understanding
of this book, though it might enhance your grasp of chapters
two and three. Perhaps, if you haven't read these great tales,
my book will excite you to do so. What's that you say? Not
enough time? Good Heavens, if that is the case, put this text
aside and read the masterwork first! There, that's better.
Wake me when you're done:

In a hole in the ground there lived a hobbit ...

CHAPTER ONE

EXCITING TIMES

May you live in exciting times.
—Ancient Chinese Curse

∞ ∞ ∞

EXCITING TIMES INDEED.

In the decades since the close of Vatican II we have seen a decline in the Catholic Faith such as history has never imagined. Decline did I say? Collapse might be a better word. Disintegration. Pick your favorite synonym for the debacle we have witnessed in our generation. It's enough to make the stout of heart tremble and the otherwise docile sinfully furious.

If my reader is blinking with puzzled eyes—"What are you talking about? Everything looks fine to me!"—it's time for a Reality Inventory.

Simply put, we faithful Catholics have been defrauded of our religious heritage by those who were called to protect it: our popes, bishops, theologians, priests and nuns. We have been deprived of the Holy Sacrifice of the Mass as it was celebrated for centuries, unchanged in its essentials since the reign of Pope Gregory the Great (590-604 AD). The defined morals, dogmas and doctrines of the Roman Catholic Faith have been obfuscated by an influx of modernist theologians and scholars who seek to undermine all that ever made the Church transcendent and holy. And now the bishops and priests who orchestrated this tragedy are falling like so many dried leaves, tossed upon the fire not on account of manly sins for which we can summon some degree of compassion, but putrescent perversions such as pedophilia for which we can only feel re-

vulsion and nausea. Catholic parents are pulling their children out of their own parish schools in droves to protect them from the pagan frenzies of nuns-turned-witches, deeming the burdens of home-schooling preferable to the dangers of exposure to Sister Aphrodite of the New Crystalline Age.

Yes, I'd say these are exciting times.

And guess what? You and I are invited by Divine Providence to live during them. And get this: the tickets are non-refundable.

What's to be done? Well, if you're like most people—including me—your first impulse is anger. A draught of righteous fury has its medicinal value, but do not forget:

> Be angry, and sin not. Let not the sun go down
> upon your anger.
> —Ephesians IV:26

In other words, get ferocious and be done with it. Express your outrage and then let it go like sand through your fingers. Do not harbor your wrath. Do not let dark thoughts eat their way into your soul like smoldering worms.

> Put ye on therefore, as the elect of God, holy, and beloved, the bowels of mercy, benignity, humility, modesty, patience:
> Bearing with one another, if any have a complaint against another: even as the Lord has forgiven you, so do you also.
> But above all these things have charity, which is the bond of perfection:
> And let the peace of Christ rejoice in you abundantly ...
> —Colossians III:12-16

Remember that God requires of us not just to be right, but to be holy. If the state of the Church—or rather our reaction to it—causes us to sin, we are doing ourselves a disservice by our lack of charity and are contributing to the problem rather than the solution.

So, our anger being expressed and assuaged, the next step is to focus our energy on prayer. When all is said and done, our primary duty is not to bemoan the ills of the world but to

save our souls. We cannot help save anyone else until our personal piety is intact. Prayer is our only true weapon; prayer and humble devotion. All else is dust in the wind; or worse, baubles in the enemy's purse. God gave us knees—let's use them.

Thirdly, having accepted these exciting times as God's curse against a faithless generation, I suggest we turn our attention to the blessings which Grace provides in ages of upheaval. It is in times such as these that God raises up Saints. We would not have examples like Sts. Francis of Assisi, Ignatius of Loyola, Thomas More and Athanasius if not for exciting times. It is from the likes of us that God will do likewise in these tumultuous days. So don't just get angry, get excited! Many Saints looked to our day with longing, yearning to stand up for the Lord of Hosts against the forces of evil. They are backing us with their prayers. How thrilling! How utterly glorious!

Ponder the exhilaration that permeated King David's soul as he wrote:

> For though I should walk in the midst of the shadow of death, I will fear no evils, for thou art with me. Thy rod and thy staff, they have comforted me.
>
> Thou hast prepared a table before me against them that afflict me. Thou hast anointed my head with oil; and my chalice which inebriateth me, how goodly it is!
>
> —Psalm XXII:4-5

And lest all this bombastic militaristic language troubles some of us, we may rest assured that we spring from a long line of valiant soldiers. We are the Church Militant, after all; but our weapons are not of iron and steel, but of sterner stuff:

> Therefore take unto you the armour of God, that you may be able to resist in the evil day, and to stand in all things perfect.
>
> Stand therefore, having your loins girt about with truth, and having on the breastplate of justice,
>
> And your feet shod with the preparation of the gospel of peace:

In all things taking the shield of faith, wherewith
you may be able to extinguish all the fiery darts of
the most wicked one.

And take unto you the helmet of salvation, and the
sword of the spirit (which is the word of God).

—Ephesians VI:13-17

Onward!

CHAPTER TWO

THE ROAD MUST BE TROD

"At least for a while," said Elrond. "The road must be trod, but it will be very hard. And neither strength nor wisdom will carry us far upon it. This quest may be attempted by the weak with as much hope as the strong. Yet such is oft the course of deeds that move the wheels of the world: small hands do them because they must, while the eyes of the great are elsewhere."
—J.R.R.Tolkien
The Lord of the Rings

∞ ∞ ∞

EVERY TWO OR THREE YEARS I blow the dust off *The Lord of the Rings* along with its prequel, *The Hobbit,* and treat myself to a generous dose of Middle Earth. I would not be exaggerating to say this is my dozenth time or so. What makes my current quest through Lothlórien significantly different from all previous journeys, however, is that this time around I am returned to the Catholic Faith.

"Prophecy" is not a word I apply lightly, especially in these confusing times, but I can't help but note a remarkable parallel between the state of the Roman Catholic Church today and the shadow that brooded over Middle Earth in Tolkien's imagination. His own Catholicity shines forth throughout the work, as does his insight into the nature of evil and—most significantly to us—the stuff of those who are called to combat it. Hear Gandalf's answer to Frodo's pitiful cry of "Why did it come to me? Why was I chosen?"

"You may be sure that it was not for any merit that
others do not possess: nor for powers or wisdom, at
any rate. But you have been chosen, and you must
therefore use such strength and heart and wits as you
have."

—J.R.R.Tolkien
The Lord of the Rings

Not the answer any of us wants to hear, to be sure. Who of
us feels up to the awesome task of holding firmly to the One,
Holy, Catholic and Apostolic Faith against all odds, challenging all persecutors, defending the honor of Our Lady when
only a few still call Her blessed? Reading about the Ignatius
Loyolas and Athanasiuses of past ages is all very uplifting before settling down into a comfortable bed, but finding ourselves actually living in equally horrific times is quite another
matter! Who—we ask ourselves in all sincerity—are we?

Did not Francis of Assisi feel the same bewilderment when
he found himself surrounded by a veritable pigsty of sacerdotal excess and gluttony? Or Athanasius when he was excommunicated by the majority of the world's bishops because
he fought the Arian heresy which they embraced? Or Pope
Pius V as the Muslim hordes encircled Christendom? Or
Louis Marie de Montfort as he was driven out of diocese after
diocese by those in ecclesiastical authority? Surely in times of
weakness, humiliation, and frustration they must have balked
at the sheer audacity of their predicament. Who were they to
take on the world?

And who are we?

We, as it turns out, are all that is left; and we must do all we
can with what modicum of strength and courage we possess to
carry on till the end. We cannot sit back and wait for knights
and warriors to wage war in our stead. Such luxury is lost to
us. Those who should be our defenders busy themselves with
other matters.

My friends, welcome to Reality. Out of all possible centuries during which you and I could have been born, God in His
Omnipotence knew that this would be the optimum time for
each of us to effect our Salvation. Think about that. Let it
percolate deep down into your being. No human life is an
accident or a throw of the dice. Each soul is infinitely precious and profoundly significant in the eyes of God.

"But if only I'd been born in a safer, saner age," I have sometimes sulked with trembling thumb inserted between pouting lips. "Why couldn't I have landed in some peaceful medieval hamlet built by the sweat of simple peasants around a lovely church run by a devout priest who just leaked awe for God everywhere he went and who would instantly drop pen, fork, or hammer to hear the confession of a penitent sinner, day or night ...?"

Let us be frank. Honesty requires it and the situation demands no less. I know myself better than that, and God's insight is keener still. Life in such a quaint setting would have bored me to nooks. Any faith I would have managed to summon would have been complacent at best and vacuous at worst. Who knows? I may have ended up as the town drunk.

But look at me now: pounding my desk in outrage, poring over tattered volumes of doctrine and history discarded by seminary libraries, debating Dogmas with others of the same ilk, denigrating dim bishops for their heresies and clacking the keys of this computer with ebullient abandon. My Faith is alive; I'm having a ball!

For this I was born. This is my time.

> "... Do we walk in legends or on the green earth in the daytime?"
>
> "A man may do both," said Aragorn. "For not we but those who come after will make the legends of our time. The green earth, you say? That is a mighty matter of legend, though you tread it under the light of day!"
>
> —J.R.R.Tolkien
> *The Lord of the Rings*

And it's also your time. Many were the Saints who looked forward to this age and yearned to take part in the conflict we face. Instead of feeling sorry for ourselves, rather than crying over the spilled milk of post-conciliar apostasy, instead of wringing our hands in despondent dismay, we should rejoice in the honor that God has bestowed upon us—*us!*—to defend the Faith, to stand up to the enemies of the Church, and to endure whatever comes.

Let us never forget this profound promise bequeathed to us in the writings of St. Paul:

> And we know that to them that love God, all
> things work together unto good, to such as, according
> to his purpose, are called to be saints.
>
> —Romans VIII:28

All that is happening around us in the world today, in society, in the Church, in our personal lives—everything is
working together for our explicit good. We must love God
with all our hearts, all our souls, all our strength, and all our
concentration; and hold onto this promise for dear life. It is
all for our good. If we view the dementia around us through
the lens of this truth, we will find that it does make sense after
all. And when our resolve wobbles and we feel the self-
sniffles coming on again, we can recall another promise, this
one uttered by the Savior Himself:

> The things that are impossible with men, are pos-
> sible with God ...
> Amen, I say to you, there is no man that hath left
> house, or parents, or brethren, or wife, or children, for
> the kingdom of God's sake,
> Who shall not receive much more in this present
> time, and in the world to come life everlasting.
>
> —St. Luke XVIII:27, 29-30

Yes, welcome to Reality. It will be very hard, but the road
must be trod.

CHAPTER THREE

BUT TO WHAT END?

> Gandalf laughed grimly ... "There is only one way:
> to find the Cracks of Doom in the depths of Orodruin,
> the Fire-mountain, and cast the ring in there, if you
> really wish to destroy it, to put it beyond the grasp of
> the Enemy for ever."
>
> —J.R.R.Tolkien
> *The Lord of the Rings*

∞ ∞ ∞

FRODO WAS GIVEN A SIMPLE ORDER: to take a golden Ring
and throw it into a volcano. Such a task was not particularly
difficult, nor did it require extraordinary intelligence, military
prowess, or physical strength to carry out. Of course, there
was a catch: the fiery mountain was deep in the heart of
Sauron's territory. Between Frodo's home in the Shire and
the Cracks of Doom in the unspeakable wasteland of Mordor
lay many miles of dangerous territory. The road was treacherous, and the countryside was inhabited by all sorts of vile
characters and deadly vermin. Sauron's eyes and ears were
everywhere. And worst of all, the Enemy was aware that a
hobbit had his precious Ring of Power. He had sent his
henchmen to find him.

Ah yes, the catch. The deed was simple, but the problem
of getting there to do it was another matter.

And so it is with us in these days of spiritual decline. Our
quest is simple: to save our souls, and in so doing, to help others to do likewise. But the task is also very hard, for the path
is the road to Calvary. "There is only one way," as Gandalf

said, but in our case the "way" is Jesus Christ, and the vehicle is the Cross.

We must learn to look at the matter through different eyes than our own. We tend to concentrate on the here and now, on things immediate such as sorrow and comfort, pain and pleasure. But the life Jesus calls us to lead is not concerned with our proximate needs, wants, and desires. These things are secondary, tertiary, all the way to googoliary:

> He that taketh not up his cross and followeth me, is not worthy of me.
> He that findeth his life, shall lose it: and he that loseth his life for me, shall find it.
> —St. Matthew X:39

> Amen, amen I say to you, unless the grain of wheat falling into the ground die,
> Itself remaineth alone. But if it die, it bringeth forth much fruit. He that loveth his life shall lose it; and he that hateth his life in this world, keepeth it unto life eternal.
> —St. John XII:24-25

While this viewpoint does not jibe with the concessions of most of our current prelates—indeed, it wasn't well-received by the powerful in Jesus' day, either—it is nonetheless the decision of the Master, and it is up to us to mold ourselves according to His wishes rather than cater to our own. We must not concern ourselves about rewards, certainly not of the material kind, but not even of the congratulatory kind. These things feed greed and vanity. Our minds must be set on other ends.

> For they that are according to the flesh, mind the things that are of the flesh; but they that are according to the spirit, mind the things that are of the spirit.
> For the wisdom of the flesh is death; but the wisdom of the spirit is life and peace.
> —Romans VIII:5-6

For some of us this is a new thing, a great hurdle. But like it or not, it is *required*. We must seek the spiritual life rather than the carnal. Everything concerned with the body will die, but the things of the spirit will not.

Devotion to the spiritual life brings a great reward: peace. Not the mere cessation of noise and dissolution of anxiety, but profound tranquility of mind, soul and spirit. The peace of God ...

> ...which surpasseth all understanding ...
> —Phillipians IV:7

... cannot be equated with anything the world can offer. It is a peace which endures as long as we focus our minds and hearts on God; but it will crack, splinter and shatter if our attention returns to the things of the world, if we focus on our imminent trials and circumstances.

No matter what hardship we may encounter on our journey, no matter what complication tempts us to be fearful, no matter how deeply we are wounded in mind or in body, we must keep our eyes on Jesus Christ and never lose our peace. Impossible? Certainly—if we were to try to summon such uncommon virtue on our own. But it is quite achievable, and on extraordinary levels, when we accept it as a gift from God:

> Peace I leave with you, my peace I give unto you: not as the world giveth, do I give unto you. Let not your heart be troubled, nor let it be afraid.
> —St. John XIV:27

If we try to grasp this with our intellect alone, it will slip between our synapses like water through a colander. By its very nature, the Peace of Christ defies comprehension. There is no imitation, no substitution, no quick and painless method, no easy detour. When we find it, we will know it; even though the taste is unfamiliar. Those who have not experienced it, yearn for it; while those who have found it, cherish it.

It is such Peace, such focus on the things of God rather than the immediate circumstances, on life eternal rather than physical consequence, that prompted St. Thomas More to write in the Tower of London as he awaited his death:

> Give me Thy grace, good Lord,
> To set the world at naught;

> To set my mind fast upon Thee ...
> To think my most enemies my best friends;
> For the brethren of Joseph could never have done so
>   much good with their love and favor as they did
>   him with their malice and hatred.
> —St. Thomas More
> *The Sadness of Christ*

To regard our most abusive and inimical enemies as our friends—(!!!)—because through their violence upon us they bring us closer to God: now that is the kind of Peace a man could live with. And die with.

"D-d-die with?" you say.

Let us again be frank. The reality is that the times in which we live are serious. The stakes are not just life and death, but eternal life and eternal death:

> For those of us left behind, the question remains:
> How necessary to us is our religion? The litmus
> question is this—would we die for it? Could we, like
> St. Thomas More, sacrifice everything in its defense?
> —Charles A. Coulombe
> *Everyman Today Call Rome*

We may be called upon to sacrifice our property, our careers, our families, our very lives for the Faith. This is nothing new. It has always been the case.

I well remember the prickle of sweat that gripped me when I first read the following exchange between Frodo and his companion, Samwise, as they approached the land of Mordor:

> "About the food," said Sam. "How long's it going
> to take us to do this job? And when it's done, what
> are we going to do then? ..."
> "I don't know how long we shall take to—to fin-
> ish," said Frodo. "... Sam, my dearest hobbit, friend
> of friends—I do not think we need give thought to
> what comes after that. To *do the job* as you put
> it—what hope is there that we ever shall? And if we
> do, who knows what comes after that? If the One
> goes into the Fire, and we are at hand? I ask you,
> Sam, are we ever likely to need bread again? I think

not. If we can nurse our limbs to bring us to Mount Doom, that is all we can do. More than I can, I begin to feel."

—J.R.R.Tolkein
The Lord of the Rings

To go forward with no hope of return: no frivolous flight of happy-ending fantasy, this. Here we snap into the high-contrast of stark Reality. It is all very well to practice our Faith because it brings us comfort in the difficulties of daily life, but it is another thing entirely to hang one's soul so completely upon it that one is willing to sacrifice everything for its sake. Everything.

I repeat, we must learn to look at the world around us with different eyes, looking for that which we have never sought before. We have a *duty* to perform, a thing which has lost its meaning in our modern, hedonistic culture. The duty to which Christ calls us is to follow Him, not serve ourselves. As we make this arduous journey, we must bear in mind that:

> The disciple is not above his master: but every one shall be perfect, if he be as his master.
>
> —St. Luke VI:40

No cheers of congratulation awaited Jesus on top of Golgotha. No presentation of tributes, laurels, and medals. And so with us. There must be no thought of accolades, decorations, and well-dones. What we are called to do is the same as that which is required of every Catholic believer in every century:

> But which of you having a servant ploughing, or feeding cattle, will say to him, when he is come from the field: Immediately go, sit down to meat:
>
> And will not *rather* say to him: Make ready my supper, and gird thyself, and serve me, whilst I eat and drink, and afterwards thou shalt eat and drink?
>
> I think not. So you also, when you shall have done all these things that are commanded you, say: We are unprofitable servants, we have done that which we ought to do.
>
> —St. Luke XVII:7-10

When all is said and done, we must do that which we ought to do. That is all. Every man and woman with the prefix "Saint" added to their name by the Church has done no less and no more.

Ultimately, there will be an accolade, but it waits on the other side of Calvary, beyond the veil of death. Only there will we hear the words:

> Well done, good and faithful servant ...
> —St. Matthew XXV:21

We will then be Home, the place where our hearts and minds and souls have longed to be all along. Having sought the peace the world could not provide, having faced the trial head-on and stood our ground, having given our all to Him who gave it all to us to begin with, we will enter His House and warm our hands by the fire in the hearth. How comforting it will be to pull up a chair beside Master Samwise:

> He drew a deep breath. "Well, I'm back," he said.
> —J.R.R.Tolkien
> *The Lord of the Rings*

Home sweet home.

15

CHAPTER FOUR

OKAY, FROM THE TOP

It's the job that's never started as takes longest to finish, as my old gaffer used to say.

—J.R.R.Tolkien
The Lord of the Rings

∞ ∞ ∞

BEFORE WE GET TO THE END, we must start at the beginning. Traipsing off to seek out the treasure of Thrain, King under the Mountain, peer into the mirror of Galadriel in Lothlórien, circumvent Minas Morgul by way of Shelob's Lair, or venture into Gorgoroth via the Stairs of Cirith Ungol is all well and good, but one must first have a reason for doing so. Curiosity alone will not sustain the adventurer through the thick and thin of the journey. It certainly won't fill the belly on a cold night or ward off cowardice when danger threatens.

So first things first, as they say. Prior to trudging off to Mordor, it would help if we assent to the purpose of the quest. Searching for the Grail makes little sense if we deny its existence or that it once held Something Precious. Before we can appreciate the action of a novel or play, we must first agree with the author's premise, as well as accept as valid—in theory, at least—the status and attributes of his characters.

> There is no doubt that Marley was dead. This must be distinctly understood, or nothing wonderful can come of the story I am going to relate. If we were not perfectly convinced that Hamlet's Father died before the play began, there would be nothing more remarkable in his taking a stroll at night, in an easterly

> wind, upon his own ramparts, than there would be in
> any other middle-aged gentleman rashly turning out
> after dark in a breezy spot—say Saint Paul's Church-
> yard for instance—literally to astonish his son's weak
> mind.
>
> —Charles Dickens
> *A Christmas Carol*

As with Marley's ghost, as well as Hamlet Senior's, nothing marvelous can come of the story if we don't have something absolutely clear in our minds before we go further. In
our case, however, the Thing in Question that we all must understand is far more lively—and in many ways more unsettling—than magic rings, crumbling castles, or ectoplasmic ap-
paritions.

It is funny—in the pejorative sense—how the last generation of the twentieth century has come to view the whole question of God. Our tendency is to assume that He is benign, but
this to a degree that is beyond goodness and on its way to
harmlessness. In truth, we very much want to go about our
business in our own way, to "do our thing" without the inter-
ference of the Old Codger. We seem to have incorporated
into our scheme of things the idea that if there is a Man Upstairs, we hope He will be so kind as to remain up there,
creaking in his eternal rocking chair, out of harm's way. And
if He does care, He will understand that if we *had* put our
minds to it, we might have gotten around to seeking Him with
all our hearts, and though we *didn't* we're still pretty much
okay without his help anyway.

If there is an afterlife (of which we're not at all sure) and
if there is a Heaven (of which we're even less sure) then we are
destined for it (of this we are quite sure).

Religion is perceived as one big mishmash of individual
opinions, no one's more reliable or trustworthy than anyone
else's. It begins with the sophism that each of us is whole and
complete unto ourselves, and is inflamed with the cherished
conviction that we must respect each other's beliefs, no matter
how quaint, no matter how bizarre.

> "Well, now that we *have* seen each other," said the
> Unicorn, "if you'll believe in me, I'll believe in you.
> Is that a bargain?"

> "Yes, if you like," said Alice.
> —Charles Lutwidge Dodgson (alias Lewis Carroll)
> *Through the Looking Glass*

This kind of solipsistic thinking, unleashed, leads to something more than confusing and less than intelligent:

> "What the hell are you getting so upset about?" he asked her bewilderedly in a tone of contrite amusement. "I thought you didn't believe in God."
> "I don't," she sobbed, bursting violently into tears. "But the God I don't believe in is a good God, a just God, a merciful God. He's not the mean and stupid God you make Him out to be."
> Yossarian laughed and turned her arms loose. "Let's have a little more religious freedom between us," he proposed obligingly. "You don't believe in the God you want to, and I won't believe in the God I want to. Is that a deal?"
> —Joseph Heller
> *Catch-22*

Such nondiscriminate retro-reasoned pan-pantheism gets us nowhere, yet it is precisely this kind of quasi-anti-sanctimonious lunacy that prevails in our society. It will come as no surprise that the following was the conclusion of a sermon given by a self-proclaimed "Christ-worshiping agnostic" in an Episcopalian Church:

> This has no doubt been a silly sermon. I am sure you do not mind. People don't come to church for preachments, of course, but to daydream about God.
> I thank you for your sweetly faked attention.
> —Kurt Vonnegut
> *Palm Sunday*

It *was* a silly sermon, I'm afraid—though when I first read it some years ago I thought it profound. That was during a time when I was "away from the Church," as I often put it. Why I left and what brought me back I will leave for later. The important thing is that I am back, and the more important

thing is that the road Home is wide open and available to anyone who has the good sense and Good Will to seek it.

With all the confusion and pseudo-solutions slopping
around us like foam on a churning sea, how can we get
through the storm? How can we see clearly to get to dry land?
The key lies in a question asked almost two thousand years
ago, *the most significant question ever asked in the history of
all the world:*

> Jesus saith to them: But whom do you say that I
> am?
> —St. Matthew XVI:15

Everything, absolutely everything from this moment on
hangs on how we answer it. I am dead serious. Be very clear
about this; I am not being facetious. Virtually every religious
argument, every hindrance, every doubt, every victory—all of
it hinges around the answer to this simple query of eight
words, the biggest of which is composed of only four letters.

Some will reply, "Well, Jesus was a good man who said
some really wonderful things." This is what is known as a
"safe answer." It sounds all right while not committing the
respondent to much of anything. But watch out: it is only a
short step from this seemingly safe position to the conclusion
that Jesus was either insane or a consummate liar.

Whoa. How did I jump from "good man" to "lunatic"
and "liar"? The trek is all too brief. What else can be said
about a man who stands in a public place and proclaims:

> I and the Father are one.
> —St. John X:30

Now before anyone thinks, "Jesus was just being poetic,"
we must take into account His audience's reaction:

> The Jews then took up stones to stone him.
> Jesus answered them: Many good works I have
> shewed you from my Father; for which of those
> works do you stone me?

> The Jews answered him: For a good work we stone
> thee not, but for blasphemy; and because that thou,
> being a man, makest thyself God.
> —St. John X:31-33

They understood Him to be anything but poetic. His
goodness was not at issue, but the fact that He had just declared Himself to be God. To a people whose whole cultural
identity pivoted around the Commandments given to Moses
on Mount Sinai—

> I am the Lord thy God, who brought thee out of the
> land of Egypt, out of the house of bondage.
> Thou shalt not have strange gods before me ...
> Though shalt not adore them, nor serve them ...
> Thou shalt not take the name of the Lord thy God
> in vain: for the Lord will not hold him guiltless that
> shall take the name of the Lord his God in vain.
> —Exodus XX:2-3, 5, 7

—this man Jesus had just committed an unspeakable crime.
Notice their similar reaction to another of His statements:

> Abraham, your father, rejoiced that he might see
> my day: he saw it, and was glad.
> The Jews then said to him, Thou art not yet fifty
> years old, and hast thou seen Abraham?
> Jesus said to them: Amen, amen I say to you, be-
> fore Abraham was made, I am.
> They took up stones therefore to cast at him ...
> —St John VIII:56-59

His claim of being able to transcend time almost got Him
killed. And later, in spite of the darkly looming consequences, He didn't change His story when He was reduced to
a prisoner standing before Caiphas, the high priest, His life
hanging in the balance:

> ... And the high priest said to him: I adjure thee by
> the living God, that thou tell us if thou be the Christ
> the Son of God.

> Jesus saith to him: Thou hast said it. Nevertheless
> I say to you, hereafter you shall see the Son of man
> sitting on the right hand of the power of God, and
> coming in the clouds of heaven.
> Then the high priest rent his garments, saying: He
> hath blasphemed: what further need have we of wit-
> nesses?
>
> —St. Matthew XXVI:63-65

So He certainly wasn't being poetic. His audience understood that, in declaring Himself the Son of God, He was assuming equality with God—that He was, in fact, God. Blas-
phemy, the thing that caused Caiphas to rip his clothing, is not
just showing irreverence to God, but claiming His attributes.

If, then, Jesus made such a claim, what can we make of
Him? What else could He be? Well, if He was sane, He
couldn't be a "good man" because good men don't lie, and
to knowingly say He was God when He was only a man would
not be true. Are you comfortable answering the question,
"But whom do you say that I am?" with "Jesus, you're a
liar?" I most certainly am not.

So what else is there? He could be a lunatic, a megaloma-
niac with delusions of deity. There are beatific loonies
bumping around rubber rooms in every corner of the globe
missionized by the shamans of psychiatry. Would derange-
ment not be our assessment of a man standing on a street corner declaring himself to be God making a personal appearance?

In this regard there is a practical question we need to include: could a drooling lunatic—or even one better versed in
etiquette—design a complex theology aligned with a philosophy so profound it would capture the minds and hearts of
geniuses and dolts, kings and paupers, men and women—not
just for a decade or two, but for centuries to come? Frankly,
this cannot be swallowed. It would be rash and irresponsible
to look Christ in the eye and answer His question, "Jesus, you
are a nut."

Of course, there is always the supra-intellectual fall-back
position of those who buy into the whims of so-called "higher
criticism" foisted on us by self-proclaimed experts in Scrip-
ture-equivocation: "So many scribes, so many translations, we
don't really know what Jesus said in the first place." (Practice

saying it with an academic lisp.) This, of course, reduces the question to a non-issue so it can be safely tucked away in a mildew-scented cabinet in the basement archives. A word of advice to those who try this solution: it will come back to haunt you sooner or later. Like the evidence the murderer tries to sink in the lake, it keeps bobbing back to the surface.

What most people try to do is ignore the question entirely, because the last alternative is simply too preposterous for consideration:

> Simon Peter answered and said: Thou art Christ, the Son of the living God.
>   —St. Matthew XVI:16

This poor rabbi, son of a carpenter, companion of fishermen, friend of harlots and tax collectors ... What if—just "what if," mind you—what if Jesus was exactly who He said He was ...?

Quick! We must brace ourselves for an explosion. Here it comes—*BOOM!*—The shock waves will ripple through every facet, every detail, every thought, word, deed, negligence, nook, and cranny of our existence from this moment on and through the entirety of our eternal continuation. The consequences are that awesome.

For, you see, if Jesus Christ was—is—God, then *we* become the nuts and the liars and the charlatans if we do anything else but fall down and worship Him, hanging onto every word that issues from His mouth, obeying every command He utters. If He is God then He saw to it that His words and their precise meaning were preserved, in writing and tradition, right down to the present day for our benefit. If Jesus is God then the Church He founded is indefectible, destined to last until His return, shepherded by a Pope in a long line of descent from the man He renamed Peter. If Jesus is God then, by gum, we'd better get our spiritual and moral acts together and follow Him as if our lives depended upon it—because they do.

This, of course, is the ramification we've been avoiding all along. We've become comfortable in the lazy confusion of our generation. Jesus calls us to make an abrupt about-face. Whereas we have been calling the shots, He wants to guide our paths. We want to have our secrets, and He demands access.

We want to be left alone, but He is on our tail, hunting us down with merciless Mercy:

> For, though I knew His love Who followed,
> Yet was I sore adread
> Lest, having Him, I must have naught beside.
> —Francis Thompson
> *The Hound of Heaven*

Perhaps the time has come to stop running. Something must be prompting us to reconsider our answer to the question we've been avoiding. Certainly, we can turn tail and flee yet again, but aren't we getting a wee bit weary of the chase?

He has all the time in the world, since He made it—

> All things were made by him: and without him was made nothing that was made.
> —St. John I:3

—but we do not. Our span is limited. Do we really want to risk facing our death without confronting He Who Follows? Do we want to be counted among those of whom it was written:

> And the light shineth in darkness, and the darkness did not comprehend it.
> —St. John I:5

I pray not. The Light of God is so much more refreshing, invigorating and pleasing than the cold, dank dreariness of Satan's shadow. It would be foolish to persist in our arrogant malaise. Sure, change is hard, but preferable to an eternity spent in the excruciating fires of Hell, pondering for all time the waste of our defiance.

This is why our answer to His question—"But whom do you say that I am?"—is so crucial: how we answer it will define the kind of people we will be, the kind of lives we will live, and ultimately the kind of Eternity we will experience.

So, we might wonder, what will happen if we dare to acknowledge the Divinity of Our Lord Jesus Christ? This cannot be predicted with specificity. Each and every convert has a different story to tell. What we can expect, and what the Lord

Himself guarantees, is that our lives will change because our hearts will be transformed. What happens beyond that is anyone's guess, and the Lord's good pleasure.

Look at the example of the first man who answered the Great Question correctly:

> Simon Peter answered and said: Thou art Christ, the Son of the living God.
>
> And Jesus answering, said to him: Blessed art thou, Simon Bar-Jona: because flesh and blood hath not revealed it to thee, but my Father who is in heaven.
>
> And I say to thee: That thou art Peter; and upon this rock I will build my church, and the gates of hell shall not prevail against it.
>
> And I will give to thee the keys of the kingdom of heaven ...
>
> —St. Matthew XVI:16-19

He became the first Pope.

Perhaps it is time we stop pretending to be our own self-appointed popes and embrace the Roman Catholic Church, the only Church founded by the Son of God. The time is now, the question is asked.

Go ahead—answer it.

CHAPTER FIVE

NICE AND HOLY

God loves you just as you are—that's pure heresy
right from Hell. To tell you the truth: God can't
stand you just the way you are! He has to sanctify
you. He has to change you and put a new nature into
you, which we keep trying to slough off. Eighty
percent of alleged Catholics under fifty in the United
States of America reject the Doctrine of the Holy
Eucharist. God loves them just the way they are?
Come off it!

> —Father Paul Trinchard
> "What If Anything Can Be Done with Rome"
> VNI Conference, Monrovia, CA; August 1993

∞ ∞ ∞

I SHALL NEVER FORGET the first time I went to Confession to
a priest who was my junior. (You know you're getting old
when ...) It was about a month after my return to the Faith
after a hiatus of twelve years. He was "new"—fresh out of
the "really new" seminary. The air in the face-to-face "reconciliation room" was thick with his cologne.

When I had finished telling my sins, he took the opportunity to explain his brand of theology: "I did not become a
priest to upset people about Hell," he said with a self-assured
twiddle on the word "I." "Ultimately, God in his goodness
and mercy will bring everyone into Heaven."

"Even Satan?" I asked.

"If he exists, yes."

I was so unprepared for this curious turn in the confessional that I was halfway through my so-called penance—"Sit

and think about God's kindness for a while"—before I realized what had just happened.

I did not become a priest to upset people about Hell?!?!?

It had been my understanding since childhood that in addition to offering Solemn Sacrifice at Mass, the priest's *raison
d'être* was to assist his flock in their interminable struggle
against sin. But this new protégé of the modern age had just
said that everyone goes to Heaven.

Even Satan—if he exists!?!?!

I almost marched back to the booth to ask why the man
bothered to hear confessions, since the logical and obvious
outcome of his theology was that sin doesn't matter.   My
spirit was darkened by the thought that his absolution had
been insincere. In a shameful moment of cowardice, I fled the
place and sought absolution elsewhere.

Such sacerdotal incidents, I fear, have become typical in
the moral malaise of the contemporary Church. The age-old
tenets of the Catholic Faith have been replaced with fresh
ideas, up-to-date concepts, more innovative thinking.   Thus,
many Catholics have come to the conclusion that sin is meaningless, since God is so good that He couldn't possibly send
anyone to Hell. They have re-written the Bible, preferring
their diaphanous insights to those of Saint John who only
wrote down what he had seen with his own eyes:

> There shall not enter into it any thing defiled, or
> that worketh abomination or maketh a lie, but they
> that are written in the book of life of the Lamb.
> —The Apocalypse XXI:27

If Saint John's eyes were playing tricks, then Saint Peter
was unduly concerned when he wrote:

> And if the just man shall scarcely be saved, where
> shall the ungodly and the sinner appear?
> —I St. Peter IV:17-18

Poor Saint Peter—a lifetime wasted on the search for
sanctity. But then, he and the other Apostles had attended the
words of Jesus Christ. How myopic of the Master to declare:

> Enter ye in at the narrow gate: for wide is the gate, and broad is the way that leadeth to destruction, and many there are who go in thereat.
> How narrow is the gate, and strait is the way that leadeth to life: and few there are that find it!
> —St. Matthew VII:13-14

... and ...

> Not every one that saith to me, Lord, Lord, shall enter into the kingdom of heaven: but he that doth the will of my Father who is in heaven, he shall enter into the kingdom of heaven.
> —St. Matthew VII:21

So we come to a conspicuous junction in the road. Either, as the modernists assert, everyone goes to Heaven; or, as Christ and His Apostles and the Fathers of the Church and the great Saints held, the majority go to Hell. Which position is the most plausible?

To put it bluntly: someone is lying. They have lost their Faith and are covering their tracks. If Jesus was God, then surely He knew what He was talking about. These perfidious folks, who no longer believe this of Jesus, claim to understand the Mind of God better than He. Meanwhile they twist the sublime and urgent message of the Gospels into a vague, mucilaginous blur in their own image.

> One reason why Catholic theology has degenerated so much since the High Middle Ages is because theologians are now rarely saints, and mysticism has become divorced from scholarship. It is impossible for the carnally minded to discern the world of the spirit. This is why reliance on the Fathers and Doctors of the Church is so important. They were not always the best "educated," but they had the light of holiness which provides its own illumination.
> —Charles A. Coulombe
> "Communion of Saints"
> *The Angelus,* November 1993

With all due respect to the moderns (*i.e.,* none), I will stand with Saint John, Saint Peter, Saint Augustine and Jesus Christ any day, even if their doctrine does grate against my selfish wish for conscience-alleviation. As I have said repeatedly, this is a perilous age, and in such times we must take our religion seriously.

Somebody has to.

Those who do not take it seriously wish us to focus, not on personal holiness, but on nurturing the quality of being "nice." Nice is good, nice is practical, nice will keep you out of trouble. Nice people are totally non-confrontational. They never bother anybody, would rather die than offend, and they never ever make waves. Virtually every automaton at a teller window, check-out stand, fast-food counter, bar, or passport photo shop is diligently trained to exhibit this useful, saccharine quality. It is useful in that it keeps the wheels of meaningless conversation turning, and it is saccharine in that it is phony as all get-out.

Grab a dictionary and look up this curious four-letter word. It has seven meanings in mine. But take a moment and examine its revealing etymology:

> **nice** \'nis\ *adj* **nic·er; nic·est** [ME, foolish, wanton, fr. OF, fr. L *nescius* ignorant, fr. *niscire* not to know—more at NESCIENCE]
> —*Webster's Ninth New Collegiate Dictionary*

This is the word that has earned a place of esteem in our non-culture: a word which is historically synonymous with "ignorant." Think about that the next time you say, "Have a nice day!"

Then think about the times you have refrained from discussing your Faith with someone because you were afraid that it would make them—or you—feel uncomfortable, that you would not be perceived as a nice person.

Then ask yourself the question: "Was Jesus nice?"

First hint: do nice people almost get themselves thrown off cliffs by angry mobs?

> And they rose up and thrust him out of the city;
> and they brought him to the brow of the hill,

> whereon their city was built, that they might cast
> him down headlong.
>
> —St. Luke IV:29

Second hint: would a nice person scandalize his audience
by criticizing them publicly?

> Woe to you scribes and Pharisees, hypocrites; be-
> cause you are like whitened sepulchres, which out-
> wardly appear to men beautiful, but within are full of
> dead men's bones, and of all filthiness.
> So you also outwardly indeed appear to men just;
> but inwardly you are full of hypocrisy and iniquity ...
> You serpents, generation of vipers, how will you
> flee from the judgment of hell?
>
> —St. Matthew XXIII:27-28,33

Not a very good method for becoming popular at parties.
Nor did He ingratiate himself with the community leaders
when He disrupted their commercial tranquility in the most
intrusive and confrontational way:

> And when he entered into the temple, he began to
> cast out them that sold and bought in the temple, and
> overthrew the tables of the moneychangers, and the
> chairs of them that sold doves ...
> And he taught, saying to them: Is it not written,
> *My house shall be called the house of prayer to all
> nations? But you have made it a den of thieves.*
>
> —St. Mark XI:15, 17

Was Jesus nice? Last and final hint:

> But they were instant with loud voices, requiring
> that he might be crucified; and their voices prevailed.
>
> —St. Luke XXIII:23

No, my Friends, they don't crucify people for being nice.
Jesus was far from nice. He was anything but nice. He was
holy, and holiness infuriates the ungodly who so easily camouflage themselves under a veneer of well-rehearsed nice.

So we come to the next question: do we dare follow the mandate of Saint Paul who tells us to ...

> ... put ye on the Lord Jesus Christ ...
> —Romans XIII:14

... that is, to imitate the Master? Dare we follow Him in the path of holiness rather than hide in the camouflage of niceness?

Whatever its proponents pretend, nice deals with the immediate, while holiness occupies itself with the eternal. Nice seeks at all costs to cast good light on oneself, to convince the other guy you're just swell; holiness assumes that we are swill in the sight of God and demands the taming of personal pride. Nice will back down from an argument, regarding opinions as things subject to change; holiness holds to principles, and would die rather than compromise them.

Nice seeks happiness; holiness spawns joy. Nice employs charm; holiness requires courage. Nice fosters happy feelings; holiness engenders awe. Nice is easy; holiness is hard.

Nice twinkles, "Have a nice day!"; holiness asks, "Where will you go when you die?"

Nice pouts, "What a lack of charity—you've destroyed my peace"; holiness replies, "To hold my peace would be a sin against charity."

Nice says, "I don't want to upset people about Hell." Holiness says, "Why? You don't want to be there all by yourself?"

Nice or holy: it's your choice and mine to make.

I pray we choose wisely.

CHAPTER SIX

SIN

The trouble with being wicked is you don't know
you're wicked. That's the worst thing about being
wicked. And you say, "I'm right, I'm doing right,
I'm doing the best thing according to my conscience."
Yeah, and you're going to go straight to Hell, too.
That's the curse of being wicked: that you think
you're right when you're totally wrong.
> —Father Paul Trinchard
> "Overcoming a Dysfunctional Church"
> VNI Conference, Monrovia, CA; August 1993

∞ ∞ ∞

AS I SAID IN THE PREVIOUS CHAPTER, somebody is lying.
Unfortunately, the job of teaching the Faith too often falls into
the hands of the liars, and how clever they are in their deception. They profess things that on the surface sound profound,
even enlightened to the unwary ear, but which in reality only
confuse the seeking soul. Take this proposition, which is currently used in the instruction of Catholics, as an example:

> Sin is a refusal to love. It is also a refusal to be
> loved by God.
> > —*RENEW*
> > "Small Group Sharing," option 3, week 2

On some level this statement may be true, but why teach
vagaries? In their blatant condescension, they have decided
that the Old Faith is too hard for ordinary people to under-

stand, when they themselves fail to grasp its awesome simplicity.

> Do you know of anyone who refuses to love? Even Hitler apparently loved the human race and desired to rid it of defective stock. Sin isn't a refusal to love ... It is a refusal to love God by disobeying Him. More specifically, actual sin is any willful thought, word, deed, or omission contrary to the law of God. What's so vague or difficult with the truth?
>
> —Father Paul Trinchard
> *Apostasy Within*

It is hard for a person who no longer believes in the reality of the soul to understand the consequences of sin upon the soul.

They tend to say, "If you really didn't intend to do wrong, it couldn't have been a sin." That's like the dieter who says, "I didn't really mean to eat that chocolate sundae, therefore it doesn't count." The stomach is real, and so are calories. Whether you meant to eat dessert or not, or were driven by impulses beyond your control, you gained weight. Regret afterwards is a good sign, but the damage is done. Extra effort tomorrow will be required to undo it.

In like manner, whenever we sin we scar our souls. Our sins are real, as are their repercussions on our very real souls. Each sin separates us farther from God. Each sin repulses Him eternally, for He is infinite in His perfection. Each sin damages us, as sure as a sledgehammer affects a windshield. Try as we might, we can't ignore the soul away. It is not just as real as our physical bodies, but more so; for it is eternal, while our bodies are destined to decay.

What the modernists have done is to take the distinctions originally intended to aid the sinner in his examination of conscience—grievous matter? sufficient reflection? full consent?—and stretch them so thin as to render them transparent and meaningless. These things were meant as clarifications, not excuses. Even those men and women who have not been taught the specifics of moral theology are bound by the Natural Law available to everyone through their senses and reason:

> For the wrath of God is revealed from heaven against all ungodliness and injustice of those men that detain the truth of God in injustice:
> Because that which is known of God is manifest in them. For God hath manifested it unto them.
> For the invisible things of him, from the creation of the world, are clearly seen, being understood by the things that are made; his eternal power also, and divinity: so that they are inexcusable.
> —Romans I:18-20

"Ignorance of the Law," then, becomes a lame alibi when one is standing before the Throne of Almighty God who sees and knows all—not a defense on which I'm prepared to rely, in any case.

> It does not suffice to say : "If I had known that such a thing were forbidden by the law of God, I would have conformed to it." St. Paul, in persecuting the Christians, previous to his conversion, did not think he was committing evil; on the contrary, he acted through zeal for the law of Moses; he did not know then that Jesus Christ was the Son of God and that the Christian religion was divine. The same may be said of very many Jews who persecuted and crucified Jesus Christ. And yet, St. Paul and these Jews were not excusable and innocent. If they had died in this state they would never have been saved, since they ought to have carefully examined His doctrine and, above all, His works and miracles. They would have seen that they were in error. Hence, St. Paul, despite the good faith on which he acts, acknowledges that he was at that time a blasphemer, an unjust man, a persecutor of the Church. If, therefore, a person be ignorant of what is commanded or of what is forbidden, and he is ignorant of it because he has not studied the law of God, his ignorance does not excuse him from sin.
> —Saint Alphonsus Liguori
> Quoted in *The Apostolic Digest*

Another popular tactic among the enlightened liars: "Sin, as the old fogies used to define it, no longer exists. We, the self-sapient, now know that many things which used to be called sins—birth control, masturbation, gluttony, pride, and so on—these are no longer considered sins. They are merely expressions of our self-awareness. They are, in fact, good for us."

How many modern minds have bought into this moral somersault? The hourglass is overturned and the sand is running in the opposite direction. Sin, which was to be shunned, is now good for us. How enticing this concept is to our selfish tendencies. How easy it is to buy into this insidious lie.

But down this road lie severe consequences. Do not disregard the warning of Saint Peter, our first Pope:

> But there were also false prophets among the people, even as there shall be among you lying teachers, who shall bring in sects of perdition, and deny the Lord who bought them: bringing upon themselves swift destruction.
> And many shall follow their riotousnesses, through whom the way of truth shall be evil spoken of.
> And through covetousness shall they with feigned words make merchandise of you ...
> —II Peter II:1-3

Make *merchandise* of us? What a chilling prospect, and yet what does the exaltation of sex in magazine advertising, billboards, on TV, in the movies, in virtually every aspect of our daily lives—what does that do to us? It makes us mere consumers, entities driven by our passions and therefore easily manipulated, pawns to be pushed here and there on a chessboard not of our own choosing. The glorification of sin, be it licentiousness, greed, dishonesty in business, adultery, homosexuality, you name it, bombards us at every turn.

> Hell and destruction are never filled: so the eyes of men are never satisfied.
> —Proverbs XXVII:20

The advertisers know which buttons to push, and push them they do. If we do not keep our guard up constantly, the ideas seep in, the temptations gain hold, and before you know it we're sliding down the mountain away from God and into the lake of fire.

> Let not sin therefore reign in your mortal body, so as to obey the lusts thereof.
> Neither yield ye your members as instruments of iniquity unto sin ...
> ...For the wages of sin is death.
> —Romans VI:12-13, 23

Do we want to be merchandise or human beings? This is not melodrama. This is the cold, hard result of buying into lies. Death of spirit, mind, and soul loom at the end of this path.

Yes, the most pernicious lie of all is this: "It isn't a sin if I don't think it's a sin." Of course! Why didn't I think of that before? How can God (if there is one) possibly punish me (wonderful me) for something that I (with all my heart) didn't think was wrong? That's like saying, "How can I possibly get a sunburn if I honestly don't believe in ultraviolet rays?" or "How can the liquid in this flask hurt me if I assure myself it isn't poison?"

First off, either something is real or it isn't. Something can't be so and not so at the same time. Reality is not an opinion, it is simply so.

And second, what incredible pride is manifested in this attitude, that any mere creature can make up his own rules. God made us just as He made the planets. If the heavenly orbs violated the laws of gravity the universe would degenerate into chaos. If we ignore the boundaries God has set for us, we fall into sin. And sin, like it or not, is sin.

> God doesn't care whether you think contraception is right or wrong. He really doesn't care. He didn't even consult me, why should he consult you?
> *Well, I think it's all right to have premarital sex; we really love each other*—God doesn't care what you think, honey. You can be thinking that for all eternity in Hell.

*Well if I was God I wouldn't send anybody to
Hell*—Well I hate to break this to you, honey, beautiful little child, but you aren't God, stupid.

You've got the most perverse thinking in this generation than probably has ever existed on the face of
the earth.

—Father Paul Trinchard
"Overcoming a Dysfunctional Church"
VNI Conference, Monrovia, CA; August 1993

Does this seem unfair?   To the modern mind it certainly
does.   We are so used to having our own way.   Even to the true
seeker it can be a terrible frustration:

For we know that the law is spiritual, but I am
carnal, sold under sin.

For that which I work, I understand not.   For I do
not that good which I will; but the evil which I hate,
that I do.

—Romans VII:14-15

Nonetheless it is a given that we are creatures, not the
creators, therefore we do not make the rules.   We did not design the parameters of our bodies, nor the limits of our lives.
None of us wished ourselves into existence.   All of these
things are the possession of God.

He makes the rules.   We, therefore, should follow them.
Otherwise we're like the locomotive who thought he was an
airplane.   He didn't get very far.

Our First Parents made that mistake.   They were told the
rules:

Of every tree of paradise thou shalt eat:

But of the tree of knowledge of good and evil, thou
shalt not eat.   For in what day soever thou shalt eat
of it, thou shalt die the death.

—Genesis II:16-17

What could possibly be more simple?   Eat anything you
want—anything, that is, except this one thing over here.   This
will kill you.   'Nuff said—or so it should have been.

But the serpent planted other ideas in Eve's head:

> No, you shall not die the death.
> For God doth know that in what day soever you
> shall eat thereof, your eyes shall be opened: and you
> shall be as Gods, knowing good and evil.
> —Genesis III:4-5

How familiar that sounds—how much like the modern liars. Evil is never very creative, but it is nonetheless highly effective.

To what in Eve did the serpent appeal? Pride. What do the faithless liars of today appeal to? The same thing. And we, like our Parents, are oh so vulnerable to the thought of our own wonderfulness.

> And the woman saw that the tree was good to eat,
> and fair to the eyes, and delightful to behold:
> —Genesis III:6

Is not sin always alluring and delightful? Does it not beckon to our senses, taunt our desires? Does it not trick us into saying, "This will make me happy—this is good for me"? Why else would anyone proceed with it?

> ... and she took of the fruit thereof, and did eat, and
> gave to her husband who did eat.
> —Genesis III:6

And so do we. In no other way is the reality of Original Sin more manifested than in our own susceptibility to fall ourselves. Such is our tendency: to carry on in the footsteps of our First Ancestors. Sin is so much a part of us that we cannot seem to avoid it even for a little while.

> And the eyes of them both were opened ...
> —Genesis III:7

As must ours be also. The time has come—indeed, it is now—to recognize exactly what we are: creatures; and to look to God rather than ourselves to provide the instruction manual.

And provide it He gladly does.

CHAPTER SEVEN

BE YOU THEREFORE PERFECT

> Because it is written: You shall be holy, for I am
> holy.
>> —I St. Peter I:16

∞ ∞ ∞

WHATEVER LOCUS OF HONOR "nice" has found in our society, there is absolutely no place for insincerity in the hearts who propose to enter the Holy of Holies, the House of Almighty God. Rather, God requires perfection in those who dare to approach Him. Jesus did not say, "Be nice," but ...

> Be you therefore perfect, as also your heavenly Father is perfect.
>> —St. Matthew V:48

Perfect? Did He say perfect? How can we ever hope to be perfect? On our own, of course, we cannot. But only the man who has lost his Faith would think himself alone.

We are most certainly not alone. We must get that straight in our minds; let it sink in deep. We are not now, nor have we ever been—even in the most desperate, dark moments when despair all but crushed us—anywhere but in the direct gaze of our loving Creator.

> Are not five sparrows sold for two farthings, and
> not one of them is forgotten before God?

> Yea, the very hairs of your head are all numbered.
> Fear not, therefore: you are of more value than many
> sparrows.
>
> —St. Luke XII:6-7

This is not poetry, this is a glimpse into the concern God has for every detail of His creation. No animal flies, gallops or crawls without His knowledge and consent. No meteor which plunges into the atmosphere and flares into an ash escapes His attention and direction. No proton, electron, or stray neutrino is outside His constant scrutiny.

If He concerns Himself with such minutiae, so much more is He involved with us. To those who say, "How can God keep all that straight? How can He possibly care about each and every one of us?" I respond, "How dare you bring God down to your level? Open your mind to His limitlessness."

God is infinite. Beside Him, the vast expanse of the universe which so impresses us is nothing. For all its tremendous volume and mass, it has its boundaries. It is governed by irrevocable laws, fueled by gravity, entwined in space and time. Space and time are created things, a media in which we are meant to operate. But God is beyond them, outside them more than a sculptor is removed from his statue or a painter his painting. He is in no way bound by His handiwork. Anything so limited, from king to quasar, when set beside He Who Knows No Limits, dwindles to nothing like skyscrapers shrinking on the horizon as your plane flies in the opposite direction. It boggles the mind, but that's okay. There's nothing like a good boggling to blow the dust off the grey matter so we can get down to some clear thinking.

Because God is infinite, He is infinitely perfect. Next to His blazing purity, the slightest imperfection is abhorrent. Utterly abhorrent. Yet—wonder of wonders—He yearns to have fellowship with us. He truly cherishes us with unquenchable love. Our souls, however, are marred with sin. That sin must be flensed from us before we can approach His penetrating Light.

> For thou, O God, hast proved us: thou hast tried us
> by fire, as silver is tried.
>
> —Psalm LXV:10

Silver and gold do not begin as shiny metals. They are mined from the ground as ores: mineral deposits of which only a small constituent is the desired metal. The ore must be fired, refined, melted down; so that the precious metal separates from the residue and rises to the surface. This is what "refined" means: to be reduced to a pure state, to be freed from moral imperfection. We must be refined to enter into fellowship with God, otherwise we would be annihilated by His indescribable Holiness.

Perfection is required, therefore we aspire to it. It cannot be achieved in the blink of an eye, nor the in passing of one night. It takes a great deal of time, attention, and effort—commodities our microwaveable generation does not spend with a flourish. Nonetheless we must overcome the inertia of our culture and become something new: individuals—thinking, believing, earnestly seeking individuals.

So how can we even begin to be perfect?

First we must recognize the reality of the state of sin in which we find ourselves. If a person won't accept the fact of his disease, he won't seek a cure. If we deny the actuality of sin, we cannot begin our journey to God.

Perhaps the hardest thing for the current generation to swallow is the truth of Original Sin. "Why should we be held responsible," we declare defiantly, "for something our ancestors did?" This sentiment changes abruptly when a rich uncle dies and the disposition of his estate commences.

We owe our physical characteristics to our ancestors, of this there is no doubt: I have my dad's physique—such as it is—and my mother's nose.

But man is more than body: I also seem to have inherited Dad's penchant for books and Mom's tendency to forget peoples' names. Since painting was the forte of neither parent, it seems to have percolated down from further up the chute. And as for musical interest, I'd say there must be a whole orchestra of progenitors in my genetic panoply. Would that I had inherited my grandfather's knack for organization, but one can't have everything. In any case, I derived more from my parents than appearances.

But man is still more, much more. It is our nature to be a union of body and soul, straddling the fence between two entirely different realms. We have one foot, so to speak, in the physical plane and the other in the spiritual. If we inherit physical traits, why not spiritual ones? If I can inherit my father's money, my grandfather's hairline, and my great-grandmother's predilection for poetry, why should I exclude sin from the estate?

We must not slough off the story of the Fall of Adam and Eve, nor discount Genesis as mere myth. A sober assessment of the first book of the Bible is an absolute prerequisite for understanding everything to do with Salvation. On this we must stand firm and not be swept away by winds of doubt hotly blown by self-aggrandizing scholars and self-proclaimed experts. We must heed, rather, the words of Jesus Christ Himself:

> For if you did believe Moses, you would perhaps believe me also; for he wrote of me.
> But if you do not believe his writings, how will you believe my words?
> —St. John V:46-47

He had too much at stake to waste time on euphemisms or epic poetry. He came into the world to repair the damage done to the whole Human Race by the Fall of our First Parents as told in Genesis. The "why" of Salvation is to be found there.

Just because we may balk at the idea of Original Sin doesn't make it not so. We all share in Adam's sin—period. Original Sin is like a disease, a terrible fatal congenital disease. If a baby is born in a hospital with a correctable heart problem, do not the parents move Heaven and Earth to get the necessary surgery performed immediately? What would be our reaction if the parents instead said, "We refuse to believe that our precious little baby is anything but perfect?" Well, each and every human being is born with a spiritual disease: Original Sin. And make no mistake, Original Sin is mortal, deadly, and ugly in the sight of God. It is correctable, but not if we swoon in a state of self-righteous denial.

Saint Paul was not indulging in hyperbole when he wrote:

> As it is written: *There is not any man just.*
> *There is none that understandeth, there is none that seeketh after God.*

*All have turned out of the way, they are become
unprofitable together: there is none that doth good,
there is not so much as one.*
— Romans III:10-12

Nor was King David, whom Saint Paul was quoting, when he
sang:

The Lord hath looked down from heaven upon the
children of men, to see if there be any that understand
and seek God.
They are all gone aside, they are become unprofitable together, there is none that doth good, no not
one.
— Psalm XIII:2-3

Or, as a twentieth century priest has so succinctly put it:

You and I are rotten sinners going to Hell.
— Father Paul Trinchard
"All About Salvation"
VNI Conference, Monrovia, CA; January, 1994

This is why Jesus Christ came into the world: to affect a
cure on our congenital disease which would otherwise land us
in Hell.

For by a man came death, and by a man the resurrection of the dead.
And as in Adam all die, so also in Christ all shall
be made alive.
— I Corinthians XV:21-22

Once we recognize the stone-hard reality of Original Sin,
we must rid ourselves of it in Baptism:

And he said to them: Go ye into the whole world,
and preach the gospel to every creature.
He that believeth and is baptized, shall be saved:
but he that believeth not shall be condemned.
— St. Mark XVI:16

Do not be put off by the simplicity of this Sacrament.
Why God chose to cleanse us of Original Sin by a mere dose
of water on the head is beyond our purview. Nonetheless, it is
in keeping with His pattern. In the Old Testament, for example, a Syrian general named Naaman sought the help of Eliseus the prophet to cure his leprosy. Eliseus' instruction was
simply:

> Go, and wash seven times in the Jordan, and thy
> flesh shall recover health, and thou shalt be clean.
> —IV Kings V:10

Naaman, expecting more dazzle, stomped away furious.
He wanted more kick, more *shtick,* more pizzazz for his trouble. But his servants, who were perhaps more used to the less-
than-spectacular, said to him:

> Father, if the prophet had bid thee do some great
> thing, surely thou shouldst have done it: how much
> rather what he now hath said to thee: Wash, and thou
> shalt be clean?
> —IV Kings V:13

Only when Naaman got down off his high horse and
washed in the Jordan did God effect a cure.

Baptism, then, is the simple pouring of water and the utterance of a few words: "I Baptize you in the Name of the Father, and of the Son, and of the Holy Ghost." As with all the
Sacraments, God chooses simple actions and ordinary materi-
als to effect profound Realities.

> Here, then, in one sacrament, we find the whole
> plan of salvation. Christ in the gospel ordered it as
> clearly as He did the Mass. Baptism cleanses us of
> original sin, and thus accomplishes the goal of regen-
> eration, of restoring us to God's grace. All the sac-
> raments become available to us, and we are incorpo-
> rated into the Mystical Body of Christ.
> —Charles A. Coulombe
> *Everyman Today Call Rome*

The need for water Baptism cannot be overemphasized. Those who quote Scripture out of context—

> Amen, amen I say to thee, unless a man be born
> again, he cannot see the kingdom of God.
> —St. John III:3

—are editing the story to fit their own conclusions as to what should be necessary for Salvation. They want to dodge the embarrassment of having water poured on their heads, or the hassle of having it done to their kids. They want to "just believe" and be done with it. There's no way around it: coming to God requires humility—something few of us can muster without Herculean effort. But if mighty Naaman could learn the lesson, so can we. In any case, this oft-quoted line—from which "born-again Christians" derive their handle—is only the beginning of the story. We must look further for the whole truth.

As soon as Jesus spoke the words, "Unless a man be born again," Nicodemus, a Pharisee and an important man in the Jewish community, revealed his lack of comprehension:

> How can a man be born when he is old? can he enter a second time into his mother's womb, and be born again?
> —St. John III:4

Nicodemus had his eyes and understanding set on what he was willing and able to visualize rather than on the new possibilities Christ proposed. Like so many people then and now, his expectations were material rather than spiritual. In response to his quandary, Jesus explained Himself in more detail:

> Amen, amen I say to thee, unless a man be born
> again of water and the Holy Ghost, he cannot enter
> into the kingdom of God.
> That which is born of the flesh, is flesh; and that
> which is born of the Spirit, is spirit.
> —St. John III:5-6

So the rebirth of which Jesus spoke was not the same as the physical birth through which we enter the world, though it is every bit as real. There is a breach between the physical and the ethereal, between the flesh and the spirit—a chasm which somehow must be bridged. Being "born again" is not just a mental decision to cross over, but a physical action involving "water and the Holy Ghost."   At the moment of Baptism a miracle takes place—not just of belief, but of total rebirth. The water signifies that a change is occurring, while the Holy Ghost breathes new life into the soul. This transformation is genuine, not imagined, not theoretical. It is akin to resuscitating a stillborn baby. The soul, once dead through Original Sin, is now awakened to a whole new life. If we understand the dynamics, we should not be surprised at all by His initial declaration of the need for rebirth.

> Wonder not, that I said to thee, you must be born again.
> —St. John III:7

Baptism—the application of water and the action of the Holy Ghost—is not just some innocuous ritual that we dig up when we have our own kids because we have some vague sense of tradition, or because our in-laws put pressure on us. Like the cure of Naaman's leprosy, it marks a profound turning point in a person's health, only more so. The healed flesh, like the rest of the body, will eventually wear out, die, and decay. The soul is immortal, and will live on for eternity. It is the quality of that eternity that is at stake.

Of course, none of this makes any sense if we don't believe in the soul, or eternity, or the divinity of Jesus Christ. If we cannot look beyond our carnal nature, we remain like Naaman pouting at Elesius' tent, tied to that which we can see and touch, oblivious to the blessings that abound in God's kingdom.

> Lay not up yourselves treasures on earth: where the rust, and moth consume, and where thieves break through and steal.

But lay up yourselves treasures in heaven: where
neither rust nor moth doth consume, and where
thieves do not break through, nor steal.
For where thy treasure is, there is thy heart also.
                                        —St. Matthew VI:19-21

Heaven provides a much better bank than the savings and
loan on the corner. The security is awesome, the options phe-
nomenal, and the interest rates—incredible!   I suggest we
transfer our accounts immediately.

CHAPTER EIGHT

AND WALK IN HIS WAYS

> Wherefore, my dearly beloved ... with fear and trembling work out your salvation.
> For it is God who worketh in you, both to will and to accomplish, according to *his* good will.
>
> —Philippians II:12-13

∞ ∞ ∞

BAPTISM, THEREFORE, CLEANSES US from Original Sin. Through reception of this simple Sacrament, our souls are given the new life of Sanctifying Grace by which we become children of God and heirs of Heaven. Now we are members of the Catholic Church. We are subject to Her laws and eligible to receive Her other Sacraments. This being accomplished, we proceed to the next phase: spiritual growth.

If the whole point of the exercise is to become pleasing to God so that we may one day stand in His Holy Presence free from stain and agreeable to His infinite purity—and thus avoid annihilation—it is reasonable that we should follow the advice of Saint Paul and ...

> ... put ye on the Lord Jesus Christ, and make not provision for the flesh in its concupiscences.
>
> —Romans XIII:14

That is, we must imitate the Master; learn to deny our very selves of that for which we naturally hunger. After all, it was of Jesus Christ that God the Father said:

> Thou art my beloved Son; in thee I am well
> pleased.
>
> —St. Mark I:11

What better example to follow than that of Jesus Christ,
beloved Son of the Father?

Ah, but now the already ponderous road becomes impos-
sibly steep—at least to the beleaguered soul looking for excuses to quit. We must remind ourselves again and again: we
are not alone. God does not expect us to make it on our own.
He is more aware than we of our hopelessness. Remember
that Jesus didn't just sit up in Heaven, crooking a condescending finger at us ...

> But emptied himself, taking the form of a servant,
> being made in the likeness of men, and in habit found
> as a man.
> He humbled himself, becoming obedient unto
> death, even to the death of the cross.
>
> —Philippians II:7

He met us more than halfway, descending from Heaven to
be in our midst, to live as we live, to share in our humanity.
What more could a Creator do to prove His ardent desire to
have fellowship with His creatures?

> Behold, I stand at the gate, and knock. If any man
> shall hear my voice, and open to me the door, I will
> come in to him, and will sup with him, and he with
> me.
> To him that shall overcome, I will give to sit in
> my throne: as I also have overcome, and am set down
> with my Father in his throne.
>
> —The Apocalypse III:20-21

There's a knock at the door. Dare we not answer it? And,
having asked Him into our lives, are we not bound to recipro-
cate by entering into His? We must reform ourselves, spurn-
ing the sins that drag us back toward the tendencies we left
behind.

> Know you not that all we, who are baptized in
> Christ Jesus, are baptized in his death?
> For we are buried together with him by baptism
> into death; that as Christ is risen from the dead by the
> glory of the Father, so we also may walk in newness
> of life.
>
> —Romans VI:3-4

Original Sin is like a disease that, though cured, leaves the body weakened, prone to re-infection. So too our soul, and our weak human nature. Baptism brings us new life, but our flesh is still weak and our desires askew.

> Let not sin therefore reign in your mortal body, so
> as to obey the lusts thereof.
> Neither yield ye your members as instruments of
> iniquity unto sin; but present yourselves to God, as
> those that are alive from the dead, and your members
> as instruments of justice unto God.
>
> —Romans VI:12-13

Just as He renounced His own will in deference to His Father—

> Father, if thou wilt, remove this chalice from me:
> but yet not my will, but thine be done.
>
> —St. Luke 22:42

—so do we conform our wills to His.

We must cast aside such thoughts as, "If He really loved me, He would love me just as I am." That's the talk of a spiritually spoiled child. What good mother would allow her toddler to sit in a mud puddle for the rest of his life, just because he's happy there for the moment? What loving father would indulge his daughter's every selfish whim, teaching her to expect everything and work toward nothing? A parent does not love his child less when he denies his offspring opportunities for stagnation. Will the child be ungrateful when the parent so loves? Of course, for the child does not see the whole picture. Growth requires discipline, and correction is often painful, but the end result is a mature human being rather than a blathering brat.

God calls us to an even higher level, to become Saints. The time has come to stop stalling and start actively pursuing a life of holiness.

> The disciple is not above his master: but every one shall be perfect, if he be as his master.
> —St. Luke VI:40

What was good enough for Jesus is certainly the right course for us. He beckons us to follow, the road peppered with signposts of guidance in the Scriptures, Saints for examples, the Church for support, and Sacraments as refreshments for reviving the tired spirit. But make no mistake, to walk in His shoes is the greatest challenge we have ever faced:

> For unto this are you called: because Christ also suffered for us, leaving you an example that you should follow his steps.
> *Who did no sin, neither was guile found in his mouth.*
> Who, when he was reviled, did not revile: when he suffered, he threatened not: but delivered himself to him that judged him unjustly.
> Who his own self bore our sins in his body upon the tree: that we, being dead to sins, should live to justice: by whose stripes you were healed.
> For you were as sheep going astray; but you are now converted to the shepherd and bishop of your souls.
> —I St. Peter II:21-25

With a goal so lofty, we must be prepared for failure. And fail we will, being weak and fragile, prone to all sorts of temptations.

Of course, the Good Lord has provided for that contingency, too. Funny, do we begin to see a Divine Pattern in the making? Does the delightful thought begin to form that maybe, just maybe, God does have us figured out and has already seen to our needs before we perceive them ourselves? That maybe He knows what He's doing?

Perhaps it made sense after all to put our trust in Him. How about that?

CHAPTER NINE

CAPSICUM

He who hides his sins shall not prosper, but he who shall confess and forsake them shall obtain mercy.

— Proverbs XXVIII:13

∞ ∞ ∞

"CAPSICUM" IS THE GENUS of tropical herbs of the night-shade family widely cultivated for their many-seeded, fleshy-walled berries, also known as chili peppers. I chose it as the title for this chapter because 1) it is appropriate to the "hot" subject at hand, 2) it sounds sort of Latiny, like it could be the name of an order of minor friars or fit nicely after the word "Dominus," and 3) if I had called this chapter "Confession" some of my readers would have skipped over it.

Some may think to do so now—but please don't. This is something we really do need to look into. It isn't just a matter of religious theory, but of solid, concrete necessity.

Here we come to the meat of the topic. This is the sacrament concerned with sin. We young moderns, of course, have none. Before the great stupefaction of the 1960's, however, sin was very much a problem. People did all sorts of things. They lied, they cheated, they stole. Some drank, took drugs or gambled, to the detriment of their families, while others cheated on their wives, or selected lovers of the inappropriate sex. Some fornicated while others embezzled, and all had pride, envy, jealousy, and a ton of other little flaws. It was into such a world Our Lord

came, and began, upon repentance, to forgive sins.
His Church, following His mandate, continued to do
so.

—Charles A. Coulombe
Everyman Today Call Rome

The standard argument against the Sacrament of Penance—I say "standard" because it's used so often one begins
to think everyone's been coached by the same heretic—goes
like this: "Why should I tell my sins to a priest? Why can't I
just pray directly to God for His forgiveness?" Those more
Scripturally proficient will then produce a verse from the Bible as "Dissenter's Exhibit A":

For there is one God, and one mediator of God and
men, the man Christ Jesus.

—I Timothy II: 5

The key to their objection is not to be found in the direct-
ness of one's prayer to God, or the applicability of the citation
from Scripture—which we will address in a moment—but in
the word "I."

Why should the great "I" have to admit to anyone else
the things "I'm" ashamed to even think about? How humiliating. "I" would rather just forget my mistakes, thank-you
very much. My pride would be much better accommodated if
"I" just said a quick, "Sorry, Lord," and went on about my
business.

It is not enough that a man acknowledge his sins to
God, from Whom nothing is hidden; he must also
confess them to the priest, God's representative. The
Redeemer Himself does not forgive sins without penance.

—Saint Augustine
Quoted in *The Apostolic Digest*

The method of the Sacrament, that is, saying our sins
aloud to another human being, addresses these very issues that
we would rather avoid. We *should* be ashamed of our sins. If
they repulse us in the telling, and shame us before our fellow
man, how much more abhorrent must they be to Almighty

God. We need to recognize the sheer ugliness of our sins. If
we keep them secret, hidden within our hearts, we will in time
become accustomed to them. We will learn to live with them,
and thus be more comfortable with ourselves. If we get too
complacent, if our sins no longer grate against the sensitive
membrane of our consciences, we run the risk of denying our
sinfulness altogether.

> Today, due to the realization of self-perfection oc-
> curring about the time of Haight-Ashbury and the
> Summer of Love, many, if not most, Catholics in
> America have abandoned the practice [of Confession].
> It is to be hoped that God will see them as sinless as
> they see themselves on the day of judgment.
> —Charles A. Coulombe
> *Everyman Today Call Rome*

The next part of the sacramental method which so per-
turbs us is that the human being to whom we must reveal our
tarnishes has been given power through Holy Orders to wipe
them clean—or *not*—depending on his judgment as to
whether we are sincere in our repentance. For example, I
might confess that I spread untruths in anger against a friend
who betrayed a confidence. The priest might, if he's
sharp—and believe it or not, there are a few left—ask something intolerable like, "Have you forgiven her?" Gulp. I
hadn't thought of that. If the honest answer—and we must try
hard to be honest—is no, then he must refuse absolution.
How appalling. How embarrassing. Here I thought I'd made
a clean breast of things and this nosy provocateur comes up
with something I missed. Who does he think he is? Why, I'm
so furious I'm on the verge of another sin ...
        But wait. If I go off half-cocked like that I'm missing a
salient point: the priest just rendered me a service. We are,
after all, seeking the perfection of the Father in order to be
pleasing to Him. Do we really suppose that we, fallen as we
are, corrupt as we are, are truly capable of ferreting out the last
drop of our own sinfulness? Have not the lessons of life
taught us that we are the poorest judges of our own character?—that often it takes another point of view to cut through
the camouflage with which we protect ourselves from our own
vileness? We should be grateful to encounter such a priest, a

man with the courage to do his job, to help his flock seek out
and overcome sin.

Put an extra five bucks in his collection plate.

And then—assuming we are contrite of heart and he gives
us Absolution—there's the Penance. It's not that bad: a few
prayers to say, an act of charity to perform. I wonder how
many people who want the "quick fix," the direct-to-God
approach, bother to do anything extra as an offering to demonstrate their sincerity?

In any case, the point is that we come to recognize our sins
for what they are: offenses against God for which we should
feel shame and sorrow. If we can't muster genuine remorse,
then fear of Divine Punishment will do—imperfect contrition
is covered by the Grace of the Sacrament. Fear of Hell suf-
fices when Love of God is running thin.

We must tell all—repeat all—our mortal sins. A sure way
to blow the Sacrament is to knowingly hold back something.
Tell all and don't make excuses—no matter how convincing
your rationalization is to you, the priest will see it as lame.
Then say your penance and walk away with a clean slate. It's
very simple, really.

> Be converted to me with all your heart, in fasting,
> and in weeping, and in mourning.
> And rend your hearts, not your garments, and turn
> to the Lord your God: for he is gracious and merciful,
> patient and rich in mercy ...
>
> —Joel II:12-13

In all our discussions we must remind ourselves of the
question we considered a few chapters back:

> Jesus saith to them: But whom do you say that I
> am?
>
> —St. Matthew XVI:15

How we answer this question affects everything in our lives
thereafter. One of the wonderful things about genuine Catholicism, as opposed to the artificial variety so prevalent today, is that it is entirely reasonable—reasonable not in the
sense of agreeable, but in the classic sense of rationally sound.
It is reasonable to believe that Jesus Christ is God, therefore we

are compelled to do so. If Jesus is God, then it is reasonable for us to heed what He has to say.

On the very day He rose from the dead, Jesus went and stood before the Apostles and said,

> ... Peace be to you. As the Father hath sent me, I also send you.
>
> When he had said this, he breathed on them; and he said to them: Receive ye the Holy Ghost.
>
> Whose sins you shall forgive, they are forgiven them; and whose *sins* you shall retain, they are retained.
>
> — St. John XX:21-23

Notice the sense of mission in His words, "As the Father hath sent me, I also send you." He is sending them out into the world to accomplish a task. Notice, too, the involvement of the Holy Ghost, Who was also the catalyst in the Sacrament of Baptism along with the outward sign of water. Then He gives them the power to forgive sins — and *not* to forgive sins.

In the Gospel of Saint Mark, Jesus told a man with palsy:

> Son, thy sins are forgiven thee.
>
> — St. Mark II:5

Immediately the scribes and Scripture experts thought to themselves:

> Why doth this man speak thus? he blasphemeth. Who can forgive sins, but God only?
>
> — St. Mark II:7

Jesus' response was to heal the man of palsy in order to prove that He also had the power to forgive sins — a power reserved only to God. Just as a king can appoint a delegation as an extension of his royal authority, so could Jesus as God designate the Apostles and their successors as emissaries with diplomatic powers.

This is precisely what He did. He gave the Apostles the power to forgive the sins of repentant sinners, and refuse absolution to those whose remorse was insincere. Thus the Sacrament of Penance was established. We who follow Christ are required to admit our sins aloud to a priest, whose power to forgive our wrongdoings has been passed down by the laying on of hands from bishop to priest for two thousand years. We may not like it, but it's one of His stipulations.

And, wonder of wonders, it works.

How certain can one really be of the direct-to-God approach? Were we penitent enough, was our sincerity intact? As imperfect as we are, can we ever be sure our internal prayer to God was truly adequate? On the other hand, saying the Act of Contrition, hearing the priest's words of Absolution, saying the Penance—these outward signs give us a tangible reference on which to hang our Faith. Sometimes we're very sorry for our failings indeed, other times it's hard to muster a true sense of remorse. But as long as we give it our best shot, no matter our mood, no matter the distractions, we can count on the efficacy of the Sacrament because Jesus established it. There is great consolation in this: a sense of relief, of completion, of "Okay, that's behind me—now for another try."

As for the appeal to Saint Paul's First Epistle to Timothy, also known as "Dissenter's Exhibit A," Paul was not talking about Confession or anything of the sort. If we read the whole passage, we realize that the verse in question is actually said in passing:

> I desire, therefore, first of all, that supplications, prayers, intercessions, and thanksgivings be made for all men.
>
> For kings, and for all that are in high station: that we may lead a quiet and a peaceable life in all piety and chastity.
>
> For this is good and acceptable in the sight of God our Savior,
>
> Who will have all men to be saved, and to come to the knowledge of the truth.
>
> For there is one God, and one mediator of God and men, the man Christ Jesus;
>
> Who gave himself a redemption for all, a testimony in due times.
>
> Whereunto I am appointed a preacher and an apostle
> ...
>
> —I Timothy II:1-7

Let us look at this passage soberly. Saint Paul begins by encouraging everyone to pray for one another. Now consider: when someone asks you to pray for their needs, and you comply by making said request to God on their behalf, what are you doing? You are *mediating*. Interceding for others in prayer is an act of mediation, and this is deemed "good and acceptable in the sight of God." If there is one and only one possible mediator in the strict sense that some detractors give to this verse, then praying for our loved ones becomes meaningless. Yet I've never heard a Protestant say, when asked to pray for an intention, "No, there is only one mediator. You're on your own. Pray to Him yourself!"

So yes, Jesus Christ is the *primary* mediator, but just as we are called upon to imitate Him in perfection, we are also required to imitate Him in deed. It is our duty to pray for one another.

After telling us that there is one God and one mediator, Saint Paul goes on to explain his commission as a preacher and Apostle. "Whereunto" in the last verse means "to that purpose," the purpose being that all men be saved and come to the knowledge of the truth as God wishes. If Paul's role as preacher and Apostle includes Jesus' mandate to forgive or retain sins, and his Christ-appointed purpose is to help men be saved, then there is no contradiction between Jesus Christ being the "one [primary] mediator" and Paul himself an Apostle.

Appeals to Scripture, when taken out of context, are of questionable use. My guess is that most people who purse their lips and say, "There is only one mediator," heard someone else say it, and use it themselves because it sounds like a pretty good line to thrust against the practice of the Sacrament of Penance. If they had searched the Scriptures for themselves they might not have given so much weight to the verse, or at least not used it to support this particular argument.

It is also patently clear that the Fathers and Bishops of the early Church understood that the Sacrament of Penance was absolutely necessary. These were the men who were the disciples of the disciples. They perceived the Savior's wishes from a perspective much closer to the Source than we who are many generations removed. To quote but a few:

Consider that, unless you confess your sin, you will go to Hell.

—Saint Augustine (354 - 430 AD)

It is necessary to confess our sins to those to whom the dispensation of God's mysteries is entrusted.

—St. Basil the Great (c. 330 - 379 AD)

Confession removes the burden of sins; concealment adds to it ... If you draw back from Confession, reflect in your heart on that fire of Hell which Confession will quench for you.

—Tertullian (c. 150 - c. 230 AD)

Sin is to be confessed, in order that pardon may be obtained.

—Saint Hilary of Poiters (d. 367 AD)

For those who prefer Saints of later centuries:

Mortal sins must be confessed not only to God, but also to the priest who has the power to forgive them.

—Saint Robert Bellarmine (1542 - 1621 AD)

If, then, your souls are ulcerated with sin, do not be ashamed to confess it; otherwise, you are lost.   For those who have sinned grievously, there is no means of salvation but the confession of their sins.

—Saint Alphonsus Maria Liguori
(1696 - 1787 AD)

And for those of you who don't buy anything that doesn't have the seal of approval of the great Summist:

The sinner is not restored to the Church except by the decree of the priest ... If anyone has Perfect Contrition before the absolution of the priest, he obtains the remission of his sins by the fact that he intends to subject himself to the keys of the Church, without which intention there is no real contrition.

—Saint Thomas Aquinas (1225 - 1274 AD)

All the above quotes are from
The Apostolic Digest.

"Why should I tell my sins to a priest? Why can't I just pray directly to God for forgiveness?"
Oh come now.

CHAPTER TEN

FLESH AND BLOOD

> I cannot omit taking notice of what S. Chrysostom
> and S. Cyril, in their commentaries on this place,
> have left us on these words, *How can this man do
> this?* These words call in question the almighty and
> incomprehensible power of God, would hinder them,
> says S. Chrysostom, from believing all other myster-
> ies and miracles: they might as well have said: *How
> could he with five loaves feed five thousand men?*
> This question, *How can he do this? Is* a question of
> infidels and unbelievers. S. Cyril says that *How,* or
> *How can he do this?* cannot, without folly, be applied
> to God.
>
> —Haydock Footnotes; St. John VI:52
> *Douay-Rheims Bible*

∞ ∞ ∞

"OH, I CAN'T BELIEVE THAT. It's just supposed to be symbolic."

The sands on the shore are almost as numerous as the
times this irritating phrase has raised its irksome head during
discussions about Holy Communion. It is bothersome for two
reasons: 1) here's the all-powerful "I" again, passing judgment on things obviously not understood, and 2) "I" cites as
his authority a mere supposition with no foundation whatsoever. Who, we'd like to know, decided it's supposed to be
symbolic? On whose authority was this conclusion reached?

"You don't mean you actually believe that bread can become Christ's body, do you? That's impossible. Jesus never
meant that."

Grrrrrr.
Okay, once more—from the top:

> Jesus saith to them: But whom do you say that I
> am?
>
> —St. Matthew XVI:15

If Jesus is God, as He clearly claimed to be, then we must acknowledge everything He did and said as being the Action and the Word of God. There's no way around this stumbling block, which is why we keep going back to square one.

As we have seen, much of what Jesus had to say infuriated people, especially the hypocrites and know-it-alls. More than once crowds threatened to stone Him, and they weren't above trying to throw Him off a cliff. There was one time, however, when He said something that so befuddled everyone that they just ... went away. They, like, split. Let us examine this incident carefully. It is found in the Gospel of Saint John.

It began with a large crowd following Jesus into the mountains.

> And a great multitude followed him, because they
> saw the miracles which he did on them that were dis-
> eased.
>
> —St. John VI:2

They were already impressed with His miracles and, naturally, they wanted to see more. We would no doubt do likewise in their place. And He did not disappoint them. At hand were only five barley loaves and two fishes. In response to the crowd's need for sustenance ...

> ... Jesus took the loaves: and when he had given
> thanks, he distributed to them that were set down. In
> like manner also of the fishes, as much as they
> would.
>
> —St. John VI:11

When the leftovers were gathered up after the people had finished eating, they filled twelve baskets. The crowd was duly impressed—

> Now those men, when they had seen what a miracle
> Jesus had done, said: This is of a truth the prophet,
> that is to come into the world.
>
> — St. John VI:14

— so impressed, in fact, they were ready to make Jesus king
right on the spot. He therefore slipped away to the mountains
to be alone.

Later that night, His disciples went down to their boats and
set out across the Sea of Galilee. But *en route* a great storm
caught them unawares. We turn to the Gospel of Saint Matthew, where the events of that strange cruise are told in more
detail:

> But the boat in the midst of the sea was tossed with
> the waves: for the wind was contrary.
>
> And in the fourth watch of the night, he came to
> them walking upon the sea.
>
> And they seeing him walking on the sea were trou-
> bled, saying: It is an apparition. And they cried out
> for fear.
>
> — St. Matthew XIV:24-26

As we saw earlier on, there is a breach between the physical world and the ethereal, between the flesh and the spirit — a
chasm which somehow must be bridged. We must avert our
attention from the input of our senses, the immediately tangible, and try to grasp that which our senses cannot provide, the
eternally intangible. Peter — good old lovable, brash, reckless,
impulsive Peter — was about to learn a lesson in this regard:

> And immediately Jesus spoke to them, saying: Be
> of good heart: It is I, be not afraid.
>
> And Peter, making answer, said: Lord, if it be thou,
> bid me come to thee upon the waters.
>
> And he said: Come. And Peter, going down out of
> the boat, walked upon the water to come to Jesus.
>
> But seeing the wind strong he was afraid: and when
> he began to sink, he cried out, saying: Lord, save me.
>
> — St. Matthew XIV:27-30

What a treasure is Peter! Perceiving the approach of the Lord, he challenged Him: if You're really You, prove it—make it so I can walk on the water, too. Jesus, as He so yearned to do, complied. Peter, in a burst of well-meaning courage, lunged out into the stormy sea and found himself supported on the insupportable.

Huh? Me?!? Walking on water? Impossible! It can't be! I should be sink …….

Kerplunk!

……… ing.

As soon as he turned his attention back to the input of his senses, Peter's determination failed. He lost faith. Jesus intervened.

> And immediately Jesus stretching forth his hand, took hold of him, and said to him: O thou of little faith, why didst thou doubt?
>
> And when they were come up in to the boat, the wind ceased.
>
> —St. Matthew XIV:31-32

As so often happens, once the crisis is over, things settle down; and when the danger has passed, we wonder why we weren't more faithful and courageous when we needed to be.

With all this in mind, we now come to the opposite shore of the Sea of Galilee and pick up with Saint John's account again. The multitude, waking to find Jesus gone, went looking for Him. When they realized He'd crossed the sea, they followed Him in boats. They found Him in the synagogue in Capharnaum. Their enthusiasm knew no bounds—or so they thought. They said they'd found their prophet, but what they really wanted was a king who would keep their bellies full.

> Jesus answered them, and said: Amen, amen I say to you, you seek me, not because you have seen miracles, but because you did eat of the loaves, and were filled.
>
> Labour not for the meat which perisheth, but for that which endureth unto life everlasting, which the

> Son of man will give you. For him hath God, the
> Father, sealed.
>
> —St. John VI:26-27

Taken aback, and their curiosity roused, they asked:

> What shall we do, that we may work the works of
> God?
> Jesus answered, and said to them: This is the work
> of God, that you believe in him whom he hath sent.
>
> —St. John VI:28-29

The "Work of God" is not a task of muscle and skill, but
a choice in the mind and heart to believe in His Son. Hardly
the "work" they expected. Caught off guard, they tried to
get Him back on their level, away from this lofty stuff and
back to that which they could touch and taste.

> They said therefore to him: What sign therefore
> dost thou shew, that we may see, and may believe
> thee?
>
> —St. John VI:30

As if multiplying the loaves and fishes was not enough!
More, they still wanted more. So they fell back on the old
stand-by, the glorious past, the works of Moses:

> Our fathers did eat manna in the desert, as it is writ-
> ten: *He gave them bread from heaven to eat.*
>
> —St. John VI:31

Here is where Jesus started to throw them the curve ball,
the pitch that would prove so difficult for them to catch.

> Amen, amen I say to you: Moses gave you not
> bread from heaven, but my Father giveth you the true
> bread from heaven.
> For the bread of God is that which cometh down
> from heaven, and giveth life to the world.
> They said therefore unto him: Lord, give us always
> this bread.
>
> —St. John VI:32-34

Manna on their minds, bread on their brains, they were not at all prepared for His next statement:

> I am the bread of life: he that cometh to me shall not hunger: and he that believeth in me shall never thirst.
>
> —St. John VI:35

This got them murmuring. What on earth was He talking about? They thought they had Him pegged, but He slipped between the cracks of their understanding. Annoyed, they kept trying to bring Him back to their own level.

> And they said: Is not this Jesus, the son of Joseph, whose father and mother we know? How then saith he, I came down from heaven?
>
> —St. John VI:42

As much as they tried, He stood His ground and insisted that they rise to His:

> I am the bread of life.
> Your fathers did eat manna in the desert, and are dead.
> This is the bread which cometh down from heaven; that if any man eat of it, he may not die.
> I am the living bread which came down from heaven.
> If any man eat of this bread, he shall live for ever; and the bread that I will give, is my flesh, for the life of the world.
>
> —St. John VI:48-52

Their confusion mounting, they struggled with His strange words. "How can this man give us His flesh to eat?" they grumbled. "What He says makes no sense."

There can be no doubt that when He said "eat," He meant *"eat."* He did not say "partake" or "share" or "experience." The word He chose was synonymous with "gnaw" or "chew." To a people bound by strict dietary laws, the idea was utterly repulsive.

Undaunted, Jesus continued. He did not back off in the least, but rather surged forward, expanding on each point. Not just His Flesh was involved, but His Blood as well:

> Amen, amen I say unto you: Except you eat the flesh of the Son of man, and drink his blood, you shall not have life in you.
> He that eateth my flesh, and drinketh my blood, hath everlasting life: and I will raise him up in the last day.
> For my flesh is meat indeed: and my blood is drink indeed.
> —St. John VI:54-56

We, too, may be repelled. Like many disciples in the synagogue, we can complain:

> This saying is hard, and who can hear it?
> —St. John VI:61

We can pound our fists, we can snarl all we want, we can climb the walls and swell the veins on our necks. The one thing we must *not* do is change what He said into something more agreeable to us. It dishonors Him and throws the veil of dishonesty upon ourselves. If we are to follow Jesus or abandon Him, the decision must be based on what He said, not what we wished Him to have said, or what we would have said if we were in His place. This kind of proud mendacity is the root and heart of the confusion which prevails in the Church today: "I"—the great and powerful "I"—can't believe that, therefore it cannot be so.

> The Dogma of Faith: that's the God-given-ness of Faith—everything that comes from God—that's what seems to be lost to this generation. Most people think that God begins with them and ends with them ... Well, stupid, you're not God.
> —Father Paul Trinchard
> "Overcoming a Dysfunctional Church"
> VNI Conference, Monrovia, CA; August 1993

Would a loving God say anything less than the Truth, just to make things easy for us? Should a mother say, "It's okay, Honey, electricity won't really hurt you," because her child is fascinated with the outlet and refuses to leave it alone? Jesus, as God, had to tell the Truth, even though He knew there would be those who would refuse to accept it. He could do no less, for His Love knew no limit.

The breach between the physical world and the ethereal, between the flesh and the spirit, has to be bridged. There is no detour, no back road, no sleight of hand, no way around—there is only one way to the Father, and that is through Jesus Christ. And He says to us, as He said to them:

> It is the spirit that quickeneth: the flesh profiteth nothing. The words that I have spoken to you, are spirit and life.
> But there are some of you that believe not. For Jesus knew from the beginning, who they were that did not believe, and who he was, that would betray him.
> —St. John VI:64-65

This is when most of His followers left him. They turned their backs and walked away wagging their heads. If He had been weaving poetry and parables, wouldn't He have said at this point, "Wait, come back—you misunderstood"? But He did not, for they had not. He had told the Truth; He could do no less. They had responded; He could do no more.

> Then Jesus said to the twelve: Will you also go away?
> —St. John VI:68

Peter did not know that in a short time Jesus would institute the Sacrament of the Holy Eucharist at the Last Supper. Peter had not heard of "Transubstantiation," the word which the Church would later coin to explain the miracle Jesus proposed. He was standing on the brink of the chasm, his feet on solid ground, his eyes on the far side which appeared nebulous, shrouded in mist, unclear. Did he dare jump?

Peter searched the world as he knew it, scrutinizing the backs of the receding disciples, the boats lolling in the lake, the waves lapping on the shore, everything he could touch and feel and taste and understand. There it was, and yet as he looked around he suddenly realized that what he thought was real was not so definite and solid after all.

Perhaps the sight of twelve baskets of bread fragments drifted behind his tearing eyes. Perhaps words came back to him, words from the night before that had been barely audible above the roar and rush of the storm at sea:

> O thou of little faith, why didst thou doubt?
> —St. Matthew XIV:31

Peter's next words did not reflect a leader who understood where he was going, but rather a bewildered man who was backed into a corner. For once, Peter decided, he would act according to Faith. He would do the Work of God.

> And Simon Peter answered him: Lord, to whom shall we go? thou hast the words of eternal life.
> —St. John VI:69.

Peter put his trust, not his comprehension, in the hand of the Lord. He did not understand, but he believed anyway. He leapt over the chasm.

And this is precisely what we are required to do today. It does not matter that eighty percent of Catholics in America don't believe in the Real Presence of Christ in the Blessed Sacrament. It does not matter that pastors all over the world have moved the Tabernacles to out-of-the-way niches in the dark recesses of their industrial-grey churches. It does not matter if everyone walks away wagging their heads. Truth is not arrived at by majority vote. Truth is Truth even if no human being anywhere accepts it—though hopefully a handful in a dungeon somewhere will.

No matter the opinions and attitudes of the rest, our job is to do the Work of God, to believe in Him Whom He Has Sent.

> I say unto you ... but yet the Son of man, when he cometh, shall he find, think you, faith on earth?
> —St. Luke XVIII:8

What do we think?

Our answer will not change the Reality of What Is. It will only determine what side of the breach we choose to stand upon. It doesn't matter—irritating, but true—what we think or what we're willing to believe. Jesus said it all very clearly:

> Amen, amen I say unto you: Except you eat the flesh of the Son of man, and drink his blood, you shall not have life in you.
>
> —St. John VI:54

Look around. Is there any place else to go?

CHAPTER ELEVEN

SOLEMN SACRIFICE

The Lord hath sworn, and he will not repent: Thou
art a priest for ever according to the order of Melchisedech.

—Psalm CIX:4

∞ ∞ ∞

FROM THE VERY BEGINNING, the most appropriate form of
worship due Almighty God was Solemn Sacrifice: to take the
finest of what we have and give it back to God. The offering
must be the foremost result of our labors, the cream of the
crop, the firstlings of our flock; for He is worthy of nothing
less than the very best. And there must be no thought of giving it with our lips and taking it back again for our use. It
must be destroyed, killed, butchered, burned—reduced to
ashes by fire on an altar. May the rising smoke be pleasing to
God.

In these modern times many of us have grown complacent
about the idea of "offering," lulled into philanthropic non-
chalance by the impersonal collection plate, the tax-deductible
donation, the "one eight hundred number" on the screen,
and the automatic deductions from our paychecks to worthy
causes. The thought of incinerating a basket of the best
vegetables from our backyard garden, or killing the first pup
of our dog's litter, or torching rather than framing a term paper that got an "A+" from a teacher who is usually a grade-
miser, might seem a bit barbaric, "out of touch" with our
level of cultural refinement.

We would do well to consider that we, by virtue of the
sterile, antiseptic, labor-saving predilection of our society, are

the ones who are out of touch with the cold, hard, dirt-under-the-fingernails realities of life. Most of us eat produce we never planted and drink water from sources we've never seen. The result of our labor is a piece of paper called a "pay-check"—and with "direct deposit" we may not even see that. We enjoy chicken as a main dish, but without enduring the preliminary task of plucking feathers from a freshly-killed hen or disemboweling the carcass. Strange, isn't it, that "natural childbirth" is something *new?* Couples are so oblivious to the thing they have to go to *classes* to learn about it. This, because even something as real and proximate as childbirth has been removed from our everyday experience, secreted behind hospital doors, dabbed with alcohol, and bur-ied under mountains of red tape. To most of us, blood is something we give reluctantly to the Red Cross—that red stuff counted in "units" and stored in hanging plastic bags. To the ancient Israelites, the strictures of God made them see it in a very different light:

> ... thou shalt kill of thy herds and of thy flocks, as
> I have commanded thee, and shalt eat in thy towns, as
> it pleaseth thee ...
> Only beware of this, that thou eat not the blood,
> for the blood is for the soul: and therefore thou must
> not eat the soul with the flesh ...
> —Deuteronomy XII:21, 23

When we read the Old Testament, we are confronted with graphic scenes in which animals are slaughtered, blood is poured out on the altars, and flumes of dense smoke rise up to God as the flesh is consumed in roaring holocausts. Such things were part of everyday experience, and absolutely cen-tral and necessary to worship. We must not dismiss these things as barbaric, primitive, or savage. They were *real life*.

If we do not come to terms with this critical aspect of wor-ship, we will never understand the significance of the Holy Sacrifice of the Mass. It is unfortunate today that the Novus Ordo obfuscates this principle, as we will see in a couple of chapters hence. Young people who have been raised in its shadow are generally oblivious to the sacrificial nature of the Mass, having been given the impression that it's a ceremonial "meal."

Whatever the prevailing misconception, the heart of the Mass, and of Old Testament worship, has always been Solemn Sacrifice.

We read in Genesis that ...

> ... Cain offered, of the fruits of the earth, gifts to the Lord.
>
> Abel also offered, of the firstlings of his flock, and of their fat: and the Lord had respect for Abel and to his offerings.
>
> But to Cain and his offerings he had no respect: and Cain was exceedingly angry ...
>
> —Genesis IV:3-5

The Scriptures are not clear as to what it was about Cain's offering that displeased God. Something in his intention or in the offering itself must have been lacking. In any event, Cain's fury over this incident resulted in the First Murder.

A few chapters later, we have Noe exiting the ark after the waters of the Flood had subsided. Looking around at the devastation, he surely realized his resources were severely limited. Yet his first act was to offer Solemn Sacrifice to God, the best of what he had:

> And Noe built an altar unto the Lord: and taking of all cattle and fowls that were clean, offered holocausts upon the altar.
>
> And the Lord smelled a sweet savor, and said: I will no more curse the earth for the sake of man.
>
> —Genesis VIII:20-21

Almost four centuries later, the Lord brought Abram out of the land of Haran, promising:

> And I will make of thee a great nation, and I will bless thee, and magnify thy name, and thou shalt be blessed.
>
> —Genesis XII:2

Abram was seventy-five years old at the time, and without any children.

Shortly thereafter, Abram was involved in a war between Sodom and Gomorrha (this was before God unleashed His wrath upon them) and four invading kings, in which he turned the tide and defeated the invaders. Immediately after the battle, Abram was approached by Melchisedech, the king and high priest of Salem (the original name of Jerusalem, long before the Israelites would claim it as part of their territory). No genealogy or history of this man is recorded, nor was he or his city involved in the battle, yet he suddenly appeared and gave Abram his priestly blessing:

> But Melchisedech the king of Salem, bringing forth bread and wine, for he was the priest of the most high God,
> Blessed him, and said: Blessed be Abram by the most high God, who created heaven and earth.
> —Genesis XIV:18-19

No other mention is made of this enigmatic figure in the Old Testament until King David wrote the Psalm which is quoted at the beginning of this chapter. Notice, however, his choice of offerings: bread and wine. Melchisedech was the prefigurement of the new priesthood instituted by Jesus Christ twenty centuries later.

Twenty-five years passed before Sara, Abram's wife, bore him his first and only son, Isaac. By that time God had changed Abram's name to Abraham, and had seen him through many trials and difficulties. Isaac, as far as Abraham was concerned, was the future. Out of this long-awaited son would issue the great nation promised by God. But God suddenly presented Abraham with an unexpected command:

> Take thy only begotten son Isaac, whom thou lovest, and go into the land of vision: and there thou shalt offer him for an holocaust upon one of the mountains which I will shew thee.
> —Genesis XXII:2

One can only imagine the turmoil in Abraham's mind as he gathered Isaac, some firewood, and headed for the place of sacrifice. Isaac was the only visible, tangible result of God's lofty promise—

> ... I have made thee a father of many nations.
>
> And I will make thee increase, exceedingly, and I will make nations of thee, and kings shall come out of thee.
>
> And I will establish my covenant between me and thee, and between thy seed after thee in their generations, by a perpetual covenant ...
>
> —Genesis XVII:5-7

—yet the Lord had just told Abraham to kill him. How could the prophecy come to pass if the boy died?

Two thousand years later, Peter would be faced with the same kind of dilemma, as we saw in the last chapter. He did not know how Jesus' flesh could be the Bread of Life, but he had to make a leap of Faith without understanding, to trust that somehow Jesus would make it possible. Once we have our eyes riveted on God, we cannot falter by looking at physical circumstances.

We cannot ease Abraham's burden by suggesting that he knew God would somehow intervene. The tradition of sacrifice was well-established. He knew his son would be reduced to ashes. He also knew God had made a promise. In spite of the incompatibility of the two things, Abraham kept his eyes on God, right up to the point of raising his sword. Only in the last instant, when his resolve was final, did God intervene:

> Lay not thy hand upon the boy, neither do thou anything to him: now I know that thou fearest God, and hast not spared thy only begotten son for my sake.
>
> —Genesis XXII:12

Abraham had passed the most caustic of acid tests. Then something interesting happened. Abraham caught sight of a ram whose horns were stuck in the briars nearby. He killed the animal on the altar in place of his son.

Four centuries later, after the seed of Abraham had been brought out of Egypt, Moses, under the direction of God, established the rituals and rubrics for Solemn Sacrifice, the slaughter of animals to expiate the sins of the people. These complex ceremonies and elaborate rituals were detailed in the

Pentateuch, stored in the Ark of the Covenant, and were me-
ticulously practiced for many generations, down to the time of
Jesus Christ.

Why?

When Adam fell, mankind was plunged into the darkness
of sin. God's Justice demanded retribution; but how could
any man, being a fallen and limited creature, ever adequately
repay the omnipotent eternal God? Everything man has, everything he produces, is, like himself, a created thing; and God
ultimately created everything out of nothing.

The sacrifices of the Old Testament taught man the principle of sacrifice, but the blood of animals could not wash
away the stain of Original Sin. Even if a man should be sacrificed—which in any case would have been against the
Law—the offering would be insufficient.

Jesus provided the solution. He, as Man, shared in our
nature, our created-from-nothing-ness.   He, as God, would
offer Himself to God the Father as a bloody sacrifice on the
Cross for the atonement of our sins. Like the ram Abraham
slew in place of Isaac, Jesus would die in our stead. He was
without sin, and would therefore be the Perfect Sacrifice, a
victim without blemish. In addition, this Sacrifice would be
carried on in the Holy Sacrifice of the Mass, as Jesus' Body
and Blood under the form of bread and wine, and would be
offered by the new priests of the Catholic Church. The mysterious Melchisedech prefigured Christ in that his offering was
an unbloody offering of bread and wine. Melchisedech had
no apparent lineage, and the new priests would not be heredi-
tary, as were the Levites of Israel, but called from many nations and clans by vocation.

The nature of the Sacrifice is beautifully summarized, and
the historical priestly succession is commemorated, immediately after the Consecration in the Traditional Mass:

> Mindful, therefor, O Lord, not only of the blessed
> passion of the same Christ, Thy Son, our Lord, but
> also of His resurrection from the dead, and finally His
> glorious ascension into heaven, we, Thy ministers, as
> also Thy holy people, offer unto Thy supreme maj-
> esty, of Thy gifts bestowed upon us, the pure Victim,
> the holy Victim, the all-perfect Victim: the holy

Bread of life eternal and the Chalice of unending salvation.

And this do Thou deign to regard with gracious and
kindly attention and hold acceptable, as Thou didst
deign to accept the offerings of Abel, Thy just servant, and the sacrifice of Abraham our patriarch, and
that which Thy chief priest Melchisedech, offered
unto Thee, a holy sacrifice of thanks, and a spotless
Victim.
> —Prayers of Offering after the Consecration
> The Tridentine Mass

Unfortunate, isn't it, that Catholics are no longer exposed
to this truth every Sunday? Would not many of our basic
questions about and attitudes toward the Faith be different if
we were?

And now for yet another mystery: at every Mass the priest
performs the rituals, says the words, does the actions, but it is
in reality Jesus Christ who is the High Priest—it is He who is
offering Himself as God to God. The priest offers in His behalf, but the action is Christ's. This whole idea can send one's
mind spinning, but the meditation is worth the effort.

There can truly be no more glorious vocation in
this life than the call to be a priest of God. A Catholic priest is entrusted with powers denied to the greatest of archangels; he has the power to make God the
Son present upon the altar of sacrifice and offer Him
as a pure oblation to the Holy Trinity; he has the
power to forgive or retain the sins of his fellowmen.
The Catholic priest is another Christ, an *alter Chris-
tus,* an instrument used by God the Son to impart to
men the grace He won for them upon the Cross. A
layman can only wonder that any human being dares
to accept so fearful a responsibility and to thank God
for those who do.
> —Michael Davies
> *Pope Paul's New Mass*

When the priest says the words of Consecration, he does so
in persona Christi, in the person and capacity of Christ. He
does not say, "This is *his* body," but rather, "This is *my*

body." In the Traditional Rite, the priest submitted himself completely to the rubrics of the ritual. His every movement and utterance was specifically laid out in the Missal. He was in a very real sense depersonalized, so that he could take on the person of Jesus Christ. So awesome was this responsibility, and so necessary that the soul be absolutely pure during Mass lest sacrilege be committed, that historically the priesthood was not always considered a "welcome job."

> St. Gregory Nazianzen says: "No one rejoices when he is ordained a priest." In his life of St. Cyprian, Paul the Deacon states that when the saint heard that his bishop intended to ordain him priest, he through humility concealed himself. It is related in the life of St. Fulgentius that he too fled away and hid himself. St. Athanasius also, as Sozomen relates, took flight in order to escape the priesthood. St. Ambrose, as he himself attests, resisted for a long time before he consented to be ordained. St. Gregory, even after it was made manifest by miracles that God wished him to be a priest, concealed himself under the garb of a merchant, in order to prevent his ordination ...
>
> It is known to all, that St. Francis remained a deacon, and refused to ascend to the priesthood, because he learned by revelation, that the soul of a priest should be as pure as the water that was shown to him in a crystal vessel.
>
> —Saint Alphonsus De Liguori
> *The Dignity and Duties of the Priest*

Sobering words. One can only wonder how many of today's sacerdotal country club set considered the seriousness of the position before applying. Many seem to be unaware of the gravity of their calling throughout their entire careers and into retirement.

How far we have fallen—priests and laity alike—in our understanding of the enormity of what is really happening at Mass, what Jesus Christ is accomplishing for our Salvation. In most parishes today, the priests are at the mercy of "liturgy committees," bodies of untrained, short-tempered parish "leaders" who dictate to the clergy how the Mass is going to be celebrated, what prayers will be said, what processions will be endured, what songs will be sung, and any manner of on-the-spot innovations. Never in the history of the Church was such a situation dreamed of.

The lines of demarcation between priest and laity have grown hazy, undefined. Whereas the priest used to say at the *Oratre, fratres*—

> Pray, brethren, that my sacrifice and yours may become acceptable to God the Father almighty.
> —The Offertory of the Tridentine Mass

—he now refers to "*our* sacrifice,"* as though his offering and the peoples' were exactly the same. It is only one of many tiny changes in wording that have encouraged the idea that it is the "community" that confects the Consecration, when this is patently not the case:

> Our word liturgy is derived from the Greek *leitourgos*, which originally designated a man who performed a public service ... In Hebrews 8, 1-6, Christ is referred to as the *Leitourgos* of holy things. The liturgy is *His* public religious work for His people, *His* ministry, *His* redeeming activity. It is above all *His* sacrifice, the sacrifice of the Cross, the same sacrifice that He offered on Calvary still offered by Him through the ministry of His priests. He is the principle offerer of the sacrifice of the Mass and to offer Mass nothing is necessary but a priest, the bread, and the wine. There is no necessity whatsoever for a congregation; when defining the essence, the nature of the Mass, the presence of the faithful need not be taken into account; while it is obviously desirable it is not necessary.
> —Michael Davies
> *Pope John's Council*

Try telling that to the local "liturgy committee"—then prepare to flee.

---

* At least, in the current English translation used in the United States. In other vernaculars, *i.e.*, Spanish, the correct wording is maintained.

What is to be done? There is no simple answer. But certainly a starting point for us as individual Catholics would be to meditate on the stark, harsh, reality of the bloody sacrifices practiced in ancient times. Browsing through the Old Testament would be most efficacious in this regard.

Another thing would be to get hold of an old Latin-English Missal and read through the Mass. The summation of the Catholic Faith is stated right there. Better still, if there is a Tridentine Rite Mass anywhere near us and we have the means to get to it, there we should go. If at first it seems alien, we must persevere. Its self-contained Truth will gradually imprint itself in our hearts. It can and does transform lives.

Most of all, of course, we must pray to God for guidance, for wisdom, for understanding, and for heroic Faith in these bleak and spiritually depleted times.

CHAPTER TWELVE

OLD WIVES' TALES

How can anyone receive Our Lord and not die of happiness?

—Blessed Imelda Lambertini
As told by Mary Fabyan Windeatt
Patron Saint of First Communicants

∞ ∞ ∞

THE WAY THE PRIESTS, nuns, and lay teachers have been telling it of late, we know very little about the actual events of Christ's life. Surely with the passage of time details were gradually obscured, events got amplified in the retelling, details got lost, and agendas were inserted along the way by people in high places. Surely in our own experience, a bit of information told in confidence to one neighbor can come back a week later from somebody else so garbled and blown out of proportion as to be the opposite of what we originally said. The Church, then, has been passing on a pack of ever-expanding, always-changing lies—

—this, at least, according to the priests, nuns and lay teachers since they were "enlightened" by the "spirit of Vatican II" (whatever that is). These are the same priests and nuns who abandoned their vows, got married to each other, became lay teachers, and are now spending their lives justifying their breach of faith. They seem Hell-bent on jettisoning every trace of the past, every tie and connection with anything before 1960. It doesn't take a whole lot of research to discover who's doing the "creative story telling."

The fact is: we know quite a bit about the details and facts of Jesus Christ's life. True, the Gospels are sketchy—but

that's because the men writing them were addressing people
who already knew the details. The details, however did not get
lost. They became part of Church Tradition. Are we really so
lame as to think that the followers of Christ would somehow
"forget" such important places as where He was born, where
he performed what miracles, the site of His burial and Resurrection? What foolishness.

The fate of every Apostle, their close relatives, the itiner-
aries of their travels, and their final resting places are well
known and documented. The men and women whose lives
Jesus touched did not just vanish after His Ascension, swallowed up by the maw of time, covered over with the sands of
history. The nuances of their lives were preserved for the edi-
fication of those who would come later. For example:

> Fourteen years after Our Lord's death, Saint Mary
> Magdalen was put by the Jews in a boat without sails
> or oars—along with her brother and sister, Saint
> Lazarus and Saint Martha, and Saint Maximin, who
> baptized her, and Saint Sidonius, "the man born
> blind," and her maid, Sara, and the body of Saint
> Anne, the mother of the Mother of God—and sent
> drifting out to sea.
>
> The boat landed on the southern shore of France.
> Saint Mary Magdalen lived the whole rest of her life
> in France, as a contemplative in a cave known as
> Sainte-Baume, near a little town named Saint Mixi-
> min.
>
> —The Slaves of the Immaculate Heart of Mary
> *Saints to Remember*

Many people who were nameless in the Biblical accounts
went on to become recognized saints. Places, too, which were
not specified in the Gospels, are preserved to this day, woven
into the elegant tapestry of living history:

> Saint Mary was the mother of Saint Mark the
> Evangelist, whose full name was John Mark. She
> was a wealthy woman who lived in Jerusalem. It was
> at her house that the Last Supper was held, and the
> Blessed Sacrament instituted. It was at her house that

the Holy Ghost descended upon the Apostles at the first Pentecost. It was at her house that Our Lady lived, in Jerusalem, until she died in the year 58. It was at her house that Saint Peter, the first Pope, often visited, and to her house he immediately went on his deliverance from prison in Jerusalem, as we are told in the Bible. It is simple to say and easy to prove that Saint Mary, the mother of Mark, was the greatest hostess in the history of the Catholic Church. Her house after the Last Supper was called "the Cenacle."
> —The Slaves of the Immaculate Heart of Mary
> *Saints to Remember*

The Cenacle is still preserved in the Holy Land.

Also left out of the Gospels are many details regarding ceremonies and rituals. What we read there, fortified by the "Life of Christ" movies pumped out by Hollywood on sprocketed celluloid, gives us a rather sparse idea of the rather memorable and enriching events which surrounded the Passion.

Over three million people from all over the known world flooded the streets of Jerusalem, drawn there to celebrate Passover in the Holy City. It was into this throng that Jesus rode an ass, and it was to these crowds that he preached on the Temple steps. When the high priests passed the death sentence on Him, He and His followers hid at night in a place called the Grotto of the Creed, a cave near the summit of Olivet, and a short distance from the tombs of the Hebrew prophets who had fortold His coming.

On the Day of Atonement, which would have been Holy Thursday, Jesus and the Apostles entered the Temple. Jesus, if He followed custom, which is all but certain, carried a lamb on His shoulders as their leader. In an elaborate ceremony, wine was poured on the lamb before its legs were tied together, right forefoot to left hind foot, left front to right hind, the cords forming a cross. The lamb was then washed with water. Meanwhile, in the Priest's court, five hundred priests wearing rich garments of white, green, violet, and red—colors that would be adopted by the Catholic Church to denote the liturgical seasons and vestments—faced the Holy of Holies, praying to God and awaiting His Messiah.

> They did not know it, but they faced toward that
> Calvary, 1,000 feet west, outside the walls, where the
> next day their Savior was to die.
> > —Father James L. Meagher, D.D.
> > *How Christ Said the First Mass*

There is an Oriental tradition of dubious origin, but it is worth mentioning if for nothing else than to stimulate my reader's intrigue, that before he died, Adam asked his son not to bury him until God had shown him the place where the Seed of the Woman who would crush the serpent's head would come. Adam's skull was said to have been passed down by his descendants, and was taken aboard Noe's ark. It was then entrusted to Sem, Noe's son, who was guided shortly before his death by an angel to the appropriate place for burial.

> For full many a day they went west, till they came
> to a little hill, whereon he entombed our first father's
> relic, and called it Golgotha, a Babylonian word
> meaning "The Place of the Skull." Greeks later ren-
> dered it Cranion, and the Romans Calvaria—Calvary.
> > —Father James L. Meagher, D.D.
> > *How Christ Said the First Mass*

Other traditions place the site of Abraham's near-sacrifice of Isaac on the same spot. Old wives' tales? Perhaps ...

> "Then I need say no more," said Celeborn. "But do
> not despise the lore that has come down from the dis-
> tant years; for oft it may chance that old wives keep
> in memory word of things that once were needful for
> the wise to know."
> > —J.R.R.Tolkein
> > *The Lord of the Rings*

Of course, visitors to the Holy Sepulchre in Jerusalem walk past the Tomb of Adam every day ...

CHAPTER THIRTEEN

THE GOOD BOOK

> Faith then cometh by hearing; and hearing by the
> word of Christ.
>
> —Romans X:17

∞ ∞ ∞

"IS IT IN THE BIBLE?"

"No, it isn't. It's part of Tradition—"

"Well, if it isn't in the Bible, then I don't want to hear it."

"Why not?"

"Because the Bible is the Word of God. Everything else is the fabrication of mere men." This is often accompanied by a glance that says, "Aha!—that settles that."

So end many conversations between Catholics and Protestants.

But in truth, nothing was just settled. It's sad, too, because as we've seen—and as we'll continue to discover—many verses of the Bible on which "Bible Christians" hang their beliefs are taken out of context, leading to serious misunderstandings and errors in theology. This, because they recognize no teaching authority which can tell them otherwise.

To the Protestant, the Bible is really everything, the be-all and end-all of Revelation. To the Catholic—especially those who truly understand their Faith—the Bible, while certainly inspired by the Holy Ghost, is but one part of a vast resource.

This is a serious subject, and a highly sensitive one; and no claim is being made that we can settle this matter up in a single chapter. There are, however, a few things that need clarification, especially if we're trying to come to grips with holding the Catholic Faith.

The first is a simple matter of historical record:

> The New Testament was not completed until 65
> years after Peter and Paul and most of the other Apos-
> tles were dead; many of their immediate successors
> had been martyred, and it is likely that the third or
> fourth successors of the several Apostles were con-
> verting souls without the Bible when St. John com-
> pleted his writings. In fact, the whole Roman Em-
> pire was Christian, at least ten million people re-
> mained true to Christ and suffered a martyr's death,
> and the Church was enjoying her golden age, before
> anybody ever saw the New Testament bound up into
> one volume. For four centuries people received their
> faith by *hearing* it preached in Catholic churches.
> *—Letter to a Fallen-Away Catholic**

In other words, the first Christians were certainly not "Bible Christians" for the simple reason there was no Bible.
While the collection of books we now call the Old Testament
was somewhat established, it wasn't until the Councils of Car-
thage and Hippo (393, 419 AD) that the definitive list of
books to be included in the Old and New Testaments was
agreed upon. Before this there were a great number of questionable epistles and gospels in circulation. Even when that
was sorted out, the printing press was not developed until the
fifteenth century. In the meantime the Scriptures were copied
painstakingly by hand—specifically by Catholic monks in
monasteries. A single Bible, the Old and New Testaments
combined in one volume, was the result of years of work.
These manuscripts were an invaluable resource to the world,
but the fact is that even with their distribution, most people
were illiterate and couldn't read them anyway.

The point is that the Gospel, the "Good News," was ini-
tially, and for many centuries, spread by word of mouth, not
by the dissemination of books.

Jesus' parting words to His Apostles were:

---

* *Letter to a Fallen-Away Catholic* was a marvelous little tome published by
Catholic Treasures in Monrovia, California. It and its companion, *Letter to
a Non-Catholic Friend,* have unfortunately gone out of print. The author
chose to remain anonymous.

> Going therefore, teach ye all nations; baptizing
> them in the name of the Father, and of the Son, and
> of the Holy Ghost.
> Teaching them to observe all things whatsoever I
> have commanded you: and behold I am with you all
> days, even to the consummation of the world.
> — St. Matthew XXVIII:19-20

He did not say, "Go write a book, spread it around, and let
every man judge for himself what he's willing to accept."

Even a cursory exploration of the Epistles will show that
they were written to congregations of people who already believed, people to whom the message had already been
preached. The letters of Saints Peter, Paul, James and John
were not intended as complete expositions of the Faith, but as
letters of clarification and encouragement to those who had
already accepted the Gospel.

It is obvious from Saint Paul's words and tone that his
second letter to Timothy is an instruction, among other things,
on how to preach:

> Hold the form of sound words, which thou hast
> heard of me in faith, and in the love which is Jesus
> Christ ...
> And the things which thou hast heard of me by
> many witnesses, the same comment to faithful men,
> who shall be fit to teach others also ...
> Preach the word: be instant in season, out of sea-
> son: reprove, entreat, rebuke in all patience and doc-
> trine.
> — II Timothy I:13; II:2; IV:2

In it we also find clear evidence of the Apostolic succession via the laying on of hands, the Tradition by which the
power of bishops is passed on in the Catholic Church through
an unbroken chain leading all the way back to the Apostles:

> For which cause I admonish thee, that thou stir up
> the grace of God which is in thee, by the imposition
> of my hands.
> — II Timothy I:6

In Saint Paul's Epistle to the Romans, which he wrote at
Corinth about twenty-four years after Jesus ascended to
Heaven, he had much to say about the spoken word, but his
only reference to the written word was a brief quote from
Isaias. Indeed, Paul's emphasis was most certainly on the oral
teaching of the Good News, since "Faith cometh by hearing."

> For whosoever shall call upon the name of the
> Lord, shall be saved.
> How then shall they call on him, in whom they
> have not believed? Or how shall they believe him, of
> whom they have not heard? And how shall they hear,
> without a preacher?
> And how shall they preach unless they be sent, as
> it is written: How beautiful are the feet of them that
> preach the gospel of peace, of them that bring glad
> tidings of good things!
> But all do not obey the gospel. For Isaias saith:
> Lord, who hath believed our report?
> Faith then cometh by hearing; and hearing by the
> word of Christ.
> But I say: Have they not heard? Yes, verily, their
> sound hath gone forth into all the earth, and their
> words unto the ends of the whole world.
> —Romans X:13-18

None of this, of course, is a denial that Epistles and Gospels were in circulation within a few years of Jesus' Ascension.
Saint Peter wrote his Second Epistle in Rome shortly before
his martyrdom, about thirty-five years after Our Lord's departure. In it we find the only reference in the New Testament
of one Apostle to another's writings:

> ... as also our most dear brother Paul, according to
> the wisdom given him, hath written to you:
> As also in all his epistles, speaking in them of
> these things; in which are certain things hard to be
> understood, which the unlearned and unstable wrest,
> as they do also the other scriptures, to their own de-
> struction.
> —II St. Peter III:15-16

Yes, Paul's Epistles were already causing "trouble" way
back when. Still, it is likely that when Peter spoke of prophecy earlier on in the same letter—

> Understanding this first, that no prophecy of scrip-
> ture is made by private interpretation.
>
> —II St. Peter I:20

—he was referring to the Old Testament writings. His own
letters, and those of his brothers in the Faith, would not be
formalized as "Scripture" for several centuries.

It is also important to realize that everything Jesus said and
did was not recorded in the Bible, even when all the reliable
texts were gathered into one book. He lived with His disciples
for three long years, working miracles, preaching to the
crowds, eating and drinking, all the while instructing His closest followers in the specifics of the Faith. By no stretch of the
imagination can it be said that there are three years of dis-
courses, dialogues, and informal talks recorded in the New
Testament. Saint John, in concluding his remarkable Gospel
some sixty-three years after the Ascension, thoughtfully wrote:

> But there are also many other things which Jesus
> did; which, if they were written every one, the world,
> itself, I think, would not be able to contain the books
> that should be written.
>
> —St. John XXI:25

It would be absurd to hold that the entirety of the Faith is
to be found within the pages of the New Testament, or between the covers of the whole Bible for that matter. Yet this is
what an astonishing number of people believe.

Where, we might ask, is the Biblical explanation of the
Blessed Trinity?—or even the word, "Trinity"? While we can
certainly extrapolate the Triune aspect of God from His si-
multaneous manifestation in three distinct forms—

> And Jesus being baptized, forthwith came out of
> the water: and lo, the heavens were opened to him:
> and he saw the Spirit of God descending as a dove,
> and coming upon him.

> And behold a voice from heaven saying: This is my
> beloved Son, in whom I am well pleased.
> —St. Matthew III:16-17

—this can hardly be considered an explanation. The fact is that the word, "Trinity," was first recorded by Theophilus of Antioch about 181 AD. This is not to say he "invented" the term, or that the early Christians did not have a grasp of the concept, but that the explanation is left to oral Tradition, not the Bible.

If we wish to learn about that Tradition, we have to go beyond the covers of the Bible and into the archives of the Roman Catholic Church. A large deposit of early Christian thought was written by the Fathers of the Church—the disciples of the Apostles, and their disciples, and theirs. In their sermons to their flocks, their books, and their letters amongst themselves, we find how the Faith was presented from the onset.

More than once I have been asked, "If Mary is so important, why isn't she more prominent in the New Testament? Why didn't Paul even mention her?" The Blessed Mother's presence throughout Scripture will be explored in detail in a later chapter. For now, let us learn about Her from Tradition:

We find Her in the writings of Saint Denis the Areopagite*, for example, who described his introduction to the Blessed Mother by Saint Paul in Jerusalem:

> "If faith would not instruct me, and if the under-
> standing of what I see would not teach me, that is
> God, who has conceived Her in his mind, and who
> alone could and can in his Omnipotence form such an
> image of his Divinity, if all this were not present to
> my mind, I might begin to doubt, whether the Virgin
> Mother contain not in Herself Divinity."
> —Quoted by Sister Mary of Jesus of Agreda
> "The Conception,"
> *Mystical City of God*

---

* Whatever strange speculations the term may spark in the imagination, St. Denis was called "the Areopagite" because before his conversion by St. Paul (Acts of the Apostles XVII:34) he had been a judge of the Areopagus, the prime council of Athens.

This gives us a clue as to how utterly pure and perfect She was, that She radiated such serene and awesome power that She was almost mistaken for Divinity. Saint Denis went on to become the first Bishop of Athens, and then of Paris. He is the patron of France. In the year 58 he was miraculously transported to Jerusalem to witness Mary's death, along with all the Apostles, save James the Greater who had already been martyred, and Thomas who arrived, also miraculously, three days later. At Thomas' insistence Her grave was opened so that he could see Her one last time. That was how they learned that She had been assumed into Heaven.**

One could answer the question, "If Mary is so important, why didn't Paul mention her?" with the reasonable deduction that he assumed everyone *already knew*. Saint Paul wrote letters to various churches and individuals to address specific problems. He was certainly not writing comprehensive theology or dictating creeds. The same can be said of the other authors of the New Testament as well.

We know from experience that little if any of this is going to be received favorably by our Protestant friends. This is unfortunate, for they have cut themselves off from a wealth of fascinating history and enriching religious customs, not to mention a wealth of knowledge with respect to the Faith.

By the same token, can we as honest seekers of the Truth be favorably impressed with the wholesale rape of the Scriptures perpetrated by the instigator of the Protestant Reformation, Martin Luther? Not only did he defy the teaching authority of the Church, thereby establishing the unprecedented anti-doctrine of *sola scriptura* (the belief that Sacred Scripture is the only and sufficient guide and is subject to private interpretation), but he went on to alter the same Scriptures to promote his personal theology that *faith alone* is sufficient unto Salvation, since good works, in his opinion, were superfluous. He inserted or deleted key words. For example, in this passage Luther eliminated the words in brackets.

> Wherefore, brethren, labor the more, that [by good works] you may make sure your calling and election.

** These details were garnered from various entries in *Saints to Remember* by the Slaves of the Immaculate Heart of Mary.

—II St. Peter I:10

Here he added the word in brackets:

> For we account a man to be justified by faith
> [alone], without the works of the law.
> > —Romans III:28

When reproached for the latter bit of Scripture-twisting, Luther wrote:

> You tell me what a great fuss the Papists are making because the word "alone" is not in the text of Paul. If your Papist makes such an unnecessary row about the word "alone," say right out to him:—"Dr. Martin Luther *will have it so,"* and say:—"Papists and asses are one and the same thing." *I will have it so, and I order it to be so, and my will is reason enough.*
> > —Quoted by John L. Stoddard
> > *Rebuilding a Lost Faith*

Where minor creative editing was not practical, Luther simply tore out the entire book. It is often noted that the Catholic Bible contains more books than the Protestant Bible...

> Why? For the same reason that it contains any of the writings within its covers. As already explained, and no man in the world can refute it, the writings which the Protestants accept as inspired, they know to be so *only on the authority of the Catholic Church.* The Protestant Bible omits the following seven books from the Old Testament: Judith, Ecclesiasticus, Baruch, Tobias, Wisdom, and the two books of the Machabees. (Luther originally threw out 11 entire books!) These books are inspired Sacred Scripture, and for twenty centuries, from the compilation of the Old Testament canon by Esdras and Nehemias in 430 B.C., until the rebellion of the Protestants in the Sixteenth Century, they were accepted by the

faithful as God's revelation to His people. They are still in the *Catholic* Bible.

—Letter to a Fallen-Away Catholic

One would certainly question the integrity of such behavior on the part of a president or federal judge who similarly edited the Constitution, and the reports issued by such leaders would be regarded with grave suspicion. Why, then, is not the same common sense applied to the antics of Martin Luther? As we shall see in two chapters hence, changing Sacred Texts was not peculiar to him. Key phrases throughout in the King James Bible were reworded to dilute the traditional Catholic interpretation. Yet this is The Book held high by most Protestants as the source of Truth.

With this in mind, what can be said of *sola scriptura,* the Protestant tenet that all Revelation is contained in Scripture? And even if all the discrepancies in their Bible were purged, there is still the problem of private interpretation:

There are not hundreds but *thousands* of Protestant sects, all of them founded on some innovative interpretation of the same Scriptures read by all the others. Could it really be that the Holy Ghost, the changeless and eternal Third Person of the Blessed Trinity, is directing such chaos, telling one group "This is so," and another, "No, that is so"?

This fractionalization percolates down into the very fiber of Protestant thinking, of which "Bible studies" are a natural outgrowth. A group of believers comes together and reads a passage from the Bible. All fine and good, but then they each explain it in light of their own insights. While certainly every time we read the Bible we will be struck by different ideas, we'll make new connections with other passages, derive personal consolation and so on, do we really think that we, living in the twenty-first century, can explain the writings of men dead for thousands of years? Do we have the historical, cultural, social, economic, archaeological and otherwise background to grasp the nuances of their language, the details of their apparel, the workings of their implements, the rate of exchange of their currency?

If we could discern all Truth by ourselves, would Peter have admitted that in Paul's Epistles there are ...

> ... certain things hard to be understood, which the
> unlearned and unstable wrest, as they do also the other
> scriptures, to their own destruction.
> > —II St. Peter III:16

Private interpretation leads inevitably to Pandemonium, for at its heart is the denial that there is One Truth. That Truth was not relegated to each and every individual to ferret out for themselves. Rather Jesus told Peter ...

> And I say to thee: That thou art Peter; and upon
> this rock I will build my church, and the gates of hell
> shall not prevail against it.
> > —St. Matthew XVI:18

... and in so doing established the Church ...

> ... the house of God, which is the church of the
> living God, the pillar and ground of truth.
> > —I Timothy III:15

The modern mind, beset with four centuries of Protestant thinking and its ramifications, finds it hard to give up the throne, to admit that the power to interpret Scripture is not within ourselves, but rests with the Throne of Peter. Clearly, however, this is what Jesus set up, this is what the Fathers of the Church understood to be His intention, and this has been the teaching of the Catholic Church ever since. The Church has the authority from Christ to interpret Scripture—after all, it was the Church that assembled the Bible in the first place.

As we observed at the beginning of this chapter, this is a serious and highly sensitive subject. Certainly we have merely touched lightly on a few key topics. The point that should be driven home here is that Catholics need not be cowed by Bible Christians. We have nothing to be ashamed of with respect to the Traditions of the Church. While it is a great shame that most of this knowledge has been, shall we say, swept under the rug in this century, it is far from lost. A little digging, a little time spent browsing through musty old books, and these things start shining like diamonds in the light of day.

Pass me the magnifying glass.

CHAPTER FOURTEEN

THE BAD BOOK

> When thus reflecting I feel compelled to look to a
> First Cause having an intelligent mind in some de-
> gree analogous to that of man; and I deserve to be
> called a Theist. This conclusion was strong in my
> mind about the time, as far as I can remember, when I
> wrote the "Origin of Species," and it is since that
> time that it has very gradually, with many fluctua-
> tions, become weaker. But then arises the doubt, can
> the mind of man, which has, as I fully believe, been
> developed from a mind as low as that possessed by
> the lowest animals, be trusted when it draws such
> grand conclusions?
>
> —Charles Darwin
> *Life and Letters of Charles Darwin, Vol. I*
> Francis Darwin, editor

∞   ∞   ∞

A CENTURY AGO, CHARLES DARWIN wrote a very bad book
called *The Origin of Species*. It was bad because it gave an
apparently scientific alternative to the creative powers of God.
Though many of his theories have since been discredited or
furiously transformed to fit new data (information which has
for the most part been ignored by the popular culture), his
work continues to muddy the waters to this day.

Tackling the theory of evolution was one of the hardest
things I had to deal with on my road back to the Catholic
Faith. I realize that many churchmen over the last hundred
years have tried to come to some kind of compromise in this
regard by saying that evolution and the Genesis story are

somehow "compatible," but resorting to poetics and vagaries will only get a person so far.

The Genesis story specifies that God created the heavens and the earth, populated the earth with plants and animals, then made Adam, then Eve from Adam, and that shortly thereafter they disobeyed Him.

The theory of evolution proposes that man developed over many years and through slow stages from primitive life forms, and gradually became self-aware. Carried further the theory says that the primitive life forms slowly developed out of more primitive forms, and those came from simple organic matter, which came from inorganic matter, and so on. Carried to extremes, the planet earth and the sun evolved out of the debris of many exploded suns, which condensed out of rarefied hydrogen and other simple gasses, which originated from the explosion of a unique black hole (essentially a point occupying no space but having infinite mass)* from which all known matter erupted in an event called the Big Bang.

The mental somersault necessary to bridge the gap between these two propositions is rather staggering, yet many people manage to slough it off with a wave of a hand or a shrug of shoulders.

I do not propose to solve the problem here. Superb books have been written on the subject, and many of them are still in print. They are full of observations, objections, and clarifications that most people don't stop to think about, such as:

> The General Theory of Evolution is teaching that primitive gas evolved into humans by natural processes. It postulates innumerable intermediate stages and enormous time spans; but these are merely distractions from the essential question of thermodynamics: could it happen? From gas to man would involve such staggering decrease in entropy (disorder) as to mock the 2nd Law of Thermodynamics. Therefore the scientific answer to the question can only be: it could *not* happen.

---

* "Ha!" writes Mike Malone in the column of the rough draft. "The definition of God!"

> Darwin's hypothesis broke the 2nd Law of Thermodynamics, because Darwin was saying that the simple could produce the complex.
> —J. W. G. Johnson
> *Evolution?*

Interesting revelations that inquiring minds would want to know, if the information was only readily available:

> In the domain of Paleontology, various candidates for the Missing Link have been put forward during the past century, but they had to be discarded one after the other for various reasons. The Neanderthal Men were found to have a larger average brain capacity than modern man; they were skilled hunters, they manufactured tools, buried their dead with ceremony and finally disappeared altogether at the time of the *hiatus* (or Deluge) ... The Piltdown Man went down in disgrace; the Australophithecinae or African Ape-Men put forward by Drs. Dart, Broom and Robinson were shown to be just great apes ... the original Java Man has been rejected by such authorities as Marcellin Boule; and Dr. Dubois, who found the fossil of the skull, admitted before his death that it was part of the skull of a gibbon ...
> —Father Patrick O'Connell, B.D.
> *Science of Today and the Problems of Genesis*

The above paragraph from Father O'Connel's book opens the chapter on the so-called Peking Man which, along with the Piltdown Man, formed the "scientific" basis for Teilhard de Chardin's theories—and both fossils were later proved to be out-and-out frauds. Was Teilhard "in" on the deception? Hmm.

How many times have we been told on *National Geographic* and other "nature" shows that animal populations die out slowly over many years as the climate changes gradually over geological time? In light of this, how can the following be explained:

> In 1901 a mammoth was dislodged from the permafrost near Beresovka in Siberia and was subsequently

examined by a team of scientists. Twenty four
pounds of undigested vegetable matter were found in
the stomach, and a comprehensive list was compiled
of the wide range of shrubs, herbs, meadow grasses,
mosses and plants found in the food. The color of the
leaves of one plant was still intact, as if freshly
picked ...

The type of food found in the stomach of the
mammoth cannot grow in that area today; the climate
must have been much milder before the change. Further, since the mammoth lacked oil-producing glands
in the skin and hair-erector muscles, it could not survive in a very cold environment. This also means
that the climate must once have been quite temperate.

It seems that the creature was suddenly overwhelmed in the middle of summer, within a half-hour
of eating the food, and instant death then occurred,
followed by a rapid deep freeze. The sudden death is
proved by the unchewed bean pods, still containing
the beans, that were found between its teeth; the deep
freeze is suggested by the well-preserved state of the
stomach contents and the presence of edible meat.
Some of the carcasses were thawed and fed to dogs in
the expedition party, who then ate it with great relish
and with no after effects.

—G. J. Keane
Creation Rediscovered

(There's even a photograph of the critter—or what's left
of him—in the book!) So much for the slow onslaught of the
Ice Age. And here's something of interest regarding the
theory that our solar system formed from a swirling cloud of
gas and dust:

The particles would not accumulate to form planets. Science knows of no process whereby grains of
dust will stick together, and accumulate to a size
where gravity will take effect ...

The Sun is rotating much too slowly to satisfy the
theory. The Sun's mass is more than 99% of the total mass of the solar system. If it had condensed from
a cloud, the Sun should have 99% of the rotational

momentum of the solar system. Instead, we find that
the lazily turning Sun has less than 1% of the rotational momentum, while the insignificant planets
have more than 99%. How could the Sun have trans-
ferred almost all its rotational momentum to the tiny
planets? Geniuses have tried to answer that; and still
they try.

> —J. W. G. Johnson
> *Evolution?*

And so on and so forth. This is what is called "bait."
Hopefully your curiosity is now sufficiently piqued. There
are many books on the subject awaiting your scrutiny. Happy
reading.

For now, I would prefer to go back to something more basic. Yes, square one: one more time from the top:

> Jesus saith to them: But whom do you say that I
> am?
> —St. Matthew XVI:15

Funny how we keep ending up there, but everything else
does indeed proceed from it. It's hard, I know, and frustrat-
ing, because we haven't been trained to look at the universe
through the lens of this question, but if we endure the annoyance for just a little while, we begin to see that it makes infinite
sense. "The world" tells us to test things according to our
ability or willingness to understand them. Jesus tells us
something radically different, to see all things in His light:

> I am the way, and the truth, and the life. No man
> cometh to the Father, but by me.
> —St. John XIV:6

"The world" would question the wisdom of assuming that
Jesus and this "religious stuff" has anything to do with science. And yet this same Jesus made everything science claims
to explain:

> All things were made by him: and without him was
> made nothing that was made.
> —St. John I:3

So we're propelled back to square one, forced to answer His question yet again, this time hopefully with a little more experience, a little more confidence, a little stronger Faith under our belts:

> But whom do you say that I am?

If our answer is still—

> Thou art Christ, the Son of the living God.

—then we have to come to grips with something else that He said:

> For if you did believe Moses, you would perhaps believe me also; for he wrote of me.
> But if you do not believe his writings, how will you believe my words?
> —St. John V:46-47

Let us try to tear away the debris from our windshields so we can face this clearly. Jesus became a man and entered human history in order to rectify the damage done by Adam and Eve. Evolution tells us we had no "first parents," but rather an endless succession of gradually evolving ancestral primates. There would have been no particular couple out of which the human race would develop, but a clan or tribe or perhaps a whole species. Compromise breeds compromise, and if we try to meld these two opposing concepts together, the chances are we'll end up toppling over into the evolutionists' camp down the road. The more we think evolutionarily, the more evolutionary our thinking will become. And the moment we embrace evolution, the following chain of dominoes is set toppling:

> Because if evolution is true, then Adam and Eve did not exist.
> And if Adam and Eve did not exist, then there is no such thing as Original Sin.
> If there is no such thing as Original Sin, there is no need to be redeemed from Original Sin.

And if there is no need for a redeemer, then there is no need for Christ, the Second Person of the Blessed Trinity, to die on the Cross for our sins.

And if there is no such thing as the Sacrifice of the Cross, then there is no such thing as the Sacrifice of the Mass.

—John Vennari
"Evolution, Secularism,
and the Modern Church of Compromise"
VNI Conference, Monrovia, CA; August 1993

Before evolution came along, the believer could always ask of the unbeliever: "Then where did you come from?" While there was no easy comeback to this question, there was still hope for conversion. But once evolution was introduced, and then gained widespread acceptance, the atheist had his answer. He can dodge God by claiming "natural selection" as his maker. Within that realm, "survival of the fittest" is the law, a law which raises self-preservation above all else. Self-interest, as a first principle, promotes greed, avarice, and a lack of concern for our fellow man. It reduces morality to rationalization and ethics to obsolescence. It is absolutely incompatible with the selfless charity demanded by Jesus of those who follow Him.

Evolution has been granted the attributes formerly reserved to God alone. It is omnipresent and omnipotent, in that it has invaded all the sciences and is now considered the driving force behind every natural process in the universe. It has taken on the nature of religion. It has become a god in its own right, a proud and overbearing one at that, and woe betide any who dare to blaspheme or apostatize:

The tyranny of the *Zeitgeist* in the matter of evolution is overwhelming to a degree of which outsiders have no idea; not only does it influence (as I must admit that it does in my own case) our manners of thinking, but there is the oppression as in the days of the "terror." How very few of the leaders of science today dare tell the truth concerning their own state of mind! How many feel themselves forced in public to do a lip service to a cult they do not believe in! As Professor T. H. Morgan intimates, it is only too true that many of these who would on no account be guilty of an act which they recognize as dishonest, nevertheless speak and write habitually as if evolution were an absolute certainty as well established as the law of gravitation.

—Thomas Dwight
Thoughts if a Catholic Anatomist
Quoted by Robert T. Clark & James D. Bales
Why Scientists Accept Evolution

Yet evolution is clearly not an established fact because it describes processes which cannot be verified by laboratory experiment. It is based on the uniformitarian assumption that natural processes we observe today have always been occurring at the same rate, such as uranium decaying into lead. Of this there is no, and can never be any, proof. Who's to say that the rate of uranium decay doesn't accelerate or decelerate over time? Men haven't been around long enough to observe such things. The whole evolution thing is based on guesswork, assumption, and presumption. And its effect on our culture, our ethics, our way of thinking, even our religion, have been devastating:

The apparent innocence of the theory of evolution is perhaps its greatest strength. And most people were unaware of its long-term devastating consequences. Evolution is a pantheistic, naturalistic religion parading as science; and the parade is long, and the parade is loud; to the point where in most peoples' minds, evolution has made a charade of the True Religion, and this is the most diabolic aspect of the whole thing. Evolution is a proud counterfeit creed that has the audacity to point to the genuine credo and accuse it of being an impostor. It is a myth, taken to be true fact, which causes the true facts of Genesis to be regarded as myth. It smacks of all the backwards topsy-turviness of the Satanic and has produced our upside-down modern Church, where what was right before is wrong now, and what was wrong before is right now; and the upside down Church immediately brings to mind the upside down Crucifix, which is

the symbol of witchcraft and the centerpiece of the
Black Mass.

—John Vennari
"Evolution, Secularism,
and the Modern Church of Compromise"
VNI Conference, Monrovia, CA; August 1993

Strong words, but not uncalled for.

If we find ourselves poisoned by this insidious thing called
evolution, perhaps we should heed the admonition of Saint
Paul:

> ... Know you not that a little leaven corrupteth the
> whole lump?
> Purge out the old leaven, that you may be a new
> paste, as you are unleavened. For Christ our pasch is
> sacrificed.
> Therefore let us feast, not with the old leaven, nor
> with the leaven of malice and wickedness; but with
> the unleavened bread of sincerity and truth.
> —I Corinthians V:6-8

We must pray to God for the Grace to recognize the
Truth. We must seek out good books that explain the theory
of evolution *honestly*. Any honest presentation will state that
it is an unprovable hypothesis. We must go further and educate ourselves regarding the Catholic Faith and Her teachings.
We cannot stand up against the onslaught of the modern world
if we are not prepared with the Truth. If we don't have time
to do the research, we should gravitate toward people who do,
so they can distill the information for our consumption.

The one thing we must never do is sit back complacently
and let whatever happens happen. That's what dough does
while the leaven within makes the whole lump rise ...

CHAPTER FIFTEEN

HOORAY FOR DOUAY

As Brother Francis readily admitted, his mastery of pre-Deluge English was far from masterful yet. The way nouns could sometimes modify other nouns in that tongue had always been one of his weak points ... He had finally learned that *house cat* did not mean *cat house* ... But what of a triple appositive like *fall-out survival shelter?*

—Walter M. Miller, Jr.
A Canticle for Leibowitz

∞ ∞ ∞

A WORD REGARDING "NEW" translations of the Bible. Or, rather, let us start by examining the old and see how it has been supplanted by the new.

Few Catholics today realize that one and only one version of the Bible was ever declared to be the official text of the canonical Scriptures by a council of the Church (Trent, 1546 AD) and free from error by a pope (Pius XII in his encyclical letter *Divino Afflante Spiritu,* 1943). I am speaking of the Vulgate which St. Jerome (342-420 AD) translated into Latin from the original languages at the request of Pope Damasus. A linguistic genius, a holy man, and a Doctor of the Church, St. Jerome spoke Latin, Greek, Hebrew, and Aramaic. He was fifteen hundred years closer to the ancient languages than today's self-proclaimed experts, which made him a far better judge of their subtleties.

No other extant version—not the Septuagint, nor any of the other ancient Greek manuscripts, nor the Syriac, nor the

Masoretic texts—no other version carries the Church's solemn pronouncement, the protection of the Holy Ghost. Yet virtually every modern translation is derived from these unofficial versions rather than the Vulgate. Why? Because modern scripture scholars would rather cater to the errors of their Protestant colleagues than stand up for the true teachings of the Catholic Faith, assuming they even know them.

> The Masoretic texts are Hebrew bibles copied down from memory by an ancient guild of rememberers called Masoretes. At the synod of Jamnia about 90 A.D., the most influential rabbis of the Jews, led by one Akiba, revised the Old Testament to excise references which pointed to Christ as the Messias. Older texts were destroyed whenever they could be found. When, in the 300s, St. Jerome commenced his work he employed not only the unchanged Greek Old Testament, the Septuagint; he combed the remoter regions of Palestine to find pre-Jamnia texts, a quest in which he was successful. At the Reformation many of the Protestants (including the translators of the King James Bible) used the Masoretic text, as did the creators of the New American. But the discovery of the Dead Sea Scrolls, buried since 70 A.D. vindicated the antiquity of the Vulgate.
>
> —Charles A. Coulombe
> "Return of a Classic"
> Review of the *Douay-Rheims Bible*
> with Haydock footnotes.

The English version most faithful to the Latin Vulgate is without doubt the *Douay-Rheims Bible*, the New and Old Testaments of which were first published in 1582 and 1609 respectively. Being a translation, it is not covered by the decrees of Trent and Pius XII as is the Vulgate. We can nonetheless rest assured that the translators did not have an heretical agenda in the back of their minds as they did their work. They produced a literal translation, not a paraphrase based on private opinion as in the case of other versions.

Let us focus our attention on that profound moment when the Angel Gabriel appeared to the Blessed Virgin Mary to announce that Her time had come:

> Hail, full of grace, the Lord is with thee: blessed art
> thou among women.
>
> —St. Luke I:28
> —*Douay-Rheims Bible*

So reads the Douay-Rheims. Notice the Angel bestows upon Her the solemn title, "Full of Grace." How different this is from:

> Hail, thou art highly favoured, the Lord is with
> thee: blessed art thou among women.
>
> —*King James Version*

> Hail, favored one! The Lord is with you. (The sec-
> ond phrase is deleted.)
>
> —*New American Bible*

> Rejoice, so highly favored! The Lord is with you.
> (The second phrase is deleted but alluded to in a foot-
> note.)
>
> —*The Jerusalem Bible*

And for the Club Med set, there's the ever-popular ...

> Congratulations, favored lady! The Lord is with
> you. (The second phrase is deleted.)
>
> —*The Living Bible*

Notice that all these "new" translations have something in common: the obfuscation of Mary's Immaculate Conception. To call Her "favored" is nothing at all like recognizing Her remarkable state of freedom from Original Sin. Day after day, the New American Bible's outright capitulation to Protestantism is read from the pulpits in the United States during the Novus Ordo Mass. Small wonder our children grow up without a clue as to Mary's role in our Salvation. (I know of a young woman who lost her Faith by reading the *footnotes* in the New American version—they're that insidious!)

Let us look at another Biblical word-shift, one with which we are bombarded every year at Christmas time. This is how the Douay-Rheims translates the Angels' announcement of Christ's birth to the shepherds:

> Glory to God in the Highest; and on earth peace to men of good will.
>
> —St. Luke II:14

Regarding this verse, St. Augustine tells us:

> The birth of Christ giveth not peace of mind, or salvation, but to such as are of good will, because he worketh not our good against our wills, but with the concurrence of our will.
>
> —Haydock Footnotes, St. Luke II:14
> *Douay-Rheims Bible*

In other words, as with *pro multis* (see Chapter Sixteen), God's salvific gift, though freely given, is not ladled upon anyone who does not seek it. We must take an active part in the process. But notice how other translations present an entirely, albeit subtly, different picture:

> Glory to God in the highest, and on earth peace, good will toward men.
>
> —*King James Version*

> Glory to God in the highest and on earth peace to those on whom his favor rests.
>
> —*New American Bible*

> Glory to God in the highest heaven, and peace on earth to men who enjoy his favor.
>
> —*The Jerusalem Bible*

> Glory to God in the highest, and peace to his people on earth.
>
> —The mistranslation of the *Novus Ordo Missae* currently in use in the United States

Isn't the change in orientation intriguing? How nice of God to shower His peace upon everyone, regardless of their response to Him or it.

Rest assured that the closest thing to the time-honored, Trent-decreed, pope-approved Vulgate —

> Gloria in excelsis Deo. Et in terra pax hominibus bonæ voluntatis.

—is the Douay-Rheims translation. If you haven't got one, I suggest you put it at the top of your must-get list ...

Oh, and by the way, here's a complaint I often hear when I give my spiel on the benefits of the Douay Bible. It goes something like this: "It's too awkward to read. You know, all those *thee's* and *thou's* ..."

Well, my degree in English may render me prejudiced, but it occurs to me that the Douay translation was roughly contemporary with the works of a playwright named William Shakespeare. The Bard wrote at a time when the English language had reached a peak in lyrical expression, rhythmic meter, and robust imagery. We would do well to understand that his plays were attended by common folk, most of them illiterate. The fact that they understood and enjoyed his plays—while we bumpkins of the Nintendo Age do not—demonstrates the deterioration of the English language over the past four hundred years. In case you haven't noticed, we have become a mediocre people who strive for nothing and revel in our ignorance. We are all too used to our goals descending to us rather than us struggling toward them. Of course, as I said, I may be prejudiced.

In any case, even if the language of the Douay style is cumbersome to you, I strongly suggest you learn to live with it. The challenge will do you good, and the True Faith even more so.

CHAPTER SIXTEEN

TURNS OF PHRASE ...

Confusion hath devoured the labour of our fathers
from our youth, their flocks and their herds, their
sons and their daughters.

We shall sleep in our confusion, and our shame
shall cover us, because we have sinned against the
Lord our God, we and our fathers from our youth even
to this day, and we have not harkened to the voice of
the Lord our God.

—Jeremias III:24-25

∞ ∞ ∞

IT IS AMAZING WHAT SWITCHING a couple of words around
can do. Insert a word here, delete a word there, swap them,
and the meaning of a sentence changes radically.

In the Dim Ages before the ambiguous enlightenment of
Vatican II, the Catholic Church used to be accused of being
too nitpicky. Every word, every gesture, every motion of the
priest during Mass, for example, was observed *scrupulously*.
Sloppiness in this regard was considered a sin. There was a
reason for this: to preserve continuity, to insure the passing on
of the Faith in its entirety to the next generation. What our
ancestors understood with such intensity, and our liberal hierarchy has abandoned without a care, is that a tiny change can
have profound implications over time, especially if the previous underlying theology is not consistently applied.

Perhaps the most glaring example of such an imprudent
switcheroo is the wording of the Consecration of the wine in
the English translation of the *Novus Ordo Missæ*. Let us first

examine the words honored by centuries in the immemorial Tridentine Rite (note that in the altar missal they are always capitalized):

> HIC EST ENIM CALIX SANGUINIS MEI,
> NOVI ET ÆTERNI TESTAMENTI:
> MYSTERIUM FIDEI:
> QUI PRO VOBIS ET PRO MULTIS
> EFFUNDETUR
> IN REMISSIONEM PECCATORUM.

Which is rendered:

> FOR THIS IS THE CHALICE OF MY BLOOD
> OF THE NEW AND ETERNAL CONVENANT:
> THE MYSTERY OF FAITH,
> WHICH SHALL BE SHED
> FOR YOU AND FOR MANY
> UNTO THE REMISSION OF SINS.

The key words at issue here are *pro multis*, "for many." Catholics attending the Novus Ordo are presented with something entirely different—the insertion of "for all" in place of "for many" (note the lack of capitalization):

> Take this, all of you, and drink from it:
> this is the cup of my blood,
> the blood of the new and everlasting covenant.
> It will be shed for you and for all
> so that sins may be forgiven.
>
> —The Novus Ordo

"So what?" say a great many people, sincere Catholics among them.

So quite a lot! The difference is actually profound if you give it some consideration.

Let us say we're at a dinner party and the hostess rises after the main course and announces, "My very special dessert will now be served, and there is enough for many of you." Would we not react to her words with anticipation, even anxiety, especially if her reputation for splendid sweets precedes her?   On what basis, we would want to know, do some guests get served and some go without?

On the other hand, how would we respond if the hostess were to say, "Okay, it's time for dessert; there's plenty for all!"...?   More than likely we would sit back, undo our belts, and await our portion with confidence.   Our anticipation would be of an entirely different kind, arising from presumption rather than uncertainty.

So, too, with "for all" in replace of "for many" in the Mass.   It tends to promote casual passivity rather than a definitive participation in the Salvation process.   Why bother striving for that which will be delivered on a platter?

On a doctrinal level, what is at stake here is the difference between Redemption and Salvation.   When Jesus died on the Cross, He *redeemed* us all—that is, He "paid the ransom" to the Father for all our sins and transgressions.   He "repurchased us" from the clutches of Satan.   But what He did *not* do was *save* us all—rather, He opened the doors for the *possibility* of Salvation.   As we will see later on (in Chapter Forty-nine), Salvation has a very specific meaning, namely gaining the Eternal Happiness of Heaven.   In the Tridentine Mass, the emphasis during the Consecration is on the salvific achievement of Jesus Christ; whereas the Novus Ordo turns our attention to the Redemptive.   But since Catechetics are in a shambles and few Catholics—priests included—know their terminology, most people today assume that Jesus Christ, in shedding His Blood "for all," has *saved* us all—which is patently not the case.

> ... allow this writer to try to clarify things by reaching for an analogy. As good a one as comes to mind is the TWA hijacking of a couple of years ago. Remember it? Lebanese Shi'ite Moslems took captive a U.S. civilian aircraft and all its passengers. They landed in Beirut. As we all know, the hostages eventually were freed. Although the U.S. media downplayed or obscured what it was that accounted for their liberation, they were *redeemed* by President Assad of Syria. The *price he paid* was giving his word to the captors that Lebanese Shi'ites held in Israeli prison camps would be freed ...

Now suppose that the TWA hostages had simply
been redeemed—i.e., freed by Assad's paying a price.
Suppose, in other words, that they had simply been
let go in an alien land; that there was no food for
them; no doctors ready to treat their possible medical
needs; no means provided for them to contact loved
ones in the U.S.; above all, no transportation fur-
nished for their return home. They would have been
redeemed, but they certainly would *not* have been
saved.

In the same way, Christ redeemed us—He paid for
our sins—with His precious blood, but not even that
by itself would have saved us. He provided other
means for getting us home, which is to speak of
Heaven. They are the Church and the sacraments she
uniquely makes available.

—Gary Potter
In Reaction

As we examine the modern Church with a discerning eye,
we find many such examples of word play which ultimately
produce a languid populace, a lazily confused herd that
couldn't care less and eventually does. In challenging these
"little" details, the concerned Catholic is perceived as petty
and boorish.

"What's the big deal?" yawns the chairperson of the liturgy committee. "What's in a word?"

Sometimes an Eternity.

CREDO IN UNAM DEUM
Patrem omnipotentem ...

I BELIEVE IN ONE GOD,
the Father almighty ...

—The Creed of the Tridentine Mass

Historically, there have been three major Creeds, or statements of the Faith: the Apostle's Creed which we say in the
Rosary, the Nicene Creed which is said during the Tridentine
Mass, and the Athanasian Creed which few have heard of today because of its incompatibility with the bleeding heart of

the modern Church. In none of them were Catholics called upon to say:

> We believe in one God,
> the Father, the Almighty ...
>
> —The Novus Ordo

"We" as opposed to "I."   While the use of the plural may certainly help to build this nebulous thing called "community" that has so captured the imagination of the New Age Church (or "newage" as I prefer to call it due to the obvious rhyme potential), the real point of the exercise is lost. Each individual human being must embrace the Faith in order to save their soul. Such a decision is private, not collective. My reward in Heaven will be based on what I believe and how I put that decision into action. When I go before God I will not be called to account for the aggregate acts of the community. My Salvation is my own responsibility.

All this brouhaha over the idea of "community" seems to stem from an overemphasis on one verse in the New Testament:

> For where there are two or three gathered together
> in my name, there am I in the midst of them.
>
> —St. Matthew XVIII:20

While this is indeed a profound mystery, it is an entirely separate issue from the true heart of the Mass: the Sacrifice of Jesus Christ on the Altar. This shift of emphasis has moved the spotlight from the Body, Blood, Soul, and Divinity of Christ present in the Holy Eucharist to the "body of believers," this community thing. The Mass has deteriorated into an excuse to worship *ourselves*.

Why was "Holy, holy, holy, Lord God of hosts!" commuted to "... God of power and might"? Was this change for the sake of change, or did the framers of the new deal no longer believe in Angels? Did they feel that beating their breasts and saying, *"mea culpa, mea culpa, mea maxima culpa"* ("Through my fault, through my fault, through my most grievous fault") was out of style, or did they no longer believe in sin and so scratched it? Was the Last Gospel deleted because it made the Mass too long, especially with all the extra readings they'd upholstered into the front, or could they not tolerate the indictment hurled at them from the pen of the Beloved Disciple of Jesus:

> And the light shineth in the darkness, and the darkness did not comprehend it.
>
> —St. John I:5

While the liturgical reformers—may God have mercy on their souls—were at it (indeed they continue to hack away), they also dispensed with public gestures of reverence. In the Old Mass, the priest made fifty-three Signs of the Cross, now relegated to a scant handful. Instead of genuflecting out of respect for the Incarnation during the Creed, the congregation is now directed to bow—an instruction which has been ignored altogether.

> For us men ["men" has since been deleted by popular, or at least, pastoral demand on sexist grounds] and for our salvation he came down from heaven:
>
> By the power of the Holy Spirit he was born of the Virgin Mary and became man [we're waiting to see how this second appearance of the objectionable allusion to masculinity will be modified—perhaps He only became a "person" ...?]
>
> —The ever-evolving Novus Ordo

Then the people were told to stand, not kneel, for the *Agnus Dei* (Lamb of God) and the *Domine, non sum dignus* (Lord, I am not worthy). Kneeling for Communion was abandoned with ease. What ever happened to the perception that kneeling was good for the soul? Or do they even believe in souls anymore?

Bit by bit these "little" details, these tiny drops of water, are gathering into a raging torrent. The current is carrying so much human flotsam right out of the Church and into the maw of Hell.

And to think it all started with a few simple turns of phrase.

CHAPTER SEVENTEEN

... TURN THE TIDE ...

An accepted principle in regard to liturgical worship is that the doctrinal standpoint of a Christian body must necessarily be reflected in its worship. Liturgical rites should express what they contain. It is not necessary for the Catholic position to be expressly contradicted for a rite to become suspect; the suppression of prayers which had given liturgical expression to the doctrine behind the rite is more than sufficient to give cause for concern.

—Michael Davies
Pope Paul's New Mass

∞ ∞ ∞

WE MUST GIVE CREDIT, albeit grudgingly, to those who planned the insidious attack on our Mass. To swindle us out of our birthright was heinous enough; to leave us with the bland broth of the Novus Ordo in its stead was unconscionable.

By entangling those of us who truly care in the details discussed in the previous chapter, they have made us seem petty, rigid, and meticulous to the point of distraction. In a culture which caters to hastiness and imprecision such qualities are not tolerated. Our resulting outbursts of rage and frustration are seen as severity, a lack of love, an absence of with-it-ness. They call us Pharisees and legalists. We are *personae non gratae*, strangers in our own sanctuaries, unacceptable intruders in the all-accepting "newage" Church. Yet we cannot help but bristle as sacred phrases are snipped and swapped, twisted into something they were never intended to be.

Meanwhile, they tore pages and pages of beautiful prayers out of the Mass, replacing them with tepid tracts of questionable orthodoxy—all of which has spurred a wholesale descent into mediocrity. They understood the meaning of the principle—

> *Legem credendi lex statuat supplicandi.*
> Let the law of prayer fix the law of faith.

—or "how we pray is how we believe." If we pray bilge, we will come to believe bilge.

Only the most pernicious fiend could have taken out this reverent prayer said by the priest at the Offertory—

> Accept, O holy Father, almighty and eternal God, this spotless victim, which I, Thy unworthy servant, offer unto Thee, my living and true God, to atone for my numberless sins, offenses and negligences; on behalf of all here present and likewise for all faithful Christians living and dead, that it may profit me and them as a means of salvation unto life everlasting.
> —The Tridentine Mass

—and replaced it with a Jewish *berakhah*, or table blessing:

> Blessed are you, Lord, God of all creation, through your goodness we have this bread to offer, which earth has given and human hands have made. It will become for us the bread of life.
> —The Novus Ordo

Technically, at least on the surface, one can't argue too much against it, but that's because it doesn't really say anything controversial—and it certainly doesn't call attention to our sins or our desperate need for God's help in effecting our Salvation. But "how we pray is how we believe." If we pray nothing in particular, we will believe nothing in particular.

Beneath the surface, however, we find a labyrinth of implied heresy. Since when has the Church or Her priests ever offered *bread* to God at Mass? In the Tridentine Offertory, the priest holds up the host and says, as quoted above, "Accept, O holy Father, almighty and eternal God, this *spotless victim* ..."

> Suscipe, sancte Pater, omnipotens æterne Deus,
> hanc *immaculatam hostiam* ...

The Latin word *hostia* means "victim." Even though the Words of Consecration haven't yet been uttered, the priest *anticipates* the perfection of the Victim to be sacrificed at the altar, Jesus Christ Himself. True, some of the old missals translated *immaculatam hostiam* as "spotless host," and this may have led to a general misconception of the term. We tend to think of a "host" as a little round piece of tasteless bread—even Webster's defines it as "eucharistic bread." Our priests should have known better. However the shift came about, in the Novus Ordo the emphasis on Christ as Victim Without Blemish is virtually erased. I can't imagine any casual observer gleaning the sacrificial nature of the Mass from the New Rite, especially if the priest uses "Eucharistic Prayer No. 2."

I've had a hunch for some time that the retirement of pure white wafers and the introduction of the whole grain variety was in some way a part of this doctrinal shell game. The mottled texture and color of the new hosts could hardly be described as "spotless." I was delighted, at least intellectually, when Bishop Forester made the same observation in Bryan Houghton's poignant apocryphal work, *Mitre and Crook*.

And am I the only person on whom the ambiguity of ...

> It will become *for us* the bread of life.

... is not lost? To be sure, "for us" could simply and innocently refer to God's favor rendered on our behalf. But it can also slip us into the relative realm of the never-quite-settled: does it only become the bread of life *for us*, because we're here, and not *for others* because they're not? If an unbeliever slipped into the church and received Communion, would it then not be the Body of Christ "for him" because he didn't believe? Subjective possibility vs. objective reality. Can it really be a coincidence that this ambiguity is stated yet again

in "Eucharistic Prayer No. 2" which, being the shortest, is
most often used?

> Let your Spirit come upon these gifts
> to make them holy,
> so that they may become *for us*
> the body and blood of our Lord, Jesus Christ.
> —The Novus Ordo
> (Emphasis mine, the lack of caps is theirs)

What we're seeing here is not just a loss of clarity, but of
integrity. The prayers of the Old Rite, having been solidified
in the stone of the Latin language and proven true by the test
of centuries of scrutiny, accurately stated the intentions of the
priest, the purpose of the Mass, and the Faith of the Church.
Don't think for a second that the people, especially those who
run the liturgy committees and parish councils, haven't caught
on. To those losing the Faith, the downhill momentum can
become exhilarating.

> This principle is embodied in the phrase *"legem
> credendi lex statuat supplicandi*—let the law of prayer
> fix the law of faith." In other words, the liturgy of
> the Church is a sure guide to Her teaching. This is
> usually presented in the abbreviated form of *lex
> orandi, lex credendi,* and can be translated freely as
> meaning that the manner in which the Church wor-
> ships *(lex orandi)* must reflect what the Church be-
> lieves *(lex credendi).*
> —Michael Davies
> *Pope Paul's New Mass*

Can it possibly be said that the New Rite fits this criteria,
that in its manner of worship it truly reflects what the Church
believes? Or rather, is the Novus Ordo a departure from the
Faith imposed on us by those who have lost it themselves and
wish us to do likewise? Has exposure to its tepid mediocrity
and shifting ambiguities transmuted the character of the people into something just as vulgar and unsound? I fear this to
be the case. As they pray, so shall they believe. As they believe, so shall they live.

But what did the beat generation, in their haste to be trendy, leave us? A watered down rite that is as uninspiring as it is insipid. What reflection of the glory of God is it? Even a junior high student would know that "All glory and honor *is* yours ..." is poor usage. Not content with stealing the majesty and solemnity of the mass, they took its grammar too. Even Luther and Cramner stopped at that.

—Charles A. Coulombe
Everyman Today Call Rome

Thus the nobility and grandeur of the cathedral has been replaced with the utilitarian shoe-box ecclesial-community meeting building, the Gregorian choir received their pink slips while the Dylan-Baez look-alikes were awarded microphones in the sanctuary, meticulous care of the Holy Eucharist became lackadaisical handing out of dry, crumbly bread from wicker baskets, and as for the Faith it all represented ...

Sad to say, the Church of Our Fathers has become the Convention of the Ho-Hum.

And as they live, so shall they die.

Turn the phrase, and you turn the tide.

CHAPTER EIGHTEEN

... GENTLY, GENTLY AWAY

> You seem to have defined with wonderful clarity
> the basic difference between the new rite and the old.
> If you think of Mass as "mediating religion to the
> people" then clearly it should be comprehensible, i.e.
> in the vernacular, and didactic, i.e. with lots of scrip-
> ture readings and homilies; moreover, the people
> should demonstrate that they have received the mes-
> sage by constant "participation" at every level and in
> diverse forms—exclamations, hymns, gestures.   If,
> on the other hand, you think of Mass as "mediating
> the religion of the people to God," then, as a matter
> of fact, there is nothing for it but silence.
> —Bryan Houghton
> *Mitre and Crook*

∞ ∞ ∞

THERE WAS A TIME not so long ago, during the first quarter
of my lifetime, when the local Catholic church differed from
all the Protestant churches not just in ceremony, artistic grandeur, taste, and minor things like being part of the only
Church outside of which there is no Salvation, but in something which has become the rarest of treasures these days:
    Silence.
    You went into a Protestant church before a service and it
sounded like a movie theatre before the flick.* Jabber, jabber,

---

* Several of my Protestant friends have objected to this portrayal of their
services, but I swear that I am speaking from my personal experience.

jabber. You removed yourself from First Presbyterian to St. Andrew's or St. Jude's or Queen of the Angels, and you knew what you would find: the awesome stillness one would expect in the House of God. Right up to the moment the priest followed the altar boys out to start Mass you could hear a pin drop. Immediately upon their exit at the conclusion a hush descended like a warm summer rain. Even during the Mass itself the priest said many of the prayers in secret.**

The Catholic church was a place you could go to sort out your thoughts. In times of difficulty you could walk the Stations and restore your courage. When things were going well you could kneel before the statue of Saint Anne, or whichever Saint had been helpful in the past, and express your gratitude. When death took a loved one you could sit in the shadows and let the tears flow.

No one would have dared to disturb your prayer. No one even said, "Excuse me," if they made an accidental noise. Their immediate cessation was apology enough. It wasn't that it was a sin to make an unnecessary sound, it was unfitting. The candle in the red sanctuary lamp declared that Jesus Christ was there in the Tabernacle, that God Himself was present. Awe was the only appropriate human response.

True, God chooses to speak to us in many different ways, but most often He chooses to whisper.

> And he said to him: Go forth, and stand upon the mount before the Lord: and behold the Lord passeth, and a great and strong wind before the Lord overthrowing the mountains, and breaking the rocks in pieces: the Lord is not in the wind, and after the wind an earthquake: the Lord is not in the earthquake.
>
> And after the earthquake a fire: the Lord is not in the fire, and after the fire a whistling of a gentle air.
>
> And when Elias heard it, he covered his face with his mantle ...
>
> —III Kings XIX:11-13

** Actually, in the Old Rite there were three degrees of "loudness," vs. two in the New Rite.

So did Elias come to understand, and the Psalmist, and many who have desired to hear the voice of God. Sometimes He speaks in thunderous tones, but more often He communicates in a language without words.

> Be still and see that I am God ...
>
> —Psalm XLV:11

There was a time when everyone in a Catholic church acted as though they saw.

There was also a time when we weren't required to "participate" at Mass but to "assist," which simply meant to be present. In light of today's drive to invade each and every person's space with syrupy greetings, folk-rock ditties, microphones on the verge of feedback, insincere handshakes, half-hearted responses, and quasi-tonal sing-along-singing, the thought of sitting and listening—or worse, *kneeling* and *praying*—seems downright alien. Perhaps extraterrestrial—planetary, not Angelic.

It certainly is anachronistic. (Not that they're being *judgmental* or anything like that.)

When I think of those pastors and nuns who brought the twangy-guitar amateurs, over-vibratoed debutantes and garish felt banners into the sanctuary to compete for our attention, I am reminded of a letter I once read from a master devil to his nephew, Wormwood, a "junior tempter":

> Music and silence—how I detest them both! How thankful we should be that ever since our Father entered Hell—though longer ago than humans, reckoning in light years, could express—no square inch of infernal space and no moment of infernal time has been surrendered to either of those abominable forces, but all has been occupied by Noise—Noise, the grand dynamism, the audible expression of all that is exultant, ruthless, and virile—Noise which alone defends us from silly qualms, despairing scruples, and impossible desires. We will make the whole universe a noise in the end. We have already made great strides in this direction as regards the Earth. The melodies and silences of Heaven will be shouted down in the

end. But I admit we are not yet loud enough, or anything like it. Research is in progress ...

—C. S. Lewis
The Screwtape Letters

Do none of the liturgical innovators notice that the people—though they're trying their best to cooperate in the
"spirit of reform"—are losing interest no matter how much
ballyhoo the "music ministry" musters? Change for the sake
of change becomes boring.

The thought that we might not all have to jump through
hoops in unison rankles against the "spirit of community"
which seeks to bring everyone to the same mediocre level.
But the fact is that true prayer is not orchestrated, it is lived.
True devotion is a state of being, not just a mode of action.

> ... I said to Mrs D.: "I notice that at Mass you
> don't use a rosary or missal or anything. What do
> you do, Mrs Donkin?" Without a moment's thought
> or hesitation the answer came: "I sits there and I
> loves." When anyone starts criticizing the piety of
> the laity, the harsh voice of Mrs Donkin rings in my
> ears: "I sits there and I loves." St Teresa of Avila
> could say no more.
>
> —Bryan Houghton
> *Mitre and Crook*

Catholic devotion as it was practiced for many centuries is
lost on the modern mind, for which everything must come
packaged, stamped with approval by some scrutinizing bureaucratic agency, and scientifically explained. Mysteries are
verboten. Ecstasy is achieved by absorption into the bloodstream of synthetic drugs, or switched-on quasi-Oriental body-
posture contortions, not by listening in silence to God.

For us "ecstasy" is the wrong word because our walk with
God is not based on feelings but on choices, on Faith rather
than emotions. For the most part, and for most people, we do
not "feel" God's presence in the Tabernacle, we accept it;
and behave accordingly. We do not hear whirlwinds and sense
the ground buckling under our feet, but we do meditate on
God's unimaginable glory and our aspiration of complete
submission to Him. By all outward appearances, we might

appear bored.   But inside, ah inside, some marvelous things are quietly happening inside.

> What do I, Edmund Forester, imagine is happening during Mass in the old rite? Quite simple. After a bit of back-chat, Epistles and Gospels and things, I uncover the instruments of my craft and lay on the sacrifice of Man's Redemption in much the same way as a plumber lays on water. Yes, but the people? They start subsiding. Some meditate for a moment but soon give up; some thumb a prayer book without much conviction; some finger a rosary without thinking; the majority just sit or kneel and become empty. They have their distractions, of course, but as far as they are able they are recollected. You see, the state of prayer of the overwhelming majority of the faithful is that of "simple regard."
>
> —Bryan Houghton
> *Mitre and Crook*

I miss that a lot these days.   Arriving at St. Elizabeth's a few minutes before Mass to get in a decade or two is like trying to think in the midst of a K-Mart at Christmas time. It is easier after Mass to get into my car and drive away with the windows rolled up than to sit in a pew and try to pray amidst the frenzy of gossip and idle banter that erupts as soon as the priest says, "The Mass is ended—have a nice day!"

Well, my friends, the day is coming when the silence will return to the Catholic churches. A pin dropped at the front will be heard in the back. No doubt about it. Of course, there will be no sanctuary lamp, for there will be no Tabernacle in the building. There will be no statue of Saint Anne or Stations around the nave because such antiquated paraphernalia will have long been sold off to assuage the higher cost of living enjoyed by the clergy. There will be no kneelers or pews, the parish council having decided that easy chairs are more fit for modern persons—the front three rows will even be recliners. And in the midst of it all, lo and behold the gossiping and blathering will have stopped.

There will be no noise because there will be no people. They will all have left: the liberals in search of new thrills, the priests in search of spouses, and the Traditionalists in search of catacombs in which to practice their Faith as their forefathers had done.

Silence will in the end prevail.

And the tide turns gently, gently away.

CHAPTER NINETEEN

ALTARLUDE

> And Noe built an altar unto the Lord: and taking of all cattle and fowls that were clean, offered holocausts upon the altar.
> And the Lord smelled a sweet savour, and said: I will no more curse the earth for the sake of man: for the imagination and thought of man's heart are prone to evil from his youth ...
> —Genesis VIII:20-21

∞ ∞ ∞

THE NEXT FEW CHAPTERS have titles that play on the word "altar." This sets them apart in the table of contents, as indeed they are somewhat different in tone from the rest of the book, being of a more personal, reflective, and self-historical nature. They may provide some readers an "interlude." Nonetheless they are part of the whole, and so are not set too far apart, as in a separate section.

Every time I tried on the idea of dividing this book into sections, my instincts whispered, "Don't." One of the profound glories of the Roman Catholic Faith is that every doctrine, every dogma, every bit of history, rubric, hue of vestment and dab of ash join together to make an interconnected, mutually-supporting, all-encompassing latticework. Each detail hangs suspended in the influence of every other, like all the stars in the heavens joyously dancing in the ambient cosmic aura of light and gravity.

In its way, the entirety of this book is an attempt to reflect—admittedly "through a glass in a dark manner"* —the
Catholic Faith, the safe harbor in which I have sought refuge.
As these "altarludes" are of a journalistic nature, close to the
marrow, I decided the fitting place for them was near the heart
of the book.   All the other celestial orbs, from my humble
perspective, dance around this.

My adolescent years were rather a muddle, and I can't be
sure all my time placements are accurate.   I may have some
things out of sequence, and some details askew.   But this is
how my middle-aged mind remembers them.   If anyone out
there recognizes Sister MC and Father Q from the context and
wants to volunteer corrections, I welcome letters from old
classmates.

---

* I Corinthians XIII:12

CHAPTER TWENTY

ALTARED EGOS

[P]	*Introibo* *ad altare Dei.*	[P]	I will go to the altar of God.
[R]	*Ad Deum* *qui laetificat* *juventutem meam.*	[R]	To God, who gives joy to my youth.

—The Ordinary of the Tridentine Mass

∞ ∞ ∞

I'M GOING TO TELL YOU a little secret known only to altar boys who have served the Tridentine Mass: peoples' tongues are as distinct and unmistakable from one another's as fingerprints. Some are austere yet fidgety, some are wide and beneficent, some are cocky and venturesome, some are so shy the priest has to go on safari to find them. Tongues extended to receive Our Lord have as much personality as their owners. You may laugh, but it's absolutely true.

I say this, not to embarrass anyone, but to open the door to a rare insight into the wisdom and acumen of Holy Mother Church ... at least, in the past.

I became an altar boy when I was ten. The nuns who ran the parochial school I attended lived in a nearby convent. Since the school and convent were not attached to a parish, priests came from the surrounding churches to say daily Mass for them.

Poor Dad! His head, weary from late hours at the railroad, had hardly touched the pillow when I would drag him from bed before dawn to drive me to the convent so I could serve

Mass. Actually, he was pleased to do so, if not always openly enthusiastic. Not only was he proud of me, but the convent chapel was one of those marvels of dark, pungent, polished wood prayerfully accented with elaborate but unobtrusive carvings. And how they would sing! There is no sound to be found above the earth or below it which compares to that of fifty nuns chanting reverent hymns to their Beloved Spouse.

What made the situation more interesting was that these nuns were also my schoolteachers. These were the very women who, in a few short hours, would be bossing me around, correcting my grammar, scolding me for my sloppy penmanship, and punishing me for my boyish indiscretions. With some notable exceptions, I did not like them. There were a few I even despised. But all such peripheral considerations were moot when it came time to assisting at Mass.

Teacher, student; principal, culprit; father, child—we were all there, kneeling before the altar of God, to acknowledge our mutual unworthiness. All beat their breasts in shame at the words *"mea culpa,"* all genuflected unpretentiously for the *Incarnatus*, all gazed at the Elevation, attempting to pierce the impenetrable with limited intellects. And all received the Body, Blood, Soul and Divinity of Our Divine Savior on the tips of their extended tongues. I'm not claiming everyone present was, in fact, humble; but certainly everyone was trying to be.

Consider what it felt like for me to stand there, holding the paten (a golden plate designed to catch any crumbs that might fall while Holy Communion was distributed) under the chin of the nun who, only yesterday, had reprimanded me for the messy condition of my desk. Imagine what it was like for her to kneel there, mouth open and tongue sticking out, before the kid who so tested her patience. In that instant, we were both admitting our puniness before God.

Don't think that didn't have an impact.

Don't think it didn't have some influence later on in the day when I would indeed be disobedient and Sister or Mother*

---

* The Sisters of the Holy Child Jesus were unique in that they were called "Sister" until they took their final vows, after which they were called "Mother." This was indicative of the purpose of their order: the education and formation of children. The aspiration of their foundress, Mother

would have to punish me. Whatever occurred between us, we had both been kneeling before Almighty God that morning, just as we would be the following morning. However much we couldn't stand each other, we would both be admitting our lack of charity in the confessional within the week. Everything, you see, fit into the larger picture. Every moment in life had a purpose because the Mass and the Sacraments constantly reminded us of this unavoidable Truth.

I remember how the word "my" was rarely used by the nuns. "Please put the book on *our* desk." "Oh dear, I hope this stain will come out of *our* habit." It seems a bit awkward in the retelling, but at the time it reinforced their vow of poverty, of ownership-in-common in every detail of their lives; not just for them but as an example to us. The personal possessive singular was reserved for occasions such as, "Yes, class, I must confess all *my* sins to the priest, too."

There was a time, and some of us still do remember it, when nuns wore wedding rings because they were married to Christ. As with all devoted wives, their first duty was to their Spouse; loving Him, honoring Him, and obeying Him unto death. Only in their case, death would not pull them apart but bind them together forever.

There was a time when every priest was subservient to the rubrics of the Mass. I can't tell you how many times the priest—we never knew who it was going to be each morning, but somehow one always showed up—would arrive five minutes late, unshaven and cranky, or yawning and puffy-eyed. Sometimes "Good morning, Father" was met with a warm hand on the shoulder; and sometimes it would have been wiser to go light the altar candles and stay out of his way. From my perspective as the altar boy, it really didn't matter once the Mass began. Whether the priest was kindly or fierce, saintly or seemingly not so, he would say the Mass exactly the same as every other priest. He would hold his hands just so, he would make his fifty-three Signs of the Cross, and he would kneel at the words—

ET VERBUM CARO FACTUM EST
AND THE WORD WAS MADE FLESH

Cornelia Connelly, was to treat every child as if he or she were the Holy Child.

—during the Last Gospel.

There was a time when all our egos were transformed by the Presence of God among us in the Holy Sacrifice of the Altar. His Presence in the Tabernacle affected my strike-out on the playing field as well as my "right on" in a history exam. Struggling with the concept of Transubstantiation taught me the world is not always what it seems. Learning to recognize each person's tongue not only helped develop my sense of humor, but also my sense of humanity. Yes, there was a time when every facet of life was as mingled with the Blessed Sacrament as the water was with the wine.

> O God, who hast established the nature of man in wondrous dignity and even more wondrously hast renewed it, grant that through the mystery of this water and wine, we may be made partakers of His divinity, who has deigned to become partaker of our humanity, Jesus Christ, Thy Son, our Lord, who liveth and reigneth with Thee, in the union of the Holy Ghost, God, world without end. Amen.
> —The Offertory of the Tridentine Mass

For myself, there was no more sublime moment than when the priest would lean over the large, white host and whisper—

HOC EST ENIM CORPUS MEUM
FOR THIS IS MY BODY

—so softly that only God and I could hear. There was an honor in that, and a pride unlike any other I've ever known. When I shook those bells, I rang them for joy.

CHAPTER TWENTY-ONE

ALTARATION

[P]	*Emitte lucem tuam*	[P]	Send forth thy light
	et veritatem tuam:		and thy truth;
	ipsa me deducerunt,		they have led me
	in montem sanctum		and brought me to
	et in tabernacula tua.		Thy holy hill
			and thy dwelling-place.

[R]	*Et introibo*	[R]	And I will go
	ad altare Dei:		to the altar of God,
	ad Deum qui		to God who
	laetificat juventutem		gives joy to my youth.
	meam.		

| [P] | *Confitebor tibi* | [P] | I shall yet praise Thee |
| | *in cithara, Deus ...* | | on the harp, O God ... |

—The Ordinary of the Tridentine Mass

∞ ∞ ∞

A SHORT TIME AGO I got the opportunity to serve a private Mass in a friend's home. One of those noble and mobile renegade priests who have returned to the Tridentine Rite was in town. Being slightly rusty, and thinking a missal a bit clumsy, I remembered the drawer in which I had stored my Mass Server's Card. Burrowing through the detritus of a quarter century, I finally found it under some mementos of my early adolescence.

I don't think I'd ever taken it out since the day I thrust it there so angrily in the seventh grade. It was a simple stiff card folded in half, with the priest's words in red and the server's responses in black. Each line was supported by the phonetic equivalent, or somebody's idea of it:

Ad	Deum	qui	lætificat	juventutem	meam.
Ahd	Day´oom	quee	lay-tee´fee-cott	yoo-ven-too´tem	may´ahm.

Memories of my brother Jim, older by four years, tapped on my forehead seeking entrance. I tried to fend them off, but they slipped in between the cracks, flooding my mind with bittersweet memories of air-headed pre-adolescence. I must have been ten when he grilled the pronunciation of these alien words into me with that ferocity and masked pride peculiar to older brothers ...

I was one of those kids who made an altar out of my dresser when I was seven. One of Dad's empty cigar boxes on its side became the tabernacle, a little silver baby's cup was my chalice, a Ritz cracker served as the host, and the large cardboard box in which my toys reposed (when I bothered to clean them up) was my pulpit. Poor Mom was my only congregation—Dad was on night shifts and Jim was nowhere to be found.

I'm not claiming the childhood sanctity of Saint John Vianney or Saint Anthony Mary Claret, but I was certainly fascinated with "church stuff." Exposure to the nuns at parochial school had a profound impact on me. I even used to visit the Blessed Sacrament in the chapel during recess because I preferred prayer to the playfield. There was a statue there of the Blessed Virgin Mary bigger than me standing on a globe encircled by a snake, and I loved the gooey smell of the sanctuary candles. I think I saw hopes of the priesthood for me in Dad's eyes, in fact I know I did, though we didn't talk about it till years later.

Anyway, I was in the fifth grade when Father D showed up to teach the boys how to serve Mass. Our parochial school wasn't connected to a parish church, so the nuns relied on local parish priests for First Friday Masses, May Parades, and altar boy indoctrination. Sister MC just brought him in one day, wound him up, and let him go at us. She left the room. The Mass, after all, was the domain of men. Even nuns who had dedicated their lives to God could not serve. It felt right that it was so; not out of vanity but an unspecified sense of propriety.

It didn't take Father long to realize that I was his absolutely most-enthusiastically dedicated and inexhaustibly in-his-face star pupil. I clung to every word he said, my eyebrows crunched in formidably serious rubric absorption.

He was probably relieved when I broke my left arm attempting the high-jump one day. From that moment on, Father D turned his entire attention to the other boys. The day I was to have served my first Mass, which had been quickly approaching all too slowly, was postponed in his mind to some vague time without definition. Certainly it had to wait until the cast came off.

Unless you've been an altar boy you wouldn't know this, but there's actually a division of labor up there on the altar. The boy on the left, or "Gospel side," hefts the big missal from one side of the altar to the other. The first time the boys approach the priest during the Offertory, he carries the wine cruet. The second time he carries the water cruet to pour over the priest's fingers and the bowl to hold under them. The boy on the right, or "Epistle side," rings the bells, carries the water cruet first, and then the towel. The trick was to watch for the priest's subtle signals and to be in the right place at the right time. A scolding after Mass by an irate priest was never a pleasant way to face the rest of the day.

With my left arm in a cast, there was no way I could transport the altar missal. And—just my luck!—some unspoken tradition required that when you served your first Mass, you enjoyed the honor of being on the Gospel side. There were no exceptions. That meant my chance wouldn't come for weeks after everyone else was an old pro.

I realize these are little things in the grander pecking order of life, but when you're ten and in love with the Mass as I was, this was the monumental stuff of which mountains were made. It also provided the pool out of which priests would some day be drawn by the call of Holy Orders.

So there I was, devastated. Father D had decided that I would be the last in my class to serve. I sat and watched as pair after pair of boys went through the motions during our practice sessions, switching off to make sure they learned both parts. It was more than my poor melodramatic heart could bear.

One night I poured out my misery to Jim over dinner. Dad was at work and Mom was in the kitchen. Jim was not normally the kind of guy who did things that could get him into trouble, or even close to controversy. In a few years he would enter college to study Police Science in hopes of becoming a cop. But every now and then he came up with a doozie to make up for his otherwise clean-cut straight-and-narrow routine.

I would have my chance, he proposed, *not only to serve my first Mass with a cast on, but to do so before any of the other boys.* I think I broke out in a sweat. His idea was marvelous:

The nuns had nothing to do with Father D's instruction classes, so hopefully they did not know his feelings about my broken arm. They would, however, expect me to serve on the Gospel side for my first Mass. Jim had gone to the same school, so the nuns knew him well. They would be delighted at the thought of my big brother serving my first Mass with me. Jim used to be an altar boy, so he knew all the routines. All we had to do was work up our own rubrics, our own little ballet. Jim would kneel on the bell side. When the missal needed toting, he would simply cross over and do it. He would hold the cruets and I the drying cloth. If we did it smoothly and purposefully, no one would notice: the nuns were too busy praying and the priest was usually half-asleep anyway.

Ah, but there was one weak chink: we had no way of knowing which priest from which parish would say Mass for the nuns on whatever day. If anyone but Father D came to the convent, we'd get away with it. But if Father D came in that particular morning ...

As I write this tale, I can't believe that little guy with my young face had the *chutzpah*, but he did. I actually called up the Mother Superior and told her the time had come to serve my first Mass.

"Does Father think you're ready?" she asked.

"He said I'd be ready in three weeks," I lied. "And that's in two days."

Come to think of it, I've never confessed that lie, or the unmitigated arrogance behind it. I wanted to be first, that was all. I felt the Mass meant more to me than to the other guys, who seemed more interested in baseball than altar bells. Hard to say. But a lie's a lie and behind every sin lurks the shadow of pride. I'll make a note to clear the slate this weekend.

Anyway, I hardly slept the night before the big event. Jim and I had worn furrows in the living room carpet rehearsing our movements. Our departure for the convent in Dad's car was delayed by my having to go to the bathroom for the twentieth time that morning. Hey, I was nervous.

I was in my garb waiting in the sacristy for the priest to arrive, praying it wouldn't be Father D. Jim was out at the altar busying himself with a stubborn candle that refused to stay lit. Then came the sound of the car in the driveway, and the footsteps up the stone walk. The need for a bathroom struck me again as the outer convent door opened, but I held my ground. Muffled voices echoed through the arched corridors of the stately convent—impossible to tell whose—the sweet high lilt of a nun and the low, gravelly grumble of the priest as they exchanged good mornings on the porch. A door closed, another opened ... closer, closer. Footfalls came down the hardwood hall. Then the kitchen door opened and the Man in Black entered.

It was *not* Father D.

In fact, I was so relieved that morning, and so moved in the retelling, that I can't remember whether it was Father A, B, C or X, Y, Z. The important thing was that it wasn't Father D.

Long story short, Jim and I pulled it off.

Later that day, Mother MC interrupted class to present me with my Altar Boy Pin, a tradition at the school when a boy served his first Mass. It was just a little gold- and enamel-plated somethingorother that made holes in your shirt collars. Every male eye in the classroom turned and glared at me icily.

I didn't care.

Did I mention the pin was also in the dresser drawer, in a little cardboard box beside the Mass Server's Card? It was worth keeping. And the Mass was worth serving.

Long live the Mass ...

... and little boys who love to serve it.

CHAPTER TWENTY-TWO

ALTARCATION

[P]	*... quare tristis es, anima meam et quare conturbas me?*	[P]	... why art thou sorrowful, my soul, and why dost thou trouble me?
[R]	*Spera in Deo, quoniam adhuc confitebor illi: salutare vultis mei, et Deus meus.*	[R]	Trust in God, for I shall yet praise Him, the salvation of my countenance and my God.

—The Ordinary of the Tridentine Mass

I DON'T THINK I'VE MET a faithful Catholic since my return to the Church two years ago who didn't have a horror story to tell. Here is mine.

So there I was just a few days ago, standing on the threshold of the past, looking at this old Mass Server's Card—a piece of cardboard folded in half, on which was printed all the altar boys' responses for the entire Mass. You'd think a memento this old would be discolored and frayed, splotched with the stains of random childhood incidents. But no, it was still white with only one dented corner. That tiny nick was probably there when Father D handed it to me all those years ago. Spurred by memories of bells and incense, I opened it up and looked inside—and there it was: the beginning of the end. A landslide begins with a dislodged pebble, a flood with a few drops of rain. This catastrophe, which was to derail my life

for almost thirty years, began with a few scratches of a pencil
...

I had been serving at the convent for about two years,
when one day Mother MC gathered all the altar boys for an
important meeting. This was unusual because, as I said earlier,
the Mass and everything connected with it was man's domain.

"I want you to open your server's cards," she said.
"You see where it says *Kyrie, eleison?* Take a pencil and
cross that out ..."

Huh?

"... and write 'Lord have mercy' above it. Now change
Christe, eleison to 'Christ have mercy' ..."

As I had been taught and nurtured, I obeyed.

Deo gratias became "Thanks be to God," *Laus tibi,
Christe* became "Praise to you, O Christ," and so on down
the card. That's how the virus of change entered my personal
experience. Cross out that and put in this. I don't really remember how I felt at that moment, perhaps a bit uneasy, perhaps not. The following morning at Mass, however, when the
priest turned from the altar and said, "The Lord be with
you," and I heard myself respond, along with all the nuns,
"And with your spirit," *then* I knew something was very
wrong.

At twelve years of age, it would not have occurred to me
that inserting these English phrases into an otherwise ancient
setting was like drawing happy faces on a Rembrandt with a
crayon. But I wasn't hungry for breakfast afterwards, and the
rest of the day just didn't go right.

Over the ensuing months, more and more changes crept
in. Meanwhile my interest in the Mass waned, my religious
fervor dimmed, and my private visits to the chapel slowed to a
trickle.

Basically I felt cheated, and I felt it with the self-centered
intensity of a youth on the threshold of puberty. I missed the
subtle humor of the two *tu's* in *Et cum spiritu tuo*—albeit a
joke no one has ever gotten but me. I missed the mystery of
the long Latin prayers. I didn't like the "new" English
prayers, either. They had a different flavor than the passages I
was used to seeing in my old Latin-English missal, and they
left things out:

THE OLD	THE NEW

I confess to almighty God,
to blessed Mary ever virgin,
to blessed Michael
   the archangel,
to blessed John the Baptist,
to the holy apostles,
   Peter and Paul,
to all the saints,
and to thee, Father,*
that I have sinned
   exceedingly in thought,
   word and deed,
through my fault
through my fault
through my most grievous
   fault.
Therefore I beseech
   blessed Mary ever virgin,
blessed Michael
   the archangel,
blessed John the Baptist,
the holy apostles,
   Peter and Paul,
all the saints,
and you, Father,
to pray to the Lord
   our God for me.

I confess to almighty God,
and to you,
   my brothers and sisters,

that I have sinned
   through my own fault
in my thoughts
   and in my words
in what I have done,
   and in what I have
   failed to do,
and I ask blessed Mary,
   ever virgin,
all the angels
   and saints,

and you, my brothers
   and sisters,
to pray for me
   to the Lord our God.

Glory to God
 in the highest
And on earth peace
   to men of good will.
We praise Thee.
We bless Thee.

Glory to God
 in the highest
And peace to his
   people on earth.
Lord God,
   heavenly King,

---

* "Father" in this case meant the priest.

We adore Thee.
We glorify Thee.
We give Thee thanks for
  Thy great glory.
O Lord God,
  heavenly King,
God the Father almighty.
O Lord Jesus Christ,
  the only-begotten Son.
Lord God, Lamb of God,
  Son of the Father.
Who takest away
  the sins of the world,
  have mercy on us.
Who takest away
  the sins of the world,
  receive our prayer.
Who sittest
  at the right hand
  of the Father,
  have mercy on us.
For Thou alone art holy.
Thou alone art Lord.
Thou alone, O Jesus Christ,
  art most high.
Together with the Holy Ghost,
  in the glory of
  God the Father.
Amen.

We worship you,
  we give you thanks,
We praise you
  for your glory.

Lord Jesus Christ,
  only Son of the Father,
Lord God, Lamb of God,

You take away the sin
  of the world
  have mercy on us;

You are seated
  at the right hand
  of the Father:
  receive our prayer.
For you alone are
  the Holy One,
You alone are the Lord,
You alone are the Most High,
  Jesus Christ,
  with the Holy Spirit,
  in the glory
  of God the Father. Amen.

It was subtle, but it was there—and because it was so elusive, it was hard to define when I tried to protest: "Sure, the Latinized phrases were awkward and repetitive, but the Englishized prayers don't have the same ... I can't think of the word."

The phrase "change for the sake of change" occurred to me in some dark moment, and stuck. There didn't seem to be any purpose to the ongoing changes other than the decision to change.

Perhaps, most of all, I missed being *necessary*. With the congregation elbowing in on more and more of the action, there was less and less for the altar boys to do. When they finally turned the priest around to face the people throughout the entire Mass, the office of altar boy essentially evaporated.

Perhaps it's impossible for someone younger than myself to understand. From infancy, I grew up going to Mass, and yet never saw what the priest was actually doing during the Consecration—none of us did. The motion of an elbow here, a shift of vestment there, a genuflection in the middle—except for the moments when he held up the Sacred Host and the Chalice for adoration, his actions remained hidden. Many of the priest's prayers were inaudible, with only a phrase here and there emphasized so we would know where we should be in our missals. The missal showed pictures of what he was doing, and when I grew old enough to go to school the nuns explained it as best they could, but it remained something that I had never seen with my own eyes.

It was a *mystery*—that which was out of reach, beyond carnal bounds; something that only the priest was privy to, something to which the people gained access by assent, by their presence. It was something outside the ordinary person's purview. It reminded us that the things of God are holy and that we are not.

It was not the people's Mass, it was the priest's Mass. He said it on our behalf, but it was still his Sacrifice. Like the priests in the Old Testament, he was set apart for this purpose. He was in a class by himself. This is something lost on most people today, for we have become lulled into a sense of our own adequacy. It rankles the modern sensibility that anyone can be set apart, a step above, and a notch removed from everyone else. (It just ain't democratic!) Nonetheless, whatever we may choose to believe, the things of God are holy, and we most assuredly are not.

I can't impart the emotion I felt during my first and subsequent experiences as an altar boy, kneeling there beside the priest. I had the best vantage point in the house—better than Mother MC had ever had. Better than Mother Superior! From my angle I could see the host in his hands as he leaned over it to whisper the Words of Consecration. I watched as the accidentals remained the same but the substance changed. There was nothing more profound, more stimulating, more enriching in my life than those moments when I grasped the bells and announced the arrival of Christ in Person yet again.

O taste, and see that the Lord is sweet: blessed is
the man that hopeth in him.
Fear the Lord, all ye his saints: for there is no want
to them that fear him.

—Psalm XXXIII:9-10

Sweet indeed. It was the core of my life—
—and it was snatched away without so much as an apology or explanation. The word "rape" comes to mind, but I
won't linger on it. Since the Mass and God went together in
my mind, there was only one altar on which to present the
smoldering coals of my wrath. God should not have allowed
this to happen; how could He do this to me?—to Dad?

If ever a man was bewildered by events, it was Dad. He
loved the Mass with the passion of a convert. He had lost
much when he became a Catholic in midlife, and now he was
losing that, too. The look in his eyes after Father J or K announced another change—it still gives me a chill. The cutting
and pasting was done with the cold precision of a surgeon, or
rather a butcher; without regard for the likes of those who
found the changes unnecessary, distasteful, or even harmful to
their Faith.

And it was dishonest. They never said, "Okay, everybody,
the old Latin Rite is hereby abolished and is being replaced
with this here New Order." No. They conned everyone into
thinking they were just making a few changes here and there,
fluffing a few pillows, sweeping the cobwebs, so to speak.
Nothing major, nothing to worry about. The Mass was the
Mass, after all. But the truth is that they were robbing us of
our heritage, lying about it in the process, and then telling us
we should be grateful to them for doing it.

The eighth grade proved pivotal. I remember the moment, though not the exact words, when I went to Mother MC
and told her to remove my name from the list of altar boys.
She didn't seem surprised, and I don't recall her saying anything memorable. What she did not know was that in so doing, I was severing myself from my own heart. Any childhood thoughts of the priesthood died at that moment, too.

I did not know the theological implications of what was
going on. I could not organize my thoughts into anything I
could adequately explain. When I tried to tell Mother MC or
Mother ME about my concerns, they looked at me with blank

incomprehension. Mother JA, who had apparently minced some words with Dad over another matter—he vehemently disagreed with her choice of textbooks—was no help at all. Even Mother MB, the nun I truly liked the most, suggested my conservatism was imposed on me by "someone else," since in every other way she found me to be "liberal" in outlook.*

I took that to mean that my reputation as an electric guitarist in a garage band had preceded me. I had been fined once or twice for hair length which exceeded the dress code standards. Some liberal outlook. I just liked the Beatles and the Rolling Stones.

Shortly thereafter, as the devastating loneliness of "Eleanor Rigby" captured the imagination of the American airwaves, the nuns announced that our next First Friday Mass was going to be a "Guitar Mass." Mother MC cornered me and said she wanted me to bring my guitar.

I refused.

"That kind of music belongs in the garage," I told her. "That's where I intend to keep it."

Then Mother JA, who had just become principal, told me that as student body president it was my job to lead the whole school in the latest set of new responses that was about to hit the fan.

Not only did I refuse to help indoctrinate others in this madness, but—and I must say I admire my spunk as I look back on all this—I refused to attend Mass at the school, period.

Since I was the only child out of four hundred who was having this problem—no doubt due to some kind of dysfunctional hormone-induced psychological repression—they

---

* I must insert a bit of information here that I did not have at the time, nor when I was writing this book in 1993. Mother MB, herself alarmed and dismayed by the changes within her order, had submitted her request to Rome to leave the convent. While she awaited her answer, she was under a vow of obedience not to mention her intention to anyone, including the other nuns. They even sent her to a shrink, but her traditional attitudes could not be so easily adjusted. She was living a strained and lonely life. I do not know what prompted her comment about "someone else" influencing me. Perhaps in my agitation I misinterpreted her words completely. Permission was granted and she left shortly after my graduation. She and I reconnected recently after she saw an ad for my book, *The Endless Knot*. All of that is a story in itself that I hope to tell some day.

could think of nothing better than to leave me alone in a classroom while everyone else sang "Kum-Ba-Ya" in the audito-
rium.

The school janitor, a sweet old Mexican by the name of
Angel—I kid you not!—looked in on me. He even brought
me a cup of coffee.*

"I agree wit ju," he said subversively. "When I hear the
guitarrr, I theenk of fiesta, not God."

Out of the mouths of janitors ...

Well, there I stood some twenty-five years later, looking at
my Mass Server's Card, icy talons clenching my heart as salty
pools gathered in my eyes. A lot of the pieces of my life
started to make sense in light of these memories. Funny how I
had forgotten them.

Of all those nuns and priests and other kids, no one understood except a kindly janitor—the significance of his name
was not lost on me—and of course there was Dad. Poor Dad.
His picture is in the same drawer as the Mass Server's Card.

---

* Not to belabor the point, but it shows how abnormally the nuns were be-
having. I was not a notorious troublemaker, I was the student body president. Their order was dedicated to the care and formation of children, yet not
a single one of them tried to help, comfort, explain, or even check in on
me. I, like Mother MB, was left strained and lonely in an impossible situation that no one could have anticipated. I think that perhaps they all found
themselves in a quandary, torn between the reasons they had entered the
religious life and the orders to change now raining down on them from
above.

CHAPTER TWENTY-THREE

ALTAR·NADIR

Absolve, O Lord, the souls of all the faithful departed from every bond of sin. And by the help of Thy grace let them be found worthy to escape the sentence of vengeance, and to enjoy the full beatitude of the light eternal.

—The Gradual of the Tridentine
Mass for the Dead

∞ ∞ ∞

MY CHILDHOOD ENDED on August 8, 1968 at 8:20 p.m. Everything before that evening came under the comfy umbrella of airy, unaffected innocence. From that night on, life became a deadly serious thing. It was the first time I remember thinking, "Perhaps there is no God."

That was the night my brother, Jim, died.

I will spare my reader the details of his demise. The surrounding story was that he spent the day at the beach, specifically to put down a deposit on a shorefront bungalow for the two of us to share for the last weeks of summer vacation. His first year at college had been a time of many changes for him, and we had drifted apart as brothers. A couple of weeks at the beach seemed like just the thing to get us back in touch. He came home in good spirits, had a glass of Burgundy wine while chatting with Mom in the kitchen, and went to his bedroom to rest a bit after a long day. Two hours later he was dead.

Close friends have come to realize that I cannot drink Burgundy. I gag on any food laced with it—it simply won't go down. The reason is that when one applies mouth-to-mouth resuscitation to an unconscious person, one comes into intimate proximity to whatever that person last consumed. I include this detail, not to repulse my reader, but to show how death touches not just the emotional aspect, but the whole person. If ever there was a "point of no return" in my life, it was the night Jim died. And I will never enjoy a glass of Burgundy again.

The following morning I woke up dizzy from a pill the doctor had given me to help me sleep. All it did was make the memory of the night before come back in nauseating whirls. Anyone who has experienced death in their immediate family knows that suddenly there is a lot to do, and though it is a pain in the neck, the forced activity provides a welcome buffer against the unspeakable black wall of grief that so wants to surround, to engulf, to smother you.

One painful detail was finding a priest to say the funeral Mass. Dad did *not* want our pastor to do it. The devious monsignor had coaxed large amounts of money out of the parishioners' wallets to build a "beautiful new church," and erected instead a modern monstrosity so hideous, so angular, so clashing to the eye—like some of the new buildings going up in downtown LA—that some of my friends referred to Sunday Mass as "going to the bank." The stained glass windows looked like chunks of broken bottles imbedded in rough cement, with no attention to hue or shade. Heck, there wasn't even a discernible pattern except for a general tumble of chaos from the upper right of the nave—if you could still call it that—to the lower left. And there was no Crucifix. Instead, a huge statue of a Glob that was supposed to be the Resurrected Christ was bolted to the wall above the altar.

No, Dad did not want the monsignor.

He called the friars who ran my high school for assistance, but was told that everyone was away or going away on vacation.

"After putting one boy through your school," I heard him say on the telephone, "and another a sophomore, you mean to tell me not one of you could spare a morning to bury my son?" The quaver in his voice made my blood freeze.

I went down to the friars' cloister to implore in person. My tears were finally answered. There was an old friar there who was an alcoholic in the fine Irish tradition. Few of the students took him seriously, and frankly, much of his classroom behavior did not warrant respect. Nonetheless, it was Father JB who told me he would delay his trip to San Francisco to say the Mass.

"In Latin, Father," I begged. It may have been a bit melodramatic, but I was desperate. In fact, at this point I was relying on instincts I didn't know I had. "Could you please say the Requiem in Latin?"

There was a long silence.

"Please."

"Of course," he said at last, smiling kindly. "Jimmy was a good boy."

"And I want to serve," I said, wiping my nose. "Jim served my first Mass with me, and I want to serve his last Mass … with him."

That was where Father drew the line. He riveted me, a rare look of insight in his eyes. "I don't think that would be wise. I doubt you'd be able to get through it."

After a brief stare down, I relented. He was right, of course, but the idea would have had a certain poetic symmetry.

Jim's Requiem was the last Latin Mass I was to attend for two dozen years. The thing that amazed me most about it—beside the fact that it was happening at all—was that no one in the congregation, and there were many in attendance, remembered when to stand or sit or kneel. If Dad hadn't been in the front row, leading them, they would have been lost. In fewer years than I've got fingers on my right hand, the collective memory had been wiped clean. A complete data purge—I was appalled.

How quickly we forget.

CHAPTER TWENTY-FOUR

BALTARCHISM

It is as impossible for anyone to be saved outside
the Catholic Church as it was for anyone to avoid the
deluge who was outside Noah's Ark.
—The dying words of
Blessed James Duckett (1602)
Saints to Remember

≈ ≈ ≈

LASTING IMPRESSIONS—the kind that worm their way deep
into our minds where they penetrate the innermost core of the
self and begin to affect our decisions and, by inexorable extension, the course of our lives—defy prediction. We never
know what event, conversation or quarrel is going to sear our
psyche with the burning intensity of a red-hot iron. I'm not
referring here to cataclysms—earthquakes, floods, fires, hail-
storms and other upheavals which used to be called "acts of
God." True, these things devastate persons and their property, and can be particularly harrowing, say, in the case of
earthquakes, to those who are singularly sensitive or phobic
with respect to tremblers. But most of life is composed of the
seemingly inconsequential, the trivial, and the ordinary; and it
is here that we do the majority of our absorbing and responding. While the catastrophe may occupy the bulk of our
attention for a week or a season—as did my brother Jim's un-
timely death, which knocked my life clean out of orbit—it is
the off-handed remark, the momentary look of rebuke or af-
firmation in a friend's eye, the misplaced or purposefully dis-
placed emphasis on a word in an otherwise innocuous phrase;

these are the things that leave their own kind of subtle but penetrating mark for years and years.

Two such events occurred to me in a single week when I was sixteen. The first was in religion class. Father E, who was perhaps more conservative than most of the other Capuchin friars at my high school, was using, of all things, the *Baltimore Catechism*. We had just come to the questions dealing with Salvation:

> **166. Are all obliged to belong to the Catholic Church in order to be saved?**
> All are obliged to belong to the Catholic Church in order to be saved.

> **167. What do we mean when we say, "Outside the Church there is no salvation"?**
> When we say, "Outside the Church there is no salvation," we mean that Christ made the Catholic Church a necessary means of salvation and commanded all to enter it, so that a person must be connected with the Church in some way to be saved.

"In some way," caught my eye. It was one of those curious phrases, like "seems to suggest," "in all probability," and "maybe" (the accent on the "may" but the "be" stretched out in an uncertain lilt) which had been creeping into the vocabulary of religious instructors over the last few years.

There was a little drawing on the page of Noe's Ark floating on a calm sea—one of those poorly drawn cartoons that had become so popular in religious texts. We knew it was Noe's Ark because the old patriarch had apparently painted "NOE'S ARK" on the side of the boat in huge letters bigger than elephants. Beneath it was the suggestion that we consult a passage in Scripture which made it clear that Baptism into the Church by water was as necessary for the life of the soul as being aboard Noe's boat had been necessary to survive the Deluge:

> ... in the days of Noe, when the ark was a-building: wherein a few, that is, eight souls, were saved by water.

Whereunto baptism being of the like form, now
saveth you also ...
                                   —I St. Peter III:20-21

Off to the side was a paragraph in a different type style
which had apparently been inserted by the editor of this edition for clarification:

No one can be saved except by being united
to the Catholic Church. It is like Noe's Ark,
which saved men from the flood. Only
through Christ and His Mystical Body can
men be saved. They must be either in the
Ark of the Church or at least hanging onto
the ropes which trail from its sides. (See
Question 321.)

My eyes went back to the cartoon: there were no "ropes"
dangling from the sides. I had never heard of anyone surviv-
ing the great Flood by "hanging onto the ropes" which
trailed from the Ark. Only the eight survived who were *inside*.
Where did these supposed ropes come from?—or the people
hanging onto them? Was this what was meant by "a person
must be connected with the Church in some way"?

Admittedly, my mind was more entangled in the reels of
the tape recorder with "sound-on-sound" capability I wanted
to buy at Dick Charles' Music Store than on this stuff. By this
time in my life religion was hardly a central issue. I wouldn't
have expressed it in these terms, but in retrospect I no longer
trusted the Church, so I no longer trusted Her teachers. When
you've been robbed, beaten, and left for dead—and then told
how wonderful it's all been—it's hard to revere the muggers.

When I was a child of six in grammar school, the sisters
had said, "It is written." By the time I was sixteen in high
school, the priests were saying, "It might have been written."
"Question everything" had become the motto of the mottled
in spirit, as they clunked their lopsided clay chalices together
with self-aggrandizing gusto. "Don't inculcate: equivocate."
In attenuating rather than amplifying everything connected
with the Faith, they did not reveal inner strength as they supposed, but rather deficiencies in their resolve.

Suppose you are interested in meeting Angela. I tell you I'll introduce you, but as we walk toward her house I bombard you with a tirade of remarks which bring into question her integrity, ancestry, and mental health.   Nothing about the woman is above my derision: her credentials, her choice of apparel, or her taste in food.   By the time we are standing on her welcome mat, you would know precious little about Angela, but quite a lot about me.

That's the kind of introduction to Jesus Christ and His Church the priests were shoveling in the classroom a year after the "Summer of Love."   We could be sure of nothing because there was nothing to be sure of.   Welcome to the New, Improved Church!

Anyway, there I was drifting between Noe's Ark and day-dreams of tape recorders—my waning interest in God vs. my blossoming passion for music and its production.   The next question in the catechism—and the question its answer raised—drew me back to the reality of the classroom.

168.   **How can persons who are not members of the Catholic Church be saved?**

Persons who are not members of the Catholic Church can be saved if, through no fault of their own, they do not know that the Catholic Church is the true Church, but they love God and try to do His will, for in this way they are connected with the Church by desire.

"In other words," explained Father E, his rolling brogue combining with his lofty gaze to give an impression of generous condescension, "a Protestant or Hindu or whatever, who doesn't understand the Catholic Faith or never heard of it, is of course united to the Church by their desire to please God in their own way."

This is when Mike, one of my classmates, asked the question which would leave the first of the two lasting impressions which concern me in this chapter. It was his tone of voice and puzzled eyes that made it so memorable:

"Their own way?   If they can all get to Heaven, why should I go to Mass on Sunday and fast during Lent and all that hard stuff?   Why should I be a Catholic?   Why don't I just become a something else?   It'd be easier."

Father E hesitated.

It was just a moment, but that's all it took. Though he re-
covered his wits and went on to deliver a convincing oration
about how the Catholic Faith is "better" even if it is
"harder" because the Sacraments were of such great benefit
and such, for one brief second the confusion in his eyes
amidst the blank expression on his face had given him away.
That had said it all.

What Father E had so magnanimously proclaimed, in perfect harmony with the ever-evolving spirit of Vatican II, was
that people outside the Catholic Church who "through no
fault of their own ... do not know that the Catholic Church is
the true Church," were "of course" united to Her by their
desire to please God "in their own way"—this in spite of the
fact that Jesus had established an entirely different set of rules:

First, that water Baptism was essential to Salvation:

> He that believeth and is baptized, shall be saved:
> but he that believeth not shall be condemned.
> —St. Mark XVI:16

> Amen, amen I say to thee, unless a man be born
> again of water and the Holy Ghost, he cannot enter
> into the Kingdom of God.
> —St. John III:5

Second, that the Sacramental Life was an essential part of
the salvific process:

> Then Jesus said to them: Amen, amen I say unto
> you: Except you eat the flesh of the Son of man, and
> drink his blood, you shall not have life in you.
> —St. John VI:54

Third, that few, not many, get to Heaven. Presumption in
this regard was to be considered dangerous:

> And a certain man said to him: Lord, are they few
> that are saved? But he said to them:
> Strive to enter by the narrow gate; for many, I say
> to you, shall seek to enter, and shall not be able.
> —St. Luke XIII:23-24

Fourth, that we do not have the power or the right to interpret the rules according to our own whim:

> Understanding this first, that no prophecy of scripture is made by private interpretation.
> For prophecy came not by the will of man at any time: but the holy men of God spoke, inspired by the Holy Ghost.
> —II St. Peter I:20-21

And fifth, that we are bound to observe all His rules, not pick and choose as we wish:

> Going therefore, teach ye all nations; baptizing them in the name of the Father, and of the Son, and of the Holy Ghost.
> Teaching them to observe all things whatsoever I have commanded you ...
> —St. Matthew XXVIII:19-20

True, I did not have all these citations memorized when I was sixteen; but these are the concepts in which I had been steeped as a child by the nuns before they changed; these were the concepts that were being eroded at every turn by Father E and others of his kind. How to deal with the plight of the hypothetical "native on the desert island" whom everyone was so concerned about, I did not know. What I did understand, albeit in the most rudimentary terms, was the simple logic I had been learning in geometry:

$$\text{If } a = b,$$
$$\text{and } a = c,$$
$$\text{then } b = c.$$

The criers of the "new church" were proposing a different logic with respect to Salvation. Into the above equations they were inserting the following—

$a = $ *Salvation is achieved*
$b = $ *inside the Catholic Church*
$c = $ *outside the Catholic Church*

—and even as a sixteen year-old I could see that with these values in the equation, *b* could not possibly be the same as *c*. Being inside the Church and being outside the Church could not mean the same thing.

$$b \neq c$$

For the sake of hypothetical people who "through no fault of their own ... do not know that the Catholic Church is the true Church," the Father E's were willing to deny the necessity of the Church. What they failed to realize is that if the Church is not absolutely necessary for each and every human being to be saved, it is therefore necessary for absolutely no one—and thus, should be done away with. Mike was absolutely right: why be Catholic, why put up with all the disciplines and devotions and such, if I can be saved by going about my business, paying lip service to God "in my own way"?

I did not like what I had just heard. It was another stone falling from its place in the crumbling wall of my Faith. Yet it is a curious phenomenon of humankind that over time we often emulate that which we hate. As much as I hated the changes in the Church, they provided me with the excuses to do as I pleased. In retrospect, I now realize how deeply Mike's question and Father E's answer affected me in that they became the justification of a great many terrible things that I did later on in my life. As long as I was being "honest with myself," and honoring God "in my own way," what had I to fear?

Of course, at sixteen, my immediate response—well, twenty minutes later—to this devastating development was to order two sloppy joes for lunch instead of one at the school's "greasy spoon." When the mind is burdened, the stomach requires fuel. Or better still: indigestion provides distraction.

The second thing that made a lasting impression on my life that week occurred in "Dad's Den" a few days later. Dad spent most of his spare time sitting in a chair by the window in the corner of his downstairs library, a book in one hand and a pipe in the other. Many were the volumes that lined the shelves of his haven, sagaciously staring from an assortment of mismatched bookcases which had been added to his collection over the years. It would have pleased Dad no end if there had been nothing else required of him than to sit there with curls of smoke orbiting his balding head, with no interruption save the ritual of stuffing and relighting one or another of his dozen or so pipes. My favorite was the calabash with the meerschaum bowl—he would give me one just like it for my seventeenth birthday (he figured if I was going to smoke, and smoke I did, I might as well do so in style).

I always felt guilty interrupting his quiet time but rarely enough not to do so. I enjoyed talking with him about "things," and though he invariably set aside his book with a sigh of reluctance, I think he rather enjoyed my company, too. Ever since the Mass was taken from us, he and I had developed a kind of camaraderie—fellows in the foxholes, cronies in the catacombs, that sort of thing. All talk of what was going on in the Church pained him, yet we somehow usually ended up on that subject.

I forget what started this specific conversation that was to impress me so, or how it ended for that matter. Somehow, in the middle, we got on the subject of Baptism.

"There are three," I was saying.

"No, there is one," he was insisting. "Even the New Mass"—his face always went a little grey when he mentioned Pope Paul VI's liturgical experiment—"says 'one Baptism for the remission of sins.'"

I scurried upstairs and retrieved my *Baltimore*. "Here it is," I panted triumphantly, more involved in the argument than Realities. It wasn't often I could one-up my Dad. "Right here."

320. Why is Baptism necessary for the salvation of all men?

Baptism is necessary for the salvation of all men because Christ has said: "Unless a man be born again of water and the spirit, he cannot enter into the kingdom of God."

321. How can those be saved who through no fault of their own have not received the sacrament of Baptism?

Those who through no fault of their own have not received the sacrament of Baptism can be saved through what is called baptism of desire or baptism of blood.

There was a little cartoon of a boat on the page—not Noe's Ark, this time, but a much smaller affair—manned by a smiling priest who was looking down at several people bobbing in the water. They were holding onto ropes which trailed from the side of the boat. The words "Baptism of Blood" and "Baptism of Desire" were connected to them with arrows.

322. How does an unbaptized person receive the baptism of blood?
An unbaptized person receives the baptism of blood when he suffers martyrdom for the faith of Christ.

323. How does an unbaptized person receive the baptism of desire?
An unbaptized person receives the baptism of desire when he loves God above all things and desires to do all that is necessary for his salvation.

"The *Baltimore Catechism* says that?" he said incredulously. "I had no idea."

"Why?" I said, my triumph deflated by the look on his face. "I thought everyone uses it. It's like, you know, the *standard* or something."

Dad was shaking his head slowly, eyeing the throw rug under his feet. "That isn't what I was taught when I came into the Church. I had to take an oath ..."

"An oath?"

"An abjuration of heresy when I was conditionally baptized."

"Heresy" was a word that made me uncomfortable. Sister MC* had once accused me of it in the second grade when she found the books in my desk in unabashed disarray. After a moment's thought I asked, "Conditionally?"

"Hm? Oh, it was the Church's practice to baptize everyone coming into the Faith, even if they'd been baptized in a Protestant denomination, just in case any of the form was missed."

---

* She was still "Sister" at the time because she hadn't yet taken her final vows.

"Oh."   An uncomfortable silence enveloped the room. What was eating him? Perhaps in his own way, he was mulling over a few equations of his own:

$a=$ Baptism

$b=$ is necessary because Christ has said: "Unless a man be born again of water and the spirit, he cannot enter into the kingdom of God."

$c=$ is not necessary because those who through no fault of their own have not received the sacrament of Baptism can be saved through what is called baptism of desire or baptism of blood.

Did Jesus, or did He not, mean what He said? If so, why did He not indicate that there would be exceptions to His rules? If not, who had taken it upon themselves to change them? Anyway you looked at it, $b \neq c$. b was not even $\approx$ to c.

Somebody was lying.

Perhaps Dad was reviewing the oath he had taken a score of years earlier, upon entering the Catholic Faith:

I, ——, having before me the holy Gospels, which I touch with my hand, and knowing that no one can be saved without that faith which the Holy, Catholic, Apostolic, Roman Church holds, believes, and teaches, against which I grieve that I have greatly erred, inasmuch as I have held and believed doctrines opposed to her teaching—

I now, with sorrow and contrition for my past errors, profess that I believe the Holy, Catholic, Apostolic Roman Church to be the only and true Church, to which I submit myself with my whole soul. I believe all the articles of Faith that she proposes to my belief, and I reject and condemn all that she rejects and condemns, and I am ready to observe all that she commands me ...

And, I believe in everything else that has been defined and declared by the sacred Canons and by the General Councils, and particularly by the holy Council of Trent, and delivered, defined, and declared by the

General Council of the Vatican, especially concerning
the Primacy of the Roman Pontiff, and his infallible
teaching authority.

With a sincere heart, therefore, and with unfeigned
faith, I detest and abjure every error, heresy, and sect
opposed to the said Holy, Catholic, and Apostolic
Roman Church. So help me God, and these His holy
Gospels, which I touch with my hand.

—Abjuration of Heresy or Profession of Faith
The Priest's Ritual, 1914

Or perhaps he was remembering what the priest—an old
college chum of Dad's, as it turned out—was required to say
over him while he knelt after making the above declaration:

By the Apostolic authority, which I exercise here, I
absolve thee from the bond of excommunication
which thou hast incurred; and I restore thee to the
holy Sacraments of the Church, to the communion
and unity of the faithful, in the name of the Father,
and of the Son, and of the Holy Ghost. Amen.

—*The Priest's Ritual,* 1914

"Dad?"

"Wha—? Oh, I was just thinking. There was a priest by
the name of Feeney who was excommunicated a few years
ago. Boston, it was. Yes, he was nailed for holding that there
is no Salvation outside the Church*, the very thing I had to
swear to when I embraced the Faith."

Feeney ... excommunicated. These two words burrowed
themselves deep into my mind and memory. Twenty-three
years later I would recall this conversation and thank God for
it. As I said up front, we never know what event or comment
is going to leave its mark.

I don't remember what he or I said after that. No doubt
we changed the subject.

---

* Dad, like so many Americans, was misinformed as to the specifics of Fr.
Leonard Feeney's excommunication. He was indeed so punished, but for
disobedience, not heresy. He was reconciled in the end without having to
rescind or denounce any heresy at all. See Chapter 50 for more details.

CHAPTER TWENTY-FIVE

ALTARGETHER NOW

One is forced to think of the hireling who abandons his flocks to the wolves when one reflects on the lethargy of so many bishops and superiors who, though still orthodox themselves, do not have the courage to intervene against the most flagrant heresies and abuses of all kinds in their dioceses or in their orders.

But it is most especially infuriating when certain bishops, who themselves show this lethargy toward heretics, assume a rigorously authoritarian attitude toward those believers who are fighting for orthodoxy, and who are doing what the bishops ought to be doing themselves!

—Dietrich von Hildebrand
The Devastated Vineyard

1969. HIGH SCHOOL RELIGION CLASS.

There it was in black and white, printed on a page in a book published by Paulist Press, chosen by the faculties at many Catholic schools as *the* book for religious instruction throughout the archdiocese:

There are other ways of being united to God besides baptism. An adult who believes in God and basically desires to do his will, and who has sorrow for his sins out of love of God, has God's grace-presence by this sincere desire. Many men come to God in this way through other, non-Christian religions. So, too, one

> who cannot believe in a personal God, through no
> fault of his own, but is committed to following his
> conscience, receives God's grace-presence.
> — Anthony J. Wilhelm
> *Christ Among Us*

Some years later, after the damage was done, this volume
would be condemned by the Holy Office in Rome, and the
bishop involved ordered to remove his *imprimatur* from the
book. The Paulist Press would obediently cease printing it,
but in their deep concern for souls would sell the rights to
Harper and Row, who would continue to pump it out into the
parochial schools of America for several more years. By the
time it was finally purged from the system—some seventeen
years from its original publication—its vociferous poison had
been read and absorbed by more than 20,000,000 Catholics.
They would go on to teach the same errors to their children—if they had any, since the book also taught:

> In practice there are circumstances in which couples
> feel that they cannot now comply with the pope's
> teaching. The standard the church proposes is not
> possible for some ... In effect, today many Catholic
> couples—and certainly the great majority of young
> people—feel justified in conscience in using contra-
> ceptives.
> — Anthony J. Wilhelm
> *Christ Among Us*

The author, a priest, would eventually—wouldn't you
know?—leave the priesthood.

At the time this notorious volume was in my adolescent
hands, how was I to know that when Jesus said—

> Beware of false prophets, who come to you in the
> clothing of sheep, but inwardly they are ravening
> wolves.
> — St. Matthew VII:15

—He may very well have had the author of this book in mind?
My teacher, a Capuchin friar who had selected the book from
a shelf brimming with others of better quality and more sound

orthodoxy, was not without blame, having shirked his responsibility as a spokesman for the Faith.

No matter. There it was. I knew Dad believed otherwise about the necessity of water Baptism for Salvation, and I remembered the nuns saying the same thing back in grammar school before they went loony; but here I was in high school, and everything was being turned upside down by the "spirit of Vatican II." So what if this new enthusiasm was of quite a different spirit than that of Vatican I?

> This is why We reprove and execrate the teaching, as impious as it is contrary to reason itself, which professes indifference in religious matters. In the name of such a theory, the children of our time, suppressing the distinction between truth and falsehood, affirm that the gate to eternal life is open to all from whatever religion they come, or they maintain that with regard to religious truths it is only possible to formulate more or less probable opinions, without ever arriving at certainty.
>
> We reprove likewise the impiety of those who are shutting the gates of the Kingdom of Heaven to men, assuring them under false pretexts that it is not honorable, and is in no sense necessary to salvation, for them to abandon the religion—though false—in which they were born ... and who hold it against the Church herself for proclaiming that she alone is the true religion ... as if there could ever be the possibility of participation between justice and iniquity, or of association between light and darkness, or of compromise between Christ and Belial.
>
> —Pope Pius IX
> Schema of a Dogmatic Constitution on the Church
> prepared for Examination of the Fathers
> of the First Vatican Council

What could I do? Besides, who cared? Well I did, but I was trying hard not to. I was full of my own self-importance, ravaged by hormones, plagued by zits, mesmerized by Jimi Hendrix and reveling in the recent release of the "White Album" and *Yellow Submarine* by the Beatles. My war with the New Mass was giving way to the wish to just sing "Ob-La-Di,

Ob-La-Da" and move onto other things. Maybe I had been wrong, maybe Dad was wrong, maybe Pope Pius IX was wrong, maybe the nuns were wrong before they tore off their habits and became non-entities; maybe all these priests were right after all. Who knows? I didn't know.

Besides, the religion they presented was getting easier and easier by the minute, and thus more tempting to the budding hedonist within me. No more fish sticks on Fridays. Down with grilled cheese sandwiches and macaroni casseroles at the end of a hard week. Lent—who needs it? Let's party. Invited to a non-Catholic wedding? Sure, you can go—we're one big happy family, all us lovable Christians; and hey, non-Christians are the People of God, too. Why should I be the only grump in the class who thought otherwise?

"Desire," in retrospect, was the key to much that was going to mutate in my head in the coming years. A curious word for so profound a religious anti-concept, it cast a whole new light on the Sacramental Life of the Church:

Baptism—no longer necessary, not really, as long as a person led a "good life." If I wanted to pass the religion exam I didn't answer "immersion, aspersion, and infusion" when asked to name the three kinds of Baptism. Those methods all referred to Baptism of water; but now there were also baptisms of blood and desire. They made sense, of course, since they covered the loopholes which Christ had apparently left unsettled in His haste to ascend back to Heaven.

Confession—the new "Sacrament of Reconciliation" was more like a conversation with a pal, even though everyone knew priests were weird and could never really be your friend. Oh well. Unlike the "bad old days before Vatican II" when you couldn't go to Communion if you were in a state of mortal sin, the new improved opinion was that if you were really sorry for your sins—if indeed they were sins (there are all kinds of evolving theories about the reality of sin, so don't sell yourself short)—you could receive Communion now and go to the "reconciliation booth" later. And if you forgot to carry through on that, well, you had planned to go, hadn't you? That's all that really counted: your intention. Whether you actually went or not is beside the point. Introducing: "confession by desire."

Father C, who taught us this remarkable concept, was fresh from the Capuchin seminary in Ireland. Brimming with the "new theology," he was not unaware of the pronouncements of the Council of Trent back in the sixteenth century:

> If anyone saith that faith alone is sufficient preparation for receiving the sacrament of the most holy Eucharist; let him be anathema. And for fear lest so great a sacrament may be received unworthily, and so unto death and condemnation, this holy synod ordains and declares that sacramental confession, when a confessor may be had, is of necessity to be made beforehand, by those whose conscience is burdened with mortal sin, how contrite even soever they may think themselves. But if anyone shall presume to teach, preach, or obstinately to assert, or even in public disputation to defend the contrary, he shall be thereupon excommunicated.
>
> —The Council of Trent
> Session XIII, Canon XI
> On the Most Holy Sacrament of the Eucharist

In fact, it was Fr. C who taught us to scoff at the word "anathema," which he deemed a symptom of the narrow-mindedness of less competent religious thinkers of bygone centuries. In his public profession of "absolution by desire," he apparently reasoned that he could avoid *de facto* excommunication by simply not taking such things seriously. We proudly present: "acquittal by desire," or simply "by lack of interest."

Holy Eucharist—what did we really mean by "Body, Blood, Soul, and Divinity"? Were we saying Jesus' *proteins* are present on the altar? Hmmm, did we actually believe that? (The inflection of the question suggested, of course, that anyone answering in the affirmative was a dullard and a troglodyte.) And as for the Mass, hey, what could be said? Change for the sake of change had become experiment for the sake of contrived amusement. The attention span of the average Catholic was considered so short that innovation was thought to be the only way to keep him occupied and thus get his collection money. There was much talk of returning to the

"Primitive Church," thus altars might be replaced with tables, and Crucifixes with ... nothing.   The warnings of an earlier pope were discarded for the sake of frivolity and "new insights":

> The liturgy of early ages is worthy of veneration;
> but an ancient custom is not to be considered better,
> either in itself or in relation to later times and cir-
> cumstances, just because it has the flavor of antiquity
> ... the desire to restore everything indiscriminately to
> its ancient condition is neither wise nor praiseworthy.
> It would be wrong, for example, to want the altar re-
> stored to its ancient form of a table, to want black ex-
> cluded from the liturgical colors, and pictures and
> statues excluded from our churches.
>
> —Pope Pius XII
> *Mediator Dei*, 1947

I wonder what this deceased pontiff would have said if he were around in the late sixties ...?

Of course, it was with the onslaught of "flower power" that the centrality of the Holy Eucharist at Mass began to be eroded in favor of the all-powerful congregation by the applied overemphasis of—

> For where there are two or three gathered together
> in my name, there am I in the midst of them.
> —St. Matthew XVIII:20

—mixed with generous amounts of:

> Amen I say to you, as long as you did it to one of
> these my least brethren, you did it to me.
> —St. Matthew XXV:40

The first, of course, was an injunction to gather together with other Catholics; it was an encouragement to pray in groups in addition to praying in private. The second was yet another mystery, in that Jesus was somehow presented to us in every human being that we encounter. Both suggested that Jesus was present in a special way among us. But neither thing—Christ in community   or   Christ in   our   fellow man—should vie for prominence with the Blessed Sacrament of the Mass, as was the case with the shift of emphasis onto the laity. The Sacrament is not merely a spiritual concept but a physical reality—or have we forgotten?

Worst of all, from my point of view at that time in my life, was the sudden fascination—I'm not sure whose—with pointless folk tunes. To those of us guys who played electric guitars in powerhouse bands, "Sons of God" and "Amen" were—how do I put this?—beneath us.

> When he was treated to a demonstration of Edison's talking machine in 1888, Arthur Sullivan instantly understood its potential for vulgarity: "For myself, I can only say that I am astounded and somewhat terrified at this evening's experiments. Astounded at the wonderful power you have developed—and terrified at the thought that so much hideous and bad music may be put on record forever."
>
> —Robert Pattison
> *The Triumph of Vulgarity*

We rockers spent our spare time scrutinizing Jimi's and Eric's licks. Why should we waste our time on these simplistic three-chord ditties? So the task of inane strumming on cheap out-of-tune guitars went to those who were willing but not so able. And the singing went to those who wished they could but couldn't. And the tambourine was often snatched up by the priest when no one was looking. Rarely does a priest come along who has any clue about rhythm. To see everyone patting each other on the back during the silly "sign of peace" to indicate how wonderful everything was and how good they all felt about what they were doing made me ill. If this was enlightenment, I'd take the cultural depravity of Gregorian Chant any day.

Confirmation—probably the least understood of the Sacraments. Hard it is to pin down the Holy Spirit. It had been rumored that Pope John XXIII had called Vatican II because of a mystical experience:

> As regards the initiative for the great event which gathers us here, it will suffice to repeat as historical

documentation Our personal account of the first sudden bringing up in Our heart and lips of the simple
words, "Ecumenical Council" ... It was completely
unexpected, like a flash of heavenly light, shedding
sweetness in eyes and hearts. And at the same time it
gave rise to a great fervor throughout the world in ex-
pectation of the holding of the Council.

—Pope John XXIII
Opening Statement, Vatican II

The Church had always turned a wary eye upon private
revelation, be the recipient a shepherd girl, a hermit in the
mountains, or a Vicar of Christ. While it was certainly agreed
that Pope John had the power and right to call a council—he
was, after all, Peter—his rationale was somewhat iffy, since it
was based on a personal revelation, and visions—even "approved" visions—weren't covered by infallibility. Councils
had always been called to clarify dogma, to fight heresy, or
something of the sort. This council had an entirely new purpose, something for which a general council had never been
called in the history of Christendom:

The salient point of this Council's work is not,
therefore, a discussion of one article of the fundamental doctrine of the Church ... which is presumed to be
well known and familiar to all. For this a Council
was not necessary ...

But from the renewed, serene, and tranquil adherence
to all the teaching of the Church in its entirety and
preciseness, as it still shines forth in the Acts of the
Council of Trent and First Vatican Council, the
Christian, Catholic and apostolic spirit of the whole
world expects a step forward toward a doctrinal pene-
tration and formation of consciousness in faithful and
perfect conformity to the authentic doctrine, which,
however, should be studied and expounded through the
methods of research and through the literary forms of
modern thought. The substance of ancient doctrine of
the deposit of faith is one thing, and the way in
which it is presented is another.

—Pope John XXIII
Opening Statement, Vatican II

So the *substance* of ancient doctrine was one thing; and the *way it was presented* was another. Hmm.

This was to be a "pastoral council," a term which the council itself and the pope who convened it never defined, and which has therefore never been clearly understood. It was not called to clarify doctrine, but to explore ways of presenting it to the modern world.

Oh, but didn't a pope declare a century earlier—

> 80. [It is anathema to believe that] The Roman Pontiff can and should reconcile and adapt himself to progress, liberalism, and the modern civilization.
> —Pope Pius IX
> *The Syllabus of Modern Errors,* December 8, 1864
> (Denzinger* : 1780)

—? Oh, never mind.

Pope John's "flash of heavenly light," his mystical premise of the council, was not lost on the world. With the pope as their example, many people would feel that they, too, could tap into this New Pentecost. The door was opening for a whole generation of self-proclaimed spiritually-aware prophets and seers to start responding to the "voice of God."

Traditionally, the Holy Ghost came to us in Confirmation, which involved anointing with oil, kneeling before the bishop, and up until Vatican II, a slap on the face to symbolize joining the ranks of the Church Militant. Of course, the Church Militant was fast becoming the Church Effervescent, and slaps were considered anti-social. Glossolalia was on the horizon, as was the rise of "spirit-filled" worshipers, some of whom would claim to be direct channels to the Almighty. They

---

* "Denzinger," also known as *The Sources of Catholic Dogma,* also known as *Enchiridion Symbolorum,* is the standard handbook for sources of Catholic Doctrine. The number 1780 is the paragraph number in the thirtieth edition which, unfortunately, was edited by Karl Rahner, SJ, a celebrated modernist and one of the most influential "experts" at Vatican II. The good Father managed to insert several documents into the book which were of dubious origin, but which supported his personal theological agenda. I have taken care to quote only documents that are verifiable from other sources.

would gather in "prayer meetings" and invoke the Holy
Spirit, the Third Person of the Blessed Trinity, who would always come dutifully at their call and manifest Himself obediently with signs and wonders. For two of my college years I
would be among them—embarrassing as it is to admit today—arms uplifted in prayer, never asking the salient questions until circumstances forced them upon me: "Who said we
could do this? Who, be it Jesus Christ as quoted in the Bible
or the Fathers as preserved in Tradition, ever said we laymen
have the power to summon the Holy Spirit into our midst at
the time and place of our choosing? Is this not an unauthor-
ized eighth sacrament, a kind of 'confirmation by desire'?"

I know charismatics—some of them friends—who will vehemently refute the implications of the last paragraph.   I
would present their rationale if I understood it, but I don't so I
can't.

I saw many young Catholics abandon their Faith to join
the charismatic dance of indifferentism. I listened as one person "spoke in tongues" and another "translated" the in-
comprehensible mumblings into less-comprehensible gobble-
dygook.   I watched a "prayer leader" switch to the King
James Bible and eventually join the Protestants.   I attended
"Spirit-filled Masses" where Protestants went up and received
Holy Communion without the Catholics batting an eye. All
this was perceived as the "movement of the Holy Spirit."

Perhaps this heated topic is better left alone for now. My
charismatic acquaintances tell me my unfortunate brush with
the "charismatic renewal" was a deplorable, a-typical fluke. I
can't say. All I know is that for me it was bad, bad news.

In any case, a year after my graduation from high school,
the reigning pope would have this to say about the fruits of
the Second Vatican Council:

> The devil has done it.   Through some crack the
> fumes of Satan have entered the temple of God.
> —Pope Paul VI
> Discourse of June 29, 1972

Quite an admission on the part of the Supreme Pontiff.
Whatever the purpose of the Council, or the intentions of the
bishops who attended, or the involvement of the Protestant
"observers," one would be hard-pressed to disagree with the

sad words of Pope Paul VI with respect to its overall results. My high school days were irradiated by its fallout.

Holy Orders—the storm clouds were gathering and it was about to rain on somebody's party. How vast numbers of priests could so easily abandon the old Mass for the new put me, personally, at odds with the whole lot. The general attack on the priesthood by the priests themselves and the usurpation of power by the laity would gear up to full force a decade later. First things first, however. That meant doing everything they could to forget, hide, or eradicate the traditional understanding of the priest's role at Mass.

> The unbloody immolation by which, after the words of consecration have been pronounced, Christ is rendered present on the altar in the state of a victim, is performed by the priest alone, and by the priest insofar as he acts in the name of Christ, not insofar as he represents the faithful.
>
> —Pope Pius XII
> *Mediator Dei*

In other words, the Church of Old understood that it was the priest acting *in persona Christi* who made the Divine Victim present on the altar and sacrificed Him. The people looked on and assented, but had no power to Consecrate.

> Our word liturgy is derived from the Greek *leitourgos,* which originally designated a man who performed a public service ... In Hebrews 8, 1-6, Christ is referred to as the *Leitourgos* of holy things. The liturgy is *His* public religious work for *His* people, *His* ministry, *His* redeeming activity. It is above all *His* sacrifice, the sacrifice of the Cross, the same sacrifice that He offered on Calvary still offered by Him through the ministry of His priests. He is the principle offerer of the sacrifice of the Mass and to offer Mass nothing is necessary but a priest, the bread, and the wine. There is no necessity whatsoever for a congregation; when defining the essence, the nature of the Mass, the presence of the faithful need not be

taken into account; while it is obviously desirable it
is not necessary.

—Michael Davies
Pope John's Council

You could put all the Catholic laymen in the world in one
colossal stadium and have them say the Words of Consecration
over bread and wine, and nothing would happen.   For Transubstantiation, the priest was absolutely necessary.   There was
no "Consecration by desire" yet—I said "yet" because as
time went on this distinction between priest and laity would
grow faded, fuzzy, and almost undetectable.   The term
"priest-presider" was eventually invented to further confuse
the sacerdotal position. The loss of understanding of the true
role of the priest and his function would result in women
wondering what on earth prevented them from donning the
robes and doing likewise.   And the loss of understanding that
there were, indeed, explicit differences between men and
women would cause still more havoc in other quarters.   And
on and on.

Matrimony—"marriage by desire," or what was commonly referred to as "shacking up," was on the rise.   The
priests hemmed and hawed, but in general they were unoffi-
cially beginning to say that premarital sex was okay.   After all,
the sex drive was greater than anyone's ability to resist.   No
mention was made that people had, indeed, found the where-
withal to resist temptation for many centuries, and without detriment to their mental or physical health—in fact, self-control
was once considered a virtue.   I distinctly remember Father C,
the young friar from Ireland of anti-anathema fame, telling
my religion class that "maybe" reading *Playboy* was not im-
moral.

The topper, of course—and here's an illustration of
priestly example if there ever was one—was that never in my
hearing did any of the good fathers defend Pope Paul VI's
Humanae Vitae, his landmark encyclical against birth control.
They had already decided amongst themselves, it would seem,
that the primary purpose of marriage was sex.   Nothing as insignificant as a papal encyclical which defended traditional
Church teaching was going to convince them otherwise.   Small
wonder some of them left to give it a try.

Extreme Unction—now called the "Sacrament of the Sick" was virtually useless. There was no need for Baptism, nor the other Sacraments, since they were all accessible just by wanting them. "Heaven by desire" was the logical end of the whole business, and was borne out by the text of the new funeral liturgy.

"Desire"—that said it all.

If intention was all that was required, and not the doing of the thing, then why bother lifting a finger? Design was easy, implementation was another matter. The concept of "desire" so saturated the theology, morals, and lingo of the time that it's small wonder I finally caved in and embraced it wholeheartedly. I'm reminded of a parallel paradox, an example of what might be called "agriculture by desire":

> Major Major's father was ... a God-fearing, freedom-loving, law-abiding rugged individualist who held that federal aid to anyone but farmers was creeping socialism ... His specialty was alfalfa, and he made a good thing out of not growing any. The government paid him well for every bushel of alfalfa he did not grow. The more alfalfa he did not grow, the more money the government gave him, and he spent every penny he didn't earn on new land to increase the amount of alfalfa he did not produce.
>
> —Joseph Heller
> *Catch-22*

All I needed to do was to want to do the right thing, and that was enough. Actually doing it became superfluous. If this sounds like some kind of joke, it wasn't. As I look back on my later teens and all my twenties, I see nothing but halfhearted desire—well, maybe an occasional full-fledged flare-up of wholehearted desire, too—but few if any real moral or material accomplishments.

When Jesus posed this question—

> But what do you think? A certain man had two sons; and coming to the first, he said: Son, go work to day in my vineyard.

> And he answering said: I will not. But afterwards,
> being moved with repentance, he went.
> And coming to the other, he said in like manner.
> And he answering, said, I go, Sir; and he went not.
> Which of the two did the father's will? They say to
> him: The first.
>
> —St. Matthew XXI:28-31

—was He not demonstrating that the mere intention of doing something is not as worthy as actually doing it? Doing the Will of God means exactly that: doing it. Yet in the decades following Vatican II, many of the Faithful—myself most of all—were so full of so many good intentions, but alas, our good deeds slowed to a trickle. Why bother?

> It may be said in their favor, however, that their
> hearts were in the right place. They meant well!
>
> —Charles A. Coulombe
> *Everyman Today Call Rome*

Certainly any thought of "spreading the Faith," what little I had, was immediately dismissed. Why try to tell anyone else that their religion is lacking when they're going to go to Heaven for honoring God "in their own way" anyway? Why bother to struggle against disbelief and sin if Jesus never really meant what He said? And if He was pulling the wool over our eyes, what did that say about Him in the first place?

Yes, "desire" was the key.

"Desire"—and a whole lot of "self" on which to pin it.

Chapter Twenty-six

Altar Skelter

I opened the bolt of my door to my beloved:
but he had turned aside, and was gone.
My soul melted when he spoke:
I sought him, and found him not:
I called, and he did not answer me.
—Canticle of Canticles VI:6

∞ ∞ ∞

WHAT BRINGS A YOUNG MAN to the point of apostasy?

That, my friend, is a question which would require an answer much weightier and longer than this book. On these few pages I can only scratch the skin on the surface of the surface.

I was twenty-seven years old. It was a weekday—Tuesday? Thursday? (it doesn't matter)—when I walked into my parish church in Pasadena for the last time. Saint Andrew's was a big old building, constructed at a time when churches were built to honor and glorify God rather than aggrandize and patronize man. The floors were marble, and the nave was lined with towering pillars of swirling multicolored stone. Of course, the Tabernacle had been relegated to a side altar, removed from its former place of prominence under the graduated canopy of polished white stone supported by four great columns above the main altar.

As had been my daily custom, I knelt down before the side altar and tried to pray, or at least to open my mind and heart to God. But the God to whom I stretched my hands seemed to have retreated beyond my reach. The thought had been growing in the bleak recesses of my mind that I had made excuses for Him long enough. The time had come to face the unspeakable horror that He had abandoned me.

From the moment Mother MC told me to cross out *Kyrie, eleison* on my Mass Server's Card the detachment had commenced. With each new change and innovation in the liturgy the breach had widened. The collapse of morality and the malignant twisting of Catholic theology at the hands of the nuns and priests had accelerated the process. My "charismatic experience"—all that hugging and kissing and prophesying and glossolaliating—had been but the death throes of my teetering Faith, a last-ditch attempt to fend off the inevitable. Why, indeed, had I become involved in such a thing?

> Yet it is a curious phenomenon of humankind that
> over time we often emulate that which we hate.
> —Me, two chapters back.

I no longer wanted to go to Mass, I hated it so. My confessor, Father S, had urged me to hang in there, to persevere, to "fulfill my Sunday obligation," to try to get in touch with the "essence" of the Novus Ordo. But that was the problem: I found at its center the celebration of man, which is to say the celebration of nothing, for that is ultimately the stuff out of which man is formed.

So I had turned my passions inward: to my music, painting, and writing. There was no peace there, only perpetual agitation. Not having learned to love myself, I tried to love that which I created. But what I produced was a mirror of myself, and so could not escape my own reflection: that sad face with haunted, hungry urges lurking behind desperate, searching eyes.

Everything I touched, it seemed, turned to junk. In every friendship there was misunderstanding, relationships with girls often ended in fury or confusion, every artistic endeavor ended in failure. Of course, this view was probably not shared by acquaintances who saw the carefully maintained veneer with which I cloaked my growing despair.

A few friends knew something was wrong, but didn't know what or how to help. Thirteen years hence one of my closest friends would say, "I never understood you, the way you arrived at Mass during the sermon and left as soon as Communion started without receiving, as though you were only fulfilling the minimum obligation." We had met in high school so he didn't know me back when the nuns drove the point home that no one gave a damn about my objections to "the changes." That's when I had learned to shut up and keep my feelings to myself.

The worst part of all was watching Dad deteriorate from an enthusiastic daily communicant in the old days, to a reluctant, lethargic broken old man. When he had converted to the Faith years before he met Mom, he was required to denounce his thirty-second degrees of Freemasonry and did so gladly, even though it cost him family and friends. He had understood the necessity of following Jesus Christ at the expense of everything. How shattering it must have been for him when the New Mass was promulgated. Surely he comprehended better than anyone the significant connection between the *Novus Ordo Missae* and *Novus Ordo Seclorum*, the Masonic motto. The New Order of the Ages—take a gander at the back of a dollar bill—had infiltrated the New Order of the Mass.

Dad died in 1977 after a thirteen-year battle with cancer. During the last year he was so doped up he hardly knew who he was. My ardent prayer for his recovery had become a poignant prayer that he be released. It was one prayer that God did answer finally, and I hated Him for it.

And the hatred intensified when I saw the white vestments at the funeral Mass. By the time Dad died, the immemorial canonized Requiem Mass in Latin had been outlawed. Yes, *outlawed*. Even if there had been a priest who remembered it, I couldn't find one who was enough of a lush to dare to say it. By that time Father JB had left the priesthood and settled down with a wife. Capitulation at every turn—though for Jim's sake, I wished him well. So Dad went to his grave, a profoundly confused casualty of Pope Paul VI's heavy-handed hubris.

And there were other things, so many other things that went through my mind as I knelt there at Saint Andrew's Church. The weak flame that bobbed with imperceptibly slow undulations in the red sanctuary lamp held no hope for me. The breach between me and my Creator was now a gaping chasm, with puffs of effluvial smoke rising from its murky depths like tenebrous jellyfish on boiling currents. Yes, I had made excuses for Him long enough. He had abandoned me.

Fragments of phrases from the lessons of my life drifted like diaphanous ghosts behind the tears in my burning eyes. The warning of the Angel to the Church of Laodicea—

> ... I would that thou wert cold, or hot.
> But because thou art lukewarm, and neither cold, nor hot, I will begin to vomit thee out of my mouth.
> —The Apocalypse III:16

—the promise of Jesus at the Last Supper—

> If you ask me any thing in my name, that I will do.
> —St. John XIV:14

—which I must have gotten wrong, or out of context, because things certainly hadn't worked out the way I'd asked. Even the words of Polonius to his son, Laertes, began making loop-the-loops in my darkening mind, ever spiraling, ever closing in on the inevitable.

> This above all: to thine own self be true,
> And it must follow, as the night the day,
> Thou canst not then be false to any man.
> Farewell. My blessing season this in thee!
> —William Shakespeare
> *Hamlet,* I:3

"To mine own self be true," I paraphrased. "As long as I am true to myself, You will understand."

It was just a matter of who was going to vomit out whom.

In the final analysis, the reasons had all become a blur. It did not matter that I had asked for too much in too little Faith with too much focus on myself. It did not matter that all things were working out to my good, not if nothing good worked out. It did not matter that Polonius was one of the Bard's comic figures, a meddling busybody whose incessant prattling and foolish intrigues got him killed in the end; and whose oft quoted line was merely an anomaly in an otherwise worldly soliloquy which emphasized the importance of self-interest and the shallow concern for appearances.

The only thing that mattered was that I hurt so badly I couldn't stand it anymore. I'd had enough, that was all. In all honesty, which was supposed to be a virtue, I had simply had enough. And so it was that I looked up at the gold-plated door of the disenfranchised Tabernacle, the House of the God Who Had Allowed Himself to be Set Aside, and said aloud:

"I am tired of being a worm. I am leaving. And I won't come crawling back."

CHAPTER TWENTY-SEVEN

ALTARNATIVE

I fled Him, down the nights and down the days;
    I fled Him, down the arches of the years;
I fled Him, down the labyrinthine ways
    Of my own mind; and in the mist of tears
I hid from Him, and under running laughter.
            Up vistaed hopes I sped;
            And shot, precipitated,
Adown Titanic glooms of chasmèd fears,
    From those strong Feet that followed, followed after.
            But with unhurrying chase,
            And unperturbèd pace,
    Deliberate speed, majestic instancy,
            They beat—and a Voice beat
            More instant than the Feet—
'All things betray thee, who betrayest Me.'
                    —Francis Thompson
                    "The Hound of Heaven"

∞   ∞   ∞

I CAN SPEAK FOR NO OTHER, but I know in my case the
Lord took me at my word. He never required me to crawl
back—indeed, He allowed me to skip.

It would not be prudent for me to relate my journey into
the Land of Darkness in detail. I do not wish to expound on
my sins—suffice it to say I committed many—nor do I wish to
pummel my readers with the details of my spiritual treachery.
Catharsis is not the purpose of this tome. The path I took was
indeed a twisted and dangerous one, a course I would
not—and could not, in good conscience—recommend to any-

one else. God in His infinite beneficence looked down upon my lot with solemn patience and silent understanding. He knew exactly what interests I needed to pursue, what philosophies I needed to exhaust, and what ordeals I needed to go through in order to come to the conclusion that I had missed the whole point.

Like a madman set free, when I walked out of Saint Andrew's Church for what I thought was the last time, I proceeded to embrace all that I knew to be false, hugging evil and patting it heartily on the back. I adopted atheism as my philosophy, evolution as my religion, and expedience as my moral code. I had put aside the things of a child—or so I thought—and proceeded to charge off into the sunset of liberated adulthood.

> And he said: A certain man had two sons:
> And the younger of them said to his father: Father, give me the portion of substance that falleth to me. And he divided unto them his substance.
> And not many days after, the younger son, gathering all together, went abroad into a far country: and there wasted his substance, living riotously.
> —St. Luke XV:11-13

Oh, there were occasional moments of regret. Odd instances, like going into a gift shop in an amusement park and coming upon one of those glossy, shellacked redwood plaques with a picture of a set of footprints wandering down a smooth, sandy beach. Surely you've seen something like it. You might even have one hanging in your kitchen. In my antireligious fervor I considered the accompanying words trite and sentimental—

> One night a man had a dream. He dreamed he was walking along the beach with the Lord. Across the sky flashed scenes from his life. In each scene, he noticed two sets of footprints in the sand; one belonging to him, and the other to the Lord.
> When the last scene of his life flashed before him, he looked back at the footprints in the sand. He noticed that many times along the path of his life there was only one set of footprints. He also noticed that

it happened at the very lowest and saddest times in his life.

This really bothered him and he questioned the Lord about it. "Lord, you said that once I decided to follow you, you'd walk with me all the way. But I have noticed that during the most troublesome times in my life, there is only one set of footprints. I don't understand why when I needed you most you would leave me."

The Lord replied, "My precious, precious child, I love you and I would never leave you. During your times of trial and suffering, when you see only one set of footprints, it was then that I carried you."

— Author unknown

— then I'd swallow the lump in my throat and move on before my eyes began to tear.

Those dark years were also consumed with the onslaught of illness, a disease of the spine which sapped my time, finances, energies, and endurance to their elastic limit. Over the years my intake of pain killers increased until I was buying them in lots of two hundred to save money on the insurance co-payments. The medications prescribed by the doctors, though certainly legal, ignored the real problem and concentrated on dulling the symptoms. Mainly they just fogged my mind. I came to need a cane just to walk. My face grew perpetually pale, like the underbelly of a lizard. I radiated "unwellness."

My cousin, an atheist, once asked me, "Do you ever think about praying to God about it?"

"No," I replied in all honesty. "In fact, it's a relief not to put this problem in a religious context."

Who says there are no atheists in foxholes?

Somewhere in there I wrote three novels, and even had an agent in New York who enthusiastically endorsed my work. Nothing ever got published; and today I'm glad of it—I'd be spending the rest of life saying novenas for everyone who read that awful stuff! At the time, though, lack of success was hard to swallow; but then life was just one big, awful pill anyway.

> And after he had spent it all, there came a mighty famine in that country; and he began to be in want.
>
> And he went and cleaved to one of the citizens of that country. And he sent him into his farm to feed swine.
>
> And he would fain have filled his belly with the husks the swine did eat; and no man gave unto him.
>
> —St. Luke XV:14-16

I also became fascinated with the occult, but I will say little about it. This will suffice: I was the kind of guy people would walk up to in newage book stores and say, "Could you recommend, you know, a really good book, you know, on the Kabbala?" Somehow they could tell, you know, that I was, you know? Since I always recommended the thick, heavy, expensive volumes locked in glass cabinets in the back corner rather than the cheap, sleek briefs within easy reach on the front rack, they rarely asked me twice.

But seriously: to a fallen-away Catholic, the esoteric language, the mysterious symbolism, and the elaborate ceremonials of magick* and witchcraft can be most alluring, for they counterfeit the sense of awe that Catholicism in its true practice inspires. As bitter as I was, I never forgot that sense of wonder which I had once felt kneeling beside the priest during the Consecration. In exploring the occult—of which the newage "white" fluff is but a deceptive, watered-down spin-off for the instant coffee set—I was trying to recapture that same marvelous feeling. There was a catch, however. The Lord warned us:

> He that is not with me, is against me: and he that gathereth not with me, scattereth.
>
> —St. Matthew XII:30

Magick caters to the yearning of man to alter Reality to conform to his desire. Nothing so self-centered can be a path to God. But enough on this. What is relegated to a couple of paragraphs in this book could easily turn into an entire volume at a later date. We shall see.

---

*I use the archaic spelling here to differentiate serious magical ritual from sleight-of-hand parlor tricks.

My physical illness brought me to the brink of despair. Life had become one long dull ache. I could no longer sit at my computer, play music comfortably, paint, or do anything I loved. The medications the doctors prescribed became more exotic, more exorbitant, and more toxic—and none of them really helped. One experimental medication, I learned later, is used in abortion clinics—they actually administer it to mothers to kill the baby in the womb. No wonder I felt so sick. The treatment was becoming worse than the disease!

Then someone gave me a copy of *Final Exit,* a book on how to commit suicide. No doubt they thought they were doing me a favor. In the back were tables of various prescription medications and how big a dosage was necessary to stop the heart. "Not now," I said, as I closed the book, "but soon." Life had lost its savor, and thus its meaning. When you ask yourself, "But what would such a thing do to my family and friends?" and the answer is, "I don't care anymore," you know you're pretty far down the road to oblivion.

It was December 17, 1991, when something went *pop!* in my head. The doctor had prescribed one pill too many. I had reached the point where I had to take this so I could take that so I could handle those because I needed those to take this other thing. I looked up at my shelf lined with amber bottles. Suddenly I reached out and dragged all those pills into a trash can with a wave of my arm. I did not care if I went into withdrawal convulsions; I did not care if the pain was unbearable; I simply did not care, period.

Remarkably, I suffered no symptoms of withdrawal. My pharmacist was astonished.

Then the following day, at the suggestion of a stonemason who had repaired my house after the 1987 earthquake, I went to see an acupuncturist by the name of Gou Chen Cheng. Think what you will of this prickly ancient Chinese therapy, but seven hours after the first treatment the pain went completely away. My spine was still locked up by the disease, but the pain was gone. For the first time in a decade my day did not begin and end in misery. Friends and students no longer saw me as a walking ache. My cane ended up propped in the corner with a sign scrawled in wiggly lines: "Unemployed—Will Hobble for Food."

I began to drive my students nuts. In a lecture on acoustics I would be demonstrating the physical size of sound waves made by musical instruments. The A above middle C, for example, produces 440 waves per second that are each approximately two and a half feet in length. A little blackboard math proves that the lowest note on the piano generates waves in excess of forty feet. I set down the chalk, folded my arms, and mused, "Isn't the universe fantastic?" They stared at me blankly. I stomped over to the window and threw it open. "Don't you ever stop and smell the roses?" They nodded ever so slowly, but still so blankly.

The next several weeks were, in a sense, the happiest of my natural life. Nothing bothered me. If someone thoughtlessly cut me off on the freeway, I smiled. "It really doesn't matter," I said with a wave of my hand. "After all I've been through, nothing seems all that bothersome anymore."

Then one morning, it happened. I was in bed staring at the ceiling after a deep, refreshing sleep, thinking how wonderful it was to wake up and not be in pain. I was looking forward to the events of the day, but giving into the temptation to just remain where I was a few minutes longer. I took a deep, painless breath. "I am so grateful," I said aloud, luxuriating under the covers.

I stopped.

Whom was I grateful *to?*

When all is said and done, the truly important things are infinitely simple. This was not an emotional moment, but one of the simplest, purest logic. I had just expressed gratitude. To whom was it directed?

> And returning to himself, he said: How many hired servants in my father's house abound with bread, and I here perish with hunger?
>
> I will arise, and will go to my father, and say to him: Father, I have sinned against heaven, and before thee:
>
> I am not worthy to be called thy son: make me as one of thy hired servants.
>
> —St. Luke XV:17-19

That's all it took, really. I mean, it was only the beginning of a long walk back through enemy territory riddled with mines; but that was the turning point. So simple, so obvious. Suddenly God, who had been thrust into the background, became the focus of my attention.

There are a great many details of enormous moment which I have purposely left out of my tale. Perhaps I will save them for another book. Perhaps they are best left unsaid. Again, we shall see.

What I can tell you is that within a few weeks, and after reading *Rebuilding a Lost Faith* by John L. Stoddard—an old copy which I suspect my Dad read on his own road to Damascus—I went to a Catholic church near campus. It was a bleak little Novus Ordo service with only five or six in attendance on their lunch break. I sat in the back, yearning and wondering what to do about it. I went away to do some serious thinking and even more ponderous reading.

A few days later I returned and yearned again.

The third day I went up and received Holy Communion, knowing it was a sacrilege, my soul black with sin, but I didn't think I could wait another day. I grabbed the startled priest's arm immediately after Mass and told him I needed to talk to him.

A half hour later I was walking back to campus shriven, a new man.

> And rising up he came to his father. And when he was yet a great way off, his father saw him, and was moved with compassion, and running to him fell upon his neck, and kissed him.
>
> And the son said to him: Father, I have sinned against heaven, and before thee, I am not worthy to be called thy son.
>
> And the father said to his servants: Bring forth quickly the first robe, and put it on him, and put a ring on his hand, and shoes on his feet:
>
> And bring hither the fatted calf, and kill it, and let us meat and make merry:
>
> Because this my son was dead, and is come to life again: was lost, and is found. And they began to be merry.
>
> —St. Luke XV:20-23

It was a start. After so many years away, I had much to relearn, and much to unlearn. But I had decided not to approach this thing emotionally. I had not embraced the Faith to soothe the cravings of nostalgia—indeed, there was little in the Church to which I wanted to come back. I was an adult, not a child; and I had lived my mature years amidst the academic vapors of a university. My mind was on the Shepherd, not the pastures and the fences. As I was to discover, the grass in His field was dry from lack of water and the fences were in desperate need of mending. That work would present itself in good time. For the moment, it was simply great to be alive.

Of course, there were those who did not leave the Church when things went sour. They stayed in the frying pan, rather than jump into the fire as I had done. I will always admire them, for their Faith was all the greater. They are to be commended for their steadfast courage, and great will be their reward.

> Now the elder son was in the field, and when he came and drew nigh to the house, he heard music and dancing ...
>
> And he was angry, and would not go in. His father therefore coming out began to entreat him.
>
> And he answering, said to his father: Behold, for so many years do I serve thee, and I have never transgressed thy commandment, and yet thou hast never given me a kid to make merry with my friends:
>
> But as soon as this thy son is come, who hath devoured his substance with harlots, thou hast killed for him the fatted calf.
>
> But he said to him: Son, thou art always with me, and all I have is thine.
>
> But it was fit that we should make merry and be glad, for this thy brother was dead and is come to life again; he was lost, and is found.
>
> —St. Luke XV:25-32

To those of us who bailed out, there is always the hope of return, and the journey home is a refreshing thing indeed.

I do not know if this story will be of help to anyone, but I tell it with that hope. If I, who felt so abandoned by God, who went so far astray, who never thought of returning to Him even when the going got unbearably tough—if He could draw *me* back, He can draw *anyone* back, if only they have the Good Will to respond to His call.

A few days after my "reconversion," as I call it, I happened upon a verse in Saint Paul that absolutely floored me. I sat there with my tongue on my lap, gawking at the profound goodness of God:

> I was found by them that did not seek me:
> I appeared openly to them that asked not after me.
> —Romans X:20

Yes, it certainly was great to be alive.
And in Love again.

CHAPTER TWENTY-EIGHT

BACK TO RE·ALTAR·TY

Now the Russian agent was leaning against a tree, having just removed the clip from his automatic. Napoleon couldn't quite tell what he was doing with it, though, and asked.

Without looking up, Illya said, "Napoleon, you understand that I am *not* superstitious, and I am not falling prey to the blind unthinking terror which seems to grip less sophisticated people than we."

"Yes ..."

"And I want you to be sure that I fully agree with you that there is a rational, logical explanation for everything that has been going on."

"Yes ..."

"So for the time being I have rationally and logically decided to carve a cross on each of my bullets."

—David McDaniel
The Man from U.N.C.L.E. #6:
The Vampire Affair *

∞ ∞ ∞

THIS IS THE LAST of the "altar" chapters, drawn from my personal experiences. The chapters which preceded this "interlude," and more so those that follow it, represent those parts of the Catholic Faith which I had a particularly exciting time confronting, reassessing, and reassimilating into my over-

---

* No kidding: this was the best of the U.N.C.L.E. books—really!

all perception of things. "Exciting" can be taken in some cases, such as my reevaluation of contraception and abortion, as meaning "difficult" (see Chapter 29). In other instances, such as my rediscovery of the Blessed Virgin Mary, it can be translated as "rapturous" (Chapters 31-39). With regards to great Mysteries like the Eucharist it was "intellectually challenging" (Chapter 10). Hard looks at the cold reality of Original Sin and the need for Confession (Chapters 6-9) were "stimulatingly humiliating" ... or was it "humiliatingly stimulating"? Whatever. And finally, regarding the story of the Man who went from Jerusalem to Jericho (Chapters 41-44), the operating word would be "fundamental" or "pivotal." Such are the layers of meaning with which a single word may cloak itself.

Similarly, a man may wrap his innermost self within many layers of memory, interpretation, and convenient or merciful amnesia. By this I mean that, at the time I returned to the Faith, I had for the most part forgotten the pain and bewilderment described in these "altar" chapters—not in the sense of serious clinical traumatic amnesia, but rather in the general relegation of sensitive memories to vague shadows which I rarely recalled and then without clarity. My overall recollection of grammar school and high school, for example, was positive. Academically, at least, I considered the nuns and priests good and fair teachers. My attitude toward God, though invigorated and infused with the rush of recent conversion, was nonetheless guarded, even suspicious, though I didn't really ponder the reasons why. Some kind of self-protective fog would roll in whenever I got close to the source of my unease during my meditations. Thus the acrid bitterness that had caused me to stomp away vowing never to return was eclipsed by reticence to deal with it. I remembered walking out of Saint Andrew's Church, but not the intensity of feeling roaring in my heart as I did so.

Curiously enough, I was not the only one with amnesia. Most Catholics with whom I came into contact had little or no recollection of the events that had so affected me in my youth. Whether they had been similarly traumatized by, or innocently oblivious to, the revolution within the Church I knew not. In any case, they seemed completely sold on the way things were currently going. Even the older folks spoke of the hootenanny Mass in the local parish church as "meaningful liturgy," and seemed to accept the "new theology" as the "insight of the Holy Spirit." When asked about their grown-up children they invariably shrugged. "My Eleanor married a Lutheran, and Joey is a Buddhist; and my ex-husband Al hasn't been inside a church in years." There was no mention of concern for their souls, or novenas for their return to the safety of the Church or the Sacraments. It seemed that apostasy was an inevitable "good fruit" of the "joyous renewal" inspired by the "spirit of Vatican II." Since all human beings were somehow members of the "People of God"—even those who were ardent atheists, outright pagans, or Satanists who spat upon Crucifixes—there was no sense at all that anyone's soul was in peril, that anyone would go to Hell, or that there was any real need to mortify oneself in the quest for humility and discipline. Did I say humility? Discipline? Talk about lost arts. Modesty, both of body and spirit, was a "thing of the past," since "standing up for yourself" superseded any notion of humility. Discipline meant doing whatever it takes to get ahead.

It also seemed that everyone was perfectly happy with the Novus Ordo. In fact, as I soon discovered, any mention of "that Old Mass" was verboten:

"I just recently returned to the Church," I told a squat woman behind a card table outside the church as I registered after Sunday Mass in my local parish.

She looked up at me impassively. "Hm."

"You know, I really do miss the Latin Mass. I might have come back sooner if it was still—"

"People who talk that way," she interjected unpleasantly, "want to crawl back into the crib." She emphasized her point by inserting her thumb into her mycophagous mouth. Her lipstick left a purple ring around her thorny thumb as she removed it to add, "They need to grow up."

I turned away silently, my face burning and my mind momentarily inundated with inarticulate echoes of protest from somewhere in the recesses of my memory. Today I would challenge such insolence, but at that time I was unsure of the ground on which I stood.

Try as I did—and believe me, I really did try—I just could not get enthusiastic about the Novus Ordo. It remained for me an innocuous ceremony with little class and less guts, qualities which overflowed the banks of liturgy and flooded the spiritual landscape. Everything of symbolic or intrinsic significance in Catholic ethos—as well as anything that smacked of Tradition, beauty, good taste, integrity, devotion, moral certitude, common sense, and sincere Faith—had been systematically rooted out by the organized modernists, and with the apparent cooperation of the people.

In other words: flattery works. If you tell the people that the Mass is now "theirs," that they are in control of their destinies, that their vices are their virtues, and that God's only wish is that they be comfortable in whatever behavior they choose to engage and is not at all concerned with what they actually do or believe, the result is predictable. The world in which they live and move will have less and less to do with Reality and more and more to do with fantasy:

> Alice laughed. "There's no use trying," she said: "one *ca'n't* believe in impossible things."
> "I daresay you haven't had much practice," said the Queen. "When I was your age, I always did it for half-an-hour a day. Why, sometimes I've believed as many as six impossible things before breakfast."
> —Charles Lutwidge Dodgson (alias Lewis Carroll)
> *Through the Looking-Glass*

In fact, the process of disintegration had been progressing hilariously all the while I was away. As far as I could tell, nothing had gotten any better. Indeed, the Church to which I returned appeared to be a veritable wasteland, pulverized and defoliated by a dozen more years of the ongoing ministrations of liturgical committees, soft-soap priests, coven-trained nuns, scissors-lipped feminists, and power-hungry homophiliac bishops.

But I was stuck. Where else could I receive the Blessed Sacrament? Where else could I go to Confession? As intolerable as the situation was, there was simply no place else, no other Church established by Christ. Mine was the plight of all true seekers since the Ascension.

When I decided on the name for this chapter, the sad irony of "re-altar-ty" struck a resounding chord. The "reality" to which I returned was a Church in which altars had been "replaced" with simple tables, Communion rails had been "removed" altogether, the seriousness of sin has been "reduced" to ridicule, and the direct statements of Christ as to what was necessary for Salvation had been "re-worked" through the filter of modernist double-talk into meaningless maxims. The worst part of all was that most Catholics with whom I spoke seemed oblivious to the inherent chaos. It was like passing through a Three Stooges movie in which Larry, Moe, and Curly displayed their peculiar brand of madcap lunacy, all the while regarding themselves with utter seriousness.

For nine months I wandered through the motions of modern Catholicism, hungry for Truth and finding little. All the while, in spite of my efforts to keep them suppressed, the ethereal shadows of the past became more and more solid. The more substance they took on, the more uneasy I became. The pressure was rising in the ol' cooker.

"I really do miss the Latin Mass," I confided to a charismatic friend on the phone.

"It's an antique," he scoffed. "It belongs in a museum." To verify his thesis he asked the Eucharistic minister at his parish in Seattle. "He agrees with me," came the corroborating evidence a few days later. "It may have been a work of art, but it belongs in a gallery somewhere."

I'm glad he did not see the look on my face as I set down the receiver.

Shortly thereafter, it came to my attention that back in October of 1984—seven years before my reconversion—Pope John Paul II had actually given his permission for the Holy Sacrifice of the Mass to be offered in the Traditional Latin Rite "with the approval of the local bishop." It seems this directive had been almost universally ignored throughout the world. It certainly wasn't common knowledge. When I asked my pastor he denied ever hearing of it.

Then I discovered that on July 2, 1988, the pope had further issued a *motu proprio* (a document penned "in his own hand"), in which he stated in part:

> To all those Catholic faithful who feel attached to some previous liturgical and disciplinary tradition, I wish to manifest my will to facilitate their ecclesial communion by means of the necessary measures to guarantee respect for their rightful aspirations. In this matter I ask support of the Bishops and of all those engaged in pastoral ministry in the Church ... By vir-

tue of my Apostolic authority I Decree ... respect
must everywhere be shown for the feelings of those
who are attached to the Latin liturgical tradition, by a
wide and generous application of the directives already
issued some time ago by the Apostolic See for the
use of the Roman Missal ... of 1962.

—Pope John Paul II
Ecclesia Dei

"Rightful aspirations"?   "Respect must everywhere be
shown for the feelings of those who are attached to the Latin
liturgical tradition"??   My readers may judge for themselves
as to just how generous and obedient the bishops of the world
have been regarding the express wishes of the Supreme Pontiff.

When I heard of *Ecclesia Dei,* I immediately shot off a
note to my own arch-shepherd in Los Angeles, asking for information regarding the availability of the Latin Mass. "Before I get too excited," I wrote, "I want to verify the above
information with your office."   In reply I received a letter
from a monsignor in the Office of Worship. I had to chip the
ice away from the page before I could read the words:

> ... I am not aware of the exact report you heard
> concerning the Holy Father's favorable statement
> concerning the Missal of Pius V (the Tridentine
> Mass).
>
> I can say, however, there is no intent within the
> Roman Church to provide an alternative Order of
> Mass. The Missal of Paul VI is the normative rite
> for the church and the celebration of the Eucharist, as
> are all the other liturgical books mandated by the
> Second Vatican Council and promulgated by our Holy
> Father, Paul the VI. With this in mind, there is at
> this time no intention within the Archdiocese to ex-
> pand the usage of the Missal of Pius V beyond its
> current use. We continue to encourage our people to
> fully accept and adhere to the liturgical renewal
> authorized, legitimized and encouraged by the Second
> Vatican Council.

With every personal best wish I am
Sincerely yours in Christ,
Monsignor Ferraro, Director

Note that this frigid monsignor, who by and by left the priesthood and got married—what else is new? I *think* it was to a woman—never explained that the "current use" of the Tridentine Mass amounted to once a week in Los Angeles County, but at a different location each Sunday. I happened upon this information almost by accident. In a city the size of L.A., this meant an inordinate amount of driving—in some cases more than an hour each way, which was certainly an uncharitable hardship on the infirm and elderly, not to mention younger couples with large families. I did not bother to respond to the monsignor's disinformative missive with a quote from the Vatican II Documents regarding the precise kind of liturgical mandates stated by the Council to whose "spirit" he had appealed:

> Finally, in faithful obedience to tradition, the sacred Council declares that Holy Mother Church holds all lawfully recognized rites to be of equal right and dignity; that she wishes to preserve them in the future and to foster them in every way. The Council also desires that, where necessary, the rites be revised carefully in the light of sound tradition, and that they be given new vigor to meet present-day circumstances and needs.
>
> —Introduction to
> *The Constitution on the Sacred Liturgy*
> Vatican II *Sacrosanctum Concilium,*
> 4 December, 1963

In any event, I did seek out the Latin Mass. The first one I attended was on November 8, 1992, two dozen years and three months since my brother's funeral. It was a High Mass, complete with Gregorian Chant.

To be perfectly honest, I was lost. I had forgotten how to use a missal. I didn't recall when to sit or stand. The movements of the altar boys seemed foreign to me. And I certainly didn't remember kneeling for *so long*. Nonetheless, all the while, the shadows in my past were becoming more and more solid.

As I observed before, it is generally the little things that impact us most profoundly, that leave us with the most lasting impressions. There were two such moments during that Mass of Reawakening. The first was during the Creed when the priest came to the words:

ET INCARNATUS EST
DE SPIRITU SANCTO EX MARIA VIRGINE:
ET HOMO FACTUS EST.

And was made flesh
by the Holy Ghost, of the Virgin Mary:
and was made man.

The second was during the Last Gospel:

ET VERBUM CARO FACTUM EST,
ET HABITAVIT IN NOBIS.

And the Word was made flesh,
and dwelt among us.

In both cases, the people *genuflected*. That's all. Nothing grandiose or particularly difficult. They simply went down in unison on one knee to show respect for the fact that God so loved us that He entered our history and shared our experience.

That's when the tears began to flow. That's when the long process of healing began. That's when I began to understand that the little boy who had defied the nuns and refused to participate in their silly "changes" had not been weird, wrong or nuts. My refusal to play guitar at their modified Mass had been a noble gesture, not just a ploy of misplaced defiance. I realized that my whole life had been turned inside out and upside down by forces beyond my control, and that through it all God had heard the silent pleas of my heart and had planned all along to bring me to this moment. Suddenly the reason why that maudlin plaque with the one set of footprints so gripped me dawned as the aurora borealis of memories came flooding back with all their brilliant colors and sparkling clarity.

The Mass—that had been the crux, the unsolved riddle, the cornerstone, the key. How different my life would have been if perpetrators of rampant change had not gotten their talons into the Holy Sacrifice. But even so, it couldn't have happened if God had not allowed it. That was still hard to swallow, and continued to be so for months to come, but the more I experienced God's Love, the more I came to trust that somehow it had all worked out for my good.

My good? Yes. Perhaps if I had lived in a saner time, I never would have come to appreciate the Mass with anything approaching the same respect, awe, and fervor. As it was, because it had been snatched from me in my youth, I cherished its memory all my life. Perhaps if I had not gone through that particular Hell, I never would have come back to the Faith in the way that I did. It's hard to say.

But the tears flowed freely, and that was good. The time had come to stop running from the memories, to stand still and let the fear overtake and pass through me, to experience and then let go of my anger, to remove the great weight from my shoulders and give it to God. Yes, I cried in sobs so deep they shook my very soul. But I was not alone in my misery. Indeed, I would never be alone again.

> Come to me, all you that labour, and are burdened, and I will refresh you.
> Take up my yoke upon you, and learn of me, because I am meek, and humble of heart: and you shall find rest to your souls.
> For my yoke is sweet and my burden light.
> —St. Matthew XI:28-30

Once the tears were dried, my nose blown, and the soggy Kleenex tucked away in my hip pocket, the essential work of spiritual reconstruction began. No one understands better than I the appalling task of coming back to the Faith after years of denying all Her teachings, of somehow managing to work through denial into a state of acceptance, understanding, and enthusiasm. This, you see, is why I am writing this book. It is indeed possible to embrace the Roman Catholic Faith, in spite of oneself, and in spite of the confusion and disarray in which She finds Herself. More than that, it is absolutely *necessary*. But no one is going to be profoundly converted by nostalgia, gushing feelings, warm cuddly hugs, or vague promises. The darn thing has to make *sense*.

And indeed it does—not as the average Catholic today would define it, because the plain truth is that most Catholics aren't Catholics anymore. They don't have a clue as to what Catholicism is all about—and this indictment applies to priests as well as laity. The way I discovered this fact was by reading books that had been published before Vatican II—old books by the likes of Hilaire Belloc, John L. Stoddard and Father Joseph Prachensky. Then I turned to older books by Saint Alphonsus Liguori, Blessed Mary Agreda, and Father Jeremias Drexelius. Then I dug up even older books by Saint Augustine, Saint Ignatius of Antioch, Origen, and (aha!) Saint Athanasius.

What I learned was that these people believed something very different from the lukewarm self-indulgent broth in which most Catholics today swim. What they described was an entirely *different religion,* a philosophy of life incompatible with post-Vatican II pantheistic feel-good-ism. The intellectual integrity, philosophical humility, and profound devotion to Jesus Christ and His Blessed Mother of earlier generations of Catholics convinced me that theirs was the course worthy of study and imitation, not the desultory diversions of the spiritually-anemic dweebs of this corrupted age.

Another mark of the newage Church, something which was simply not there in ages past, is sentimentality. Adherence to sound Doctrine, and the willingness to die for the principles thereof, have been replaced by "kind feelings" and "emotional candy."

> By sentimentality is here meant thought subordinated to emotion. It is being expressed when someone says, in effect, "Because I loved my late grandfather, I believe he is in Heaven even though he was an anti-Catholic Mason." In terms of performing a religious devotion, it means doing so because it gives you a "good feeling" ...

That is what sentimentality does. If it does not simply lead from a syrupy feeling about the Little Flower to syrupy feeling, period: it can lead from the feeling to "holy-roller Catholicism." "Good" feeling is in fact leading countless persons right out of the Church. In Latin America as well as all over the U.S., charismatic-type Protestant sects are filling up with former Catholics looking to "experience" religion.

When the Church is truer to herself than She has been in recent times, She is not sentimental, neither in her beliefs nor her teaching. The saints are not sentimental, either.

Consider St. Thérèse. She did not choose as patron someone like the Little Flower of sentimentalized imagination. She chose St. Theophane Venard (he was still a Blessed in Thérèse's day). This saint was martyred for the Faith—he was decapitated—in Vietnam in 1861.

St. Thérèse herself wrote: "How happy I would have been to fight at the time of the Crusades or, later on, to fight against the heretics! Be assured that I would not have been afraid ... I want to be a warrior, a priest, a Doctor of the Church, a martyr! I want to go to the ends of the earth to preach Your name, O Jesus, to plant your glorious cross on pagan shores! ... Oh! Is it possible that I must die in bed?"

There is no syrup in those lines, no "lovey-dovey" attitudes about heretics and other enemies of God. St. Thérèse yearned to fight the good fight.

—Gary Potter
"Observations and Reflections"
The Angelus, November 1993

Even in the *motu proprio* quoted a few pages back, the pope did not address the *rights* of Catholics regarding the Tridentine Mass, but only their *feelings:*

To all those Catholic faithful who *feel attached* to some previous liturgical and disciplinary tradition ...

> I Decree ... respect must everywhere be shown for the
> *feelings* of those who are attached to the Latin liturgi-
> cal tradition ... [emphasis mine]
> > —Pope John Paul II
> > *Ecclesia Dei*

So warped has this emphasis on sentiment become in our day, that efforts to convince a non-believer of the Truth of Catholicism are often declared "uncharitable" by Catholic bystanders! It is now deemed "more loving" to let those wallowing in ignorance and sin to sink in the muck than to "upset" them with something as disturbing as the Truth. Truth has indeed been subordinated to emotion in the newage Church. Small wonder that many men and women of my generation find nothing to hold their interest here.

Most people my age who, like me, left the Church in disgust do not realize that what they denigrate is a parody, a caricature, a burlesque, but most certainly not the real thing. The dogmas they reject, and the teachers who promoted them, are *bogus*.

> [The innovators] expect to be taken for masters, al-
> though they were never even disciples.
> > —Saint Alphonsus Liguori
> > Quoted in "Sì Sì No No,"
> > *The Angelus,* December 1993

To hang a disreputable scoundrel in effigy is all very well as some sort of symbolic gesture or emotional purge, but ultimately it accomplishes little that is concrete. Rather, to seek out the ruffian and call him to account—now we are getting somewhere. But we cannot stop there. Just because we were denied the Truth does not give us the excuse to go on living without It. We must seek It out, capture It, feast on It. And since we are what we eat, when we devour the Truth, we will become absorbed in It.

And so I set about arming myself with Knowledge. There is no weapon quite like it. Before it the clouds of darkness retreat, the tongues of liars are knotted, and the bogeymen and werewolves who sought to confound us are revealed as lame and phony fools in the light of day.

∞ ∞ ∞

Illya's automatic blasted twice, and a shaggy body slammed against Napoleon's chest and drove his instinctively raised arm hard against his face ... The wolf that had hit him fell away from him again, its jaws locked in his overcoat and blood oozing from its chest ... Napoleon tore his coat from the death-grip of the fangs that had so nearly met in his throat. Then, as he swung the door open and leaped inside, he saw to his amazement that the rest of the wolf pack was disappearing—fading into the forest ...

The Russian agent had lifted the wolf's head and was examining it, running his fingers along it as though patting a dog. Something seemed to glitter amid the fur. Napoleon stared at him.

"What in the world are you doing?" he asked. "Do you want to wait for them to come back?"

"This is worth another minute," said Illya, a strange quality in his voice. "Give me a hand here—I want to get this wolf into the trunk of the car."

"Are you out of your mind?"

"Quite the contrary," said the Russian. "I think I am in it for the first time in longer than I care to consider."

Napoleon looked at him suspiciously. Illya was wearing a secret smile, and his voice hinted at unsuspected things of great interest. Napoleon got out, opened the trunk, and helped load about a hundred pounds of dead weight into it. Then he got back behind the wheel, let Illya in the other door, and started the motor. There had been no further signs of the other wolves.

He wondered about this, and commented on it to Illya, who just nodded, and kept smiling.

Napoleon scowled at him. "You're looking inscrutable again," he said. "Will you tell me your little surprise if I ignore you long enough?"

"It won't be necessary," said Illya. "I don't really *know* anything yet. But when we get back to the village I expect to be very busy in Gheorghe's kitchen for some time."

"Oh, great," said Napoleon. "I've always wanted to try barbecued wolf meat."

Illya shook his head. "Not barbecued wolf, Napoleon. I have the feeling it will be a roasted bird this time—almost certainly a cooked goose."

—David McDaniel
The Man from U.N.C.L.E. #6:
The Vampire Affair

CHAPTER TWENTY-NINE

LIFE

Yes, my Beloved, this is how my life will be consumed. I have no other means of proving my love for you other than of strewing flowers, that is, not allowing one little sacrifice to escape, not one look, one word, profiting by all the smallest things and doing them through love. I desire to suffer for love and even to rejoice through love; and in this way I shall strew flowers before Your throne. I shall not come upon one without *unpetalling* it for You. While I am strewing my flowers, I shall sing, for could one cry while doing such a joyous action? I shall sing even when I must gather flowers in the midst of thorns, and my song will be all the more melodious in proportion to the length and sharpness of the thorns.

— Saint Thérèse of Lisieux
Story of a Soul

∞ ∞ ∞

EVERY TICK OF THE CLOCK is a gift from God.

There is not a moment of my life that happens because I wish it. I did not will myself into being, and I can't will myself out of existence. True, in a moment of despair I might try to kill myself, but there is never any guarantee that I'll accomplish the deed. People have leapt from the Golden Gate Bridge, downed massive doses of noxious substances, even fallen from airplanes without parachutes, and survived. But even if I should succeed in ending my earthly life, there is still the matter of my soul which will live on and on. I have no means of stopping that.

If I cannot begin my life or end it, then I am essentially helpless with respect to my own existence. It is something that has been thrust upon me by God, and it is sustained by Him. If He were to withdraw His thought of me, I would be unmade. In fact, I would never have been.

I am in a precarious position.

I am nothing.

Yet I am.

God is.

HE WHO IS.

I AM WHO AM.

This is God's Name.

His essence is existence.

When Moses asked God His Name ...

> God said to Moses: I AM WHO AM. He said: Thus shall thou say to the children of Israel: HE WHO IS, hath sent me to you.
>
> —Exodus III:14

In giving us existence, God shares His essence with us. It is a treasure beyond measure—to be! To be alive. Unfortunately, it is something so obvious, so basic, so all-encompassing as to be easily missed. How many of us take it for granted? For myself, it took hitting rock bottom—coming to the conclusion that my life was not worth living—and then climbing back out of the pit of hopelessness, to begin to comprehend how priceless this thing called life really is.

Every moment of our lives is a gift from God. There isn't a detail of our body, our experience, or our surroundings of which He is not intimately aware. Nothing can happen around us or to us that He does not allow. Therefore we should be grateful for every second of time, and everything that happens in the time we have.

> For thou lovest all things that are, and hatest none of the things which thou hast made: for thou didst not appoint, or make any thing hating it.
>
> And how could any thing endure, if thou wouldst not? or be preserved, if not called by thee.

> But thou sparest all: because they are thine, O
> Lord, who lovest souls.
>
> —Wisdom XI:25-27

Some people seem to be born with an awareness of this Truth. I was not among them. I spent most of my life feeling that everything and everyone was out to get me. "Expect the worst," was my motto as I grew up, "then you'll never be disappointed." When I rediscovered the Catholic Faith in later years, and savored its profundities with a new mind, I came to understand life in a very different way. Whereas I used to regard every pitfall as a setback, I came to see that everything that happens is a gift from God, the seemingly bad as well as the obviously good. For the first time Job, who had been an enigma to me in the "old days," became a source of inspiration:

> ... if we have received good things at the hand of
> God, why should we not receive ill?
>
> —Job II:10

We thank God for the things that we enjoy, but why does this change when something we don't like comes along? Does He not provide both? When our mother puts food on the table, should we be less grateful to her for the Brussels sprouts than the chocolate pudding? Both are provided for us with loving care, for our nourishment. Does not God also bring an endless flow of experiences into our lives for our spiritual benefit, some of them enjoyable, some hard to endure—but all for our good?

If we are not used to seeing things in this light, it will seem awkward at first. Indeed, it may remain ungainly for quite some time. The poison of the world around us has had plenty of time to imbed itself throughout our consciousness. Deeply ingrained attitudes take time to mend. Nonetheless, when we stop gritting our teeth at life, and start relishing it, it becomes so much more ... fun.

> A great injury is done to me, you will say. But
> what sort of injury is it, let me ask? God punishes
> your sins, exercises your patience, multiplies your
> reward, and is an injury done to you? Yes, but you

say, I am filled with indignation at this wicked man,
and his will which is so thoroughly corrupt. But you
persist in looking at *man,* while I wish you to look
at *God* alone. However corrupt the human will may
be, what has it been able to do? What has it done?
You do not grieve on this account, because he *willed*
to injure you, but because he actually *did* injure you,
or was *able* to injure you. But why, I would ask, and
how could he do this? Whence did he derive the
power? And why had he the power? Was it not from
the Divine Power and Permission? And if it is Divine, is it not also just, laudable, and holy? Therefore, either hold your peace, or else direct your com-
plaints against the Divine Permission, and engrave
this on your mind, that God never would permit that
the wicked will of another should devise any evil
against you, if it were not for your good, provided
that you yourself do not become a hindrance.
                              —Father Jeremias Drexelius
                                       Heliotropium

If we try to appreciate every moment of life as a gift from
God, then every moment becomes a prayer. In this way, we
can imitate Saint Thérèse, the Little Flower, in "profiting by
all the smallest things and doing them through love." Great
blessings are awaiting those who honor God in the little things,
the minutiae of daily life. It is well and good to wish to go
forth and do great deeds for the honor of Our Lord Jesus
Christ and the Queen of Heaven, but the great battles are often
being waged over the next hill, on the other side of the lake,
beyond our reach. To stop and take stock of the here and
now, to make heroic the tiny acts, even the insignificant acts,
herein lies the path to peace and wisdom. Amazing but true,
chopping up vegetables for a salad or mowing the lawn, and
doing it while consciously giving honor and praise to God,
will not only do wonders for our spiritual life, but make the
results of our labors noticeably more pleasing. If I sharpen
this pencil, and do it for Jesus' sake, I'll sharpen it right, by
gum, like it's never been sharpened before.
     Ah, but when people say things like, "I have taken control
of my life," or "I am *empowered,*'" they are grasping at

straws. A simple case of the flu will demonstrate to anyone just how much "control" and "power" they have over the details of their lives. Not a one of us can predict with certainty that we will be alive five hours from now, five minutes, five seconds! This modern idea that "I" can somehow decide my material "destiny," and that "I" make my own "environment," is pure fantasy. True, I can educate my mind, train my body, do certain things, but all of this is contingent on my existence, which I don't have any say in; and how my actions affect my environment is a crap-shoot, because I have no control over the millions of other causes and effects that are going on all around me. I have as little say in the outcome of my endeavors as I have over the fact of my existence. An otherwise perfect day can be devastated by the intrusion of a virus into my bloodstream that I can't even see.

> ... I saw that under the sun, the race is not to the swift, nor the battle to the strong, nor bread to the wise, nor riches to the learned, nor favour to the skillful: but time and chance in all.
> Man knoweth not his own end ...
> —Ecclesiastes IX:11-12

In other words, you and I are *creatures*. It is a basic fact of life. We may not like it, we may wish at times we had never been born, or that we had been born into different circumstances, but the bottom line is that there is simply nothing we can do about it. We can run, but we can't hide. There is no escape:

> Whither shall I go from thy spirit? or whither shall I flee from thy face?
> If I ascend into heaven, thou art there: if I descend into hell, thou art present.
> If I take my wings early in the morning, and dwell in the uttermost parts of the sea:
> Even there also shall thy hand lead me: and thy right hand shall hold me.

> And I said: Perhaps darkness shall cover me: and
> night shall be my light in my pleasures.
> But darkness shall not be dark to thee, and night
> shall be light as the day: and darkness thereof, and the
> light thereof are alike to thee.
> —Psalm CXXXVIII:7-12

Given the fact of our existence and our creature-hood, we are then presented with a choice: do we decide to acknowledge our Creator, to obey His commands, to dispose ourselves toward knowing, loving, and serving Him? Or do we choose to recognize only ourselves, to see to our needs, and revel in cherishing, promoting, and pleasing ourselves?

This is the thing over which we do have control. This is the essence of Free Will. And it is something with which God chooses never to interfere. While we have nothing to say about our material destiny, we have quite a lot to do with our eternal destiny.

Given all this as a backdrop, the stage on which we play out our lives today is cluttered with a peculiar assortment of modern props. Primary among them is the idea that we have "rights." We are encouraged by our culture to demand them, fight for them, legislate more of them, and sue if we're denied them. The average person would probably define a "right" as their privilege to do as they please. This is precisely what our topsy-turvy society has led us to believe; but as is the case with so many things modern, it is a distortion of the Truth:

> *The Oxford Companion to Law* informs us that the
> term *right* is "a much ill-used and over used word" ...
> *The Random House College Dictionary* defines it as
> "a just claim or title, whether legal, prescriptive, or
> moral." The word *just* is of the greatest importance,
> for where a claim is not just there can be no right to
> make it. Catholic teaching, expressed clearly in the
> encyclicals of Pope Leo XIII, is that no man can lay
> claim justly to anything that is contrary to the eternal
> or natural law of God.
>
> In Catholic teaching, as has been explained, the
> terms *right* and *moral liberty* can be considered as
> synonymous. A right is the moral faculty of a per-
> son enabling him justifiably to perform an action,

> own a possession, or make a claim. The word *justi-*
> *fiably* indicates that we can only speak of a right
> when its object is morally licit ... There can only be
> a right, that is, the moral liberty, to choose that
> which is good and true. No man can ever have a right
> to choose what is evil or false ...
>
> —Michael Davies
> *The Second Vatican Council and Religious Liberty*

In the politically-correct lingo of our day, a woman says, "I have a right to choose." What she means in plain English is that she claims the privilege of murdering her unborn child. Since—I'm ashamed to say—there was a time in my life when I would have agreed with her completely, I do understand her position. She feels that her body is hers to do with as she pleases, and if what she pleases accidentally produces a baby inside her womb, her convenience supersedes the child's natural claim on her to carry him, give birth to him, nurse him, feed him, educate him, and otherwise encourage his existence.

She may rationalize, "I can't give this baby a good home, so he'd be better off dead." What she's really saying is that this child will be a tremendous inconvenience to her. He will put a stupendous strain on her resources and relationships that she doesn't feel equipped or willing to handle. She's already decided on behalf of the child that he will be miserable, will take out his misery on her, and that he will most likely go on to repeat her mistakes.

Or she might try, "It isn't really human, it's just a gob of tissue." I couldn't get behind this one even when I was an atheist. If it were true, that human fetuses aren't really human, then every expectant couple would be spending nine nerve-wracking months wondering what's going to pop out. Will they get a giraffe? or a llama? or maybe an ostrich? Of course it's human! What else could it be? Just because it's in an early stage of development, that doesn't change its nature. If I step on a caterpillar, the world is deprived of a butterfly. A human fetus is not defined in the medical books as a tumor. A human fetus is a human being.

Did God call something less than or other than human to be the great prophets of Israel?

The Lord hath called me from the womb, from the
bowels of my mother he hath been mindful of my
name.

— Isaias XLIX:1

And the word of the Lord came to me, saying:
Before I formed thee in the bowels of thy mother, I
knew thee: and before thou camest forth out of the
womb, I sanctified thee, and made thee a prophet unto
the nations.

— Jeremias I:4-5

While yet a fetus, was John the Baptist, the last of the Old
Testament prophets, not human either?

And the angel said to him: Fear not, Zachary, for
thy prayer is heard; and thy wife Elizabeth shall bear
thee a son, and thou shalt name him John:
And thou shalt have joy and gladness, and many
shall rejoice in his nativity.
For he shall be great before the Lord; and shall
drink no wine or strong drink: and he shall be filled
with the Holy Ghost, even from his mother's womb.

— St. Luke I:13-15

There was a time when the safest part of a man's or
woman's life was the first nine months in the womb—

But darkness shall not be dark to thee, and night
shall be light as the day: the darkness thereof, and the
light thereof are alike to thee.
For thou hast possessed my reigns: thou hast protected me from my mother's womb.

Psalm CXXXVIII:12-13

— but today the womb is one of the riskiest places on earth for
a baby.   At the rate we're killing unborn children in the
United States each year—some 1.6 million annually—we're
surpassing the Nazi slaughter of the "outlawed classes" every
four years, and there's no end in sight.   Who knows how
many great and noble souls were cut out at the root, never allowed to be born in our era?

Angry man:	God, why haven't you sent us people with cures for AIDS, cancer, world hunger and social problems?
Voice of God:	I did ... but you aborted them!

—Cartoon by Stayskai

How much do we value human life? This is the issue. If we truly think our lives are something we possess to do with as we please, then the step from selfishness to murder is all too brief. If, on the other hand, we recognize that our lives are not ours at all, that we do not possess them but rather they encompass us, that we do not make the rules, that we do not decide when life begins or ends; then protecting human life—especially when it is innocent and helpless—becomes a duty and a privilege.

On this basis alone, contraception is unacceptable.

The focus of advertising, media, and Sex Ed throws attention on the preventing of sperm from reaching the ovum. Sperm are certainly not "human," so how can anyone object to preventing a conception? The fact is that no birth control method, other than abstinence, is foolproof. Condoms break, diaphragms slip, vasectomies and tubal ligations have been known mysteriously to heal themselves. Sure, the odds of conception are reduced, but not eliminated. Contracepted acts can still produce human life. What then, when that life "accidentally" occurs despite all efforts? That brief step from selfishness to murder becomes all too inviting. Even if the odds are one in a hundred, or even in a thousand, the craving for sexual pleasure can never be judged to be more important than a human life, even a potential human life. How many of us would submit to a game of Russian roulette every time we wanted to have sex?

Notice, too, the violent language of birth control:

Contra	+	ception	= against conception
Aborta	+	facient	= to bring about termination
Sperm	+	icide	= to kill sperm

Rather nasty language when we consider that it's directed against potential children. What is it saying? *Children are a curse.*

What has happened to us? Have we so lost touch with our own humanity that we now shudder at the sound of the "patter of little feet," that we cringe at the thought of responsibility, dread the time spent in close contact, shrink from cuddling and instructing our offspring? There was a time when men and women rejoiced at the thought of raising families:

> ... behold, the inheritance of the Lord are children: the reward, the fruit of the womb.
> —Psalm CXXVI:3

> ... blessed art thou, and it shall be well with thee.
> Thy wife as a fruitful vine, on the sides of thy house. Thy children as olive plants, round about the table.
> Behold thus shall a man be blessed that feareth the Lord.
> —Psalm CXXVII:2-4

And there is no doubt that Jesus Himself placed a high value on children and their qualities:

> And they brought to him young children, that he might touch them. And the disciples rebuked them that brought them.
> Whom when Jesus saw, he was much displeased, and saith to them: Suffer[*] the children to come unto me, and forbid them not; for of such is the kingdom of God.
> Amen I say to you, whosoever shall not receive the kingdom of God as a little child, shall not enter it.
> —St. Mark X:13-15

If Jesus so loved children that He would set them apart as examples to us of a holy attitude, how great must be His consternation that we do not share in His appreciation of them.

---

[*] "Suffer," of course, is the archaic word for "let" or "allow."

Heaven help us if He punishes in a manner befitting our crime.

> A voice in Rama was heard, lamentation and great mourning; Rachel bewailing her children, and would not be comforted, because they are not.
> —St. Matthew II:18

A few words on contraception. I've heard it said more than I'd care to recall, and by parish women with anger in their eyes, "A bunch of old men in Rome aren't going to dictate to *me* what I do in my bedroom." This is, of course, a dodge. It matters not who proclaims the Truth. The Truth is the Truth. What we have here is another case of the great "I."

When Pope Paul VI wrote *Humanae Vitae*, the encyclical forbidding birth control, he was not offering an opinion, or deciding a matter of policy, he was teaching a Truth. He was restating what the Church has maintained all along, that married couples ...

> ... should conform their deeds to God the Creator's guidance, which is expressed by the very nature of matrimony and its acts and which is declared by the constant teaching of the Church.
> —Pope Paul VI
> *Humanae Vitae*

We have been lulled in this country by a perverse sense that what the majority of people want is what is right. Truth is not a matter of popular opinion. Citing these kinds of figures —

> A 1987 public opinion poll reports not only that 66% of Catholics in the United States believe one can be a good Catholic without obeying the Church's teaching on contraception but also that 57% answer similarly with respect to remarriage after divorce and 39% with respect to abortion.
> —c.f., *National Catholic Reporter*
> September 11, 1987

—does not prove a Truth, but rather demonstrates that most Catholics in America are no longer Catholics.

Traditionally, the Church has taught that every marital act must to be open to new life. Marriage was understood to be established by God for the raising of children and to allay concupiscence. Contraception, being contra-life, was considered like homicide—though not the same as homicide—in that it sought to impede the beginning of the life of a possible person. It was not considered a sexual sin, like masturbation or fornication, but rather like intended murder.

> ... killing someone is not morally wrong only because the person who is killed loses the good of life. If that were the case, it also would be morally wrong to kill anyone by accident. An essential condition of the immorality of deliberate homicide is that is involves a contralife will ...
>
> The New Testament makes it abundantly clear, against false, legalistic conceptions, that morality is in the heart. A man can commit adultery without ever touching a woman ... Indeed, any sin is in one's heart before it is in one's deed, and one's sinful deed is wrong because of one's evil heart ...
>
> Usually when people contracept, they are interested in sexual intercourse which they think might lead to conception. If they did not think that, they would have no reason to contracept. They look ahead and think about the baby whose life they might initiate. Perhaps for some further good reason, perhaps not, they find the prospect repugnant: "We do not want that possible baby to begin to live." As the very definition of contraception makes clear, that will is contralife; it is a practical (though not necessarily an emotional) hatred of the possible baby they project and reject, just as the will to accept the coming to be of a baby is a practical love of that possible person.
>
> —Grisez, Boyle, Finnis, & May
> "Every Marital Act Ought to Be Open to New Life"
> *The Teaching of Humanae Vitae: A Defense*

If more couples took the bringing of children into the world seriously, they might take their marriages more seriously. They might as individuals, beforehand, take a longer look at their possible spouse, asking such questions as, "Do I want to raise a family with him?" and "Do I want her to be the mother of my children?" The child, then, becomes an end beyond the marriage itself; and as we've seen in recent years, marriages based on only the mutual self-love between men and women are often doomed to failure.

Also to be considered are the long-range societal ramifications of contraception:

> It is also feared that the man, growing used to the employment of anti-conceptive practices, may finally lose respect for the woman and ... may come to the point of considering her as a mere instrument of selfish enjoyment.
>
> —Pope Paul VI
> *Humanae Vitae*

This papal warning has clearly been borne out by subsequent developments:

> No, not exclusively in America are men getting away from their bodies, no longer sensing the body's natural rhythms, and making of their women objects on which to perform more-or-less masturbatory acts. Nor is it only in America that more and more women, dimly sensing the violence being done their nature, are willing to pervert nature, if only to strike back spitefully, destructively, at it.
>
> —Gary Potter
> *In Reaction*

All of this, because the self-enlightened of this age have persuaded the malleable majority that the purpose of sex is self-gratification, and that any consequences arising from its free exercise are to be rationalized, legalized, and ostracized out of existence.

What business does the Church have in the bedroom? Why, the Church has every reason to be there. In what other place does the very crux of the human condition, the essence of our corrupt fallen nature, and the dark depths of our most hidden desires, erupt so vehemently and obviously? The

Church has every reason to be there, for Her purpose is not just to govern our acts, but to ennoble our purposes. Turmoils over sex and its accouterments are nothing new; nor is the holy way to deal with them:

> I say then, walk in the spirit, and you shall not fulfil the lusts of the flesh.
> For the flesh lusteth against the spirit: and the spirit against the flesh; for these are contrary one to another ...
> Now the works of the flesh are manifest, which are fornication, uncleanness, immodesty, luxury,
> Idolatry, witchcrafts, enmities, contentions, emulations, wraths, quarrels, dissentions, sects,
> Envies, murders, drunkenness, revellings, and such like. Of which I foretell you, as I have foretold to you, that they who do such things shall not obtain the kingdom of God.
> But the fruit of the Spirit is charity, joy, peace, patience, benignity, goodness, longanimity,
> Mildness, faith, modesty, continency, chastity. Against such there is no law.
> And they that are Christ's, have crucified their flesh, with the vices and concupiscences.
> If we live in the Spirit, let us also walk in the Spirit.
>
> —Galatians V:16-17, 19-25

Of course, this is hard. And none of it makes sense unless we believe with all our hearts that our lives are not ours but God's, and that everything that comes into our lives is for our good. If we turn our eyes away from God and focus on our own pleasures, we find that we can rationalize just about anything. But if we keep our attention riveted to Him, and commit our trust into His keeping, we will be in harmony with His intention for our lives; and like Saint Thérèse, we will be "profiting by all the smallest things and doing them through love."

CHAPTER THIRTY

THE ACHE

In the emphasis of every man's dream
There's a spark that wants to be seen and known
And be discovered.
In the dark of every woman's heart
There's a fire that wants to start to burn
And be uncovered.
And in answer to this call
There's a Wind that rushes 'round us all
Beckoning for us
To blossom into flame.

—William L. Biersach
"The Wind," 1978

∞ ∞ ∞

IT MAY BE AN OVERSTATEMENT, though not likely, that there is a very special Place deep within every man and woman. It is the locus of powerful and mutually contradictory forces, all converging and merging and diverging into barely-controlled chaos, or rising to a frenzied and cacophonous silence. It is the source of overpowering desire and timid hesitation, of the wish for intimacy and the dread of discovery, of hilarious generosity and miserly hunger. It is a burning and a yearning, a satisfaction and a craving, a blossoming and a withering. It is the human capacity to and for Love. For most of us, it is an Ache—an Ache so deep, profound, and compelling as to be unthinkable; yet think about it we do, endlessly.

We can only imagine how Adam and Eve experienced Love before the Fall. Created as they were in complete and

total harmony with God, within themselves, with the world
around them, and with each other, what they experienced in
their hearts was surely something sublime, pure, integrated and
awesome.   When they fell through disobedience, everything—repeat, everything—went haywire.   Their bond with
God was severed, their internal balance sent teetering, they lost
touch with the material paradise around them, and their rela-
tionship with each other degenerated into the unintelligible
hysteria with which we are so familiar today.

We have an innate sense that Love should be simple, honest, straightforward, and unwavering—though we rarely experience it as such. Our intuition also tells us that Love and God
are intimately connected—

> Dearly beloved, let us love one another, for charity
> is of God. And every one that loveth, is born of God,
> and knoweth God.
> He that loveth not, knoweth not God: for God is
> charity.
> —I St. John IV:7-8

—yet somehow our wiring gets short-circuited. If nothing else,
this mess provides playwrights, poets and minstrels a living
while their characters agonize unceasingly about it before
audiences that never seem to tire of reliving the agony
through the actors' eyes—as if their own senses were not
enough.   How rapturously Juliet's feelings for Romeo gush
ebullient on one page—

> Come, gentle night, come, loving, black-browed night,
> Give me my Romeo, and when I shall die
> Take him and cut him out in little stars,
> And he will make the face of heaven so fine
> That all the world will be in love with night
> and pay no worship to garish sun.
> O, I have bought the mansions of a love
> But not possessed it, and though I am sold,
> Not yet enjoyed. So tedious is this day
> As is the night before some festival
> To an impatient child that hath new robes
> And may not wear them ...

—only to sour in disillusionment on the next:

> O serpent heart, hid with a flowering face!
> Did ever dragon keep so fair a cave?
> Beautiful tyrant! Fiend angelical!
> Dove-feathered raven! Wolvish-ravening lamb!
> Despisèd substance of divinest show!
> Just opposite to what thou justly seem'st,
> A damnèd saint, an honorable villain!
> O nature, what hadst thou to do in hell
> When thou didst bower the spirit of a fiend
> In mortal paradise of such sweet flesh?
> Was ever book containing such vile matter
> So fairly bound? O, that deceit should dwell
> In such a gorgeous palace!
>
> —William Shakespeare
> *Romeo and Juliet*, III: 2

Ah, Love.

In spite of the confusion and stickiness of the whole business, disregarding its inherent uncertainty and unfavorable credit history, we find ourselves moved to seek it out, take the plunge, try it "one more time," again and again and again.

Let us digress for a moment to remind ourselves that in response to this Ache, there are three possible states in life to which we may be called: 1) a religious vocation, 2) the single life, and 3) marriage. Each has its own remarkable blessings and opportunities; each deals with the Ache in a different way.

The call to the priesthood is the highest thing to which a man can aspire. He is called to offer Solemn Sacrifice to God, something denied the holiest of Angels. But there is more. The priest stands in the midst of the collective Ache of his flock, setting aside his own needs for the sake of theirs. He is not his own man, he is God's, and therefore theirs. He is theirs, not in the modern sense adopted by parish councils that he is a pawn on the chessboard of their myopic agendas; but rather in the traditional sense that he is at their spiritual disposal. His job is to assist them on their path to Salvation. He makes himself available, not just to listen passively to their immediate woes like the counselors of the world, but to actively call attention to their sins so that they can free themselves of woes eternal. Whether they appreciate his input or

not, he is there to admonish them when they err, to guide them
down the right path toward the Light of God. He is spurred
by the realization that if he knowingly allows them to continue
in their sins, the guilt is accounted as his own. When beautiful
young couples come before him to wed, he must set aside any
residual lonely Ache of his own, and bless them in their union.
Their eventual children he will gladly Baptize, and later feed
the Body of Christ. And when any of his flock are near death,
he is there to assist them in their passing. So consuming is his
task, that the Roman Church in Her Wisdom has for many
centuries followed the advice of Saint Paul. (This Scriptural
passage is easier to understand if you substitute the more col-
loquial "anxiety" for "solicitude," and "anxious" for "so-
licitous:")

> But I would have you be without solicitude. He
> that is without a wife, is solicitous for the things that
> belong to the Lord, how he may please God.
> But he that is with a wife, is solicitous for the
> things of the world, how he may please his wife: and
> he is divided.
> And the unmarried woman and the virgin thinketh
> on the things of the Lord, that she may be holy both
> in body and in spirit. But she that is married thinketh
> on the things of the world, how she may please her
> husband.
> —I Corinthians VII:32-34

Would not a married man hesitate to run to the aid of a
diseased person, for example, if he fears that he might infect
his wife and children afterwards? Would not the needs of his
wife and children weigh heavily if his duty to God demands
that he risk his life to reach a sinner in a dangerous situation,
say, amidst gunfire in a ghetto? Would not the basic job description, as cited above, cut deeply into the time and energies
necessary to make a good marriage? And so, too, with women
called to the religious life. The rigors of communal existence
and the demands of the work to which their particular order is
dedicated require freedom from the ties of matrimony. Thus
the sacerdotal life, the monastic life, and the call of women to
the convent, are celibate states. The Ache is sublimated by
devotion to God and service to others.

The second calling, to the single life, is also, by definition and the requirements of morality, a celibate state. The Ache is set on "hold." Unfortunately, most people seem to have gotten it into their heads that singleness denotes some kind of failure. "Normal" people seemingly have no trouble getting married, and "holy" people obviously become priests and nuns—so single people are somehow abnormal, unfit, unloved, and weird (or else they're excessively picky). All of which is simply rot. The single person is free from the worries and responsibilities heaped upon those in the other two states. When a man is not bound by obedience to religious superiors, be they abbots or bishops, nor must he expend his energy supporting the physical and spiritual needs of his wife and children, he can concentrate his efforts on other things. When a woman is not tied to the constraints of a family, nor is she under the thumb of a mother superior or abbess, there is much she can accomplish as a free agent.

If the question arises, "What else is there?" then the asker has not given the matter much thought. The single person is free to travel, take financial risks, change jobs, try new things, make unpopular statements in public, take controversial courses of action and the like—things which the married and vowed are restrained from doing without causing harm to their dependents and offices. Moreover, the single life allows for a unique concentration on Faith, and can thus be an opportunity for many Graces and blessings. We don't normally think of the single state in these terms, but it is worth considering. More on this in a moment.

For many, of course, the Ache seems to have but one answer: marriage. Their Ache may manifest itself as a love for children, the need to take care of someone, or the desire for intimacy. On the other hand it may be felt as the fear of loneliness, an inability to organize one's own affairs, or something more basic and urgent:

> ... It is good for a man not to touch a woman ...
> But if they do not contain themselves, let them
> marry. For it is better to marry than to be burnt.
> —I Corinthians VII:1, 9

Such considerations are all normal, prudent, and certainly human—and are all addressed to some degree, in one way or another, in marriage. The potential for mutual support, emotional release, personal intimacy, the joys and pangs of raising children, are all very much there. The word "potential" is important, because none of these things come easily. The benefits of the married state are the result of patience, self-sacrifice, and a host of other difficult virtues that romance novels and passionate songs fail to address. Marriage is hard. Marriage is also a Sacrament, and thus couples have access to Divine Grace to overcome the hurdles. As with the Grace of Confirmation, the Grace of Matrimony kicks in only when actively applied. No matter how stormy a couple's internal strife may become, God can and will supply sufficient Grace to pull them through. They, of course, must will to do so and make use of the supplied help. Furthermore, their commitment goes beyond their vows to each other, for the product and blessing of shared Love is children—and to this possibility the husband and wife must both be open, honest, and willing.

As a single man myself, I am ill equipped to say much more about the sacerdotal or married states, having only tangential experience of them. Like all proud bachelors, I tend to expound on the benefits of my own state. Yes, it has its lonely moments, but is also has its freedoms. In moments of doubt all I have to do is chat with some of my married friends and in almost no time I feel vindicated.

Some attention, however, must be given to those of us who have landed in the single state, but are convinced that they would be better off married. As time passes arithmetically, anxiety grows exponentially. Despondent unwillingness to accept such a "fate" has brought many men and women to the brink of collision with the jagged reefs of despair. "If God really loved me," we may find ourselves thinking, "He would see to my needs—He would find me a spouse." We may even couch the thought in the form of a prayer: "God, if you love me, find me a partner." But this is self-deception. It is a deception in that it buys into the lie that we can dictate how God should express His Love for us—as if we knew better than He; and it assumes that God owes us something.

Admittedly, when the Ache is upon us, it is hard to remind ourselves that we came from nothing, that we are nothing, because it's hard to imagine how nothing can hurt so much. But the fact is that, as much as we wish it otherwise, we are inherently and essentially nothing. God does not need us: we need God.

No one has ever ached as much as Jesus the evening before He was to suffer and die on the Cross. So intense was His agony at the prospect of what was coming that He sweat blood. It is a great Mystery that even though He was about to do exactly what He had come into the world to accomplish, He wished to be released from His mission. And yet, as an example of the proper attitude in which all our prayers should be said, He deferred to the Will of the Father:

> Father, if thou wilt, remove this chalice from me:
> but yet not my will, but thine be done.
> —St. Luke XXII:42

His exact words can be our prayer in whatever dark circumstance we may find ourselves. It takes an inordinate amount of courage to say them—in fact, most of us who do probably don't mean them half as much as we think. The more we say them, however, and the more we try to mean them, the deeper they will work their way into our hearts. Eventually they will be like the anchor that holds a boat in place as the squall rolls by. "Not my will, but thine be done"—words such as these reflect a total commitment of the mind, the heart, and the soul to the Will of God; a surrender of our immediate desire to the long-range benefits of His Wisdom, His Knowledge, His Plan. Such profound capitulation is not arrived at without much thought, devotion, and above all, prayer. Just as we do not put our confidence in anyone until they first prove themselves to be reliable, we tend to withhold our trust from God until we learn by experience that He is truly on "our side." Many are the times in life ...

> ... when the earth shall be troubled; and the mountains shall be removed into the heart of the sea.
> —Psalm XLV:3

But the greatest lesson we can learn, in the midst of all the turmoil and chaos is to ...

> Be still and see that I am God ...
> —Psalm XLV:11

"This is not poetry," I have said again and again. And indeed, this is not. This is facing Reality.

> Patience attains all that it strives for.
> He who has God finds he lacks nothing.
> Let nothing disturb thee.
> Let nothing discourage thee.
> All things pass.
> God never changes.
> God alone suffices.
>
> —Saint Teresa of Avila
> These words are engraved in tiles
> at Santa Terecita Hospital in Duarte, California,
> where I often attend Mass in the chapel
> with the Carmelite nuns.

We must constantly remind ourselves that our main purpose in life is not to be happy, but to bring about our Salvation. There is nothing which supersedes this. Absolutely nothing. If we place our trust in God, He will guide us down whatever path is most beneficial to us:

> And we know that to them that love God, all
> things work together unto good, to such as, according
> to his purpose, are called to be saints.
> —Romans VIII:28

Marriage, we must remember, is a means to Salvation. That is why it is sanctioned by God as a Sacrament. Anyone considering matrimony must ask the question: "Will this marriage, and will this person, lead me closer to God?" There is no other reason to get married. None. All the needs and wants, all the dreams and hopes, all the romance and melodrama in the world is moot beside this one issue. Our first duty is to strive to know, love, and serve God. Once we are on that path, if marriage will work to our good, God will provide it for us. If it will not—and if we don't go off half-cocked and take matters into our own hands—He will provide another means that will be more to our benefit. We may not at first see this as a benefit because we do not see the long-range results.

But if our minds are focused on God, rather than ourselves, He will be free to work out what is ultimately best in our lives.

> Seek ye therefore first the kingdom of God, and his
> justice, and all these things shall be added unto you.
> —St. Matthew VI:33

How hard this is to grasp, and how simple to execute. Total surrender, once achieved, is such a relief!

I have, at times, resorted to a prayer which I composed one night while writing a letter to a dear friend. These words will never end up on a holy card or wall plaque, but they have been of enormous consolation and help to me, so I pass them on to you:

> Dear Lord,
> Please do whatever is necessary to make me a Saint, no matter how I kick and scream and take it back during the process. Help me to trust that each and every calamity is a gateway to Grace and a step closer to You. For the goal, after all, is not to be found in this corrupt life, but in the life thereafter. Amen.

Another thing to consider is that, in some of us, the fantasy we create of the person "out there somewhere," who is going to ride heroically into our lives and apply the healing balm to our heart's pulsating Ache, can easily become an idol. An idol is anything we come to worship in place of Almighty God. Make no mistake: harping on the deeply desired, ever-illusive lover who never seems to materialize can become as idolatrous as a golden calf—

> Thou shalt not make to thyself a graven thing, nor
> the likeness of any thing that is in heaven above, or
> in the earth beneath ...
> Thou shalt not adore them, nor serve them: I am
> the Lord thy God, mighty, jealous ...
> Exodus XX:4-5

—and just as offensive to God. Why does an omnipotent God describe Himself as "jealous"? Because He knows that anything that comes between us and Him is so terribly detrimental—not to Him, but to us. The intensity of His infinite Love arouses His jealousy on our behalf. As creatures we have no business turning to anyone or anything for sustenance other than our Creator, not even a lover or a spouse, and certainly not a dream of one.

Living for a dream is, as startling as the word may at first seem, a *trap*. Just as an unwitting animal is vulnerable to the deviously placed snare, so is the desperately searching Ache susceptible to deception, misuse, and humiliation. So consumed can we become with our yearnings that we leave ourselves wide open to those who will sense our need—unsavory sorts who don't think twice about using and discarding those they can manipulate. But even if we are spared this, do we really want to live our lives perpetually looking under every rock and around every corner, anxiously searching for a kind word, a gentle smile, a much-desired glance from that possible partner? Is it fair to ourselves or others to scrutinize every person we meet of the opposite sex with the underlying query: "Can this be the one?" Many a noble and fruitful friendship can be nipped in the bud by such initial behavior, and all because we are grasping for what might be, rather than embracing the solid Reality of each moment and detail of our lives as a personal gift from God.

About a year ago a good friend handed me a card. On it was a prayer which His Eminence Cardinal Merry del Val used to recite every day after celebrating Mass. He was secretary to Saint Pope Pius X. I got as far as the third line and—gulp!—tucked the card safely away between the pages of a book I had no intention of finishing. There it sat, patiently awaiting the day when I would remember it, realize its necessity, and retrieve it from the shelf. Two months I took. Now I keep it in my missal where I can review it every day at Mass. No one who says this prayer daily with an open heart—even if it rankles at first—can long remain unaffected. The attitude of heart which it seeks to inspire is diametrically opposed to that which is encouraged by the material and physical gluttonies of our culture. May my reader profit by its Wisdom:

THE LITANY OF HUMILITY

O Jesus! meek and humble of heart, hear me.

From the desire of being esteemed, deliver me, Jesus.
From the desire of being loved, deliver me, Jesus.
From the desire of being extolled, deliver me, Jesus.
From the desire of being honored, deliver me, Jesus.
From the desire of being praised, deliver me, Jesus.
From the desire of being preferred, deliver me, Jesus.
From the desire of being consulted, deliver me, Jesus.
From the desire of being approved, deliver me, Jesus.

From the fear of being humiliated, deliver me, Jesus.
From the fear of being despised, deliver me, Jesus.
From the fear of suffering rebukes, deliver me, Jesus.
From the fear of being calumniated, deliver me, Jesus.
From the fear of being forgotten, deliver me, Jesus.
From the fear of being ridiculed, deliver me, Jesus.
From the fear of being wronged, deliver me, Jesus.
From the fear of being suspected, deliver me, Jesus.

That others may be loved more than I,
    Jesus, grant me the grace to desire it.
That others may be esteemed more than I,
    Jesus, grant me the grace to desire it.
That in the opinion of the world, others may increase,
    and I may decrease,
    Jesus, grant me the grace to desire it.
That others may be chosen and I set aside,
    Jesus, grant me the grace to desire it.
That others may be praised and I unnoticed,
    Jesus, grant me the grace to desire it.
That others may be preferred to me in everything,
    Jesus, grant me the grace to desire it.
That others become holier than I,
    provided that I may become as holy as I should.
    Jesus, grant me the grace to desire it.

∞ ∞ ∞

Take as many months as you need, but remember where you hid this book so that when the Truth of this prayer takes root within you, you can find this page again.

CHAPTER THIRTY

THE VALLEY OF THE BLIND

For professing themselves to be wise, they became
fools.

—Romans I:22

∞ ∞ ∞

IT CAN BE SAID WITHOUT EQUIVOCATION that each and
every person reading the words on this page has been poisoned by the Protestant Reformation—the author included.
The ideals of Luther and Calvin and the other so-called reformers so permeate our culture, our lives, and our thinking
patterns that we are unaware of their influence; but their impression is imminent and very real. It matters not that we're
the most staunch Traditionalists that ever lived, that we
marched from Notre Dame to Chartres in support of the rein-
statement of the Tridentine Mass, or that we can recite the
Syllabus of Errors by heart. Like it or not, squirm as we may,
deny it with pounding fist and heaving breath, we are compromised. By virtue of the fact that we speak English, we are
subliminally disposed against the Roman Catholic Church. If
you were to say to me, "Bill, you're *pontificating* again," you
would not be paying me a compliment, even though you had
just said that I was "speaking like the pope."

Think about it—don't dismiss it out of hand. This is not
the ravings of a deranged layman in search of conspiracy
theories, but the sober observation of a serious Roman Catholic living in the United States in the early years of the twenty-
first century. For the most part the poison of which we speak

is of a subconscious nature, but the venom is nonetheless there.

The antidote to this toxin is, of course, knowledge of the True Faith—knowledge of God as it was taught by the Fathers and Doctors of the Church, not as it has been obfuscated by newage theologians who think putting sand in holy water fonts is really neat because it's "so close to the earth." What we need is to learn the Reality of the Church, to understand Her Dogmas rather than assume their irrelevance, to embrace Her teachings instead of diluting them to fit our tastes.

Perhaps the hardest thing about becoming and then being a Roman Catholic in the United States at this time in history is coming to grips with the fact that the Faith is at complete odds with the American culture. True, the modernists are busily promoting compromise, but ultimately there can be none.

> He that is not with me, is against me: and he that
> gathereth not with me, scattereth.
> —St. Matthew XII:30

The teachings of Jesus Christ are as contrary to the goals of our society as matter is to anti-matter—with the exception that the interaction of the latter produces mutual annihilation, while the former produces Saints.

The Puritans from England, who started this conundrum known as the United States, were guilty of de-babying the bath water twice. As Protestants they hated the Catholic Church and went to great lengths to rid themselves of any latent Papist tendencies—outlawing Christmas and mince pie was an obvious declaration of war in this regard. As Protestants, too, their acrimony against authority would erupt into revolution against the monarchy in order to establish a self-celebrating, self-aggrandizing democracy.

All the while, their stark view of God and their distorted view of His Reality left them deprived of the ability to enjoy life. Whereas a Catholic poet could sing—

> But Catholic men that live upon wine
> Are deep in the water, and frank, and fine;

Wherever I travel I find it so,
Benedicamus Domino.

—Hilaire Belloc
"Heretics All"

—a Puritan could not. Traditionally, and historically, Catholics enjoyed life. With Mary in their hearts and Jesus in their tabernacles, what else was there to do? What else made sense? The Joy of the Faith permeated their lives, from the heights of dedicated spiritual contemplation to the bare-bones basics of everyday life:

I would like to have the men of Heaven
In my own house:
With vats of good cheer
Laid out for them.

I would like to have the three Marys,
Their fame is so great.
I would like people
From every corner of Heaven.

I would like them to be cheerful
In their drinking.
I would like to have Jesus too
Here amongst them.

I would like a great lake of beer
For the King of Kings,
I would like to be watching Heaven's family
Drinking it through all eternity.

—"The Heavenly Banquet," c. eleventh century
Daily Readings from Prayers in the Celtic Tradition
Edited by A. M. Allchin and Esther de Waal

How strange that most Catholics today have grown up with the notion that it was *their* Church that promoted guilt as a means of controlling Her subjects. The Truth, in fact, is entirely the other way around:

The United States was originally settled by the
English Puritans, who came here to ensure that none
of their membership would have the opportunity to
enjoy himself.   Like their co-religionist Oliver
Cromwell, they outlawed Christmas, and even today
the phrase "Banned in Boston" conjures up visions of
baboonish ignoramuses outlawing Shakespeare because of the Bard's profanity ... Unfortunately, their
shortsighted love of profit, their suspicion of emotion, their speed in abandoning honor for material advantage have become seemingly indelible traits in our
national character ...
    ... Armed with the ardour of their hypocritical
faith, they did their best to wipe our all traces of the
old pre-Reformation English merriment that they
could ... God showered material riches upon those
who were saved, so that wealth became a sign of salvation.   The poor deserved their fate.   And, as the
great H. P. Lovecraft observed, "In attempting to follow in inhuman moral code, the early Puritans became adept at hiding things.   In time, they lost all
taste with regard to what they hid."
                                                    —Charles A. Coulombe
                                                    Everyman Today Call Rome

Calvinism left its mark on American thought in insidious
ways—including the "dragondizement" of Catholic priests
and nuns who fell under its influence—long after intelligent
people rejected the original tenets of the movement.   To the
Calvinist mindset, a man who loses his job has just lost his self-
worth because wealth is a sign of inclusion among the elect of
God.   Centuries later, when "of God" has been forgotten and
deleted from the equation, would not any American feel a severe sense of depreciation, desperation, depression, and even
scandal if they were fired?
    Whereas in a truly Catholic society, where God's reign is
welcome in every heart, if a man were to lose his job he would
say, as did Job in the Old Testament:

    Naked came I out of my mother's womb, and naked
    shall I return thither: the Lord gave, and the Lord hath

> taken away: as it hath pleased the Lord so is it done:
> blessed be the name of the Lord.
>
> —Job I:21

Or, perhaps in less lofty terms, he might pause and reflect, "Thank-you, Lord, for closing another door in my life. Please grant me the grace to see the next one you wish to open for me. And if poverty be my lot, so be it. Libraries are free—I will at last have time to read." The Catholic, we realize, would remember that, first off, God is in control—

> God, whose wrath no man can resist, and under
> whom they stoop that bear up the world.
> What am I then, that I should answer him, and have
> words with him?
>
> —Job IX:13-14

—and second, that His promises hold True, even when on the surface everything seems to be going awry.

> And we know that to them that love God, all
> things work together unto good, to such as, according
> to his purpose, are called to be saints.
>
> —Romans VIII:28

Food for thought as we take a moment to examine critically our religious situation.

If phrases such as "I think some people are a little too wrapped up in Mary" or "separation of Church and State is a good thing" have passed my reader's lips, I hate to tell them but they are manifesting symptoms of the Wittenburg Flu. If such thoughts as "all religions are equally valid" are crossing my reader's mind, along with wonderment at my negative, non-community-building comments concerning our Protestant "brethren," their condition has just been upgraded to serious. Very serious. And if they think the plots of *Star Trek: The Next Generation* are morally and philosophically profound, they should be put on the critical list and start intravenous novenas immediately. In the mean time, please read on.

In all seriousness, we are in the midst of a religious catastrophe. Before we can respond to a disaster, we must first accept that one has occurred. If my house has been demolished by a 9.2 earthquake, but I wander around the rubble in a state of denial, refusing to admit that my home and all my belongings have been destroyed, I will never roll up my sleeves and set to the business of rebuilding.

> *It's the job that's never started as takes longest to finish ...*
>
> —J.R.R.Tolkien
> *The Lord of the Rings*

Though the moral and theological disaster rages around us like a horrific hurricane, there are many Catholics who don't even suspect that something is wrong. There are others who have attained some partial return to sanity—their bishop having granted an occasional Tridentine Mass as a token of his "generous application" of *Ecclesia Dei** or the like—and rather than shift to a higher gear of Faith, prefer to slip into neutral and coast. They don't want to make waves lest what crumbs have been tossed their way by their condescending shepherd be snatched away again. There are others, many others, who would gladly give their lives for the Faith, if only they could find it, if only they could find someone to teach them.

Whatever our particulars, we are all compromised. Reading European history from books in English is like consulting *Pravda* for information concerning the Communist Revolution in Russia. The winner decides the morality of the outcome. Thus we were taught that monarchies were inevitably bad, that all the popes were tyrants, that movies like *The Name of the Rose* accurately portrayed monastic life, that people take a flying leap upwards when they cast off the yoke of authority and trust in themselves. But there is another point of view, one which may come as a surprise to some:

> It is difficult for us in the twentieth century—propagandized as we have been by those forces which ever since the French Revolution have been plotting the overthrow of Christianity and fomenting

---

* See chapter 28.

wars and revolutions and financial depressions, and re-
lentlessly reducing, as part of the plan, every lofty
Catholic cultural ideal to the lowest common
level—to understand Pope Innocent's extraordinary
labor and his influence on the monarchs and govern-
ments of the thirteenth century.   We have been
slowly and deliberately taught, through slanted literature and history ... that monarchies and kings are bad
things, and papal supervision of any kind in government is a *very* bad thing ...

Scarcely anyone is ever told any more, that France,
under its Saint-King, Louis IX, flowered as never before; that the Holy Roman Emperor, Henry II, who
with his Empress, Cunegunda, lived in holy and perpetual virginity, was a constant source of goodness
and benevolence toward his people; that Spain and
Portugal, Poland and Hungary, England and Sweden,
all had kings and queens who were saints, and who
ruled their lands gloriously and brought untold happiness and well-being to their subjects.

No one is told that when great monasteries were to
be found on almost every hill in Europe—peopled
with holy monks, many of them from noble and
kingly families—there was never any need of bread
lines or soup kitchens, for the hungry could always
find food and a night's lodging with the monks.   It
was only after the "Reformation" that poorhouses and
poor farms came into being, and that men were forced
to go on the dole and huddle together in dirty slums.

And it is only since the free rein given to the forces
unleashed on the world by the French Revolution that
king after king, in all the Catholic countries of
Europe, lost their thrones.   The kings were, as we
know, replaced by presidents, and the presidents by
dictators.   And now that the dictators are gone, we
suddenly become aware that something exceedingly
sinister has been put over on the Christian world ...

—The Slaves of the Immaculate Heart of Mary
Our Glorious Popes

Most people don't want to hear such things, because if the above is true, then almost everything they believe and accept and take for granted is not.

Welcome to Reality.

I am reminded of a disturbing short story by H. G. Wells called "The Country of the Blind." Normally I don't recommend Wells except to the strongly-Faithed because his rampant rationalism and fascination with the theory of evolution so permeates his works as to render them potentially dangerous to the malleable mind.* In this particular case, however, his ardent atheism perhaps makes him the best teller of the tale, because he is so close to its heart.

It involves a man by the name of Nunez, an experienced mountaineer, who became lost while on an attempt to climb Parascotopetl, the Matterhorn of the Andes Mountains. By chance he stumbled into a remarkable haven, completely isolated from the rest of the world.

> The valley ... had in it all that the heart of man could desire—sweet water, pasture, and even climate, slopes of rich, brown soil with tangles of a shrub that bore an excellent fruit, and on one side great hanging forests of pine that held the avalanches high ... In this valley it neither rained nor snowed, but the abundant springs gave a rich green pasture, that irrigation would spread over all the valley space. The settlers did well indeed there.
>
> —H. G. Wells
> "The Country of the Blind"

It was indeed a paradise, except for one curious thing. All the inhabitants were completely blind due to a disease which had struck their village centuries before. Nunez, upon meeting them and seeing their handicap, felt sure that he could turn the situation to his advantage.

> It seemed they knew nothing of sight.
> Well, all in good time he would teach them.

---

* For a serious exploration of the anti-Catholic bias of H. G. Wells, see *A Companion to Mr. Wells's "Outline of History"* by Hilaire Belloc.

His expectations, however, were immediately dashed.

> "There is no such word as *see*," said the blind man,
> after a pause. "Cease this folly, and follow the sound
> of my feet."
> Nunez followed, a little annoyed.
> "My time will come," he said.
> "You'll learn," the blind man answered. There is
> much to learn in the world."
> "Has no one told you, 'In the Country of the Blind
> the One-eyed Man is King'?"
> "What is blind?" asked the blind man carelessly
> over his shoulder.

They knew nothing of words such as "sight," "light,"
and "sun"; nor anything about the world outside their valley.
Not as a savior did they come to regard Nunez, but rather as:

> "A wild man, out of the rocks ... A wild
> man—using wild words ... His mind is hardly formed
> yet. He has only the beginnings of speech ... He
> stumbles as he walks and mingles words that mean
> nothing with his speech."

Try as he might, he could not get through to them, could
not convince them that there was something beyond the limits
of their senses, a world outside their tightly-barricaded notion
of the universe.

> Nunez found himself trying to explain the great
> world out of which he had fallen, and the sky and
> mountains and sight and such-like marvels, to these
> elders who sat in darkness in the Country of the
> Blind. And they would believe and understand noth-
> ing whatever he told them, a thing quite outside his
> expectation. They would not even understand many
> of his words. For fourteen generations these people
> had been blind and cut off from all the seeing world;
> the names for all the things of sight had faded and
> changed; the story of the outer world was faded and
> changed to a child's story; and they had ceased to con-

cern themselves with anything beyond the rocky
slopes above their circling wall. Blind men of genius
had arisen among them and questioned shreds of belief
and tradition they had brought with them from their
seeing days, and had dismissed all these things as idle
fancies, and replaced them with saner explanations.
Much of their imagination had shrivelled with their
eyes ...

Mortally frustrated, Nunez tried to flee, but could find no
way out of the valley. After several days of frantic wandering,
he was driven back to the village by the ravages of hunger.
But there was a price to pay.

They asked him if he could "*see*."
"No," he said. "That was folly. The word means
nothing—less than nothing!"
They asked him what was overhead.
"About ten times the height of a man there is a
roof above the world—of rock—and very, very
smooth." He burst again into hysterical tears. "Before you ask me any more, give me some food or I
shall die."

In order to live in peace with these stubborn blind folk, he
had to compromise everything in which he believed, everything he knew to be true. And so he did. Warily they accepted him, hoping his new "sanity" was genuine. They gave
him the name "Bogota" because that was the "imaginary
city" which he had claimed to come from when he first arrived in their midst. Nunez, in return for their "generosity"
and "kindness" did everything he could to fit in. He even
fell in love with Medina-saroté, the daughter of Yacob, the
man who took the incompetent stranger in.

Once the gears of compromise are engaged, the engine
will run on and on, feeding as it does not on the abundance of
fuel but rather on its ever-decreasing supply. The engine
shifted into high gear when Nunez-Bogota proposed marriage
to Yacob's daughter. Some of the villagers objected vehe-

mently, not wanting their race tainted with the blood of an idiot. One of the elders, a great medicine man and philosopher, came up with a solution which he proposed to Yacob:

> "Those queer things that are called the eyes, and which exist to make an agreeable soft depression in the face, are diseased, in the case of Bogota, in such a way as to effect his brain ... And I think I may say with reasonable certainty that, in order to cure him completely, all that we need do is a simple and easy surgical operation—namely, to remove these irritant bodies."
>
> "And then he will be sane?"
>
> "Then he will be perfectly sane, and a quite admirable citizen."
>
> "Thank Heaven for science!" said old Yacob, and went forth at once to tell Nunez of his happy news.

Would Nunez consent to such a thing? Would he even endure the loss of his eyes in order to "get along" with the society in which he found himself? If my readers have "inquiring minds" they will have to seek out an H. G. Wells anthology and find out for themselves. *Caveat emptor.*

But the same question needs to be addressed to all Catholics living in the United States in the present: will they choose to continue living the lie? Will they choose, for the noble cause of "not making waves," to continue affirming the unTruths of the society in which they find themselves?

> The light of thy body is thy eye. If thy eye be single, thy whole body will be lightsome: but if it be evil, thy body also will be darksome.
>
> Take heed therefore, that the light which is in thee, be not darkness.
>
> —St. Luke XI:34-35

Are we so immersed in the cauldron of concession that we have lost all sense of real priorities?

> And if thy eye scandalize thee, pluck it out. It is
> better for thee with one eye to enter into the kingdom
> of God, than having two eyes to be cast into the hell
> of fire:
> Where their worm dieth not, and the fire is not ex-
> tinguished.
> — St. Mark IX:46-47

"Mustn't bother anyone," we declare, shifting our tooth-
pick from one side of the mouth to the other. "Live and let
live, I always say. Whatever gets you through the night. If
someone gets consolation and warm feelings out of their religion, who am I to upset their applecart?"

> You are the light of the world. A city seated on a
> mountain cannot be hid.
> Neither do men light a candle and put it under a
> bushel, but upon a candlestick, that it may shine to
> all that are in the house.
> So let your light shine before men ...
> — St. Matthew V:14-16

Whom do we fear? Our fellow men and their opinions,
their derision, their laughter? Or do we fear God? Who, we
might ask, is the more Real?

> And fear ye not them that kill the body, and are not
> able to kill the soul: but rather fear him that can de-
> stroy both soul and body in hell...
> Every one therefore that shall confess me before
> men, I will also confess him before my Father who is
> in heaven.
> But he that shall deny me before men, I will also
> deny him before my Father who is in heaven.
> — St. Matthew X:28, 32-33

"But the loving thing," whine the compromising Bogotas
of today, "is to leave well enough alone. It would be uncharitable to tell them they're going to go to Hell. It might
disrupt their peace."

> Do not think that I came to send peace upon earth:
> I came not to send peace, but the sword.
>
> For I came to set a man at variance against his fa-
> ther, and the daughter against her mother, and the
> daughter in law against her mother in law.
>
> And a man's enemies shall be they of his own
> household.
>
> —St. Matthew X:28

The message of Jesus will not bring "peace," not as the world wishes it. Rather, it will cause division and strife, alienation from family and loss of friends. The true Peace of Christ is purchased at the price of everything we own, everything that we are, everything that would be convenient and easy to believe. The price of compromise is even greater, however, for the sales tax includes our very souls.

The story of Nunez is profoundly parallel to our own. He knew that there was a sun, that it emanated light, that he had eyes with which to see that light. Through no fault of his own, he was thrust into the midst of a society that regarded the sun as a legend, and all luminous things connected with it as fairy tales. They had "their truth," and he had "his." But one truth was false—it had to be, because there are no "two truths." Their ignorance, denial and incomprehension did not change the pre-existing fact that the sun, and all that proceeded from it, was real.

By the same token, while it is fashionable today to speak of "your truth" and "my truth" as if Reality was so accommodating, such a thing is preposterous to anyone with intellectual, philosophical, or moral integrity. There cannot be two mutually exclusive truths. There can only be One Truth. Anything else is compromise. And compromise, as Nunez discovered, ends in complete subjugation to the lie.

The choice before us today is simple: do we compromise with the Lie, or do we summon the courage to learn, live, and speak out the Truth as Jesus Christ our Lord and Savior commands? The clock is ticking and, unlike God, we don't have all the time in the world. Which shall it be?

CHAPTER THIRTY-TWO

WHO IS SHE?

He that awaketh early to seek her, shall not labor:
for he shall find her sitting at his door.
— Wisdom VI:15

∞ ∞ ∞

ONE ONLY NEEDS TO LOOK at a map of North America to see
that the landscape is peppered with cities and towns named
after the Blessed Virgin Mary.   Even my own metropolis of
Los Angeles was originally called the city of "Nuestra Señora
Reina de los Angeles"*—Our Lady Queen of the Angels.
Landmarks such as Point Conception also bear reference to
Her.   Surely She must have held an important place in the
lives of the early explorers for them to name so many places
with Her in mind rather than after their wives and sweethearts.
What kind of amnesia has overtaken us that we no longer un-
derstand what so moved the Spaniards, the French, and the
Portuguese that they would praise the Blessed Virgin at every
turn of coast, river, and mountain range as they explored the
New World?

Why, we might ask, are so many chapels, churches, cathedrals, shrines, monasteries, convents, hospitals, orphanages and
so on, all over the planet, named after this Woman who never
traveled far from Her place of birth, never performed any
great miracles in Her lifetime, and is only mentioned in passing in the Bible after the birth of Christ?   What is it about Her

---

* The full name was actually *El Pueblo de Nuestra Señora Reina de los Angeles de Porciuncula,* but a comprehensive explanation of this colorful bit of
historic nomenclature would take us far afield of the topic at hand.

that captured the devotion of kings and paupers, theologians and simpletons, explorers and blacksmiths, queens and scullery maids, Saints and sinners? Who could She possibly be? Could a myth carry such weight, provoke such ardor, inspire such devotion, and sustain all this over the span of so many centuries?

I remember Her statue in the chapel at my grammar school, all dressed in ocean blue except for Her flowing white veil. She was standing atop a plaster globe. I don't think I ever asked the nuns about the snake pinned under Her feet, but somehow it seemed to fit. I was six or seven. I vaguely remember Mother LM—or was it Sister MC?—telling us that Mary lived in the Temple of Jerusalem from the time She was three until She was betrothed to Joseph at the age of fourteen. There was also something about him being chosen from a group of other suitors when the staff in his hands suddenly sprouted flowers as a sign of Divine Favor ...

Certainly we learned about Her Mysteries in the Rosary, but the significance of these things, and how we came to know about such ethereal events as the Assumption and Coronation, were left unaddressed. Perhaps they thought us too young to understand. The nuns at my grammar school used to put on May Processions each year. I was chosen to carry the Cross in front of the whole line once. Most of the songs were in Latin—yes, even the first-graders learned hymns and chants in that "dead language"—and the sight of two hundred and fifty children carrying candles and flowers around the block in the evening surely caught the attention of the local neighborhood residents. We could see them looking out their apartment windows, irregular silhouettes framed in orderly squares of pale yellow light. Some of them even ventured into the night air to listen to the sweet sound of so many children singing prayers to Our Lady. Mary was part of the Faith, an integral part of our lives. We were not ashamed of Her.

Strangely, though, when the changes came, Mary was among the casualties.

There was a big-shot scholar, Monsignor P, who used to reside at my parish when I was in my early twenties. He said Mass on Sundays but spent his weekdays teaching Foundational Christology at the archdiocesan seminary. One day after Mass I stopped him and asked how we knew that Mary had been assumed into Heaven. He stared through me for several long seconds. Then he went into "scholar-speak"—the language of the pretentious pedagogue: much verbiage, no substance. He danced around Tradition—he somehow made the word rhyme with "legend"—but delivered no facts and no specifics.

My dad once told me about his conditional Baptism when he converted to the Catholic Faith. That was back when they didn't assume that Protestant Baptisms were always valid without exception. Just in case any part of the form had been incorrectly administered, they resprinkled all newcomers. Those were the days when they took Baptism seriously.   Anyway, Dad's entrance to the Catholic Faith was crowned by an intriguing sensation: "I could feel a Presence ..." he said, groping for words. He took a long, pensive puff on his pipe. "... and I knew it was Mary."   More than that he could not say.

Channel 5 used to show *The Miracle of Our Lady of Fatima* on Easter Sundays, not that the movie had anything to do with Easter, but I guess the TV station thought the title sounded Catholic. If it hadn't been for that movie, I never would have heard of Fatima until I was forty. Very few of today's Catholics know anything about it—or want to.

During my "charismatic" period I was involved in a large prayer meeting in a nearby parish. It was very "ecumenical." A fair percentage of the people that attended were Protestants. That's when I learned that, "You Catholics put too much emphasis on Mary."   After a while the prayer group "leader," himself a Catholic, began to sound more like them than us. Shortly thereafter I walked out of the Church for what I thought was for good (see Chapter 26).

Then came the Dark Years.

Most of what I heard about Mary "out there" was deflating, if not downright derogatory.   Everything I'd learned about Her as a child was called into question: Her Immaculate Conception for one thing, Her Virginity with respect to Joseph and the Birth of Jesus, and the likelihood of Jesus having brothers were all fair game, it seemed, for brutal attacks by college professors, academics, intellectuals, and just plain folks. Such things as Her Assumption into Heaven were reduced to mere myth, stories to fascinate gullible peasants when the Faith was still young. I noticed that most people did not call her "Blessed" let alone "Virgin," and one particularly obnoxious fellow once referred to Her as, "Just an incubator, that's all she was—nothing more." Even as an atheist, I was offended by much of the language used against Her. Why did they find it necessary to so vehemently attack that in which they professed disbelief? They *hated* Her—there's no other way to put it. The whole thing was most perplexing.

Finally, the Dark Years ended.

When one has been away from the Church for a dozen years, one can't expect to remember everything that was jettisoned as one leapt overboard. Nor does coming back bring about some kind of miraculous, instantaneous understanding. I had to start at "square one" over and over, as my reader is discovering throughout this book.

Unlike Dad, I could not say I "felt" Mary's presence when I embraced the Faith. It was more as though I "knew" She had a hand in it. Hard to explain; but in any case, from day one I sensed an urgency about Her. I started saying the Rosary every day, pondering the Mysteries which I hadn't considered for years. That of course brought me face-to-face with the Assumption again, and the Coronation, and so on. It bothered me that I didn't understand these things.

Well, I hadn't come back from the Land of Darkness just to sit in the back of the church with my hands folded passively in my lap, wondering. If this was to be my Home, and Mary was to be my Mother, then I wanted to know everything I possibly could about Her.

So I contacted a friend of mine, a man who had stayed in Peter's Barque all the while I had been away. He was a devout Catholic who had married a good woman and raised a family of eight children*, all of them home-schooled. They had been praying that I would find my way clear to God again; and God had heard their prayers. If anyone knew about Our Lady, it had to be him, right?

"So tell me about Mary," I said. "Who is She? What is Her place in all of this?"

His answer surprised me. "To tell you the truth, I don't know. My family and I say the Rosary together every night, and we certainly observe all Her feasts, but I really don't know much about Her."

---

* Nine as of this edition.

His Faith had been one of simple acceptance, and I appreciated that. But I knew for myself I needed more in the way of knowledge. If my Faith was not founded on rock-sound reason, I ran the risk of falling away again. Not that feelings didn't play their part—but I needed to satisfy my intellect as well.

So I started digging.

What I found *overwhelmed* me.

It was no accident that most of the Catholic churches in the world are named after Her. No mere "incubator" was She, but the most necessary and remarkable human being ever born. Clearly, She had played a part in my return to the Faith, a critical and essential part that only became obvious after the fact. There was no way I would have understood while the process was in progress, but I came to realize that Mary plays a vital role in the Salvation of every sincere follower of Christ. Every single one.

How sad it is that so many Catholics have been convinced by outsiders that we place "too much emphasis on Mary," and so purged the Faith of all things Marian. In so doing, or rather undoing, we have deprived ourselves of a spiritual resource so powerful and breathtaking as to defy imagination. Those "old fogies" who remain in the church after Mass, shunned by the modern liturgical specialists, murmuring Hail Marys amidst the chitter of so many tiny beads, are holding on for dear life to that same Mother bequeathed to us on Calvary:

> When Jesus therefore had seen his mother and the disciple standing whom he loved, he saith to his mother: Woman, behold thy son.
>
> After that, he saith to the disciple: Behold thy mother. And from that hour, the disciple took her to his own.
>
> —St. John XIX:26-27

That Mary became our Mother at that moment was understood without equivocation by the Fathers of the Early Church. That She is still our Mother has been forgotten by many, but the realization is being rekindled all over Christendom as we turn these pages.

> It was through Mary that the salvation of the world
> was begun, and it is through Mary that it must be
> consummated.
>
> —Saint Louis Marie de Montfort
> *True Devotion to Mary*

Do we dare rediscover what so many Saints understood as a matter of course, or do we choose to follow the lore of the modernists who rip their Rosaries to pieces in their tin pulpits? Should we revel in the darkness, knocking ourselves senseless against the damp walls of cold stone, or do we pursue the drafts of fresh air into the light of day? Can we continue to wallow in the mud of ignorance to please our peers, or does honor and dignity require that we seek the waters of Truth and stand tall in the warmth of the bright and fiery sun? Do we dare to uncover the Treasure, the Cache buried under the sands of contemporary indifference, the same Trove transported to the New World aboard Spanish galleons, French transports, and Portuguese frigates, carried within the very hearts of the explorers themselves?

Awaken, Church Militant! To the oars! (Orchestral flourish here.) The Catholic Faith is a grand adventure. Let us raise the anchor and depart these tepid doldrums. What awaits us over the horizon may surprise us, it may shock us, it may even arouse within our lazy hearts feelings we've never felt before.

What have we got to lose?

Our souls! Do you hear? Our very souls!

To the oars, to the oars!

244

CHAPTER THIRTY-THREE

THE EYES OF GOD

It is strange that when all attention is upon Christ's humanity and away from his divinity, his Mother should be so pointedly omitted—Events don't have mothers, nor do Meanings! I mention her here as an illustration of the way in which the atmosphere of our world seeps into us without our noticing. I wonder if that could be the reason why she is not much mentioned among ourselves: I cannot remember when I last heard a sermon about her.

—Frank Sheed
What Difference Does Jesus Make?

∞ ∞ ∞

WHO IS MARY? Why, the Mother of Jesus, of course. Ah, then that takes us back one more time to "square one." Okay, from the top. Whenever we feel inundated by the sheer immensity of God's goodness, or overwhelmed by the complexities of the immaculate latticework which is the Catholic Faith, or simply tired of trying to cram so much information into our hungry but limited minds, it is always consoling to return to the most important question ever asked. It is an ongoing source of strength, courage, refreshment, and honor, because when we face the question—

But whom do you say that I am?
—St. Matthew XVI:15

—we're renewing our belief, polishing our resolve, reminding ourselves that when Isaias proclaimed this prophecy—

> Take courage, and fear not: behold your God will
> bring the revenge of recompense: God himself will
> come and save you.
> Then shall the eyes of the blind be opened, and the
> ears of the deaf shall be unstopped.
> Then shall the lame man leap as a hart, and the
> tongue of the dumb shall be free: for waters are bro-
> ken out in the desert, and streams in the wilderness.
> —Isaias XXXV:4-6

—he was speaking of this very same man, Jesus Christ: "God
Himself will come and save you."   He was God Incarnate,
God who came among us ...

> For God so loved the world, as to give his only be-
> gotten Son; that whosoever believeth in him, may
> not perish, but may have life everlasting.
> —St. John III:16

So, having answered this fundamental question yet again
to our satisfaction and His—

> Thou art Christ, the Son of the living God.
> —St. Matthew XVI:16

—we might proceed to the next question, "What was He
like?"   Would He be indistinguishable from other men?
When He was a baby, didn't He look and behave just like any
ordinary infant? Most people these days assume this to be the
case, and are indeed rather adamant about it. Such glib conjecture only demonstrates how far we have descended into the
slop of mediocre thinking.
   The "silver screen" and the "boob tube" have had a
profound and personal impact on our generation, more than
any of us would feel comfortable admitting. Even with all the
technical advancements of the genre, Hollywood casting di-
rectors can only provide ordinary human infants for their otherwise lavish "Life of Christ" productions.   Concurrently,
modern scholars have for years been freely running with the
absurd idea that Jesus wasn't even aware of His own Divinity
until His Crucifixion. As is their custom, they present their

groundless speculations as Revealed Truths that His "God-consciousness" was submerged within His humanity until adulthood, and that it then rose gradually from subconsciousness to full awareness as His public ministry progressed. As they have done to promote their other agendas, they overemphasize one passage out of context:

> Before the festival day of the pasch, Jesus knowing that his hour was come, that he should pass out of this world to the Father: having loved his own who were in the world, he loved them unto the end.
>
> And when supper was done (the devil having now put it into the heart of Judas Iscariot, the son of Simon, to betray him,)
>
> Knowing that the Father had given him all things into his hands, and that he came from God, and goeth to God;
>
> He riseth from supper ...
>
> —St. John XIII:1-4

Because of the emphasis here on Jesus "knowing His hour had come" and that "He came from God," they suggest that He somehow didn't know who He was before this moment. In other words, God was capable of suffering from an identity crisis! They conveniently ignore another incident that occurred when He was only twelve years old, when He became separated from His parents:

> And it came to pass, that, after three days, they found him in the temple, sitting in the midst of the doctors, hearing them, and asking them questions.
>
> And all that heard him were astonished at his wisdom and answers.
>
> And seeing him, they wondered. And his mother said to him: Son, why hast thou done so to us? behold thy father and I have sought thee sorrowing.
>
> And he said to them: How is it that you sought me? did you not know, that I must be about my father's business?
>
> —St. Luke II:46-49

His Father's business? He certainly wasn't promoting Joseph's carpentry enterprise! This is hardly the response of a Child who doesn't know who He is or what He's about. And we can be fairly sure that a Man who goes around saying—

> Amen, amen I say to you, before Abraham was made, I am.
>
> —St. John VIII:58

—has a clear perception of His own Divinity; enough to risk being stoned for it. What the modernists have tried to promote, with the unwitting, and in some cases more than willing, aid of star-studded Hollywood celluloid, is the idea that Jesus was in all respects "ordinary."   The contemporary mind has lost all sense of awe and propriety, and so perpetually seeks to bring all that is sublime down to its own tacky level. We, having been born and raised in this malaise, are most surely influenced by it. But all is not lost. We can stir the ashes of our dim imaginations and coax the embers back into a roaring blaze.

How Jesus Christ could be True God and True Man is a great Mystery, and a Mystery well worth grappling with. We should not discard it or bypass it just because it is beyond us—

> Like other men, he began at the beginning—an embryo. Like the rest of us, he was born a baby, grew into a small boy, a big boy, a youth, a man. Human bodies have laws, and his way subject to them ...
>
> In other words, he did not take short cuts! He did not use the divinity of his person to bypass the difficulties of his humanity. As an infant, he had to be fed from his mother's breast. He could have nourished his infant body by an act of his divine omnipotence, but that would have been to turn his humanity, not into a farce, but to some extent into a fiction. Miracles, when he came to work them, were for others, not to save himself trouble.
>
> —Frank Sheed
> *To Know Christ Jesus*

—nor should we ever assume that our conclusions are the last word. We must always defer in the end to the dogmatic, infallible pronouncements of popes and ecumenical councils:

> For we do not say that the nature of the Word was changed and made flesh, nor yet that it was changed into the whole man (composed) of soul and body but rather (we say) that the Word uniting with Himself according to person is a body animated by a rational soul, marvelously and incomprehensibly was made man, and was the Son of man, not according to the will alone or by the assumption of a person alone, but that out of both in one Christ and Son, not because distinction of natures was destroyed by the union, but rather because the divine nature and the human nature formed one Lord and Christ and Son for us, through a marvelous and mystical concurrence in unity ... For in the first place no common man was born of the holy Virgin; then the Word thus descended upon him; but being united from the womb itself he is said to have endured a generation in the flesh in order to appropriate the producing of His own body. Thus [the holy Fathers] did not hesitate to speak of the holy Virgin as the Mother of God.
>
> —Council of Ephesus, 431 AD
> "The Incarnation," (Denzinger: 111a)

Well, well, well: "For in the first place no common man was born of the Holy Virgin." When the Word became flesh, when the eternal and infinite God took on the skin, muscle, and bone of man, the product could not have been ordinary. So let us try something new, at least, new to us (the idea itself is ancient): let us set aside all mundane expectations. Let us allow ourselves, rather, the opportunity to embrace the *extraordinary*. Let us begin by imagining the Baby Jesus, not as the drooling, writhing, whimpering baby pictured in all the "Life of Christ" movies, but rather as something quite different than what we would expect from a typical newborn.

Let us envision ourselves as one of the shepherds, holding the Christ Child in our arms, bundled in the simple wrapping of poverty. Feel His weight in our hands, the texture of His blanket, the heat of His tiny body penetrating through the cloth, warming the skin of our encompassing arms. Smell the stable straw, hear the crickets chirping outside, sense the evening chill on our cheeks, make the moment as vivid as possible. We look down at His face and into His eyes; and we see, not the blank clueless orbs we would expect of a typical newborn, but *the deep, comprehending, riveting consciousness of God looking up at us out of clear, cognizant eyes.* The infinite and omnipotent God Who made the heavens and the earth, Who caused all things to be, Who sustains our very existence from moment to moment by an act of His Divine Will, Who is without beginning or end, without boundary or limits—*God locks eyes with us!*

Imagine That. Imagine looking into a mere baby's eyes and seeing *That* looking back at us. It's enough to make the hairs on the back of our necks rise with a terrified shiver. The sheer impossibility of such a thing, and the compounding wonder of its obvious actuality, could easily bring any sane person to the brink of horror. It would be easier to imagine opening a can of beans and finding the known universe slowly swirling around inside. This Child is ... God. These tiny fingers are flexed by the Mind of God, and those wee lips are curled into a smile of confident recognition by the Will of God, because this Baby knows more about us than we know about ourselves, including the numbers of hairs on our heads, cells in our bodies, secrets in our hearts, and stains on our souls. With a mere thought He could annihilate the world, or rewrite the physical laws that order matter, space, and time.

This fragile Child is HE WHO IS.

With this realization turning like the gyre of an immense hurricane in our minds, let us turn in our imagination to the Mother who just handed us this Child: the Woman who carried Him within Her womb for nine months, Who will caress Him in Her arms and nourish Him at Her breast, Who will protect Him from harm, Who will love Him with a Mother's Love. How could She not know exactly who He is?—and all the while knowing without the slightest fear, alarm or anxiety?

> And the shepherds returned, glorifying and praising
> God, for all the things they had heard and seen ...
> —St. Luke II:20

What kind of a Woman could possibly be the Mother of this Child? To even suggest that an ordinary woman could handle such a task is to mock the intellect. Reason dictates that She had to be special indeed.

So having first asked and answered, "Whom do you say that I am?" and then, "What was Jesus like?" we are inexorably drawn to the third inevitable question: "And who is His Mother?"

When the Angel Gabriel first appeared to the Blessed Virgin, he addressed Her in a way so unique, we must pause and consider his words. The title he bestowed upon Her had never been used before, nor would ever be used thereafter, with respect to a descendent of Adam and Eve:

> And the angel being come in, said unto her: Hail,
> full of grace, the Lord is with thee: blessed art thou
> among women.
> —St. Luke I:28

Since the Fall, no man or woman had been conceived in any state other than Original Sin, void of Grace. When the Angel Gabriel dubbed Mary "Full of Grace," he was proclaiming that She was miraculously unique, set apart from every other human creature.

As we have discovered with so many other matters, this is not poetry. Mary's Full-of-Grace-ness was no trivial or metaphorical matter. The human soul is as real as the blood coursing through our veins; Original Sin is as real as a diseased kidney which ravages the integrity of our circulatory system; and Mary's being born free of the disease is as real as dialysis. Her being "Full of Grace" was absolutely necessary for the completion of the purpose for which She had been called.

In the Old Testament, the symbol of God's presence among the people of Israel was the *Shekinah*, or visible holy light, which filled the tabernacle where the Ark of the Covenant resided.

> The cloud covered the tabernacle of the testimony,
> and the glory of the Lord filled it.

> Neither could Moses go into the tabernacle of the
> covenant, the cloud covering all things and the maj-
> esty of the Lord shining, for the cloud had covered all.
> —Exodus XL:32-33

This indwelling of the Spirit of God was no mere optical illusion, but was as real as real can be; as was discovered by an unfortunate man by the name of Oza during the time of King David. The Ark of the Convenant was being transported on an oxcart, amidst a joyous procession led by David himself. The people were singing hymns and playing instruments, but the festivities were suddenly interrupted:

> And when they came to the floor of Chidon, Oza
> put forth his hand, to hold up the ark: for the ox be-
> ing wanton had made it lean a little on one side.
> And the Lord was angry with Oza, and struck him,
> because he had touched the ark; and he died there be-
> fore the Lord.
> And David was troubled because the Lord had di-
> vided Oza: and he called that place the Breach of Oza
> to this day.
> —I Paralipomenon XIII:9-11

Why was Oza struck dead—not just struck but "divided," split, torn asunder—just for trying to steady the Ark so it wouldn't fall? Because the indwelling power of the Holy Ghost was incompatible with man in his sinful state, no matter the man's good intention.

The Angel Gabriel told Mary:

> The Holy Ghost shall come upon thee, and the
> power of the most High shall overshadow thee. And
> therefore also the Holy which shall be born of thee
> shall be called the Son of God.
> —St. Luke I:35

The same holy and lethal *Shekinah* that had overshadowed the Ark of the Convenant would come upon Mary. Thus Jesus Christ would be conceived in Her womb. If She Herself had not been immaculately conceived and was therefore free from Original Sin when the Spirit of God indwelled in Her, She would have *died*.

> In the knowledge of these exalted mysteries and de-
> crees, I confess myself ravished in admiration and
> transported beyond my proper self. Perceiving this
> most holy and pure Creature formed and conceived in
> the divine mind from the beginning and before all
> ages, I joyously and exultingly magnify the Omnipo-
> tent for the admirable and mysterious decree, by
> which He formed for us such a pure and grand, such a
> mysterious and godlike Creature, worthy rather to be
> admired and praised by all beings, than to be described
> by any one ...
>   ... I am ravished in the perception of this tabernacle
> of God, and I perceive that the Author of it is more
> admirable in her creation, than in that of all the rest
> of the world, although the diversity of the creatures
> manifests the wonderful power of their Creator.   In
> this Queen alone are comprehended and contained
> more treasures than in all the rest of things joined to-
> gether, and the variety and preciousness of her riches
> honor the Lord above all the multitudes of the other
> creatures.
>
> —Sister Mary of Jesus of Agreda
> "The Conception"
> *Mystical City of God*

If these concepts shock us, then we would do well to take some time and give them serious consideration. Perhaps when we asked, "And who is His Mother?" we were not prepared for so long, glorious, ponderous, and expansive an answer, but that—in the most specific and realistic sense of the maxim—is Life. If the whole thing seems alien, then we must see our- selves in the context of a culture that steers us away from such exalted ideas at every turn. If we were not taught these things by those that should have done so, especially the priests and nuns who of all people should have known better, then we be- gin to see how successful the modernist attack on the Faith has been. So where do we go from here?

> If we are to do our duty to Christ the King, we
> must accept the challenge of Catholic reconstruction.
> To do that, we must each of us acquire the education
> denied us. We could not help being robbed; we can
> blame only ourselves if we remain poor.
> —Charles A. Coulombe
> *Everyman Today Call Rome*

There is no excuse for remaining poor. The Old Knowledge is still available, it just takes a little searching. See, our hearty assemblage of fellow travelers is now landed on this strange and holy shore, the land of our Ancestors in the Faith. We have only arrived: we haven't yet *begun* to explore the hidden riches of this magnificent and extraordinary country. Come! Let us gather up our packs and walking sticks—be sure our swords are sharp and handy under our cloaks—and continue our journey. If we thought the voyage across the sea was interesting, wait till we encounter the adventure awaiting us further inland ...

CHAPTER THIRTY-FOUR

THE TIME BEFORE TIME

The Lord possessed me in the beginning of his
ways, before he made any thing from the beginning.
I was set up from eternity, and of old before the
earth was made.

—Proverbs VIII:22-23

∞   ∞   ∞

WE MUST OPEN OUR MINDS to a Great Secret. We must do
our best to transcend the limits of our carnal perceptions to
understand—or begin to understand—this most awesome
mystery: Mary was in the Mind of God from the very beginning, from *before* the very beginning.

How can this be?

God does not exist in time. There is no time, as we know
it, for God. Time is a created thing, as is space and matter. It
was made as a vehicle or medium within which we live and
move. But He is not bound by it, any more than He is con-
fined by His universe. To God, the first beat of our heart and
the final exhale of breath are *now*. There is no past or future.
The Fall of Adam is as present to Him as the blowing of the
last trumpet in the Apocalypse. We experience time in a continuous line, as a series of sequential events. He perceives all
time and events in the eternal Now.

Bearing this in mind, we turn to the book of Proverbs in
the Old Testament. From within its seemingly loose framework of parables and similitudes there emerges an interesting
theme. Wisdom, which at first is described as a desirable virtue—

> If wisdom shall enter into thy heart, and knowledge
> please thy soul:
> Counsel shall keep thee, and prudence shall pre-
> serve thee ...
>
> —Proverbs II:10-11

—gradually takes on seemingly human traits—

> Say to wisdom: Thou art my sister: and call pru-
> dence thy friend ...
>
> —Proverbs VII:4

—and finally develops into an actual personality, Wisdom Personified:

> I wisdom dwell in counsel, and am present in
> learned thoughts.
> The fear of the Lord hateth evil: I hate arrogance,
> and pride, and every wicked way, and a mouth with a
> double tongue.
>
> —Proverbs VIII:12-13

Here—if we only have eyes to see—is where Mary
emerges as a thought in the Mind of God, a thought which He
held before the world began. Thus the Church applies the
words that follow to Her; as the thought of Mary speaking of
Herself from outside of time:

> The Lord possessed me in the beginning of his
> ways, before he made any thing from the beginning.
> I was set up from eternity, and of old before the
> earth was made.
> The depths were not as yet, and I was already con-
> ceived, neither had the fountains of waters as yet
> sprung out:
> The mountains with their huge bulk had not as yet
> been established: before the hills I was brought forth:
> He had not yet made the earth, nor the rivers, nor
> the poles of the world.
> When he prepared the heavens, I was present: when
> with a certain law and compass he enclosed the
> depths:

> When he established the sky above, and poised the
> fountains of waters:
> When he encompassed the sea with its bounds, and
> set a law to the waters that they should not pass their
> limits: when he balanced the foundations of the earth;
> I was with him forming all things: and was de-
> lighted every day, playing before him at all times;
> Playing in the world: and my delights were to be
> with the children of men.
>
> — Proverbs VIII:22-31

This is not to say that Mary pre-existed Herself, but that
God's thought of Her was so real, so complete, so loving, that
it was as if the very thought of Her could sing and play, and
indeed, could already demonstrate care and concern for the
hearts of men, those who would one day be Her children.
What power permeates these words when we perceive them
issuing from Her most pure and maternal mouth:

> Now therefore, ye children, hear me: Blessed are
> they that keep my ways.
> Hear instruction and be wise, and refuse it not.
> Blessed is the man that heareth me, and that
> watcheth daily at my gates, and waiteth at the posts
> of my doors.
> He that shall find me, shall find life, and shall have
> salvation from the Lord:
> But he that shall sin against me, shall hurt his own
> soul. All that hate me love death.
>
> — Proverbs VIII:32-36

Mary, then, is not just an historical nobody we can ignore.
She is a vibrant, powerful, integral, and compelling part of the
unfolding story of the Salvation of Mankind. "He that shall
find me, shall find life, and shall have salvation from the
Lord"—a beautiful promise of hope to those who are open to
Her message. "All that hate me love death"—sobering words
for those who would relegate Her to the status of "incubator"
or worse.

> Thus, before all other creatures, was She conceived
> in the divine mind, in such manner and such state as

> befitted and became the dignity, excellence and gifts
> of the humanity of her most holy Son. To her
> flowed over, at once and immediately, the river of the
> Divinity and its attributes with all its impetuosity, in
> as far as a mere creature is capable and as is due to the
> dignity of the Mother of God.
>
> —Sister Mary of Jesus of Agreda
> "The Conception"
> *Mystical City of God*

Before God made the Angels—"before" being a concession to the limitations of our language—He knew a third of
them would turn away. Before He made Adam, He knew the
first man would fall. Before all time, God knew His Son
would become a Man to rectify the situation. He knew He
would require a human woman for a spouse so that He could
enter human history. Having assumed the humble form of a
helpless Child, He would then need the assistance and ministrations of a Mother. And for any of this to be accomplished,
He first required a Woman who loved Him enough to obey
Him without question, with complete trust; a Woman who
would be His Handmaid.

> She originated on this little planet of ours, pertains
> to our race, our kind, is related to us not by angelic
> ties of love and thought, but by the very fibres of
> flesh and blood.
> Her alliance to God is threefold. She is the Daugh-
> ter of the Father, the Spouse of the Holy Spirit, and
> the Mother of the Son. She presents all creation with
> a baby, whose name in Eternity is God, and whose
> name in time is Jesus.
>
> —Father Leonard Feeney
> *You'd Better Come Quietly*

No other human being has ever had, or could ever have,
such a "tri-lationship" with God. What other woman in all
history possessed within herself the obedience, humility and
purity necessary to be the Daughter and Handmaid of God,
accepting His Will and Plan without question, hesitation, or
comprehension of the consequences?

What other woman was spotless, pure, perfect enough to receive the Holy Ghost as Her Spouse? In Her womb the Human and the Divine combined to form the Body of the Son of God.

No one could "look down" at the vulnerable humanity of Jesus Christ more intimately than Mary His Mother as she held Him in Her arms. She nursed Him, clothed Him, saw to His physical needs when He was a defenseless infant.

In this light, do not the reverent words of a Saint make far more sense than the mediocre renditions handed to us on paper plates by the modernists?

> In my admiration I can say with St. Dionysius the Areopagite: "If faith would not instruct me, and if the understanding of what I see would not teach me, that is God, who has conceived Her in his mind, and who alone could and can in his Omnipotence form such an image of his Divinity, if all this were not present to my mind, I might begin to doubt, whether the Virgin Mother contain not in Herself Divinity."
> — Sister Mary of Jesus of Agreda
> "The Conception"
> *Mystical City of God*

If the flowery language is a "bit much" for our twenty-first century taste, we would do well to remember that ours is the culture that caters to the lowest common element of society. Ours is the culture that over-humanizes Christ at the expense of His Divinity. Ours is the culture that celebrates the mediocre, panders the trivial, and promotes the vulgar. Yet ours is the culture that looks back on the past with disdain, as if our ancestors lacked our "class." Truly, we don't know the meaning of the word.

Another word which eludes us is "Universals." The rampant relativism of our age has all but eradicated this concept from our minds. We, as sincere Catholics, would do well to reinstate it in our vocabularies:

> The Church Fathers looked primarily to Plato as the foremost Greek philosopher. He first proposed the idea of "Universals," that is of ideal prototypes of things like "Man" and "Horse," as well as abstract

qualities like "Love" and "Honor." These Plato held
to exist in some "realm of the Types" whence they
cast reflections on our poor earth. We ourselves, for
instance, are mere reflections of the great archetype
"Man," of whose substance we all partake—hence our
"mannishness."

... Christian philosophers deduced that these
"types" did not exist in some kingdom of their own,
but in the mind of God. They were no less real for
all of that; in a certain sense they were more real than
those of their reflections which were soul-less (rocks,
etc.). Further, these archetypes share the timelessness
of God—for He has thought of them for all eternity.
So applying this idea to the Old Testament, they
found, that just as the Holy Ghost—the *Shekinah* ...
had existed from all eternity ... so too had the Son,
the divine *Logos,* although not yet incarnate. Similarly, from all eternity was Our Lady, the vessel
whereby the Logos became flesh, present in the mind
of God as the figure of Wisdom, of *Sophia.*

—Thomas A. Hutchinson
Desire and Deception

"Be that as it may," intones our fellow traveler with the
keen grey eyes, "you certainly can't base this supra-temporal
in-the-Mind-of-God Mariology on a few verses from Proverbs."

"Most certainly not," says the most talkative member of
our valiant party, the one in the rear with a notebook and quill
in his hands. "Around the bend lies the Ultimate Verse, the
majestic pinnacle from which all the rivers of prophecy flow."

"Hrmph," shrugs Sir Skeptic, gathering his azure cloak
around his shoulders and pinning it with a clasp emblazoned
with the Mark of the Wide-Open Eye. "We shall see."

And see we shall ...

CHAPTER THIRTY-FIVE

THE SQUARE BEFORE SQUARE ONE

Inimicitias ponam inter te et mulierem, et semen tuum et semen illius.
Ipsa conteret caput tuum, et tu insidiaberis calcaneo eius.

—Genesis III:15
The Vulgate

∞ ∞ ∞

OKAY, FROM THE TOP—or rather, this time we will take it from a point *preceding* the top. Let us go back, way back, all the way back to "the square *before* square one." Can there be such a place? Most assuredly so. We can never become complacent in the Land of the Faith. There is always another adventure awaiting us, if we but seek it out.

As we have seen again and again, the most significant question ever asked in the history of the world is, "Whom do you say that I am?" But proceeding from this pivotal query is yet another question regarding an event that preceded it by five thousand years: "Whom do you say *She* is?"

If we run our eyes back up the page, we find just under the chapter heading a Treasure Map disguised as a verse from the Latin Vulgate. "X marks the spot"—or in this case, "Ipsa." This particular verse is so important that it has been given its own name. It is called the *Protoevangelium,* which means the "First Good News." It is the first of all prophecies, pronounced by God Himself in the Garden of Eden. A sound case could be made that it is the most important verse in the entire Bible because all the great, wonderful, and awesome things that are to follow—the history of the Israelites, the line of descent of the patriarchs, the coming of the prophets, even the commission of Jesus Christ in His First and Second Comings—are essentially contained within it. And, curiouser and curiouser, this prophecy is addressed to, of all people, the Serpent who had just succeeded in luring Adam and Eve into the pit of Sin:

> I will put enmities between thee and the woman,
> and thy seed and her seed:
> She shall crush thy head, and thou shalt lie in wait
> for her heel.
>
> —Genesis III:15
> *The Douay-Rheims Translation*

Here we find two distinct statements. First, that the lines of battle have now been drawn: on one side stands "the woman" and "her seed," on the other, Satan and his minions. Second, that the outcome of the conflict is already determined: "she" will conquer, while Satan's defeat is deemed inevitable.

On first reading, one might assume that "the woman" is obviously Eve, and that "her seed" refers to her offspring, the human race; but as we shall see, something far more profound is at work here. This is not—as so many faithless "experts" suggest—just the moral of a fairy tale, a quaint mythological explanation for the general human aversion to things that slither on the ground. We must bear in mind that Moses, the author of Genesis, was inspired by the Holy Ghost, that God preserved this information for thousands of years specifically for our benefit, and that we have a mandate from Jesus Christ Himself to seek out and grasp its significance:

> For if you did believe Moses, you would perhaps believe me also; for he wrote of me.
> But if you do not believe his writings, how will you believe my words?
>
> —St. John V:46-47

Our quest for the Truth dies here if we do not take these words of Christ seriously. As often as we have returned to "square one," we should begin to understand this by now. God Incarnate warns us that we will not comprehend His mission if we discount the writings of Moses. If we are still

clinging to the vestiges of the theory of evolution, we will have
to cut them loose. The *Protoevangelium* is absolute and quite
specific. The identity of the "woman" in Genesis III:15 is
not a matter for idle speculation over cocktails. Her identity is
crucial to our understanding of everything else, including
"square one."

So back to this "woman." Let us take note: nowhere else
in the Bible is "seed" attributed to a woman, for "seed" is
something exclusively male. Very strange indeed. As for this
"woman" who will defeat Satan, could she possibly be Eve,
the same Eve who just moments before stumbled so easily into
the clutches of the father of lies? Unlikely—not without some
dramatic change in her character. Besides, God had other
plans for her destiny, punishments described in the very next
verse:

> I will multiply thy sorrows, and thy conceptions:
> in sorrow shalt thou bring forth children, and thou
> shalt be under thy husband's power, and he shall have
> dominion over thee.
>
> —Genesis III:16

But, we may ask, if Eve was the only woman on earth at
the time the *Protoevangelium* was uttered, who could "the
woman" possibly be? We must remind ourselves that to God
there is no time. In the Mind of God, Mary, daughter of
Joachim and Anne fifty centuries hence, was already "playing
before him at all times." The Woman of Genesis is none
other than Mary, the Virgin who would miraculously bear a
Son, not with the participation of a human male, but by the
power of the Holy Ghost. Her "seed" is none other than Jesus Christ.

The conflict described in the *Protoevangelium*, then, is
twofold. Enmities were put between "thee and the woman,"
that is, between Satan and Mary; and also between "thy seed
and her seed," between the hordes of Hell and Jesus Christ.
The war over the Salvation of Mankind is not just between
God and Satan, but involves Mary as well. More than merely
drawn in, She is pivotal. It is She that will ultimately "crush
thy head." God in His Wisdom deemed that the defeat of
Satan will be accomplished, not by a mighty army, nor even

by the Hand of His Only Begotten Son, but by the heel of His lowly Handmaid.

> God has never made and formed but one enmity; but it is an irreconcilable one, which shall endure and grow even to the end. It is between Mary, His worthy Mother, and the devil—between the children and servants of the Blessed Virgin, and the children and tools of Lucifer. The most terrible of all the enemies which God has set up against the devil is His holy Mother Mary. He has inspired her, even since the days of the earthly paradise—though she existed then only in His idea—with so much hatred against that cursed enemy of God, with so much ingenuity in unveiling the malice of that ancient serpent, with so much power to conquer, to overthrow and to crush that proud, impious rebel, that he fears her not only more than all angels and men, but in a sense more than God Himself. Not that the anger, the hatred, and the power of God are not infinitely greater than those of the Blessed Virgin, for the perfections of Mary are limited; but first, because Satan, being proud, suffers infinitely more from being beaten and punished by a little and humble handmaid of God, and her humility humbles him more than the divine power; and secondly, because God has given Mary such great power against the devils that—as they have often been obliged to confess, in spite of themselves, by the mouths of the possessed—they fear one of her sighs for a soul more than the prayers of all the saints, and one of her threats against them more than all other torments.
>
> —Saint Louis Marie de Montfort
> *True Devotion to Mary*

If the mind boggles, let it. There's nothing like a good boggling. What we must not do is dismiss this crucial point simply because it is new to us, or beyond us, or because our Protestant "brethren" balk at its implications. Understanding the ramifications of the *Protoevangelium* is more important today than at any other time in history. Why? It is crucial that we, the Church Militant, comprehend from a tactical standpoint that even though Her Son is God Incarnate, it is not He but She who is destined to crush Satan in the end.

> It was through Mary that the salvation of the world was begun, and it is through Mary that it must be consummated ...
>
> It is principally of these last and cruel persecutions of the devil, which shall go on increasing daily till the reign of Antichrist, that we ought to understand the first and celebrated prediction and curse of God pronounced in the terrestrial paradise against the serpent ...
>
> —St. Louis Marie de Montfort
> *True Devotion to Mary*

This in no way lessens the role or the power of Jesus Christ. Indeed, just the opposite, for God's unique *modus operandi* is becoming familiar to us:

> But the foolish things of the world hath God chosen, that he may confound the wise: and the weak things of the world hath God chosen, that he may confound the strong.
>
> —I Corinthians I:27

Thus He takes delight in defeating Satan by means of His Blessed Mother. God could fight the battle, but—how grand!—He prefers that the army be led by an unexpected general ...

> ... because Satan, being proud, suffers infinitely more from being beaten and punished by a little and humble handmaid of God ...
>
> —St. Louis Marie de Montfort
> *True Devotion to Mary*

Let us share His delight, luxuriating in the Divine Irony. How marvelous and gracious is God that He would so bless His children.

The promise of God, declared at the dawn of time and preserved through the ages, roars down through the centuries to engulf our hearts today with the fire of hope, courage, and solace. One cannot overstate the importance of the *Protoe-vangelium* and its significance to us in the here and now: the war is won, the devil is defeated, the victory is Hers, and we share in Her triumph. On this we can depend, on this we can hang our very souls.

In the immediate and personal sense, however, it may appear that the battle is not going our way. In point of fact, you and I may go down in smoke. The way things are going, it is not outside the realm of possibility that we will end our lives in martyrdom. To carnal eyes, what surer sign of defeat is there than execution? If we despair in our own predicament, we fall to the side of the Serpent who wants nothing more than to draw us under the shadow of Her heel to share in his eternal demise. But if we clutch the truth of the First Good News to our hearts, marching forth in confidence under Mary's banner, we will share in Her conquest. This should be our lively hope ...

> Unto an inheritance incorruptible, and undefiled,
> and that can not fade, reserved in heaven for you.
> —I St. Peter I:4

This is the stuff of Faith, that we rely not on the input of our senses, but the promises of God. As with the Transubstantiation, we believe according to the command of Christ rather than the data relayed through our optic nerves and taste buds. It follows that our hope is of a similar disposition. No matter what befalls us, no matter how bleak things may seem; even as the very life is drained from our bodies through the punctures of the Serpent's deadly fangs, we have this eternal hope, this promise on which to cling. Those who fall in battle in service to the cause nonetheless share in the glories of victory. Those who side with the Woman of Genesis will cheer as She crushes Satan under Her humble but mighty heel. And the reward for our loyalty cannot be measured by the currency of this world, for our sights are not here but elsewhere.

> Blessed shall you be when men shall hate you, and
> when they shall separate you, and shall reproach you,
> and cast out your name as evil, for the Son of man's
> sake.

Be glad in that day and rejoice; for behold, your reward is great in heaven. For according to these things
did their fathers to the prophets.

—St. Luke VI:22-23

A toast to Our Blessed Lady, the Woman of Genesis and
Crusher of serpents!

CHAPTER THIRTY-SIX

THE SERPENT CRUSHED

He was a murderer from the beginning, and he stood not in the truth; because truth is not in him. When he speaketh a lie, he speaketh of his own: for he is a liar, and the father thereof.

—St. John VIII:44

∞ ∞ ∞

SO SIGNIFICANT IS THE ANCIENT PROPHECY of the *Protoevangelium,* such a consolation to us who roam the fields of battle today, that Satan has done everything in his power to obfuscate its meaning, to rob the Church Militant of our rightful hope, courage, and solace. No other verse in the Bible has come under more scrutiny and attack, not just by those outside the Barque of Peter, but in recent times by the modernist termites who have infested her hull.

The why is obvious: to deprive us of access to a Conduit of infinite Grace, to break our spirit, to shatter our confidence, to call into question that which we hold dear. The means are insidious, but this is to be expected from a serpent. Subterfuge is a tactical assumption in war—and make no mistake, this is a deadly war in which we are engaged. Cries of "that's not fair" are meaningless on a battlefield.

Put on the armour of God, that you may be able to stand against the deceits of the devil.

For our wrestling is not against flesh and blood; but against principalities and powers, against the rul-

> ers of the world of this darkness, against the spirits of
> wickedness in the high places.
>
> —Ephesians VI:11-12

Satan has incited many scholars, first Protestant and now Catholic, to cast doubt on the integrity of the Genesis text itself. First, they play with the very word "she." They appeal to non-authorized codices such as the Septuagint, which was a translation of the Hebrew Scriptures into Alexandrian Greek by a group of Hellenistic Jews between 250 and 100 BC. In this version, the pronoun "he" is found in place of "she" in the second half of the *Protoevangelium:*

> *He* shall crush thy head, and thou shalt lie in wait
> for *his* heel.

This, along with similar pleas to other ancient texts, has caused much confusion. While the use of "he" can certainly be interpreted to be a Messianic reference—"he" being the "seed" referred to in the previous line—the "woman" then becomes Eve, and the Marian message gets discarded.

Do not be fooled by those who say this is a trivial matter. We are not "splitting hairs." We walk on extremely unstable ground if we in any way diminish the importance of Mary in the history and culmination of salvation.

Another scholarly attack focuses on the actions "crush" and "lie in wait." The original Hebrew texts are of course lost to us, but as best as we can derive from copies, it is a fact that both verbs are represented by the same word,

$$שׁוּף$$

or *shuph.* It doesn't take an inordinate amount of research to discover that *shuph* has two meanings, as do many words in English.

1. A by-form of ... *sha'aph* ... "to trample upon,
   crush"; Akkadian cognate *shapu*, "to trample
   underfoot"; Syriac. "to rub, wear out, bruise."
2. Arabic cognate *shapa*, "to see, look at, watch."
                                        —Thomas Mary Sennnott
                                        The Woman of Genesis

Nonetheless, our self-proclaimed experts seem to think they know more than St. Jerome about the nuances of these ancient languages, even though he was fifteen hundred years closer to them. Thus, under their scalpels, not only does "she" become "he" but the actions of both parties become the same:

He shall *bruise* thy head, and thou shalt *bruise* his heel.

The First Good News is reduced from a promise of final victory to a description of an interminable battle, both sides merely injuring each other endlessly. The ramifications of these kinds of verbal switches are indeed profound.

In their zeal to denigrate the Word of God, liberal scholars and theologians have produced many "new" versions of the Bible, none of which rely on the Vulgate. Thus, pronouns and verbs swirling like so much confetti, we are bombarded with such travesties as:

And I will put enmity between thee and the woman, and between thy seed and her seed;
   it shall bruise thy head, and thou shalt bruise his heel.
                                        —*King James Version*

I will put enmity between you and the woman, and between your seed and her seed;

he shall bruise your head and you shall bruise his
heel.
                    —*Revised Standard Version (Catholic Edition)*

I will put enmity between you and the woman, and
your seed and her seed:
He shall crush your head and you shall lie in wait
for his heel.
                    —*Confraternity of Christian Doctrine Version*
                    (1962)

I will put enmity between you and the woman, and
between your offspring and hers;
He will strike at your head while you strike at his
heel.
(A footnote suggests a better translation is "They
will strike ... at their heels," but concedes the
woman's offspring "primarily" is Jesus Christ.)
                    —*New American Bible*

I will make you enemies of each other: you and the
woman, your offspring and her offspring.
It will crush your head and you will strike at its
heel.
                    —*The Jerusalem Bible*

From now on you and the woman will be enemies,
as will all of your offspring and hers. And I will put
the fear of you into the woman, and between your
offspring and hers.
He shall strike you on your head, while you will
strike at his heel.
                    —*The Living Bible*

I will put enmity between you and the woman, and
between your offspring and hers:

they shall strike at your head, and you shall strike
at their heel.
                          —*Tanakh: The (New) Jewish Bible*

Enough! Enough of lies and half-truths which are worse!
As Catholics struggling to understand and keep the Faith in
these troubled times, we must remember that only one version
of the Bible was ever declared to be the official text of the canonical Scriptures by a council of the Church (Trent, 1546
AD) and free from error by a pope (Pius XII in his encyclical
letter *Divino Afflante Spiritu,* 1943): namely the old Latin
Vulgate.   Since the Douay-Rheims translation is the most
faithful to it, we can read it without concern as to its integrity.

And there is more.   Fortunately, we as Catholics are not
subject to the banal whims of theologians and linguistic hacks.
We are bound by an infinitely higher authority: the infallible
teachings of the Roman Catholic Faith and Her Supreme Pontiffs. I refer here to the *infallible* papal definition of the Immaculate Conception made in 1854:

> Hence, just as Christ, the Mediator between God
> and man, assuming human nature, blotted out the
> handwriting of the decree that stood against us, and
> fastening it triumphantly to the Cross, so the Most
> Holy Virgin, united with Him by a most intimate and
> indissoluble bond, was, with Him and through Him,
> eternally at enmity with the evil Serpent, and most
> completely triumphed over him, and thus crushed his
> head with her immaculate foot.
>
>   —Pope Pius IX
>   The bull, *Ineffabilis Deus*

Thus, Mary is here identified as the one who crushes the
Serpent's head. Furthermore, we can also examine the definition in 1950 of Our Lady's glorious Assumption:

> We must remember especially that, since the sec-
> ond century, the Virgin Mary has been designated by

the Holy Fathers as the new Eve, who, although subject to the new Adam, is most intimately associated
with Him in that struggle against the infernal foe
which, as foretold in the *Protoevangelium,* would finally result in that most complete victory over sin
and death which are always associated in the writings
of the Apostle of the Gentiles.

—Pope Pius XII
Munificentissimus Deus

Again, Mary is identified as the one foretold in the First
Good News.

The final say, of course, should go to the Woman in question. In 1531, Our Lady appeared to Juan Diego in Mexico.
She told him that She wished to be known as Our Lady of
Guadalupe. Neither Juan, nor his shepherd, Bishop Zumar-
raga, understood the request. There was no town with the
name Guadalupe near the site of the apparition, nor does the
word have any meaning in Spanish. As it turns out, *de Guadalupe* sounds very similar to the Aztec *te coatlaxopeuh* (pronounced "te quatlasupe").

Te, means "stone"; *coa* means "serpent"; *tha* is the
noun ending which can be interpreted as "the"; while
xopeuh means "crush" or "stamp out."

—Thomas Mary Sennnott
The Woman of Genesis

In other words, She wished to be called Our Lady Who
Crushes the Stone Serpent—the "stone serpent" being the
collective hierarchy of bloodthirsty Aztec deities to whom the
Indians disemboweled thousands of men, women, and children
on their altars of sacrifice every year. This ravenous religion
worshiped the same Serpent who slithered through the terrestrial paradise of Genesis. Within a decade of Our Lady's
appearance to Juan Diego, nine million Indians converted to
Catholicism—destroying the grip of the "stone serpent" on
the lives of the Indians and reaffirming Her declaration of war
against the enemy of mankind.

We must learn to stand firm against the subtle infiltrations
of Satan. We must recognize his lies and bring them into the
light of Truth where they perish. We must arrive at a place of

trust with respect to the time-honored teachings of the Catholic Church. With respect to the *Protoevangelium,* we need not be intimidated by the confusing musings of scholars who have lost their faith and wish to draw us into the vortex of their unbelief. Peter has spoken, the matter is closed. Mary has dotted the i's and crossed the t's. The only reliable rendering of Genesis III:15 is as follows:

> I will put enmities between thee and the woman, and thy seed and her seed:
> She shall crush thy head, and thou shalt lie in wait for her heel.
>
> —*Douay -Rheims Bible*

Amen. So be it.

CHAPTER THIRTY-SEVEN

PLAYING BEFORE HIM
AT ALL TIMES

> Holy Scripture was written for Mary, about Mary,
> and on account of Mary.
> —Saint Bernard of Clairvaux (1091-1153 AD)

∞ ∞ ∞

ONCE WE COME TO THE REALIZATION that Mary the Mother of Jesus Christ is the "she" referred to in the *Protoevangelium,* and that She is also Wisdom personified in the Book of Proverbs, a chain of stimulating Secrets concealed within the Sacred Scriptures throughout the ages begins to unwind like a well-spun mystery. Here's where the real fun begins.

Before the world began, Mary was in the Mind of God. As He created the world, He was thinking of Her. When Adam and Eve fell, He held Her up to the Serpent as a sign of his ultimate destruction. As the complex twine of history unraveled, Mary remained foremost in His thoughts.

> I was with him forming all things: and was delighted every day, playing before him at all times.
> Playing in the world: and my delights were to be with the children of men.
> —Proverbs VIII:30-31

Naturally, as the Holy Ghost "brooded" on His Spouse, awaiting the day when the most perfect of all creatures would fulfill Her destiny, She would emerge in His Revelation as He guided the hands and mouths of His prophets, "leaking out" between the lines and taking gradual form in the cascade of unfolding imagery.

Did the prophets who spoke the thoughts of God understand them? We cannot know for sure, but it is probable that they did not—at least, not fully. As the Spirit moved them, they obediently gave utterance. By His direction they preached to the people; through His inspiration they wrote it down. The specifics and ramifications of what they spoke and recorded would not become clear until the Light, Jesus Christ, came into the world to reveal them. Now, with the benefit of His illumination, we can retrace the thoughts of God as they unfolded throughout history. Here is where our journey becomes unbelievably exciting. We've already seen that "Ipsa"—Mary—marks the spot on our Treasure Map. Now let us trace the winding trail that leads us to Her, and through Her, to Her Son.

The Bible begins with the Act of Creation, when God formed the material universe out of the vacuum of absolute nothingness:

> In the beginning God created heaven, and earth.
> And the earth was void and empty, and darkness was upon the face of the deep; and the spirit of God moved over the waters.
>
> —Genesis I:1-2

Yet, as we noted three chapters ago, the Church understands that Mary was in the Mind of God even before this Beginning.

> The Lord possessed me in the beginning of his ways, before he made any thing from the beginning.
> I was set up from eternity, and of old before the earth was made.
> The depths were not as yet, and I was already conceived, neither had the fountains of waters as yet sprung out ...
> He had not yet made the earth, nor the rivers, nor the poles of the world.
> When he prepared the heavens, I was present ...
>
> —Proverbs VIII:22-24, 26-27

The Hebrew form of Mary, *Miryam,* can be translated "exalted," "lady," "star," or "bitterness."   When the Scriptures were translated into Latin, the Church delighted in the similarity of "Maria" to *mar,* the sea.   Do we really, after all our treks back to "square one," still believe in coincidences? Come now. God is in control. The connection of Mary and the sea goes all the way back to the very Act of Creation, long before Her name was Latinized.

When the Spirit of God moved over the waters, He was contemplating His Spouse. The Holy Ghost stirred the water, invigorating it in preparation for its eventual use in the Sacrament of Baptism. Furthermore, Mary would be the conduit through which Grace would enter the world in the Person of Her Divine Son. She therefore becomes absolutely necessary—in the immediate and personal sense—for each and every one of us, for without Her, none of us would have any hope of Salvation.

> The eternal Son of God, when He wished to assume the nature of man for the redemption and glory of man, and for this reason was about to enter upon a kind of mystic marriage with the entire human race, did not do this before He received the wholly free consent of His designated mother, who, in a way, played the part of the human race itself, according to the famous and truthful opinion of Aquinas: "Through the Annunciation the Virgin's consent was looked for in place of all human nature." Therefore, no less truly and properly may it be affirmed that nothing at all of the very great treasure of every grace, which the Lord confers, since "grace and truth came by Jesus Christ" [John I: 17], nothing is imparted to us except through Mary, God so willing; so just as no one can approach the highest Father except through the Son, so no one can approach Christ except through His Mother.
>
> —Pope Leo XIII
> The Encyclical, *"Octobri mense"*

Without Her obedient assent, He could not have entered our history, and so Grace would have been withheld from us.

This is why She is called the Dispenser or Mediatrix of All Grace.

So, while She played in the Mind of God in the beginning, the Spirit moved over the waters, uniting Her with the process of Salvation. And this was only the beginning.

In the *Protoevangelium,* we learned that a certain Woman—Mary—would have "seed." This unique Offspring would be the Messias. The first specific prophecy of the Savior, uttered by Balaam in the time of Moses, involved the rising of His "star":

> A STAR SHALL RISE out of Jacob, and a sceptre
> shall spring up from Israel ...
> —Numbers XXIV:17

Some fifteen centuries later, this verse would draw Gaspar, Melchior, and Balthasar from Persia in search of the Messias:

> ... there came wise men from the east to Jerusalem.
> Saying, Where is he that is born king of the Jews?
> For we have seen his star in the east, and are come to
> adore him.
> —St. Matthew II:2

Since "Miryam" also means "star," Her destiny merges with His. Saints down through the centuries have celebrated Mary as the "Star of the Morning" and the "Star of the Sea."

> She is most beautifully likened to a star, for a star
> pours forth its light without losing anything of its
> nature. She gave us her Son without losing anything
> of her virginity. The glowing rays of a star take
> nothing away from its beauty. Neither has the Son
> taken anything away from his Mother's integrity.
> —Saint Bernard of Clairvaux
> Quoted by Msgr. Charles Dollen in
> *Listen, Mother of God!*

Seafarers navigate by the stars. So do we sinners steer with the aid of Mary's vigilant guidance. This beautiful imagery is further explained by Saint Thomas Aquinas:

> ... as mariners, in tempestuous weather, are guided
> by the star of the sea into port, so are souls guided by
> Mary over the sea of this world into Paradise.
> —Quoted by Saint Alphonsus de Liguori
> *The Glories of Mary*

For those of us wishing to increase our devotion to Our
Blessed Mother, to access Her aid, or to better understand
Mary's place in the scheme of things, there is perhaps no bet-
ter meditation ever written than that of Saint Bernard:

> When you find yourself tossed by the raging storms
> of this great sea of life, far from land, keep your eyes
> fixed on this Star to avoid disaster. When the winds
> of temptation or the rocks of tribulation threaten,
> look up to the Star, call upon Mary!
> When the waves of pride or ambition sweep over
> you, when the tide of detraction or jealousy runs
> against you, look up to the Star, call upon Mary!
> When the shipwreck of avarice, anger or lust seems
> imminent, call upon Mary!
> —Saint Bernard of Clairvaux
> *Missus Est,* II

Traditionally in mythology and literature, the Morning
Star is the planet Venus—the last light in the sky to grow pale
and be absorbed by the growing brilliance of the rising sun.
Small wonder, then, that Mary is described in the New Testament as ...

> A woman clothed with the sun, and the moon under
> her feet, and on her head a crown of twelve stars.
> —The Apocalypse XII:1

... and in the Old Testament as ...

> ... she that cometh forth as the morning rising...
> —Canticle of Canticles VI:9

Ultimately, the title of Morning Star is claimed by Jesus Himself, when He triumphs at the end of time and all things come under His rule:

> I am the Alpha and Omega, the first and the last, the beginning and the end ...
> I am the root and stock of David, the bright and morning star.
> —The Apocalypse XXII:13, 16

Thus we discover that the roles and attributes of Jesus and Mary become intimately intertwined in the salvific process, as well as in the history of the world. They are both the Morning Star. They are both heralds: She of Her Son, He of His Father.

We see this allusion throughout the Old Testament. For example, Mary's role as the Bearer of God is foreshadowed in the construction of the Ark of the Covenant:

> Frame an ark of setim wood, the length whereof shall be of two cubits and a half: the breadth, a cubit and a half: the height, likewise, a cubit and a half.
> And thou shalt overlay it with the purest gold within and without: and over it thou shalt make a golden crown round about ...
> —Exodus XXV:10-11

This box, made of extremely dense wood and completely plated inside and out with fine gold, was to house the Pentateuch, the Scrolls of Moses. It would be the visible focus of Hebrew worship, and the vessel upon which the *Shekinah* would descend.

The durable setim wood used in the Ark was seen by many Saints as a prefiguration of Mary's body, preserved from the corruption of Sin by virtue of Her Immaculate Conception, and from the corruption of the grave by her Glorious Assumption. The gold represented the purity of Her soul, and the sanctity of Her womb. Just as the Ark contained the Law, Mary would contain the Lawgiver. Inside the Temple was a shelf under which the Ark resided. The shelf was called the Propitiatory or Mercy Seat. The quality of Mercy has long been associated with the Virgin Mary, especially by those

Saints whose devotion to Her was exemplary. For all these reasons and more the Church has come to refer to Mary as the Ark of the Convenant.

> Some of the Fathers have employed the words of the Psalmist: "Arise, O Lord, into thy resting place: thou and the ark, which thou hast sanctified" (Psalm 131: 8) and have looked upon the Ark of the Covenant, built of incorruptible wood and placed in the Lord's temple, as a type of the most pure body of the Virgin Mary, preserved and exempted from all corruption of the tomb and raised up to such glory in heaven.
>
> —Pope Pius XII
> *Munificentissimus Deus*

Just as the Ark was lined with gold, so was the Temple built by Solomon in which it was housed:

> And the house before the oracle he overlaid with most pure gold, and fastened on the plates with nails of gold.
> And there was nothing in the temple that was not covered with gold: the whole altar of the oracle he covered also with gold ...
> And the floor of the house he also overlaid with gold within and without.
>
> —III Kings VI:21-22, 30

It follows, then, that another of Mary's many titles is the House of Gold.

Whether we consider the temple of portable tents which housed the Ark in the desert in the time of Moses, or the glorious edifice erected by Solomon which was the glory of Israel, the temple was the House of God.

> Wisdom hath built herself a house ...
> —Proverbs IX:1

As such, the temple was a prefigurement of the Mother of God, who would be the *Theotokos,* the God-Bearer. With this in mind, King David's prayer to God takes on wealth of new meaning:

> I have loved, O Lord, the beauty of thy house; and
> the place where thy glory dwelleth.
>
> —Psalm XXV:8

This is the same Psalm spoken by the priest during the Tridentine Mass while he washes his hands at the conclusion of the Offertory:

> I will wash my hands among the innocent; and will
> compass thy altar, O Lord:
> That I may hear the voice of they praise: and tell all
> thy wondrous works.
> I have loved, O Lord, the beauty of thy house; and
> the place where thy glory dwelleth ...

This connects Mary not only with the House of God, but right into the heart of the Mass itself, the Holy Sacrifice of Her Son on the altar. The priest, in effect, says, "I have loved, O Lord, the beauty of Your Mother, Mary." How sweet it is to bring Her to mind, to consider Her comeliness, perfection, purity, holiness, and mercy, just before proceeding with the Consecration.

Isn't it amazing how this all ties in together?

> Mary hardly appeared at all in the first coming of
> Jesus Christ, in order that men, as yet but little in-
> structed and enlightened on the Person of her Son,
> should not remove themselves from Him in attaching
> themselves too strongly and too grossly to her. This
> would have apparently taken place if she had been
> known ... The reasons which moved the Holy Ghost
> to hide His spouse during her life, and to reveal her
> but very little since the preaching of the Gospel, sub-
> sists no longer.
> God, then, wishes to reveal and make known Mary,
> the masterpiece of His hands, in these latter times:
> 1. Because she hid herself in this world and put
> herself lower than the dust by her profound humility,

having obtained from God and from His Apostles and
Evangelists that she should not be made manifest.

2.   Because, as she is the masterpiece of the hands
of God, as well here below by grace as in Heaven by
glory, He wishes to be glorified and praised in her by
those who are living upon the earth.

3.   As she is the dawn which precedes and reveals
the Sun of Justice, who is Jesus Christ, she must be
seen and recognized in order that Jesus Christ may
also be.

4.   Being the way by which Jesus came to us the
first time, she will also be the way by which He will
come the second time, though not in the same manner ...

—Saint Louis Marie de Montfort
True Devotion to Mary,

Now—as   if   things   weren't   already   interesting
enough!—we pull back and flatten out a corner of our Treasure Map which has been curled over, concealing yet another
Secret, a more perplexing mystery, an entirely unexpected
aspect of the Mother of God. Here we read the words:

> Mary: terrible as an army set in battle array.

One does not often see the name of the Blessed Virgin
Mary beside the word "terrible."   Indeed, most Catholics
these days—those who most likely would not have come this
far in our gallant expedition—are more used to thinking of
Her as a benign maternal presence, a statue in the shadows in
the back of the chapel holding a plump infant Jesus, or a relic
of some forgotten time in the Church when such things as
Motherhood and Chastity were more pertinent.   Some have
opted to turn Her into some kind of "earth mother," a
newage amalgam of Isis, Gaea, and Mother Nature.   Some
feminists have even tried to twist Her into a leathery parodistic
symbol of their warped sense of motorcycle-chain woman-
hood, the "first truly independent woman."   All of which is
sheer foolishness.

What is it about the audacious modern mindset that so
vainly encourages such pseudo-spiritual thumb twiddling?
How dare anyone so carelessly disregard the volumes and vol-

umes of books, prayers, and meditations penned by Saints and honest scholars, popes and prophets, men and women who devoted the entirety of their lives to learning and understand Mary's unique place in the scheme of things? Let us ignore these groundless speculations, and seek out Mary as She really is.

As we noted above, most people do not associate Mary with the word "terrible." Rather, we rightly honor Her and diligently hope to imitate Her in ...

> ... her profound humility, her lively faith, her blind obedience, her continual prayer, her universal mortification, her divine purity, her ardent charity, her heroic patience, her angelic sweetness and her divine wisdom. These are the ten principal virtues of the most holy Virgin.
>
> —Saint Louis Marie de Montfort
> *True Devotion to Mary,*

But there is another dimension to Her. Picture thousands of fierce men in polished armor, their swords sharpened, spears raised in salute, banners unfurled in the crisp breeze, shields blazing with piercing light as the sun rises over the field of battle—a powerful human machine geared and ready for war. Strong words, but they—no less than the gentle words above—describe Her to a tee:

> Who is she that cometh forth as the morning rising,
> fair as the moon, bright as the sun,
> terrible as an army set in array?
> —Canticle of Canticles VI:9

The Canticle of Canticles in the Old Testament is a poetic book of heavenly mysteries. It was regarded by the Fathers as a description of the union between Christ and His beloved Church; and more specifically as the affection of Almighty God for perfect souls, every one of which He loves profoundly. Most specifically, and joyously, it is a song of the Triune God and His special Love and Devotion to the Immaculate and ever-Virgin Mary.

All who have experienced love understand the profound and perplexing mixture of emotions displayed in this quotation from the Canticle of Canticles. She comes gently but inexorably, as slow and unstoppable as the dawn. She is passively beautiful, like the cool but steady moon which reflects the rays of the sun earthward. She is also actively beautiful, the radiant source of pure, blinding light. Moreover, as with all true lovers, She is awesome in the power that She wields, dreadful in Her fury, unquenchable in Her determination to please Her Spouse and to defend His honor.

Here we see again that Mary was "playing" before the Mind of God, like a melody that sometimes captures our imagination and delightfully goes on and on. She was the closest thing to Perfection He would ever create, and thus the Holy Ghost yearned for Her as time unfolded. Perhaps the relevance of the citation which crowns this chapter is now shimmering brilliantly:

> Holy Scripture was written for Mary, about Mary,
> and on account of Mary.
> — Saint Bernard of Clairvaux

No more clearly is this idea evident, to the insightful eye, than in the Canticle of Canticles, written centuries before Mary was physically born. Here the yearning of the Holy Ghost for His Spouse become manifested in the language of passionate Love:

> Who is this that cometh up from the desert, flowing with delights, leaning upon her beloved?
> ... Put me as a seal upon thy heart, as a seal upon thy arm, for love is strong as death, jealousy as hard as hell, the lamps thereof are fire and flames.
> Many waters cannot quench charity, neither can the floods drown it: if a man should give all the substance of his house for love, he shall despise it as nothing.
> — Canticle of Canticles VIII:5, 6-7

Anyone who thinks that God is the least bit diminished when we give honor and devotion to His beloved Spouse has an incredibly small-minded idea of God and an atrophied perception of the power of Love—not to mention a nincompoopish lack of understanding regarding the wish every true Lover has that His Beloved be cherished and admired by all.

Furthermore, it is not maudlin to suggest that Jesus Christ cherishes His Mother: it is only right. Just because our ungracious, unceremonious generation has decided, in its lust for self-gratification, that motherhood is passé there is certainly no reason to assume that God thinks likewise. Indeed, the carnal mind hasn't a clue about the deference and sincere regard God has for His Handmaid, Mother and Spouse. After all, Mary agreed to His indwelling, carried Him in Her womb, nourished Him at Her breast, clothed and fed Him as He grew up, witnessed His first miracle, stood by Him as He suffered on the Cross, and buried Him when the dreadful deed was done. Only a simpleton would think such holiness, obedience, and integrity on Her part would go unrewarded, uncherished, and unproclaimed. Only a fool on an ingrate would deem Her "just an incubator."

> ... it is an infallible mark of reprobation to have no esteem and love for the holy Virgin; while on the other hand, it is an infallible mark of predestination to be entirely and truly devoted to her.
> —Saint Louis Marie de Montfort
> *True Devotion to Mary*

If ever there was a crime in this age, is has been the despicable dishonor paid this Woman by those who would deny Her the prominence that is rightly Hers. To think that the role of Mary in Salvation has been so downplayed, that Her Virginity has been called into question, that Her purity of heart should be so offended, and that devotion to Her has been offhandedly discounted by the butchers of the Faith.

This Woman, the brunt of so much vile and vehement hatred, is the humble Maiden who proclaimed at the age of fourteen:

> My soul doth magnify the Lord,
> And my spirit hath rejoiced in God my Savior.
> Because he hath regarded the humility of his handmaid; for behold from henceforth all generations shall call me blessed.

> Because he that is mighty, hath done great things
> to me; and holy is his name.
> —St. Luke I:46-49

Yes, since that time all generations have called Her "Blessed," including the current one—though our numbers have dwindled and our voices seldom manage to rise above the din of Her detractors, so outnumbered are we.

> All the true children of God, the predestinate[*], have God for their Father and Mary for their Mother. He who has not Mary for his Mother has not God for his Father. This is the reason why the reprobate, such as heretics, schismatics and others, who hate our Blessed Lady or regard her with contempt and indifference, have not God for their Father, however much they boast of it, simply because they have not Mary for their Mother ...
>
> The most infallible and indubitable sign by which we may distinguish a heretic, a man of bad doctrine, a reprobate, from one of the predestinate, is that the heretic and reprobate have nothing but contempt and indifference for Our Lady, endeavoring by their words and examples to diminish the worship[†] and love of her, openly or hiddenly, and sometimes by misrepresentation.
>
> —Saint Louis Marie de Montfort
> *True Devotion to Mary*

---

[*] Do not cringe at the word "predestination." One of Calvin's great disservices to the Church was to so taint this word with his screwy heretical theology that Catholics have been afraid to use it ever since, fearing "guilt by association." The fact is that Saint Paul spoke openly of predestination in his epistles (see Romans VIII:29-30 and Ephesians I:5 & 11). It simply means that God, being omnipotent, knows ahead of time—since He is not bound by time—who will be saved. His knowing who is among the "elect" does not negate the free will of any human being in their struggle to get there.

[†] The etymology of the word "worship" is that in Old English *weorthscipe* meant "worthiness," and denoted respect due to any person of rank, hence the title "Your Worship." The Protestant accusation that Catholics "worship Mary" is obfuscation, a distortion of the language, which modern Catholics have not been properly trained to confront.

May God have mercy on Her enemies, for just as She flies into battle for the honor of Her Lord, we can rest assured that the Holy Ghost who so yearned for Her throughout the ages, who took such delight in the very Idea of Her from the beginning, who in a very real sense "did it all for Her"—yes, Her Spouse will ride swiftly and with unspeakable ferocity to defend the Honor of His Lady.

Two guesses which side we want to be on.

Wait—what's this? As we let go of the flattened map it begins to curl up, and we see there is still *more* writing on the other side. How can this be? Is there no end to the avalanche that is Mary?

Happily, no.

> As the glorious Virgin Mary has been raised to the dignity of Mother of the King of kings, it is not without reason that the Church honors her, and wishes her to be honored by all, with the glorious title of Queen.
>
> —Saint Alphonsus Liguori
> *The Glories of Mary*

The titles, attributes, virtues, and accolades heaped upon the Blessed Virgin Mary never do end, for just as we think we've exhausted Her ongoing revelation in the Bible, we turn a page and find a whole new field ripe for harvest. And each time we think we have exhausted any given orchard, we glance over our shoulders as we pause to wipe our brows, and lo and behold the trees we thought were picked bare are again brimming with bright, colorful fruit, gleaming with the morning dew. Truly, it has been declared by many Marian Saints and scholars:

DE MARIA NUMQUAM SATIS
Of Mary, Never Enough

Indeed does it make sense, once we begin to fathom the Miracle that is Mary, to think otherwise? The same Holy Ghost who "brooded" on His Spouse throughout the Old Testament, also inspires, activates, and spurs on the Holy Catholic Church up to the present. Small wonder that the

Church has continued to ponder the Mother of God, and to diligently seek out Her many Graces, blessings, and positions within the framework of the Mystical Body of Christ. Perhaps no greater summary of Our Lady's efforts can be found than the Litany of Loreto, which dates from the twelfth century in Italy (an Irish version goes back to the eighth), and which has been gradually enhanced by the additions of popes along the way. May its recitation excite Her children to a deeper understanding of, and earnest devotion to, the Woman "playing before Him at all times," unto the consummation of all things.

∞ ∞ ∞

THE LITANY OF LORETO
also known as
THE LITANY OF THE BLESSED VIRGIN MARY

Lord, have mercy on us.
Christ, have mercy on us.
Lord, have mercy on us.
Christ hear us.
Christ, graciously hear us.

God the Father of Heaven,	have mercy on us.
God the Son, Redeemer of the world,	have mercy on us.
God the Holy Spirit,	have mercy on us.
Holy Trinity, one God,	have mercy on us.
Holy Mary,	pray for us.
Holy Mother of God,	pray for us.
Holy Virgin of virgins,	pray for us.
Mother of Christ,	pray for us.
Mother of divine grace,	pray for us.
Mother most pure,	pray for us.
Mother most chaste,	pray for us.
Mother inviolate,	pray for us.
Mother undefiled,	pray for us.
Mother most amiable,	pray for us.

Mother most admirable,	pray for us.
Mother of good counsel,	pray for us.
Mother of our Creator,	pray for us.
Mother of our Savior,	pray for us.
Virgin most prudent,	pray for us.
Virgin most venerable,	pray for us.
Virgin most renowned,	pray for us.
Virgin most powerful,	pray for us.
Virgin most merciful,	pray for us.
Virgin most faithful,	pray for us.
Mirror of justice,	pray for us.
Seat of wisdom,	pray for us.
Cause of our joy,	pray for us.
Spiritual vessel,	pray for us.
Vessel of honor,	pray for us.
Singular vessel of devotion,	pray for us.
Mystical rose,	pray for us.
Tower of David,	pray for us.
Tower of ivory,	pray for us.
House of gold,	pray for us.
Ark of the Covenant,	pray for us.
Gate of heaven,	pray for us.
Morning star,	pray for us.
Health of the sick,	pray for us.
Refuge of sinners,	pray for us.
Comforter of the afflicted,	pray for us.
Help of Christians,	pray for us.
Queen of angels,	pray for us.
Queen of patriarchs,	pray for us.
Queen of prophets,	pray for us.
Queen of Apostles,	pray for us.
Queen of martyrs,	pray for us.
Queen of confessors,	pray for us.
Queen of virgins,	pray for us.
Queen of all saints,	pray for us.
Queen conceived without original sin,	pray for us.
Queen assumed into heaven,	pray for us.
Queen of the most holy Rosary,	pray for us.
Queen of peace.	pray for us.

Lamb of God, Who takest away the sins of the world,
    spare us O Lord.
Lamb of God, Who takest away the sins of the world,
    graciously hear us, O Lord.
Lamb of God, Who takest away the sins of the world,
    have mercy on us.

V/.   Pray for us, O holy Mother of God.

R/.   That we may be worthy of the promises of Christ.

V/.   Let us pray. Grant unto us, Thy servants, we beseech Thee, O
       Lord God, at all times to enjoy health of soul and body; and by
       the glorious intercession of Blessed Mary, ever virgin, when
       freed from the sorrows of this present life, to enter into that joy
       which hath no end. Through Christ our Lord.

R/.   Amen.

CHAPTER THIRTY-EIGHT

COME OVER TO ME:
A MEDITATION

Mary, Our Blessed Mother, was the only creature in
this world who never made Love shudder. You and I
made Him shudder, but Mary never did.
—Virginia A. Kenny
Convent Boarding School

∞ ∞ ∞

ALMOST SMACK DAB IN THE MIDDLE of the *Douay-Rheims
Bible,* silently tucked away between the Book of Wisdom and
the Prophecy of Isaias, is the Book of Ecclesiasticus. It was
written in Hebrew two hundred years before the birth of Christ
by a man named Jesus son of Sirach, and was translated into
Greek by his grandson, also named Jesus. The twenty-fourth
chapter of this remarkable work provides us with a penetrating
insight into the Miracle that is Mary.

What I now write comes from the bottom of my heart,
from the deepest recesses of my being: When the insanity of
this age gets to me, as my feet slip on the loose and wobbly
cobblestones, and the howl of the wind and the thrash of the
hail unhinges my resolve, I take refuge in this beautiful and
ancient prophecy. May its secrets and soothing unguents provide a healing elixir for you as well, and may we uphold one
another as we continue on our wearying journey.

∞ ∞ ∞

> WISDOM shall praise her own self, and shall be
> honoured in God, and shall glory in the midst of her
> people,
> And shall open her mouth in the churches of the
> most High, and shall glorify herself in the sight of
> his power,
> And in the midst of her own people shall be ex-
> alted, and shall be admired in the holy assembly.
> — Ecclesiasticus XXIV:1-3

WISDOM, who needs no further introduction, is here described in terms that resonate forward in time, pre-echoing the
words She would one day say to Her cousin Elizabeth:

> My soul doth magnify the Lord,
> And my spirit hath rejoiced in God my Savior,
> Because he hath regarded the humility of his hand-
> maid; for behold from henceforth all generations shall
> call me blessed.
> Because he that is mighty, hath done great things
> to me; and holy is his name.
> — St. Luke I:46-49

True humility is the fruit of honest self-knowledge.   Mary
demonstrated the depths of Her humility by obeying God and
offering Herself as the Vessel through which His Son would
enter the world. This being accomplished, and thus sharing so
intimately in the Love and Life of Our Savior, She is free to
savor His Delight in Herself, and so rejoices in Her own exaltation. We who are corrupt cannot behave so, because our sinfulness draws us inexorably toward selfish pride when we receive accolades. But Mary's humility is complete. When She
rejoices in Herself, the glory goes straight to God. When we
share in Her Joy, we honor Her and take our minds off our
puny and prideful selves. Hence the Catholic Church exalts,
praises, and admires Her in the Holy Assembly, and with great
enthusiasm. It is right and just that we do so. And the laurels
we heap upon Her pass through Her to God, for Her profound
Humility renders Her absolutely Transparent. Nothing of our
praise sticks to Her, but goes through Her to God.

> And in the multitude of the elect she shall have
> praise, and among the blessed she shall be blessed,
> saying,
> I came out of the mouth of the most High, the
> firstborn before all creatures:
> I made that in the heavens there should rise light
> that never faileth, and as a cloud I covered all the
> earth:
> I dwelt in the highest places, and my throne is in a
> pillar of a cloud.
> —Ecclesiasticus XXIV:4-7

Again we are confronted with the mystery of Mary
"playing before Him at all times," present in His Mind as the
world was created, foremost in His Thoughts as He guided the
Israelites out of Egypt:

> And the Lord went before them to shew the way by
> day in a pillar of a cloud, and by night in a pillar of
> fire ...
> —Exodus XIII:21

Next we come to a verse that, on the surface, is a continuation of the same theme.

> I alone have compassed the circuit of heaven, and
> have penetrated into the bottom of the deep, and have
> walked in the waves of the sea ...
> —Ecclesiasticus XXIV:8

Happily, we have had Saints who could see beyond the
obvious:

> Fortunate, indeed, are the clients of this most com-
> passionate Mother; for not only does she succor them
> in this world, but even in purgatory they are helped
> and comforted by her protection.   And as in that
> prison poor souls are in the greatest need of assis-
> tance, since in their torments they cannot help them-
> selves, our Mother of mercy does proportionately
> more to relieve them.   St. Bernadine of Sienna says,
> "that in that prison, where souls that are spouses of

Jesus Christ are detained, Mary has a certain dominion and plenitude of power, not only to relieve them,
but even to deliver them from their pains."

And, first, with respect to the relief she gives. The
same saint, in applying those words of Ecclesiasticus,
I have walked in the waves of the sea, adds "that it is
by visiting and relieving the necessities and torments
of her clients, who are her children." He then says,
"that the pains of purgatory are called waves, because
they are transitory, unlike the pains of hell, which
never end; and they are called waves of the sea, because they are so bitter. The clients of Mary, thus
suffering, are often visited and relieved by her." "See,
therefore," says Novarinus, "of what consequence it is
to be the servant of this good Lady, for her servants
she never forgets when they are suffering in those
flames ..."

—Saint Alphonsus de Liguori
The Glories of Mary

Knowing our own sinfulness and the extent of the evils we
have committed throughout our lifetimes, the weight of our
past offenses can sometimes drag us down into the dust. Purgatory looms—and in this we hope, for it is the detour with
but one end, which is Heaven. Still, it is comforting to know
that we will not be alone if, with God's help, we make it that
far.

In any case, Mary not only played before the Mind of
God before Her birth, but continued to do so in the minds of
men afterwards. This splendid Lady sure does get around.

I alone have compassed the circuit of heaven ...
And have stood in all the earth: and in every peo-
ple,
And in every nation I have had the chief rule:
And by my power I have trodden under my feet the
hearts of all the high and low: and in these I sought
rest, and I shall abide in the inheritance of the Lord.
—Ecclesiasticus XXIV:8, 9-11

Yes, She has captured the hearts of kings and paupers,
philosophers and merchants, knights and dolts, queens and

flower girls. Small wonder the explorers named everything in sight after Mary, for She had trodden their valiant hearts under Her gentle feet, and rested tenderly within them.

Now we pause, take a deep breath, and let it out slowly, as we arrive at the crux:

> Then the creator of all things commanded, and said
> to me: and he that made me, rested in my tabernacle.
> —Ecclesiasticus XXIV:12

Around this revolves all else, that the God of all creation came and resided within Mary's very body; the very thought of which arouses our deepest gratitude, incites our most bewildered amazement, and enkindles our most profound hope. We can only imagine what it was like for Her to realize that "He that made me rested in my tabernacle." We, who once in a great while snatch a flash of a glimpse of the beginnings of an insight when we receive Holy Communion, would do well to meditate on Her prolonged and intimate experience. Small wonder that Her soul magnified the Lord, and Her spirit rejoiced—and we continue to call Her "Blessed."

Indeed, many are the generations who will take delight in Her:

> And I took root in an honourable people, in the
> portion of my God his inheritance, and my abode is
> in the full assembly of saints.
> —Ecclesiasticus XXIV:16

This fervor is then portrayed in blossoming imagery, reminiscent of the poetry of the Canticle of Canticles. One can easily get lost in the swirl of symbols and smells, the music of Love in bloom:

> I was exalted like a cedar in Libanus, and as a cypress tree on mount Sion.
> I was exalted like a palm tree in Cades, and as a rose plant in Jericho.
> As the fair olive tree in the plains, and as a plane tree by the water in the streets, I was exalted.
> I gave a sweet smell like cinnamon, and aromatical balm: I yielded a sweet odor like the best myrrh:

> And I perfumed my dwelling as storax, and gal-
> banum, and onyx, and aloes, and as the frankincense
> not cut, and my odour is as the purest balm.
> I have stretched out my branches as the turpentine
> tree, and my branches are of honour and grace.
> —Ecclesiasticus XXIV:17-22

Next we come to a beautiful description of how closely Mary is intertwined with Her Son in purpose, mission, and intention. Here, also, is explained the delineation between them: how their paths differ. Would that more people hungering for the Truth would seek out, find, and devour these insightful passages:

> I am the mother of fair love, and of fear, and of
> knowledge, and of holy hope.
> —Ecclesiasticus XXIV:24

How simple, and yet so complex, is Mary. As the Mother of Jesus, She is the Bearer of Love Personified. Within Her Son, and so within Herself, is knowledge and hope. After Her Son's Ascension, She would be present with the Apostles when the Holy Ghost descended upon them and the Catholic Church was born. Indeed, it was Her prayer which summoned Her Spouse on that occasion:

> Come, Holy Ghost, fill the hearts of Thy faithful
> and kindle in them the fire of Thy Love.
> Send forth Thy Spirit and they shall be created; and
> Thou shalt renew the face of the earth.

As for "Mother of fear," we would do well to recall that in an earlier age all Catholics were taught to pray for the gifts of the Holy Ghost: wisdom, understanding, counsel, fortitude, knowledge, piety, and—yes—fear of the Lord.

> In me is all grace of the way and of the truth, in me
> is all hope of life and of virtue.
> —Ecclesiasticus XXIV:25

How closely this prefigures the words of Her Son:

> I am the way, and the truth, and the life. No man
> cometh to the Father, but by me.
>
> —St. John XIV:6

But notice the subtle differences. Jesus would proclaim, *"I am* the way," whereas His Mother says, *"In me* is all grace of the way ..." Her claim is not to be the way itself, but by virtue of Grace, to be the harbinger, the precursor, the forerunner, the gateway, the bearer of Him who would be the way.

She continues:

> Come over to me, all ye that desire me, and be
> filled with my fruits.
> For my spirit is sweet above honey, and my inheri-
> tance above honey and the honeycomb.
> My memory is unto everlasting generations.
>
> —Ecclesiasticus XXIV:26-28

How much this resonates with, yet does not imitate, the words of Her Son:

> Come to me, all you that labour, and are burdened,
> and I will refresh you.
> Take up my yoke upon you, and learn of me, be-
> cause I am meek, and humble of heart: and you shall
> find rest to your souls.
> For my yoke is sweet and my burden light.
>
> —St. Matthew XI:28-30

And then we read Her disclaimer, Her absolute denial that She in any way usurps the purpose or power of Her Son:

> They that eat me, shall yet hunger: and they that
> drink me, shall yet thirst.
>
> —Ecclesiasticus XXIV:29

To feast on Mary is not enough, for She is not the end or the object of our worship. She cannot slake our thirst nor satisfy our hunger. She is but our means to Her Son, and the means by which He came to us. It is for Her Son and Him alone to fulfill our most fundamental needs:

> I am the bread of life: he that cometh to me shall
> not hunger: and he that believeth in me shall never
> thirst.
>
> —St. John VI:35

Still, it is within Her power to grant favor to those who do approach and appreciate Her; for after all, no one desires our Salvation more than She does—not even ourselves. She promises Her aid and protection to those who earnestly seek Her help.

> He that harkeneth to me, shall not be confounded:
> and they that work by me, shall not sin.
>
> —Ecclesiasticus XXIV:30

This is why concerns about someone being "too involved" or "preoccupied" with Mary are groundless. It is Her promise that they shall not be confused. If they listen to Her, She will guide them. She is, after all, Our Mother.

My reader will perhaps forgive me if I revel for a moment in the next verse:

> They that explain me shall have life everlasting.
>
> —Ecclesiasticus XXIV:31

I fully intend to make a career out of doing exactly that. For those who are jealous, I make the following suggestion wholeheartedly, and in the words of Her Son:

> Go, and do thou in like manner.
>
> —St. Luke X:37

These proclamations of Mary as Wisdom Personified are not to be taken lightly. Today, more than ever in history, we need to understand Her place in the scheme of things, and Her pivotal importance in our lives.

> All these things are the book of life, and the cove-
> nant of the most High, and the knowledge of the
> truth.
>
> —Ecclesiasticus XXIV:32

Mary is not "optional."   These things which the Holy Ghost revealed for our benefit through the hand of Jesus son of Sirach, two centuries before Mary was born, are all in the Book of Life ...

> And whoever was not found written in the book of life, was cast into the pool of fire.
> —The Apocalypse XX:15

Those who deny the importance of Mary, or flee from Her from lack of knowledge, deprive themselves of a vast resource of strength and holiness, and thus place themselves in great peril. We are called to follow the example of Christ Her Son, who was promised from the beginning, and whose line of descent was carefully preserved in the Scriptures.

> Moses commanded a law in the precepts of justices, and an inheritance to the house of Jacob, and the promises of Israel.
> He appointed to David his servant to raise up of him a most mighty king ...
> —Ecclesiasticus XXIV:33-34

Thus Moses promised through the Law that a mighty King would descend from David, who was Christ Our Lord:

> Who filleth up wisdom as the Phison[*], and as the Tigris in the days of the new fruits.
> Who maketh understanding to abound as the Euphrates, who multiplieth it as the Jordan in the time of harvest.
> Who sendeth knowledge as light, and riseth up as Gehon in the time of the vintage.
> —Ecclesiasticus XXIV:35-37

---

[*] The Phison is a river in Armenia which, like the Tigris, Euphrates, and Gehon, overflows its banks at the beginning of summer when the snow melts.

Within this beautiful prophecy is the sad realization that
everyone will not seek out the help of His Mother:

> Who first hath perfect knowledge of her, and a
> weaker shall not search her out.
> For her thoughts are more vast than the sea, and her
> counsels more deep than the great ocean.
> — Ecclesiasticus XXIV:38-39

Again we find Mary's poetic connection with *mar,* the sea.
And as Her virtues and attributes are indeed as vast and as in-
timidating as the ocean, many will cringe in fear rather than
embrace Her.

Undaunted, Wisdom flourishes, Her freely-given Graces
gushing forth in torrents of life-giving water.

> I, wisdom, have poured out rivers.
> I, like a brook out of a river of a mighty water; I
> like a channel of a river and like an aqueduct, came
> out of paradise.
> — Ecclesiasticus XXIV:40-41

Ah, Mary! Again you remind us that You are the promise
made in Eden, the Woman of Genesis.

> I said: I will water my garden of plants, and I will
> water abundantly the fruits of my meadow.
> And behold my brook became a great river, and my
> river came near to the sea:
> For I make doctrine shine forth to all as the morn-
> ing light, and I will declare it afar off.
> — Ecclesiasticus XXIV:42-44

Again you come forth ...

> ... as the morning rising, fair as the moon, bright
> as the sun, terrible as an army set in array...
> — Canticle of Canticles VI:9

... but this time armed with doctrine:

> . And take unto you the helmet of salvation, and the
> sword of the spirit (which is the word of God).
> —Ephesians VI:17

And in spite of our weakness, our cowardice, the end of our strength, and the limits of our understanding, You will come on and on, inexorably on. For as long as we sincerely seek the Truth, You will ferret us out and teach us with a Mother's tenacity, so that by Your patience and inexhaustible maternal ministrations we may come into full knowledge and holiness.

> I will penetrate to all the lower parts of the earth,
> and will behold all that sleep, and will enlighten all
> that hope in the Lord.
> I will yet pour out doctrine as prophecy, and will
> leave it to them that seek wisdom, and will not cease
> to instruct their offspring even to the holy age.
> See ye that I have not laboured for myself only, but
> for all that seek out the truth.
> —Ecclesiasticus XXIV:45-47

And so it is with the glee of playful children, the gratitude of salvaged detritus, the humility of found-out sinners, the valor of an assembled army, and love of true admirers that we join our voices with Saints throughout the ages who have prayed:

> Hail, thou star of ocean
> God's own mother blest,
> Ever sinless Virgin,
> Gate of heavenly rest.
>
> Oh! by Gabriel's Ave,
> Uttered long ago,
> Eva's name reversing[*]

---

[*] When the salutation of the Angel Gabriel, "Hail Mary," was translated into Latin, *Ave Maria*, it was immediately noticed that, not only was Mary's name similar to *mar*, the sea, but "Ave" was the reversal of *Eva*, the Latin rendering of "Eve." Mary, the Woman of the *Protoevangelium*, came into

'Stablish peace below.

Break the captives' fetters,
Light on blindness pour;
All our ills expelling,
Every bliss implore.

Show thyself a Mother;
May the Word divine,
Born for us thine Infant,
Hear our prayers through thine.

Virgin all excelling,
Mildest of the mild;
Freed from guilt preserve us
Meek and undefiled.

Keep our life all spotless,
Make our way secure,
Till we find in Jesus,
Joy for evermore.

Through the highest Heaven
To the almighty Three,
Father, Son and Spirit
One same glory be. Amen.

—"Ave Maria Stella"
The Raccolta

---

the world to reverse, to undo, to repair the damage done by the First Woman
in the Garden of Eden.

CHAPTER THIRTY-NINE

FAR FROM ME:
TOTAL CONSECRATION

Behold, I make all things new.
—The Apocalypse XXI:5

∞ ∞ ∞

HAVING CONSIDERED THE BLESSED VIRGIN MARY for the last seven chapters—indeed, we could go on for seventy times seven volumes and still only skim the gently rolling surface of the Marian Sea—there comes a juncture when we need to plan a course of action. Knowledge that is not put to use is like fruit left on a tree to wither and fall to the ground. Now that we have come to a clearer realization of the awesome power and position of the Mother of God, what are we going to do about it?—about Her?—about us in relation to Her?

Mary, as we have seen, is the most perfect creature God ever made, more glorious than all the Angels put together, more pleasing to Him than all the Saints combined. It therefore stands to reason that if we wish to be pleasing to Him, we would do well to imitate Her. When we attach and devote ourselves to the Mother of God, She in turn takes an interest in us. More than an interest, She has a Mother's deep and abiding concern for Her children, wanting what is holiest and best for them. She desires our Salvation more than we do for ourselves.

> When Mary has struck her roots in a soul, she produces there marvels of grace, which she alone can produce, because she alone is the fruitful Virgin who

never has had, and never will have, her equal in purity
and fruitfulness.

—Saint Louis Marie de Montfort
True Devotion to Mary

The most perfect way that we can attach ourselves to Our
Lady is called the Total Consecration. While this has been
practiced in one form or another over the centuries by various
Saints, the best and most precise formulation was conceived by
Saint Louis Marie de Montfort, whose feast day is April 28.

Louis Marie Grignion de la Bachelaraie was born in the
town of Montfort-la-Canne in Brittany in 1673. After his or-
dination in 1700, he became a traveling missionary wandering
through France, which was falling under the shadow of the
Jansenist heresy. Jansenism was a joy-killing severity-
instilling Calvinist-resembling kind of Puritanism which had
been condemned by the Church twice before Louis' birth, yet
continued to thrive in France. It is amazing how people will
opt for a merciless parody of God's Revelation rather than
accept with joy and thanksgiving the profound Mercy which
He expressed in the Person of His Son. It's sort of the spiritual version of walking around with a sign on our back that
says, "Kick me."

In any case, three hundred years ago, reverence to Our
Lady was on the decline as a result of the Jansenist influence,
and Louis met with serious opposition as he traveled through
France, preaching devotion to Her. His stiffest opposition
came from—who else?—bishops and clergy. Discouraged by
their antagonism toward his message, Louis took his case to
Pope Clement XI, asking whether he was doing something
wrong. The pope told him to continue his efforts, appointing
him Missionary Apostolic, and—as is always the quirk and
challenge of Catholicism—instructed him to work under obedience to the diocesan authorities. This Louis did until his
death in 1716. He was canonized in 1947.

Of Saint de Montfort's numerous works, his most important was *True Devotion to Mary*. This book is *required reading* for all Catholics who want to understand Mary's proper
place with respect to our Salvation, and it provides the best
course for nurturing and achieving a deep and abiding rela-
tionship with Her. It is also a *survival guide* for the Faithful in
times of persecution. Saint Louis Marie de Montfort under-

stood the importance of his book, for within its pages he prophesied:

> I clearly foresee that raging beasts shall come in fury to tear with their diabolical teeth this little writing and him whom the Holy Ghost has made use of to write it—or at least to smother it in darkness and silence of a coffer, that it may not appear. They shall even attack and persecute those who shall read it and carry it out in practice.
> —Saint Louis Marie de Montfort
> *True Devotion to Mary*

As it turned out, the religious order he founded was severely persecuted, and the manuscript itself was lost for a hundred years. It was found by accident in 1842, which is providential for us, since it seems eerily directed to our generation in particular:

> Mary must shine forth more than ever in mercy, in might and in grace, in these latter times: in mercy, to bring back and lovingly receive the poor strayed sinners who shall be converted and shall return to the Catholic Church*; in might, against the enemies of God, idolaters, schismatics, Mahometans, Jews and souls hardened in impiety§, who shall rise in terrible revolt against God to seduce all those who shall oppose them and to make them fall by promises and threats; and finally, she must shine forth in grace, in order to animate and sustain the valiant soldiers and

---

* Like me!!!!!!!!!!!

§ Not a very ecumenical guy, this Saint Louis de Montfort. He certainly wouldn't be welcome in the average Catholic gathering today. Nonetheless, he is a canonized Saint, and the book from which this quote is taken was wholeheartedly endorsed by Popes Pius IX, Leo XIII, Pius X (also a canonized Saint), Benedict XV, Pius XI, and Pius XII. The fact that his message would be scorned by modern Catholics is a startling proof that the religion they practice is not the same one as that practiced by their ancestors in the Faith—not to mention clear proof of the validity of his prediction. Someone is lying.

faithful servants of Jesus Christ, who shall battle for
His interests.

And lastly, Mary must be terrible to the devil and
his crew, as an army ranged in battle, principally in
these latter times, because the devil, knowing that he
has but little time, and now less than ever, to destroy
souls, will every day redouble his efforts and his
combats. He will presently raise up cruel persecu-
tions and will put terrible snares before the faithful
servants and true children of Mary, whom it gives
him more trouble to conquer than it does to conquer
others.

—Saint Louis Marie de Montfort
True Devotion to Mary,

When anyone says to me, "I'm on a limited budget; what
books do I absolutely *need* to buy?" my recommendation is:
1) the *Douay-Rheims Bible*, preferably the edition with the
Haydock footnotes if they can possibly swing it, and 2) *True
Devotion to Mary.* "Once you're consecrated to Her," I explain, "you can trust Her to lead you to whatever else you
need."

First off, we as Faithful Catholics need to recognize and
get it through our heads that the whole Protestant buzz over
"You Catholics put too much emphasis on Mary" is silly. We
should render such nonsense the response it deserves: since it
demonstrates their *ignorance,* we should *ignore* it. Truly, we
should know and proclaim that *De Maria numquam satis—of
Mary, there is never enough!* How can we overemphasize that
which is so magnificent and awesome as to be beyond comprehension? When we come to realize that ...

In this Queen alone are comprehended and contained
more treasures than in all the rest of things joined together, and the variety and preciousness of her riches
honor the Lord above all the multitudes of the other
creatures.

—Sister Mary of Jesus of Agreda
"The Conception"
Mystical City of God

... what would be the sense of minimizing Her splendor? To do anything but magnify Mary, to shower Her with praise and devotion, is to behave irrationally. Besides, if the Protestants put so much stock in the Bible, and ...

> Holy Scripture was written for Mary, about Mary, and on account of Mary.
> —Saint Bernard of Clairvaux

... then what's their problem? Enough of this. Let us move on to something sensible, reasonable, and certainly more constructive.

Secondly, we need to recognize, as so many Saints have told us, that we absolutely *need* Mary. There is nothing *optional* about this, there is no room for personal opinion on the matter. It is *de Fide*—of the Faith—so we must accept it. Listen to the declarations of great and holy Saints:

> No one can enter into Heaven except through Mary, as entering through a gate ... No one ever finds Christ but with and through Mary. Whoever seeks Christ apart from Mary seeks Him in vain.
> —Saint Bonaventure

> The salvation of everyone is left to the care of this Blessed Virgin.
> —Saint Peter Damian

> Mary is called "The Gate of Heaven" because no one can enter Heaven but through her means.
> —Saint Alphonsus de Liguori

> Sinners receive pardon by the intercession of Mary alone.
> —Saint John Chrysostom

> All gifts, virtues, and graces of the Holy Ghost are administered by the hands of Mary to whomever she desires, when she desires, and in the manner she desires, and to whatever degree she desires.
> —Saint Bernadine of Siena

All the saints have a great devotion to Our Lady:
no grace comes from Heaven without passing through
her hands. We cannot go into a house without speaking to the doorkeeper. Well, the Holy Virgin is the
doorkeeper of Heaven.
                —Saint John Mary Vianney, the Curé of Ars

O Most Holy Virgin, receive us under thy protection if thou wouldst see us saved, for we have no
hope of salvation but through thy means.
                                        —Saint Ephrem

Whoever honors, loves, serves and invokes Mary
with humility and confidence will ascend to Paradise.
                                    —Saint John Eudes

No one, not even a sinner, who devoutly recom-
mends himself to her shall ever become the prey of
Hell.
                            —Saint Catherine of Siena

Unless the prayers of Mary interposed, there could
be no hope of mercy.
                            —Saint Bridget of Sweden

For, since it is the will of Divine Providence that
we should have the God-Man through Mary, there is
no other way for us to receive Christ except from her
hands.
                                —Saint Pope Pius X

All the above quotes are from
The Apostolic Digest

Yes, yes, we know very well what Protestants have to say
about "one mediator," which was why that point was covered
back in Chapter 9. Besides, we just set their narrow-minded
claims aside on the basis of ignorance. And, as we saw back in
Chapter 36:

Therefore, no less truly and properly may it be af-
firmed that nothing at all of the very great treasure of

> every grace, which the Lord confers, since "grace and truth came by Jesus Christ" [John I: 17], nothing is imparted to us except through Mary, God so willing; so just as no one can approach the highest Father except through the Son, so no one can approach Christ except through His Mother.
>
> — Pope Leo XIII
> The Encyclical, *"Octobri mense"*

The fact is that to the degree they close themselves off from Mary, so much do they also imperil their own Salvation.

Thirdly, we need to foster devotion within ourselves to the Blessed Virgin Mary. Genuine devotion to Our Lady begins with admiration of Her greatness. The more we learn about Her, the more we are awed by all that She is. Small wonder that God took so much delight in Her throughout the ages. Admiration naturally leads to imitation, the desire to foster within ourselves the virtues we find so admirable in Her. Truly, Mary furnishes the perfect model for the life of every person, regardless of age, sex, occupation, or vocation. There is no human being who cannot benefit from mirroring Mary. The trouble is that there is no way that we can accomplish it on our own, because we are thoroughly rotten due to Original Sin. Therefore we must invoke Her intercession, ask Her to give us the Grace and Guidance to make our imitation of Her genuine and complete. On Her assistance and cooperation we can fully depend, for She loves us as Her own, and longs to bring forth Christ in us, and us in Christ.

Fourthly, we need to dedicate ourselves totally and completely to Her. We need to learn all we can about the Total Consecration, and then do it. Simple.

> All our perfection consists in being conformed, united and consecrated to Jesus Christ; and therefore the most perfect of all devotions is, without any doubt, that which the most perfectly conforms, unites, and consecrates us to Jesus Christ. Now, Mary, being the most conformed of all creatures to Jesus Christ, it follows that, of all devotions, that which most consecrates and conforms the soul to Our Lord is devotion to His holy Mother, and that the

more a soul is consecrated to Mary, the more it is consecrated to Jesus.

Hence is comes to pass that the most perfect consecration to Jesus Christ is nothing else but a perfect and entire consecration of ourselves to the Blessed Virgin, and this is the devotion I teach; or, in other words, a perfect renewal of the vows and promises of Holy Baptism.

This devotion consists, then, in giving ourselves entirely to Our Lady, in order to belong entirely to Jesus through her. We must give her (1) our body, with all its senses and its members; (2) our soul, with all its powers; (3) our exterior goods of fortune, whether present or to come; (4) our interior and spiritual goods, which are our merits and virtues, and our good works, past, present, and future. In a word, we must give her all we have in order of nature and in order of grace, and all that may become ours in the future, in the orders of nature, grace and glory; and this we must do without reserve of so much as one farthing, one hair, or one least good action; and we must do it also for all eternity; and we must do it, further, without pretending to, or hoping for, any other recompense for our offering and service except the honor of belonging to Jesus Christ through and in Mary—as though that sweet Mistress were not (as she always is) the most generous and the most grateful of creatures.

—Saint Louis Marie de Montfort
True Devotion to Mary

In other words, in giving Her everything internal and external that we would ever precede with the possessive pronoun "my," we offer ourselves as slaves to Mary. "Slaves?!?!?!" Yes, the word rankles, grates against our sensibilities, sends shivers up and down our spines, makes us want to close the book and turn on the television or reach for a scotch. Well, leave the TV off—the scotch is optional. This is indeed a hard thing to swallow, but we mustn't make the mistake of turning away from a great blessing just because we are uncomfortable with the terminology. The word "slave" is indeed disturb-

ing—especially here in the United States of America—but it is
not foreign to Catholicism, nor does Jesus ever ask of us
something which He wasn't willing to do Himself:

> There is nothing among men which makes us be-
> long to one another more than slavery. There is
> nothing among Christians which makes us more ab-
> solutely belong to Jesus Christ and His holy Mother
> than the slavery of the will, according to the example
> of Jesus Christ Himself, who took on Himself the
> form of a slave for love us (*Phil.* 2:7); and also ac-
> cording to the example of the holy Virgin, who called
> herself the servant and slave or the Lord. (*Lk.* 1:38)
> ...
> Before Baptism we were slaves of the devil. Bap-
> tism has made us the slaves of Jesus Christ: Chris-
> tians must needs be either the slaves of the devil or
> the slaves of Jesus Christ.
> —Saint Louis Marie de Montfort
> *True Devotion to Mary*

Willing slavery—consciously choosing to bind oneself to
the service of another—is not all that foreign to us. Marriage,
in its truest Sacramental form, is much the same thing. The
difference is that instead of merely committing ourselves to a
person whom we choose to love, we are freely chaining ourselves to the Mother of Fair Love. If we have learned anything in the last few chapters, it is that Mary is well worth
cherishing, admiring, honoring, and imitating. Making the
Total Consecration attaches us to Her in a solemn promise of
fealty and love.
     According to Saint Louis de Montfort's prescription, we
prepare for the Consecration over a period of thirty-three
days. For each day he suggests a reading from Scripture or
the *Imitation of Christ* by Thomas à Kempis, followed by
prayers that help to properly direct our thoughts and intentions; prayers such as:

SAINT LOUIS DE MONTFORT'S PRAYER TO JESUS

O most loving Jesus, deign to let me pour forth
my gratitude before Thee, for the grace Thou hast bestowed upon me in giving me to Thy holy Mother
through the devotion of Holy Bondage*, that she may
be my advocate in the presence of Thy majesty and
my support in my extreme misery. Alas, O Lord! I
am so wretched that without this dear Mother I should
be certainly lost. Yes, Mary is necessary for me at
Thy side and everywhere: that she may appease Thy
must wrath, because I have so offended Thee; that she
may save me from the eternal punishment of Thy justice, which I deserve; that she may contemplate Thee,
speak to Thee, pray to Thee, approach Thee and
please Thee; that she may help me to save my soul
and the souls of others; in short, Mary is necessary
for me that I may always do Thy holy will and seek
Thy greater glory in all things ...

With St. John the Evangelist at the foot of the
cross, I have taken her a thousand times for my own
and as many times have given myself to her; but if I
have not yet done it as Thou, dear Jesus, dost wish, I
now renew this offering as Thou desire me to renew
it. And if Thou seest in my soul of my body anything that does not belong to this august princess, I
pray Thee to take it and cast it far from me, for whatever in me does not belong to Mary is unworthy of
Thee.

—Saint Louis Marie de Montfort
True Devotion to Mary

—and—

---

* It is no coincidence that the concept of "bondage" has a warped porno-
graphic connotation in our culture. Satan's efforts against all things
Marian has been rampant and insidious for a long, long, time. Understanding this, we mustn't allow ourselves to be swayed from our course by a mere
dislike of certain words.

SAINT LOUIS DE MONTFORT'S PRAYER TO MARY

Hail Mary, beloved Daughter of the Eternal Father. Hail Mary, admirable Mother of the Son. Hail Mary, faithful Spouse of the Holy Ghost. Hail Mary, my Mother, my loving Mistress, my powerful sovereign. Hail, my joy, my glory, my heart and my soul. Thou art all mine by mercy, and I am thine by justice. But I am not yet sufficiently thine. I now give myself wholly to thee without keeping anything back for myself or others. If thou seest anything in me which does not belong to thee, I beseech thee to take it and make thyself the absolute Mistress of all that is mine.

Destroy in me all that may displease God; root it up and bring it to nought. Place and cultivate in me everything that is pleasing to thee. May the light of thy faith dispel the darkness of my mind. May thy profound humility take the place of my pride; may thy sublime contemplation check the distractions of my wandering imagination. May the continuous sight of God fill my memory with His presence; may the burning love of thy heart inflame the lukewarmness of mine. May thy virtues take the place of my sins; may thy merits be my only adornment in the sight of God and make up for all that is wanting in me. Finally, dearly beloved Mother, grant if it be possible, that I may have no other spirit but thine to know Jesus, and His Divine Will; that I have no other soul but thine to praise and glorify God; that I may have no other heart but thine to love God with a love as pure and ardent as thine ...

—Saint Louis Marie de Montfort
True Devotion to Mary

We're talking a time commitment of ten to fifteen minutes a day, tops. Then, on the thirty-fourth day—it's recommended that we plan ahead to that this day falls on one of Our Lady's feast days—we make a good Confession, receive

Holy Communion, and then make our formal pledge to do all our actions ...

> ... by Mary, with Mary, in Mary, and for Mary. So that we may do them all the more perfectly by Jesus, with Jesus, in Jesus, and for Jesus.
> —Saint Louis Marie de Montfort
> *True Devotion to Mary*

Simple, really. From that moment on, we hand the keys to Mary and let Her slip into the driver's seat of our lives. Since She knows the Way to Heaven only too well, we can be confident in Her sense of direction. It's something of a relief, too, when we realize even more fully than ever that our lives are not our own. In this sense the total honesty of the Consecration is most satisfying.

Before we move on to other important topics, I wish to advise my readers and friends of several important things:

First, I have yet to meet a person who made the Total Consecration who did not derive enormous benefit from it. To a man—to a woman—everyone experiences a radical change in their spiritual lives for the better.

Second, Mary will turn our lives inside out and upside down. Our Blessed Mother wants us to be pleasing to Her Son, and pleasing She shall make us. We all tend to build monuments to ourselves, often without realizing it. Many of us have erected majestic cathedrals in our own honor. When we commit ourselves to Mary, She will bring in the bulldozers and level such monstrosities. So we rebuild, this time taking care to raise our monument to God. Of course, old habits die hard, and so we think we can get away with adding a side chapel dedicated to ourselves; in which case Mary does another bulldozer sweep. This process is agonizing and requires patience, and at times we may wish She would stop handing us roses thorns first, but once we are Hers we can rest assured that everything that happens thereafter is all the more for our good.

Third—and this too, is universal—during the thirty-three days of preparation, we will go through periods of depression, often accompanied by situations that incite tension or personal difficulty. Our lives may seem to unravel before our very eyes. When this began to happen, and I told the person who had recommended the Total Consecration to me, she said sweetly, "Oh yes, I forgot to warn you ..."   So I am warning you, my devout readers: be prepared. As we approach Mary who is so perfect, so pure, so radiantly humble, yet so stunning and playfully delightful, our own impurity, imperfection, and sinfulness can get terribly gnarly by contrast. It can be very exasperating, and certainly humiliating, but it is nonetheless purifying; and we do well to endure it with patience and hope. Hang in there. She will get you through.

Now we will roll up our Treasure Map, for having found the Cache of Gold, we must pass on the Directions to others so that they, too, may find this precious Trove. As for ourselves, "Ipsa"—the "X" that marks the spot—is now part of us, for the "spot" She marks is deep within our hearts.

And now, refreshed and renewed, and so much richer, we set sail for the next great adventure ...

316

CHAPTER FORTY

"YES, BUT ..."

> And behold a certain lawyer stood up, tempting him, and saying, Master, what must I do to possess eternal life?
>
> But he said to him: What is written in the law? how readest thou?
>
> He answering, said: Thou shalt love the Lord thy God with thy whole heart, and with thy whole soul, and with all thy strength, and with all thy mind: and thy neighbor as thyself.
>
> And he said to him: Thou hast answered right: this do, and thou shalt live.
>
> But he willing to justify himself, said to Jesus: And who is my neighbor?
>
> And Jesus answering, said: A certain man went down from Jerusalem to Jericho ...
>
> —St. Luke X:25-30

∞ ∞ ∞

THE ABOVE CONVERSATION PROVIDES the lead-in to the story of the Good Samaritan, one of the most compelling of Jesus' parables. Much has been written about the "man who went down from Jerusalem to Jericho," but before we look at him, we would do well to pause and take a closer look at this brief exchange between Jesus and "a certain lawyer."

From what Saint Luke tells us, this lawyer is not a sincere seeker of the truth. No doubt he has assured himself that he is, but he has a fatal flaw: he is convinced of his own infallibility. This is not an uncommon trait for it is found in many men, from auto mechanics to presidents, from certified nin-

compoops to licensed theologians, despite their wily protesta-
tions to the contrary. Such people are most clearly and easily
recognized by the way they ask questions. After a while it
becomes apparent that, as much as they pretend sincerity in
their inquiry, in reality they already have their own answers,
presupposed solutions to which they are doggedly committed.

> Even in our own day it is a remarkable truth that
> men who are not sincere in seeking the truth are never
> done asking questions; and even if you silence them,
> as our Divine Lord did on this occasion, you have
> reason to doubt whether you have convinced them.
> "Seeing they see not, neither do they understand," for
> immediately after they will speak and act as if you
> had never said a word about the truth in their hearing.
> The ancients used to say of such, "Non persuadebis
> etiamsi persuaseris" (you will not persuade them,
> even if you persuade) ...
>
> — Father Joseph Prachensky, SJ
> *Divine Parables Explained*

Such a person is this lawyer. Full of himself, he proposes
a question to the Teacher, a question for which he already has
his own answer. It is actually a ploy to state his own position.
Jesus, on the other hand, knowing the lawyer's mindset,
counters with a question of His own. (As a teacher myself, I
have found this to be an excellent technique for dealing with
students of similar ilk.) Bound to answer, since it was after all
he who initiated the exchange, the lawyer gives the obligatory
responses from the Torah:

> Thou shalt love the Lord thy God with thy whole
> heart, and with thy whole soul, and with they whole
> strength.
>
> — Deuteronomy VI:5

... and ...

> Thou shalt love thy friend as thyself.
>
> — Leviticus XIX:18

Notice how selective is his citation, for Moses went considerably further in his treatment of both commands, as we see when we view them in context:

> Thou shalt love the Lord thy God with thy whole heart, and with thy whole soul, and with they whole strength.
> And these words which I command thee this day, shall be in thy heart:
> And thou shalt tell them to thy children, and thou shalt meditate upon them sitting in thy house, and walking on thy journey, sleeping and rising.
> —Deuteronomy VI:5-7

> Thou shalt not be a detractor nor a whisperer among the people. Thou shalt not stand against the blood of thy neighbor. I am the Lord.
> Thou shalt not hate thy brother in thy heart, but reprove him openly, lest thou incur sin through him.
> Seek not revenge, nor be mindful of the injury of citizens. Thou shalt love thy friend as thyself. I am the Lord.
> —Leviticus XIX:18

God, through Moses, was not just dictating legal statutes. He was describing a committed way of life in which sin is imminently possible within the heart even before outward action is taken: "Thou shalt not hate thy brother in thy heart ... lest thou incur sin through him." The enormity of these citations, and the extent of their ramifications, seem lost on—or rather dodged by—the lawyer. A slippery solicitor is he.

Taken aback by the turn of events, since after all it was *he* who was supposed to be asking the questions, the lawyer tries to justify himself by posing what he's sure will be the topper: "And who is my neighbor?" We can almost see the twinkle in his eye: "There, I gotcha!"

Poor man. If only he had understood to Whom he was talking. Are we not like him whenever we forget that in addressing Jesus we are speaking to Him of Whom it is written:

> All things were made by him: and without him was made nothing that was made.

> In him was life, and the life was the light of men.
> And the light shineth in darkness, and the darkness
> did not comprehend it.
> —St. John I:3-4

There is no greater darkness than our own ignorance, our arrogance with respect to it, our insidious self-esteem, and our stubborn pride.

Jesus dealt with all this foolishness by presenting the story of the Good Samaritan, which we will look at in the next chapter. At the conclusion, He asked:

> Which of these three, in thy opinion, was neighbor
> to him that fell among the robbers?
> But he said: He that shewed mercy to him. And Je-
> sus said to him, Go, and do you in like manner.
> —St. Luke X:36-37

In light of what has transpired already, it is doubtful that the lawyer really learned much from this conversation. We can imagine him going away to sulk in his room, replaying the exchange with Jesus over and over in his legalistic mind, coming up with clever objections he would have tried if he'd been quicker on his feet.

It is of vital importance that we, as Catholics, do not partake of this lawyer's proud and sinful attitude. It leads inevitably back to one's self, which is nowhere. Being in love with your reflection in the mirror is no way to draw close to God. But how deeply entrenched is this tendency in human nature.

The mother says, "Don't touch that cake, it will ruin your appetite," and the child whines, "Yes, but I'm hungry *now.*"

The professor warns, "There will be a quiz on Monday, so be prepared," and the student sighs, "Yes, but the weather's so nice, I'd rather spend this weekend at the beach."

The priest tells (or should tell) the couple, "Artificial contraception is a sin," and they counter, "Yes, but we can't afford to have a child ... not if we want maintain our present lifestyle."

Jesus said ...

> Amen, amen I say unto you: Except you eat the
> flesh of the Son of man, and drink his blood, you
> shall not have life in you.
>
> —St. John VI:54

... and the people said, as did their Protestant descendants,
"Yes, but ..."

> ... This saying is hard, and who can hear it?
> —St. John VI:61

"Yes, but ..."

The half-hearted acknowledgment followed by the clever
objection; apparent agreement then qualified by the manipu-
lative appeal to reason. You and I do it whenever we're confronted with that which goes against our precious grain. This
"Yes, but ..." tendency permeates our sinful nature, and is
aggravated to new heights by our society's deification of preoccupation with our own viewpoint. "I've got a right to my
own opinion," we are encouraged to say. "Mine's as good as
yours." We are a nation of "Yes, buts."

The Catholic Faith, however, is not an opinion. It is Revealed Truth. It is not a smorgasbord of steaming dishes from
which we can freely choose according to our acquired tastes.
It is not a marketplace of on-sale, buy-one get-one-free,
prices-subject-to-change-without-notice merchandise. The
Church was instituted by Christ as a vehicle for our Salvation,
and we are required to believe *all* that She teaches. Repeat:
all. This is not a call to mindlessness, but a command to acknowledge that if we believe in Jesus Christ, we must accept all
that He did and taught, including the establishment of His
Church under Peter and his successors:

> And I say unto thee: That thou art Peter; and upon
> this rock I will build my church, and the gates of hell
> shall not prevail against it.
> And I will give thee the keys of the kingdom of
> heaven. And whatsoever thou shalt bind upon earth,
> it shall be bound also in heaven: and whatsoever thou
> shalt loose on earth, it shall be loosed also in heaven.
> —St. Matthew XVI:18-19

There is no room within the bosom of Holy Mother Church for "Yes, buts." As Her children, we must accept and obey Her official teachings and mandates. It is only logical, since She was founded by Jesus Christ Himself.

I'm anticipating the lawyers among my readers: "Yes, but are we then to turn our minds off and stop thinking?" It is not a matter of thinking or not thinking, though these limits are the boundaries of the carnal man's comprehension. The devout man, on the other hand, through his commitment to prayer comes to understand that some things are beyond the purview of his questions. With respect to the world he knows he must practice meticulous caution and scrutiny:

> Behold I send you as sheep in the midst of wolves.
> Be ye therefore wise as serpents and simple as doves.
> —St. Matthew X:16

With respect to the Church, he must exercise trust, for he accepts that the truth is Hers, not his, to discern:

> Further, by divine and Catholic faith, all those things must be believed which are contained in the written word of God and in tradition, and those which are proposed by the Church, either in a solemn pronouncement or in her ordinary and universal teaching power, to be believed as divinely revealed.
> —The First Vatican Council, 1869-1870
> Dogmatic Constitution
> concerning the Catholic Faith
> (Denzinger 1792)

Though it may ruffle our feathers, rankle our egos, and stick in our huffy throats, we are required to accept the whole Catholic thing. With respect to the Faith, we have a responsibility to purge the "Yes, but" tendency from our systems. From the Immaculate Conception to the Incarnation to the Ascension to the Assumption; from the command not to tell lies to the proscription against homosexual activity to submission to the *ex cathedra* definitions of the Popes in matters of Faith and Morals, the body of all things Catholic forms an intricate latticework of interconnected counter-balanced and mutually supportive Truths.

In the next several chapters we will examine this unsettling but necessary business in detail, and hopefully see the Wisdom in trusting Jesus and His Church. This needs to be clearly understood and settled in our minds. We tempt God when he dare to say, "Yes, but I can't accept this or that."

One day each of us will be called before His throne. Imagine what parable He has in store for those who can only say, "Y-y-yes, b-b-but ..."

CHAPTER FORTY-ONE

A CERTAIN MAN WENT DOWN ...

> It would be a grievous mistake were we to suppose
> that the parables and sayings of Jesus Christ recorded
> in the Gospel had reference merely to those persons
> whom He addressed at the time; "for what things so-
> ever were written, were written for our learning."
> [Romans xv: 4] Hence it is that those to whom "it is
> given to know the mysteries of the kingdom of
> heaven," the members of the true Church of Christ
> well instructed in their religion, find a vast deal more
> of information in the sacred text than those without,
> to whom "it is not given, because seeing they see
> not, hearing they hear not, neither do they under-
> stand." [Matthew xiii:13]
> — Father Joseph Prachensky, SJ
> *Divine Parables Explained*

∞ ∞ ∞

SINCE I WAS A CHILD, I was always a little bit dissatisfied with
the wrap-up of the Good Samaritan story.   When Jesus con-
cluded his discussion with the lawyer—

> Which of these three, in thy opinion, was neighbor
> to him that fell among the robbers?
> But he said: He that shewed mercy to him. And Je-
> sus said to him: Go, and do thou in like manner.
> — St. Luke X:36-37

—it seemed to me that we are left with the impression that the
moral of the story is that "the man who shows you mercy is

your neighbor." Remember that the Commandment under discussion was:

> Thou shalt love ... thy neighbor as thyself.
> —St. Luke X:27

—and the lawyer's precise question in this regard was:

> And who is my neighbor?
> —St. Luke X:29

—to which the lawyer's final conclusion was:

> He that shewed mercy.
> —St. Luke X:37

He that demonstrates mercy is your neighbor? How easy it is, I thought, to love someone who treats you kindly. Where's the virtue in that? Wouldn't it have been more like Jesus to lead the lawyer to see that it was up to *him* to show mercy regardless of the response of the other person?

> But I say to you, Love your enemies: do good to them that hate you: and pray for them that persecute and calumniate you ...
> For if you love them that love you, what reward shall you have? do not even the publicans this?
> —St. Matthew V:44, 46

Yet no priest in the pulpit or classroom, in my experience, ever seemed to glean anything deeper out of the parable than precisely the opposite: "Be like the Good Samaritan: he loved his neighbor who was in trouble." Well and good as an example of moral behavior, but the question Christ asked was, "Which of these ... was neighbor to him that fell among the robbers?"—not the other way around.

I was recently relieved to find that my question regarding this denouement was not unique to me:

> Were we to adhere to the mere words of this parable, it would seem to follow, that only those who do us good were to be esteemed our neighbors; for the

context seems to intimate, that the Levite and the
priest were not neighbors to the man who fell among
the robbers, because they did not assist him. But according to the opinion of most fathers, the intent of
this parable is to shew, that every person who has
need of our assistance is our neighbor.

> —Maldonatus
> Haydock Footnotes
> *Douay-Rheims Bible*

As is often the case, we must not take verses out of context. The reason Jesus didn't press the issue can be found in
the things He had said just before the lawyer stood up to
challenge Him in the first place:

> In that same hour, he rejoiced in the Holy Ghost,
> and said: I confess to thee, O Father, Lord of heaven
> and earth, because thou hast hidden these things from
> the wise and the prudent, and hast revealed them to
> little ones.
>
> —St. Luke X:21

From what we've learned about this lawyer, he would
hardly have considered himself to be among the "little ones."
As Saint Paul would later write in one of his Epistles:

> The sensual man perceiveth not these things that
> are of the Spirit of God: for it is foolishness to him,
> and he cannot understand: because it is spiritually ex-
> amined.
>
> —I Corinthians II:14

The lawyer was such a man. All he gained from the parable of the Good Samaritan was the obvious truth, that we are
beholding to those who are kind to us. This, along with being
deflated by Jesus' keen rebuttal, was more than enough for
him to deal with.

But for the others present who honestly desired to understand things on a deeper, more spiritual and less carnal level,
Jesus had this to say:

> Blessed are the eyes that see the things which you
> see.
> For I say to you, that many prophets and kings
> have desired to see the things that you see, and have
> not seen them; and to hear the things that you hear,
> and have not heard them.
>
> — St. Luke X:22-23

For them the parable of the Good Samaritan had a much richer meaning which was not spelled out by Saint Luke in his Gospel. We have to search the writings of the Fathers of the early Church for the fuller explanation—holy and honorable men such as Origen, Saint Jerome, Saint Ambrose, Saint Austin and the like. Let us take a closer look at this parable through their eyes.

> A certain man went down from Jerusalem to
> Jericho ...
>
> — St. Luke X:30

Jerusalem, the "City of Peace," was the center of religious worship for the Israelites. It was a holy city, a center of learning, a seat of knowledge and wisdom. Jericho, on the other hand, was historically a center of idol worship. Though only fifteen miles distant from Jerusalem as the crow flies, Jericho was located in the basin of the Dead Sea—3850 feet lower in elevation, almost 1300 feet below the level of the Mediterranean Sea. The Dead Sea was the site of two infamous cities destroyed by the wrath of God eighteen centuries before Christ.

> And the Lord rained upon Sodom and Gomorrha
> brimstone and fire from the Lord our of heaven.
> And he destroyed these cities, and all the country
> about, all the inhabitants of the cities, and all things
> that spring from the earth.
>
> — Genesis XIX:24-25

The Dead Sea basin was the pit left behind, some 1300 feet deep, which slowly filled with salt water. It was, and remains, a lifeless scar on the land, and the lowest land elevation on the globe. When God pours forth His fury, beware.

The road from Jerusalem to Jericho was a steeply descending, zigzagging trail that was known to be a haven for robbers and bandits. And down this treacherous road went " a certain man"—not just any man, or Everyman, but a *particular* man.

The man was Adam.

Jerusalem represented the terrestrial paradise in which God placed the first Man, who was in total harmony with himself, with God, with his wife, and with nature. On his own volition, Adam set out for Jericho, the seat of idolatry. The serpent had promised that upon eating the forbidden fruit ...

> ... your eyes shall be opened: and you shall be as Gods ...
>
> —Genesis III:5

Adam and Eve had chosen to worship themselves as idols, rather than God. So Adam set out on a downward journey from Jerusalem to Jericho, from righteous perfection to the depravity of sin ...

> ... and fell among robbers, who also stripped him, and having wounded him, went away leaving him half dead.
>
> —St. Luke X:30

In another Gospel, Jesus said of Satan:

> He was a murderer from the beginning, and he stood not in the truth; because the truth is not in him. When he speaketh a lie, he speaketh of his own: for he is a liar, and the father thereof.
>
> —St. John VIII:44

The robbers, then, were the demons of Hell, the minions of Satan, who seduced Adam to abandon Paradise, and then waged violence upon his person. Having lured him away from God, they stripped him of his spiritual clothing, his harmony with his Creator and with his surroundings.

Consider the Creation of Man:

> And the Lord God formed man of the slime of the
> earth: and breathed into his face the breath of life, and
> man became a living soul.
>
> —Genesis II:7

The word "living" in relation to the "soul" is redundant, unless we perceive that there was a life granted the soul beyond mere natural life. When Adam fell his eternal soul became dead supernaturally, even though he continued to live physically. This is Original Sin, the state in which we all enter the world: spiritually dead.

So the demons stripped Adam of Grace, the life of the soul, and then wounded him by making his formerly harmonious body subject to disease, aging, and death. They roused his hungers and fired his passions. Worst of all, they darkened his intellect. So dim did Adam become that he forgot he was talking to an omniscient God, imagining he could hide himself from his Maker while attempting to excuse himself by blaming Eve.

> And the Lord God called Adam, and said to him:
> Where art thou?
> And he said: I heard they voice in paradise; and I
> was afraid, because I was naked, and I hid myself.
> And he said to him: And who hath told thee that
> thou wast naked, but that thou hast eaten of the tree
> whereof I commanded thee that thou shouldst not eat?
> And Adam said: The woman, whom thou gavest
> me to be my companion, gave me of the tree, and I
> did eat.
>
> —Genesis III:9-12

Having stripped and wounded him, the vicious robbers left Adam "half dead" on the road—not totally annihilated but dreadfully diminished. Too weak to crawl back to paradise, he was "on his own." At least he had the sense to call feebly for help. His plea was answered by the arrival of the priesthood and Levitical rites of the Old Covenant:

> And it happened that a certain priest went down the
> same way, and seeing him, passed by.

> In like manner, also, a Levite, when he was near
> the place and saw him, passed by.
>
> —St. Luke X:31-32

Unfortunately, they were traveling down the same road. The Law they represented testified that Man had fallen, but could not repair the damage. Their sacrifices could not atone for the sin of Adam, but nonetheless foreshadowed the arrival of a new High Priest whose offering would be acceptable to Almighty God. Ancient songs foretold the arrival of this new High Priest:

> The Lord hath sworn, and he will not repent: Thou
> art a priest for ever according to the order of Melchis-
> edech.
>
> —Psalm CIX:4

Upon His coming, Salvation would spread beyond the Israelites—indeed, it would be taken from them—and lavished upon the Gentiles:

> Who is there among you, that will shut the doors,
> and will kindle the fire on my altar, gratis? I have
> no pleasure in you, saith the Lord of hosts: and I will
> not receive a gift of your hand.
> For from the rising of the sun even to the going
> down, my name is great among the Gentiles, and in
> every place there is sacrifice, and there is offered to
> my name a clean oblation: for my name is great
> among the Gentiles, saith the Lord of hosts.
>
> —Malachias I:10-11

These verses are obviously prophetic because at the time they were written the only people who knew to offer Solemn Sacrifice to the One True God were the descendants of Abraham. As Israel lost Faith, God would turn His salvific gaze on the Gentiles. Whereas under the Old Covenant there was only the one Altar of Sacrifice, the New would bring about many Sacrifices on many Altars.

> Now on looking around we find every circumstance
> of this remarkable prophecy literally fulfilled. The

Jewish sacrifices have ceased; the Jewish people are scattered all over the earth; they have ... no priesthood, no altar, no sacrifice. The second part of the prophecy is also fulfilled. At the Last Supper, our Lord Jesus Christ, the promised Redeemer, instituted a new and pure and perfect sacrifice—that of His Sacred Body and Blood, which he substituted for the typical sacrifices of the Old Law. And now this adorable and perfect sacrifice of Our Lord's Body and Blood is offered up all over the world, at every hour of the day and every part of the night, "from the rising to the setting of the sun."

—Father Michael Müller, C.SS.R.
The Holy Sacrifice of the Mass

In other words, four hundred years before the time of Christ, the prophet Malachias foretold the rise and spread of the Catholic Church.

Ah, but we have gotten ahead of ourselves. Poor Adam is still lying on the road, stripped, wounded, and half-dead.

But never fear. Help is on the way.

CHAPTER FORTY-TWO

... AND ANOTHER MAN CAME ALONG ...

> But a certain Samaritan being on his journey, came
> near him: and seeing him, was moved with compas-
> sion ...
>
> —St. Luke X:33

∞ ∞ ∞

A "CERTAIN MAN" WENT DOWN from Jerusalem to Jericho. That particular man was Adam. Who then was the "certain Samaritan" who came along and helped Adam after the robbers from Hell stripped him, wounded him, and left him half dead?

During a different discussion in another Gospel, we find an interesting exchange between some detractors and the Lord Jesus Christ:

> The Jews, therefore, answered, and said to him: Do
> we not say well that thou art a Samaritan, and hast a
> devil?
> Jesus answered: I have not a devil: but I honour my
> Father, and you have dishonoured me.
>
> —St. John VIII:48-49

So bitter was the religious rivalry between the Jews and the Samaritans, that calling Him such was considered a gross insult. Notice, however, that while He dismissed the charge of demon possession, He did not deny their first accusation. As misunderstood and maligned as He invariably was at every turn, He had much in common with the Samaritans—indeed, He identified with them.

In another situation, He was in the city of Sichar, formerly called Sichem, where He had a conversation with a Samaritan woman at Jacob's Well. Sichar was located on the flank of Mount Garazim, and was the capital of Samaria. The Samaritans, who along with the Jews claimed lineage from Abraham, worshipped God on Mount Garazim rather than in Jerusalem, and not without precedent, because we read in the Old Testament:

> And all the people, and the ancients, and the princes, and judges, stood on both sides of the ark, before the priests that carried the ark of the convenant of the Lord ... half of them by Mount Garazim, and half by Mount Hebal, as Moses, the servant of the Lord, had commanded.
>
> —Josue VIII:33

In other words, the Samaritans were attached to a more ancient site, one which Moses himself had designated long before King David established Jerusalem as the center of Hebrew worship. This formed the basis of the woman's challenge to Jesus as a Jew:

> How dost thou, being a Jew, ask of me to drink, who am a Samaritan woman? For the Jews to not communicate with the Samaritans...
> Our fathers adored on this mountain, and you say that at Jerusalem is the place where men must adore.
>
> —St. John IV:9, 20

But Jesus did not address the issue of His Jewishness, nor refute her assumption that He was a Samaritan. In fact, His answer transcended the whole "which-mountain-is-it?" issue:

> Woman, believe me, that the hour cometh when you shall neither on this mountain, nor in Jerusalem, adore the Father.
> You adore that which you know not: we adore that which we know: for salvation is of the Jews.

> But the hour cometh, and now is, when the true
> adorers shall adore the Father in spirit and in truth.
> For the Father also seeketh such to adore him.
> God is a spirit, and they that adore him, must adore
> him in spirit and in truth.
> The woman saith to him: I know that the Messias
> cometh (who is called Christ); therefore when he is
> come, he will tell us all things.
> Jesus saith to her: I am he, who am speaking with
> thee.
> —St. John IV:21-23

As we have seen repeatedly, Jesus cannot be brought down to our level. By declaring neither mountain important, by discounting the importance of Jew vs. Samaritan, by declaring Himself the Messias, He was laying the groundwork for the establishment of His Church, which would be Universal. The old structures, which had given way before, as when Garazim was surmounted by Jerusalem, would give way again.

Therefore, it should come as no surprise that in the Parable of the Good Samaritan, it is indeed Jesus Christ who is " a certain Samaritan." As such, when He came along and saw the naked, wounded Adam—in whom is incorporated the entire human race—He did not concern Himself with whether the man was Jewish, Samaritan, Gentile or whatever nationality—nor did such things matter to the beaten man in his desperate plight.

> By this our Divine Lord teaches that charity, to be
> true charity, must be universal—that is catholic; if it
> make distinctions on account of kindred or national-
> ity, even of religion, it no longer deserves the name
> of charity: for to exclude any one who is needy, under
> such a pretext, is truly uncharitable.
> —Father Joseph Prachensky
> *Divine Parables Explained*

This "certain Samaritan," as it happened, was on an expedition of His own:

> But a certain Samaritan being on his journey ...
> —St. Luke X:33

God had become a Man, and as such was sharing our experiences, our infirmities, and our physical weaknesses. The span of His journey was limited to thirty-three years, just as our lifetimes fall within specific time parameters. His mission was indeed a humble one:

> But he debased himself, taking the form of a servant, being made to the likeness of men, and in shape found as a man.
> He humbled himself, becoming obedient unto death, even the death of the cross.
> —Philippians II:7-8

So Jesus, the traveler, came upon broken, defeated, fallen Man:

> ... and seeing him, was moved with compassion.
> —St. Luke X:33

What so moved Jesus? Was it Man's great accomplishments, his high-rise buildings, his scientific discoveries, his socio-political institutions, his endless preoccupation with himself, his gluttonous indulgence in his own desires—all the things touted as the "glory of Man" then and in our present age? Hardly. If Man were such a remarkable success, if he was indeed as self-reliant as he supposed himself to be, Jesus would have passed on. There would have been no need for Him to stop along the way, to take time out from His own journey. Rather:

> He saw the pitiful state into which sin had plunged the human race; and this excessive misery, which no one could fathom better than Himself, moved Him to compassion. He saw man stripped of the sanctifying grace of God, that nuptial garment of heavenly innocence without which no one can be ad-

mitted to the nuptials of the Lamb ... He saw him
stripped of all those supernatural gifts wherewith his
Creator endowed him, without any means on his part
to recover them.

—Father Joseph Prachensky
Divine Parables Explained

God allowed man to wallow in his dreary state for thousands of years before He came in person to intervene. It took
that long ...

... to convince this proud faculty of the soul that it
was morally insufficient of itself and needed light
from above.

—Father Joseph Prachensky
Divine Parables Explained

... for the enormity of the Serpent's lie...

... you shall be as Gods ...

—Genesis III:5

... to sink through the collective thick skull of mankind, and
even at that, the lesson was lost on the vast majority of people.

Fallen Man needed outside help, assistance from Someone
higher and stronger than himself. When Jesus Christ came
along, He was not going in the same direction as Adam, He
was not descending from Jerusalem to Jericho, from holiness
to depravity. He did not fall among robbers, nor give in to the
temptations of the flesh.

For it was fitting that we should have such a High-
Priest, holy, innocent, undefiled, separated from sinners, and higher than the heavens.

—Hebrews VII:26

His descent was from glory to humility; and at the end of His journey He would return to the glory that was rightfully His:

> And no man hath ascended into heaven, but he that descended from heaven, the Son of man, who is in heaven.
> —St. John III:13

Since no man can ascend to Heaven except the One who descended from it, namely Jesus, the only hope for Man was to somehow become united with Jesus so that he, too, could ascend with Him to Life Eternal in Heaven. But first things first. Man was broken and bleeding. Jesus had to see to Man's immediate needs:

> And going up to him, bound up his wounds ...
> —St. Luke X:34

The wounds inflicted upon Man were real, whether Man admitted the reality of his soul and the ravages of Sin upon it or not. He was bleeding to death, and the flow had to be stopped lest he perish.

> We have seen that these wounds were inflicted upon the natural faculties of the soul. The intellect was wounded, and bled errors during four thousand years; the memory was wounded, for it was weakened, and retained sensual and sinful impressions much more easily than spiritual and holy ideas; the will was wounded, for it was inclined to evil, refused to obey, and followed the impulse of its own evil inclinations rather than the dictates of reason and the holy will of God. Jesus Christ, the Good Samaritan, binds up these wounds when He binds the intellect, that restless faculty, to submit to faith and to believe the truth which He teaches, whether this limited intellect understands it or not. It must be sufficient for every created intellect to know that God said so to oblige it to comply—not only not to contradict the assertion, but not even to doubt what God says. Would to God our non-Catholic brethren would bear in mind this

> truth and give it their utmost attention! This would
> put an end to their vaunted privilege of private inter-
> pretation of the word of God. All right to discussion
> about the truth is confined to the simple question
> whether God said so or not, and not if this or that
> doctrine of Christ is true, or how it is to be explained
> in order to be understood; for if God said so it must
> be true, and even if I cannot explain how it is so,
> nevertheless it must be true when God has said so.
>
> —Father Joseph Prachensky
> *Divine Parables Explained*

Jesus well knew that some men are smart, and others not so; that some are clever, some are dullards; that some people revel in intellectual pursuits and the unraveling of hidden mysteries while others haven't the time, ability, or patience for such things. The keener the intellect, the wider a man may lead himself astray; but all of us are prone to foolishness to some degree. Even so, *all men and women are capable of believing what God says,* even if they do not fully understand it ...

> ... bringing into captivity every understanding to
> the obedience of Christ.
>
> —II Corinthians X:5

Much as we may fight it, for indeed we have been pains-takingly trained to do so by our society, we are not the final arbiters of Truth. There comes a point when we are required to submit our intellects to the Higher Authority, to the Good Samaritan who came along and bound our wounds. If we do not, our restless intellects will continue to flutter and flap like so many frantic winged things caught in a bleak and treacher-ous cave, and meanwhile we will die from dehydration as our pounding hearts continue to pump blood out of our unat-tended wounds. The demand that we submit our wills to Him is not—repeat, not—a call to mindlessness, but a directive to make a fundamental decision with regard to Jesus Christ and then live by it.

Again and again we return to "square one." And now, more than ever, as we proceed with the story of the Good Sa-maritan, we must gird ourselves with the realization that:

> Thou art Christ, the Son of the living God.
> — St. Matthew XVI:16

We must listen ever so carefully to what Jesus is telling us in this Parable, for on it hangs our possibility for Salvation.

> And going up to him, bound up his wounds, pouring in oil and wine ...
> — St. Luke X:34

Oil and wine were unlikely medicines for external wounds. Oil—or more so butter—might be a folk remedy for burns, but Adam was beaten, not scorched. Wine hasn't the alcoholic content to be truly antiseptic, so was an odd choice as an unguent for abrasions, lacerations, and bruises. No, the oil and wine which the Good Samaritan poured in the wounds were not physical medicines, but were rather the Sacraments that Jesus would institute. Wine, of course, is a reference to His Blood, which would be shed on the Cross and then commemorated in the Transubstantiation of the Wine at Mass. Oil is Sacramentally associated with healing, especially in Extreme Unction:

> And he called the twelve; and began to send them two and two ...
> And going forth they preached that they should do penance:
> And they cast out many devils, and anointed with oil many that were sick, and healed them.
> — St. Mark VI:7, 12-13

> Is any man sick among you? Let him bring in the priests of the church, and let them pray over him, anointing him with oil, in the name of the Lord:
> And the prayer of faith shall save the sick man: and the Lord shall raise him up: and if he be in sins, they shall be forgiven him.
> — St. James V:14-15

Oil also represents mercy and strength, and is so used in the Rites of Baptism, Confirmation, and Holy Orders.

The Good Samaritan, Jesus Christ, provided the spiritual unguents necessary for the healing of Man's wounds. Thus did He demonstrate the depths of His compassion.

> ... and setting him upon his own beast ...
> —St. Luke X:34

Man is a remarkable union of body and soul, the physical and the spiritual. His body, with all its material needs, belongs to the animal kingdom. To become truly one of us, Jesus took upon Himself this human body, this animal nature. This is "His own beast"—His very Body. In receiving the Holy Eucharist, Man takes into himself and is therefore joined to Jesus' human and divine natures.

> He that eateth my flesh, and drinketh my blood, abideth in me, and I in him.
> As the living Father hath sent me, and I live by the Father: so he that eateth me, the same also shall live by me.
> —St. John VI:57-58

Or, to paraphrase:

> As I, the Son of God, live by the Father, being one substance and essence with Him, and existing by Him, *so he that eateth Me,* the Son of God made man, shall be made one with Me, and *shall live by Me.*
> —Father Joseph Prachensky
> *Divine Parables Explained*

This is further expressed in the Mass when the priest adds water to the chalice of wine:

> O God, who hast established the nature of man in wondrous dignity and even more wondrously hast renewed it, grant that through the mystery of this water and wine, we may be made partakers of His divinity, who has deigned to become partaker of our humanity,

Jesus Christ, Thy Son, our Lord, who liveth and
reigneth with Thee, in the union of the Holy Ghost,
God, world without end. Amen.
—The Offertory of the Tridentine Mass

Jesus' physical Body did not cease when He ascended into
Heaven. His Body continues forward through Eternity, and is
shared with the Faithful in the Eucharist, the Source of Life
for those who receive it. Just as God provided manna for the
nourishment of the Chosen People in the desert, so does He
provide His Flesh and Blood to sustain us on our journey.

But that is not all that He did for fallen Man. Not by a
long shot ...

CHAPTER FORTY-THREE

... AND BROUGHT HIM TO AN INN

> ... and setting him upon his own beast, brought
> him to an inn, and took tare of him.
> —St. Luke X:34

∞ ∞ ∞

BY NOW IT SHOULD BE OBVIOUS that the Inn to which the Good Samaritan brought fallen Man was Christ's Holy Church. Jesus' "own journey" was only to last thirty-three years. So, having established the Sacraments to heal the wounds inflicted on Man by the minions of Hell, He chose to protect and preserve these Divine Remedies within the structure of the Catholic Church. In this way Man would continue to have access to them after He returned to the Father.

While Jesus remained on earth, He "took care of him"—him being fallen Man. He preached the Truth, healed the sick, taught His Apostles, and formulated the Sacraments. But He did not come among us only to instruct, but to die.

> Amen, amen I say to you, unless the grain of
> wheat falling into the ground die,
> Itself remaineth alone. But if it die, it bringeth
> forth much fruit.
> —St. John XII:24-25

The span of Jesus' natural life on earth was all represented by the day the Good Samaritan found and administered to the Man in the Parable. That day ended with His death on the Cross. But, breaking the chains of death, He rose gloriously from the tomb:

And the next day he took out two pence, and gave
to the host, and said: Take care of him ...
                                                —St. Luke X:35

The next day—that is, the day of His Resurrection—He
went to His Apostles to give them the "two pence" with which
they were to continue the care of Man:

> ... Jesus came and stood in the midst, and said to
> them: Peace be to you.
> And when he had said this, he shewed them his
> hands and his side. The disciples therefore were glad,
> when they saw the Lord.
> He said therefore to them again: Peace be to you.
> As the Father hath sent me, I also send you.
> When he had said this, he breathed on them; and he
> said to them: Receive ye the Holy Ghost.
> Whose sins you shall forgive, they are forgiven
> them; and whose sins you shall retain, they are re-
> tained.
>   —St. John XX:19-23

From the storehouse of Christ's mercies, He produces two
precious coins: the power to loose, and the power to bind sins.
To loose sins, that is, to absolve them, is an obvious mercy. To
refuse to absolve may seem at first harsh unless we step back
and view the larger picture, that charity is served more by ad-
monishing a sinner that his repentance is insincere than by
allowing him to "get by" with insufficient contrition. Refusal
of absolution is sometimes the tart medicine needed to snap
someone out of sweet self-delusion. Some medicines sting,
some soothe, but all real medications promote healing.

This was a reiteration, as well as a telescoping, of the loos-
ing and binding powers Jesus had already conferred on *the
Host* of the Inn, namely Saint Peter and His Successors to the
Papal Office:

> And I say to thee: That thou art Peter; and upon
> this rock I will build my church, and the gates of hell
> shall not prevail against it.

And I will give to thee the keys of the kingdom of
heaven. And whatsoever thou shalt bind upon earth,
it shall be bound also in heaven: and whatsoever thou
shalt loose upon the earth, it shall be loosed in
heaven.
                                        —St. Matthew XVI:18-19

Because Peter was the first to recognize and acknowledge
that Jesus was indeed the Christ, the Son of the Living God
(thus establishing and giving us "square one") he was
granted supremacy over the Church. The other Apostles became subordinate to him, as all succeeding bishops are subordinate to their pope.   Regarding the power of loosing or
binding, Tirinus wrote:

> The power of binding is exercised, 1st. by refusing
> to absolve; 2d. by enjoining penance for sins for-
> given; 3d. by excommunication, suspension or inter-
> dict; 4th. by making rules and laws for the govern-
> ment of the Church; 5th. by determining what is of
> faith by the judgments and definitions of the Church.
>   —Haydock Footnotes
>   *Douay-Rheims Bible*

Thus the structure and organization of the Church was
implemented by Jesus Himself, a blend of the human and the
divine. To this Church headed by the pope, this Inn run by
the Host, Jesus left the care of fallen Man:

> And the next day he took out two pence, and gave
> them to the host, and said: Take care of him; and
> whatsoever thou shalt spend over and above, I at my
> return will repay thee.
>   —St. Luke X:35

Jesus promised to return at the end of history and repay
each of the caretakers according to his works.

The Church, then, is the ongoing provision left by Jesus
Christ for the healing and nurturing of fallen Man. It is here
that he will find solace, nourishment, guidance, and ultimately
Salvation:

An inn is a place of shelter for the accommodation
of travelers. If hungry, thirsty, or weary, they are refreshed there; if sick, they are taken care of until able
to continue their journey ...

This *inn* is His holy Church which He has established in this land of our pilgrimage; here He leads
fallen man whom He wishes to save, to be guided, as
well as healed and nourished ... Fear not, then, you
who seek the truth with sincerity, though wounded in
every faculty and stripped of every supernatural gift;
still if you hunger and thirst after justice, this good
God who wills the salvation of all men will certainly
lead you to this unfailing asylum, which the storms
of time can never shatter, because He Himself has
erected it, not upon the quicksands of human opinion
about the truth, producing nothing but discord and division, and causing at length the total ruin of the
building, but upon a solid rock, chosen and consoli-
dated by Himself for that purpose, so that even "the
gates of hell shall not prevail against it." [St. John
vii. 33.]

—Father Joseph Prachensky
Divine Parables Explained

This, then, is the meaning of the Parable of the Good Samaritan that was lost on the lawyer who was too busy justifying himself to see the bigger picture. He walked away self-
assured, and satisfied with only a fraction of the Truth. Small
wonder that in our present day, an age that thrives on "ques-
tioning everything" and celebrating the supremacy of the almighty "I," the true meaning of this story has been all but
lost. Luckily the works of the early Fathers have been preserved for our benefit, for to them it was all perfectly clear.

Of course, the ramifications of this Truth are another
story. If Jesus set up this Church to be the provider of His
Remedy for Adam's Fall, what of those who choose not to
stay at the Inn?

Suppose, now, that one of the patients whom the
good Samaritan brought to the inn became dissatisfied, and, gathering together the little strength he had,
crawled away from the inn, and, with a medical book

under his arm, said to himself: "I do not want to stay any longer in that place, nor will I be any longer under the care and treatment of that host and his inferior officers. No one shall inspect my wounds or prescribe remedies for me; I care not for their *wine* and *oil,* or anything else they have to cure me. I have my book, which contains prescriptions for all my evils. If I read it every day, and trust in the goodness and mercy of the good Samaritan, I shall be cured." What, dear reader, would you say or think of such a patient? Well, the same thing can be said of all those who left the true and living Church of Jesus Christ, rejected her sacraments and the authority of her visible head, protested against her teaching and laws as being strict and binding on the conscience, believing themselves safe and their salvation secure if they but read the Bible and trusted the Savior.

—Father Joseph Prachensky
Divine Parables Explained

In other words, Jesus only set up one Inn, one Church, one Host. As Saint Paul warned, we who are staying there must be ...

Careful to keep the unity of the Spirit in the bond of peace.

One body and one Spirit; as you are called in one hope of your calling.

One Lord, one faith, one baptism.

One God and Father of all, who is above all, and through all, and in us all.

—Ephesians IV:3-6

Yet there are many who would tell us that there are many inns, not one; and many faiths other than the one established by Christ Himself; and more than the one baptism specified by Christ—

He that believeth and is baptized, shall be saved: but he that believeth not shall be condemned.

—St. Mark XVI:16

> Amen, amen I say to thee, unless a man be born
> again of water and the Holy Ghost, he cannot enter
> into the Kingdom of God.
> > —St. John III:5

—as if He had somehow "left something out."   What can be
said of those who hold this opinion?

Here we come to the most difficult part of our expedition.
If we thought the way was long and wearying, the storm was
scary, the winding mountainous road was treacherous, we must
now face the fact that all that was mere preliminaries—just
warm-up exercises! Now we come to the fork in the road, the
place at which we either continue valiantly onward or fall back
out of cowardice or complacency.   The mettle of our Faith is
about to be tested, for our goal is Heaven, and ...

> There shall not enter into it any thing defiled, or
> that worketh abomination or maketh a lie, but they
> that are written in the book of life of the Lamb.
> > —The Apocalypse XXI:27

It is all well and good to embrace the Faith.   It is another
thing to endure persecution because of it.   The degree to
which we are willing to persist in the midst of the derision of
our friends and loved ones is a keen indicator of the depths of
our commitment.   And make no mistake, when Jesus said ...

> Peace be to you.   As the Father hath sent me, I
> also send you.
> > —St. John XX:21

... the peace of which he spoke was not the cessation of inter-
personal conflicts, but rather internal certitude and calm in the
midst of external turmoil.   He knew that His Message and
Doctrines would cause division, strife, and sorrow, which is
why He also promised:

> Amen, I say to you, there is no man that hath left
> house, or parents, or brethren, or wife, or children, for
> the kingdom of God's sake,
> Who shall not receive much more in this present
> time, and in the world to come life everlasting.
> —St. Luke XVIII:29-30

Surely this is not the message proclaimed by the modernists in the Church who would have us believe that we must strive for apparent peace and numbing complacency, to be "nice" at all costs. As we've observed before, someone is lying. Let us brave the next bend in the road and try to discover *who* ...

CHAPTER FORTY-FOUR

THE HOST SPEAKS

And so do we ... teach and explain that the dogma
has been divinely revealed that the Roman Pontiff,
when he speaks *ex cathedra,* that is, when carrying
out the duty of the pastor and teacher of all Christians
in accord with his supreme apostolic authority he ex-
plains a doctrine of faith or morals to be held by the
universal Church, through the divine assistance promised him in blessed Peter, operates with that infallibility with which the divine Redeemer wished that
His church be instructed in defining doctrine on faith
and morals; and so such definitions of the Roman
Pontiff from himself, but not from the consensus of
the Church, are unalterable.

But if anyone presumes to contradict this definition
of Ours, which may God forbid: let him be anathema.
— The First Vatican Council, 1869-1870
Dogmatic Constitution I on the Church of Christ
(Denzinger: 1839, 1840)

∞ ∞ ∞

PAPAL INFALLIBILITY.
There, the words have been uttered. Most peo-
ple—especially Catholics these days—dislike them intensely,
scoff at them contemptuously, or, embarrassed, avoid them
entirely; even though they really don't know what they mean
nor have any intention of finding out. This kind of non-
integrated attitude is typical of the modern mind, concerned as
it is with self-aggrandizement and abusive as it is toward anything that suggests humility as a more viable alternative.

The opening quotation, which defines this uncomfortably controversial term, should be read carefully several times before we proceed.

Done? Okay. We need to be spotlessly clear as to exactly what it says and what it doesn't say. First, papal infallibility does *not* mean that the pope is impeccable, that is, without flaw. It does *not* suggest that he is always right, good, fair, proficient at chess, or particularly trustworthy. He can make mistakes. Indeed, the pope can be very, very wrong with respect to personal opinions, administrative decisions, political appointments, and even his own understanding of theology. Shortly after having been told that he was the rock upon which Christ would build His Church, Peter demonstrated this salient point:

> From that time Jesus began to shew to his disciples, that he must go to Jerusalem, and suffer many things from the ancients and scribes and chief priests, and be put to death, and the third day rise again.
>
> And Peter taking him, began to rebuke him, saying: Lord, be it far from thee, this shall not be unto thee.
>
> Who turning, said to Peter: Go behind me, Satan, thou art a scandal unto me: because thou savorest not the things that are of God, but the things that are of men.
>
> —St. Matthew XVI:21-23

Two chapters prior to this exchange, Peter had walked on the water. (We examined the event in detail back in our own Chapter 10.) At the end of that memorable voyage he had accepted on faith Jesus' teaching that—

> Except you eat the flesh of the Son of man, and drink his blood, you shall not have life in you.
> —St. John VI:54

—my point being that, of all the Apostles, Peter should have by now begun to learn to see the teachings of Christ through spiritual rather than carnal eyes. Yet, when Jesus explained the need for His own death as the means by which fallen mankind would be redeemed, Peter objected. He had fallen back into thinking in immediates and tangibles, and Jesus took him to task for it.

Papal infallibility does *not* mean that we must assume that the Pope is always right in whatever he does and says, and that we must follow him without question. For example, if we had been at Peter's side on the night of Jesus' trial, we would have witnessed the following:

> But Peter sat without in the court: and there came to him a servant maid, saying: Thou also wast with Jesus the Galilean.
>
> But he denied before them all, saying: I know not what thou sayest.
>
> And as he went out of the gate, another maid saw him, and she saith to them that were there: This man also was with Jesus of Nazareth.
>
> And again he denied with an oath: I know not the man.
>
> And after a little while they came that stood by, and said to Peter: Surely thou also art one of them; for even they speech doth discover thee.
>
> Then he began to curse and to swear that he knew not the man. And immediately the cock crew.
>
> And Peter remembered the word of Jesus which he had said: Before the cock crow, thou wilt deny me thrice. And going forth, he wept bitterly.
>
> —St. Matthew XXVI:69-77

If we, standing behind him and recognizing him as Pope, followed his lead and joined in his denial of Christ, we would be just as guilty of mortal sin as he. We would be equally accountable before God at the Throne of Judgment.

> It is written (Acts v. 29): *We ought to obey God rather than men.* Now sometimes the things commanded by a superior are against God. Therefore superiors are not to be obeyed in all things ...
>
> —Saint Thomas Aquinas
> *Summa Theologica*
> vol. III, Q. 104, art. 5

Our primary responsibility always rests with God. Hence the idea that we can or must always follow the moral example of any given pope is an attempt to mitigate personal responsibility; and it won't work. There have occasionally been—far less frequently than our detractors would have us believe, but still—rotten popes, unscrupulous or downright wicked men sitting on Peter's Chair. Such a situation demands a great deal of patience, prayers, and Faith on the part of all Catholics. We must always remember that the pope is a man, and therefore subject to human weakness. (Consider: do we really think we would do any better than he?) We must pray for God's mercy on his behalf. However, and this is important: just because he makes mistakes does not illegalize his papacy, nor does it give us license to decide for ourselves that he isn't really the pope just because he isn't doing what we think he should.

There is an old saying in the Church:

Qui mange le Pape, mort.
He who eats the Pope, dies.

Gulp!* A rather descriptive injunction, to say the least. The same principle, though stated with saintly sweetness, would be as follows:

> Even if the Pope were Satan incarnate, we ought not to raise up our heads against him, but calmly lie down to rest on his bosom ... He who rebels against our Father, Christ-on-earth, is condemned to death, for that which we do to him we do to Christ in Heaven: we honor Christ if we honor the Pope; we dishonor Christ if we dishonor the Pope...
> —Saint Catherine of Siena
> Quoted in the *Apostolic Digest*

We haven't the right to *slander* the Vicar of Christ. By virtue of his office, he should at least expect our respect. If he errs, he has a Greater to account to than we the Faithful—of that we can rest assured. No matter what he does or fails to do, we must pray consistently for him. Basic charity demands no

---

* This is, of course, the sound of uncanny consternation, rather than culinary satisfaction.

less, and concern for the welfare of the Church should demand even more.

> We do not belong to the Church because of pope or
> hierarchy: we may like them or dislike them, but they
> are not the point. If we think they are handling the
> Church outrageously, our first instinctive reaction
> should be grief for Christ whose work they are dam-
> aging, whose face they are obscuring. In that feeling
> we should make our protest—very much as St. John
> Fisher could say, "If the Pope does not reform the
> Curia, God will," yet die on the headsman's block for
> Papal Supremacy.
>
> —Frank Sheed
> *What Difference Does Jesus Make?*

The subjects of obedience, deference and respect can get
sticky, and should be approached with reverence and only after heaping helpings of devout prayer—never with proud undertones and self-fulfilling agendas. Nonetheless, and lest we
wander further from the original intention of this chapter, the
point here is that papal infallibility—when properly understood—is limited to a very specific arena, the one defined by
Jesus Himself, included in the power to loose and bind. We
must always harken back to "square one" and remind ourselves that it was Jesus Himself who established the Papacy and
guaranteed its infallibility through the protection of the Holy
Ghost.

> And I say to thee: That thou art Peter; and upon
> this rock I will build my church, and the gates of hell
> shall not prevail against it.
> And I will give to thee the keys of the kingdom of
> heaven. And whatsoever thou shalt bind upon earth,
> it shall be bound also in heaven: and whatsoever thou
> shalt loose upon the earth, it shall be loosed in
> heaven.
>
> —St. Matthew XVI:18-19

> This is now the third time that Jesus was mani-
> fested to his disciples, after he was risen from the
> dead.

> When therefore they had dined, Jesus saith to
> Simon Peter: Simon, son of John, lovest thou me?
> He saith to him: Yea, Lord, thou knowest that I love
> thee. He saith to him: Feed my lambs.
> —St. John XXI:14-15

The pope, as dogmatically defined, has the power to speak *ex cathedra*, which means, "from the throne." Hence, in matters of dispute or when clarification of some point of doctrine is required, he is protected by the Holy Ghost from error when he addresses the whole Church—that is, all believers in all Catholic Rites in all regions on earth—in his official capacity as Vicar, that is, Representative of Christ. This is the limit and extent of his infallibility. It only "kicks in" when the need arises—it is not some kind of infused virtue which permeates his being and protects him from the sinful acts and negligences that plague us all.

An example of such a need is recounted in the New Testament at a gathering of Apostles and elders in Jerusalem. Some there present insisted that those wishing to become Christians essentially had to first become Jews.

> But there arose some of the sect of the Pharisees
> that believed, saying: They must be circumcised, and
> be commanded to observe the law of Moses.
> And the apostles and ancients assembled to consider
> of this matter.
> And when there had been much disputing, Peter,
> rising up, said to them ...
> —The Acts of the Apostles XV:5-7

After all opinions were laid on the table, Peter stood up and settled the matter with a rather lengthy speech, thus setting the lofty tone and prolix texture of most such pronouncements down through the ages. Nonetheless, when Peter spoke, the Church listened—there was no further room for discussion.

> We have a rock of refuge in Peter, who alone has
> the absolute right of deciding in the place of God, be-
> cause he alone has the keys of Heaven. Therefore, all
> his definitions bind as coming from the Vicar of

> Christ.   Whosoever shall not abide by his instruc-
> tions is a heretic.
>
> > —Council of Chalcedon
> > Quoted in the *Apostolic Digest*

It cannot be overemphasized that when the pope speaks *ex cathedra* all Catholics are required to accept his teaching as the Truth.

Let us take a more recent example of an *ex cathedra* pronouncement.   Since the lifetime of Jesus Christ, the Immaculate Conception of the Blessed Virgin Mary has been an integral part of Catholic Tradition.   That She was conceived without the stain of Original Sin was taken for granted by most theologians and Saints.   Of course, there were those who did not agree:

> Part III, Question 27, Article 2: Whether the Blessed Virgin was Sanctified before Animation?

> *I answer that:* The sanctification of the Blessed Virgin cannot be understood as having taken place before animation, for two reasons. First, because the sanctification of which we are speaking is nothing but the cleansing from original sin: for sanctification is a *perfect cleansing,* as Dionysius says *(Div. Nom. xii).* Now sin cannot be taken away except by grace, the subject of which is the rational creature alone. Therefore, before the infusion of the rational soul, the Blessed Virgin was not sanctified.

> Secondly, because since the rational creature alone can be the subject of sin; before the infusion of the rational soul, the offspring conceived is not liable to sin. And thus, in whatever manner the Blessed Virgin would have been sanctified before animation, she could never have incurred the stain of original sin: and thus she would not have needed redemption and salvation which is by Christ, of whom it is written (Matt. i, 21): *He shall save His people from their sins.* But this is unfitting, through implying that Christ is not the Savior of all men, as He is called (1 Tim. iv, 10).

It remains, therefore, that the Blessed Virgin was sanctified after animation.

Reply Obj. 4: Consequently ... she contracted original sin, since she was conceived by way of fleshly concupiscence and the intercourse of man and woman: for Augustine says *(De Nup. et Concup. i): All flesh born of carnal intercourse is sinful.*

—Saint Thomas Aquinas
Summa Theologica

Since the matter was not a papally defined Dogma, theologians were free to speculate. However, in 1854, all such conjecture and supposition ceased with the pronouncement of Pope Pius IX:

We declare, pronounce, and define that the doctrine, which holds that the most Blessed Virgin Mary at the first instant of her conception, by a singular grace and privilege of Almighty God, in virtue of the merits of Christ Jesus, the Savior of the human race, was preserved immaculate from all stain of original sin, has been revealed by God, and on this account must be firmly and constantly believed by all the faithful.

—Pope Pius IX
Ineffabilis Deus
(Denzinger: 1641)

Note the language and wording used: "We declare, pronounce, and define that the doctrine ... must be firmly and constantly believed by all the faithful." There can be no doubt that the pope was clarifying the teachings of the Church, as the head of the Church, to the entirety of the Church. There is no further need of theological deliberation and conjecture because the matter is settled. Peter has spoken. Thus, all dispute and speculation are to end. Continued appeals to Thomas Aquinas on the matter become inappropriate. Lest the finality of this pronouncement was lost on anyone, Pope Pius continued:

> Wherefore, if any should presume to think in their
> hearts otherwise than as it has been defined by Us,
> which God avert, let them know and understand that
> they are condemned by their own judgment; that they
> have suffered shipwreck in regard to faith, and have
> revolted from the unity of the Church; and what is
> more, that by their own act they subject themselves
> to the penalties established by law, if, what they
> think in their heart, they should dare to signify by
> word or writing or any other external means.

Theologians, academians, philosophers, teachers, beer-
and-pretzel elaborators and anyone else who justifies their existence by writhing tongues or wiggling pens are *not* free to
expound to the contrary.

If such a statement seems incompatible with the spirit of
"free inquiry" and the principles of "popular democracy"
... it is. When it comes to matters of the Faith, the majority
does not rule. Popular opinion is of no consequence. When
the pope speaks "from the throne," he is speaking as the
Vicar of Christ, and what he says goes. End of discussion.

The usual response to papal infallibility by one who does
not want to accept it usually goes: "But what if one pope
contradicts the *ex cathedra* statement of a previous one?"
The answer is: it has never happened. Never. True, in their
personal opinions, in their encyclical letters (which are not
infallible unless so specified, which the vast majority are not),
in their memoirs and the like, popes have contradicted each
other—and even themselves!—down through the centuries.
Disagreement is to be expected from any sampling of two
hundred and sixty-five influential men (the number of men in
the Papal succession thus far). Some popes have even contradicted previous *ex cathedra* pronouncements in their own
non-infallible speeches and writings—putting their own souls
in peril, but not officially changing Church teaching. Shenanigans are to be expected in any sampling of men, period.

On occasion, the pope may convene an ecumenical council (from the Latin *œcumenicus,* from the Greek *oikoumene:*
"the inhabited world"). Before the word "ecumenical" became popularized to mean a warm-fuzzy and nondiscerning
attitude promoting worldwide unity and cooperation between
people of different faiths at the expense of Truth, it originally

designated a general council called by a pope to which all the bishops in the world were invited, and over which the pope presided in person or through a representative. The dogmatic pronouncements of such councils, by virtue of extension of the pope's powers (his signature ratifies their decisions), and by the unity of the successors of the Apostles, are also considered infallible. Hence the dogmatic decrees of such councils are considered binding on all the Faithful, and for all time. Councils such as Trent, Vatican I, and the Lateran Councils carry this kind of teaching authority.*

With all this in mind, we come to realize that the Catholic Church as established by Jesus Christ, the Son of God, has been granted by Her Founder the power to define Herself and Her Teachings, guided by the eternal protection of the Holy Ghost. Much of the turmoil which has gripped the Church in the present age has been due to the wholesale rejection by so many of Her members of the infallible teachings of the popes and councils of the past. Somehow the idea has taken root that anything before Vatican II is to be considered outdated, unimportant, and moot. In past centuries, such thinking would be called "heresy," but since most councils were convened to define and deal with heresies, the modern heretics make void their own definition, and so remain in their minds untouched by the term.

> ... the plain truth is that most Catholics aren't Catholics anymore. They don't have a clue as to what Catholicism is all about—and this indictment applies to priests as well as laity. The way I discovered this fact was by reading books that had been published before Vatican II—old books by the likes of Hilaire Belloc, John L. Stoddard and Father Joseph

---

* Vatican II, as declared by Pope John XXIII who convened it and by Pope Paul VI who closed it, was a "pastoral" rather than a Dogmatic council. None of its pronouncements are considered infallible and binding unless they reiterate the decrees of previous councils (and few of them do). Curiously, however, Vatican II is perceived by most Catholics as being the most infallible and binding council in history—a misconception fostered by the modernists who have taken gross advantage of the vague and imprecise wording of its copious and verbose documents to promote their liberal agendas within the Church to our spiritual and moral detriment.

Prachensky. Then I turned to older books by Saint
Alphonsus Liguori, Blessed Mary Agreda, and Father
Jeremias Drexelius. Then I dug up even older books
by Saint Augustine, Saint Ignatius of Antioch, Origen, and (aha!) Saint Athanasius.

What I learned was that these people believed something very different from the lukewarm self-indulgent
broth in which most Catholics today swim. What
they described was an entirely *different religion,* a philosophy of life incompatible with post-Vatican II
pantheistic feel-goodism. The intellectual integrity,
philosophical humility, and profound devotion to Jesus Christ and His Blessed Mother of earlier generations of Catholics convinced me that theirs was the
course worthy of study and imitation, not the desultory diversions of the spiritually-anemic dweebs of
this corrupted age.

—Me, back in Chapter Twenty-Eight

A good piece of advice for anyone struggling to grasp the
Catholic Faith, or to hold on to Her Teachings in the face of
opposition, is the same as Saint Paul's:

Pray without ceasing.

—I Thessalonians V:17

Yes: pray. We mustn't assume we can figure this stuff out
by ourselves—that what "feels right" to us *is* right. We have
popes for a reason: to define dogmas, to teach with clarity, and
to take care of Fallen Man until Christ's return. We must cultivate trust in Jesus Christ, returning frequently to the Font
from which Life flows. There is no other place to turn. If we
learn to trust Him, and the infallible pronouncements of the
Vicars He left in His stead, we will be secure in our Faith. If
we veer from this course, and allow the doubts and allurements
of the world to derail us from our Trust in God, our resolve
will dissolve and our Faith will wither.

But yet the Son of man, when he cometh, shall he
find, think you, faith on earth?

—St. Luke XVIII:8

The fact that Jesus would ask such a question is as disturbing as the question itself, for it hurls the gauntlet in our faces: will we persevere; will we hold on to the Faith no matter what—even the hard-to-accept parts?

> But know ye, that if the master of the house knew at what hour the thief would come, he would certainly watch, and would not suffer his house to be broken open.
> Wherefore be you also ready, because at what hour you know not the Son of man will come.
> —St. Matthew XXIV:43-44

In light of this warning, can we really afford to spin our wheels in idle speculation? Do we dare assume that His return is far enough off or inconsequential enough that we don't need to worry about it?—that such apocalyptic verses don't really apply to us?—that we know more than our Master?

Our job is to save our souls, and to do so we need to go to the Inn established by Jesus Christ, to become members of the Holy Catholic Church. We must subject ourselves to the teaching authority of the pope, and to accept all the tenets of the Catholic Faith. When the pope declares something infallibly that we don't understand, or that we "just can't buy," we do not have the right to appeal to our fallen intellect, our flighty feelings, or our thoroughly questionable and unquestionably sinful sense of right and wrong—as if these mercurial things can serve as the foundation for an intelligent defense. The Person we finally will have to answer to is Omnipotent, after all. What will that Judge think of our closing arguments?

Therefore, when we find the teachings of the Church hard to swallow, we need to "pray without ceasing" because Jesus told us:

> Ask, and it shall be given to you: seek, and you shall find: knock, and it shall be opened to you.
> For every one that asketh, receiveth: and he that seeketh, findeth: and to him that knocketh, it shall be opened.
> For what man is there among you, of whom if his son shall ask bread, will he reach him a stone?

> Or if he shall ask him a fish, will he reach him a serpent?
> If you, being evil, know how to give good gifts to your children: how much more will your Father who is in heaven, give good things to them that ask him?
> —St. Matthew VII:7-11

If we really want to understand the teachings of the Holy Catholic Church, which Jesus Christ established for our benefit, then all we need do is ask. In the mean time until understanding dawns, we can count on the fact that if God, our Father, provides "good things" to us, His children, then we can trust with childlike confidence whatever the popes infallibly teach because the Holy Ghost is guiding them.

God does not give his children stones when they ask for bread. A swift kick, maybe—when the situation warrants—but never stones.

CHAPTER FORTY-FIVE

IF ...

If any one abide not in me, he shall be cast forth as
a branch, and shall wither, and they shall gather him
up, and cast him into the fire, and he burneth.
— St. John XV:6

∞ ∞ ∞

IF WE BELIEVE THAT JESUS WAS GOD, then a host of ramifications radiate outward from that crucial helix. If He was God, then He meant what He said, and saw to it that His words would be preserved for us in Sacred Scripture and the Traditions of His Church. He was not impaired by the cultural and communication limitations of His time—indeed, it was He who brought about those very techno-socio-economic conditions in which He chose to be born. All claims that "we don't really know what He said or what He meant" are spurious, because they essentially claim that He lost control of His own message—which is patently and logically absurd.

Of course, they stopped teaching Logic in schools some years ago. "Sensitivity training" has been deemed more beneficial to the development of young minds by those in positions of academic power. One can only wonder why. But, formally trained in Logic or not, we must do our best to think clearly and reasonably. So:

If Jesus was God, and if He preserved and protected His message for our benefit, then we would do well to listen ever so carefully to what He had to say; constantly reminding ourselves that we are the creatures, and He the Creator. The rules are His to decide, and ours to accept. Therefore, when He said:

> He that believeth and is baptized, shall be saved:
> but he that believeth not shall be condemned.
> —St. Mark XVI:16

... and ...

> Amen, amen I say to thee, unless a man be born
> again of water and the Holy Ghost, he cannot enter
> into the Kingdom of God.
> —St. John III:5

... He was stating a simple but comprehensive requirement for entry into Heaven: water Baptism. Water is such a common and ordinary thing. Unlike the bread, wine, and oil of other Sacraments which are the result of Man's labor, water is something we already find on our planet as part of God's Creation. We cannot take credit for its manufacture. It is elemental, basic, primary, a fundamental component of life itself. Jesus commands us to take a small amount of this remarkable and readily available substance, pour it on the head of the believer, and utter a few words while doing so. To think that such an unremarkable action can bring about a profound change in a human being—the erasure of Original Sin—boggles the mind. Its very simplicity is perhaps the biggest barrier against the inflated expectations of our self-assured intellects.

256.   What is Baptism?
Baptism is a Sacrament which cleanses us from original sin, makes us Christians, children of God, and members of the Church.

258.   Who is the ordinary minister of Baptism?
The ordinary minister of Baptism is a priest; but any one may baptize in case of necessity, when a priest cannot be had.

259.   How is Baptism given?
Baptism is given by pouring water on the head of the child, saying at the same time these words: 'I baptize thee

in the name of the Father, and of the Son, and of the Holy Ghost.'

261. Is Baptism necessary for salvation?
Baptism is necessary for salvation, because Christ said, 'Unless a man be born again of water and the Holy Ghost, he cannot enter into the kingdom of God.'

—*A Catechism of Christian Doctrine*
Formerly known as the "Penny Catechism"

If Jesus had demanded that we brave a costly pilgrimage to a distant and unstable volcanic summit once during our lifetime, or that we endure unspeakable torture by fire or dull knives, or that we roam Antarctic glacial wastelands in search of rare and precious Monrovian Fire Flowers, imagine the whining theology that would have blossomed around such harsh requirements for Salvation. How abundant would be our excuses, how poignant our appeals to impossibility, how frantic our scramble for logical and merciful exceptions to so difficult and unfair a demand.

But all He stipulated was Baptism by water—so simple an act that even a child can do it, and so necessary that even an atheist can administer it:

In case of necessity, however, not only a priest or a deacon, but even a layman or a woman, yes even a pagan and a heretic can baptize, so long as he preserves the form of the Church and has the intention of doing as the Church does.

—The Council of Florence
(Denzinger: 696)

How incredibly easy, and so available. Surely, we have no problem with it. All of us dutifully and humbly submit to the necessity of performing this tiny and uncomplicated task ...

Hardly.

Appeals to theological speculations of "baptism of desire" and "baptism of blood" abound with the choking consistency and relentless fury of a hurricane. You'd think Jesus actually *did* demand that we climb volcanoes, undergo disembowelment, and scour glaciers for rare vegetables, the way

some people shriek in incredulous dismay over the sheer impossibility, arbitrariness, if not awesome unfairness, of water
Baptism.

In my travels, I have repeatedly observed that the average
Catholic today knows virtually *nothing* about the vital role of
Mary in our personal Salvation, but is overflowing with intensely stated and impressively clever arguments in favor of
"baptism of desire." I have wondered at times, considering
the understanding of Saints in past centuries, just whose agendas have been promoted and with such prevalence and precision in our time. How many of today's Catholic bishops,
priests, nuns, laymen or survivors of the insidious RENEW and
RCIA programs would say "Amen" to the following:

> Mankind was unworthy to receive the Word directly
> from God, so Mary was our Mediatrix in the Incarna-
> tion, and she continues to exercise that function. No
> one comes to the knowledge of Jesus Christ and em-
> braces His holy law except through her; no one ob-
> tains the saving gift of faith except by her prayers.
> Her mission, to which she is ever faithful, is to give
> us Jesus. He must be received from her hands, and in
> vain do we seek Him elsewhere.
>
> — Saint Peter Julian Eymard
> Quoted in *The Apostolic Digest*

Yet how many of them can spew interminable excuses for
ignorant natives on desert islands and plead vigorous cases for
"people who lead good lives but who—through no fault of
their own—never heard of Christ"?

So, back to Jesus Christ. If He was God, and He said water
Baptism is a requirement for Salvation, then is it possible He
hadn't thought the whole thing through? Did He not understand the ramifications of His own teachings? Did He not
know that there were millions of people in far-flung parts of
the world that had never heard of Him? Did He not realize
there are geographical places on earth where water is scarce?

The real question is this: *do we believe in Him enough to
accept Him at His word?* Can we let go of our frantic need to
figure everything out on our own terms, to bring everything
down to our banal and tangible level? Can we possibly relax

our desperate grip on the controls long enough to allow Him to operate in the realm suited to His omnipotent Divinity?

He is God, after all. And if He says a thing is so, then it is. When He said ...

> Be light made.
> —Genesis I:3

... it was. If He says water Baptism is necessary, then it is. And if, as He Himself also said ...

> ... God so loved the world, as to give his only begotten Son; that whosoever believeth in him, may not perish, but may have life everlasting.
> —St. John III:16

... then we can be absolutely sure that He will do all He can to provide for the water Baptism of all who are of Good Will. Are we so short in our Faith that we deem it impossible for God to get a thimbleful of water poured on the head of a man on an island, or in the middle of a desert, or on top of a mountain?—the same God who raised that island from the depths of the sea, parched that desert dry with hot arid winds, and thrust up that mountain from the very roots of the earth? Perhaps, rather than revile Jesus for making impossible pronouncements, we need to meditate on just what *is* impossible for God.

And what is Good Will? It must be very special indeed, for on the night Jesus was born the Angels proclaimed:

> Glory to God in the highest; and on earth peace to men of good will.
> —St. Luke II:14

Good Will is the fundamental hunger of a human being for the Truth. It is that which separates those who are indeed going to find the Peace of God, from those who will ignore it:

> Here too we see suggested another Platonic concept: the primacy of the Will over the Intellect. The will, according to Plato and those, Christians or otherwise, who follow him, is the basic motive force of

the personality. It is oriented at any given time to Love of Truth and Love of Self in varying proportions. The Intellect, that faculty which perceives and interprets outer phenomena (whether through learning or sense) is formed and steered as it were by the Will, and accordingly forms impressions depending on whether the Will is more oriented toward love of Truth of love of Self. So two pagans, faced with the Faith, will react differently. The one, motivated to a greater or lesser degree by love of Truth, responds immediately or gradually to the Faith, thereby embracing it despite whatever kind of unpleasantness or personal renunciations might be necessary to do so. The other, whose Will is dominated by love of Self, and reacting strictly in terms of what will please or convenience him (either personally of by means of kindred, etc.) rejects the Faith. Yet both are equipped with roughly equal intellects.

—Thomas A. Hutchinson
Desire and Deception

We need to realize that when Jesus said, "He that believeth and is baptized, shall be saved," and "unless a man be born again of water and the Holy Ghost, he cannot enter into the Kingdom of God," He was not just setting up restrictions, He was making a *solemn promise*. The man that truly believes, who is truly of Good Will, *will be baptized*. Logic assures us, as does the Church, that God provides sufficient Grace for all men to be saved. Since His Love is guaranteed, and His requirements for Salvation are clearly stated, He must provide for the water Baptism of those who truly seek Him. He will send a missionary, transport a cloistered nun, bilocate a Saint, or relocate the man of Good Will to a more propitious local. He will provide. It's really that simple. Observe:

> Now an angel of the Lord spoke to Philip, saying, Arise, go towards the south, to the way that goeth down from Jerusalem into Gaza: this is desert.
> And rising up, he went. And behold a man of Ethiopia, an eunuch, of great authority under Candace the queen of the Ethiopians, who had charge over all her treasures, had come to Jerusalem to adore.

And he was returning, sitting in his chariot, and reading Isaias the prophet.

And the Spirit said to Philip: Go near, and join thyself to his chariot.

And Philip running thither, heard him reading the prophet Isaias. And he said: Thinkest thou that thou understandest what thou readest?

Who said: And how can I, unless some man shew me? And he desired Philip that he would come up and sit with him.

And the place of the scripture which he was reading was this: *He was led as a sheep to the slaughter; and like a lamb without voice before his shearer, so openeth he not his mouth.*

In humility his judgment was taken away. His generation who shall declare, for his life shall be taken from earth?

And the eunuch answering Philip, said: I beseech thee, of whom doth the prophet speak this? of himself, or of some other man?

Then Philip, opening his mouth, and beginning at this scripture, preached unto him Jesus.

And as they went of their way, they came to a certain water; and the eunuch said: See, here is water; what doth hinder me from being baptized?

And Philip said: If thou believest with all thy heart, thou mayest. And he answering, said: I believe that Jesus Christ is the Son of God.

And he commanded the chariot to stand still; and they went down into the water, both Philip and the eunuch: and he baptized him.

And when they were come up out of the water, the Spirit of the Lord took away Philip; and the eunuch saw him no more. And he went on his way rejoicing.

Put Philip was found in Azotus; and passing through, he preached the gospel to all the cities, till he came to Cæsarea.

—The Acts of the Apostles VIII:26-40

There are other such remarkable occurrences in the Acts of the Apostles, as well as the writings of the Church Fathers, not to mention the exploits of Saints down through the ages. Of course, one must believe in miracles to accept them as true. Yes, one must believe in miracles.

A Catholic is also required to believe, as we learned in the previous chapter, that when a pope speaks *ex cathedra,* all speculation ceases and obedient belief is required of all believers. Therefore we must accept as immutable the following:

> *Ex cathedra:* "There is but one universal Church of the faithful, outside of which no one at all can be saved."
>
> —Pope Innocent III
> at the Fourth Lateran Council, 1215 AD
> (Denzinger: 430, emphasis mine)

Again: Gulp! Can such a thing be true? And could it be that all Catholics are required to believe it? Well, it certainly *used* to be considered true, and for many centuries Catholics unequivocally *did* adhere to it. How else could they possibly interpret the words during Mass:

> Et unam, sanctam, catholicam
> et apostolicam Ecclesiam.
>
> And one, holy, catholic
> and apostolic Church.
>
> —The Nicene Creed in the Tridentine Mass

The Nicene Creed dates back to the fourth century. Another statement of the Faith, known as the Athanasian Creed, arrived in the fifth. Too long to present here in full, we will examine only the beginning and end:

> Whosoever wishes to be saved, needs above all to hold the Catholic Faith; unless each one preserves this whole and inviolate, he will without a doubt perish in eternity ...
>
> ... This is the Catholic Faith; unless every one believes this faithfully and firmly, he cannot be saved.
>
> —(Denzinger: 40)

Literally hundreds of pages could be filled with quotes from various Saints on this subject. Once you start digging in libraries, pouring through brittle books that predate Vatican II and more so 1900, the evidence begins to pile up at an alarming rate—evidence that present-day Catholics are completely out of touch with the historical Mind of the Church. Here are but a few statements well worth thoughtful and suitable consideration:

> Christ has declared the unity of the Church. Whoever parts and divides the Church cannot possess Christ ... The House of God is but one, and no one can have salvation except in the Church.
>
> —St. Cyprian
> *The Unity of the Catholic Church IV*

> The Holy, Roman, Catholic and Apostolic Church is the only true Church, outside of which no one at all can be saved.
>
> —St. Alphonsus Liguori
> *Instructions on the Commandments and Sacraments*

> O beloved angel, who has been given me as a protector by the Divine Majesty, I desire to die in the Faith which the Holy, Roman, and Apostolic Church adheres to and defends, in which all the saints of the New Testament have died, and outside which there is no salvation.
>
> —St. Charles Boromeo's prayer
> to his Guardian Angel
> *Saints to Remember*

> There is no entering into salvation outside the Church, just as in the time of the Flood there was no salvation outside the Ark which denotes the Church.
>
> —St. Thomas Aquinas
> *Summa Theologica*

> What was prefigured in the Flood is now fulfilled
> in Christ's Church ... The wicked are separated from
> the good ... the heretic from the faithful. For they
> are lost, as in the Flood ... while the Church alone
> ... is sustained above the deep. And so ... we tell
> you that only those who find shelter in the bosom of
> the Ark of the Church shall escape.
>
> —St. Maximus of Turin
> *Sunday Sermons of the Great Fathers*

> All the above quotes are from
> *The Apostolic Digest*

Of course, Saints are not infallible, only popes—which is
why we began with the *ex cathedra* statement. And what, we
might ask, do the modernists have to say in this regard, those
liberal thinkers of whom Jesus remarked:

> ... for the children of this world are wiser in their
> generation than the children of light.
>
> —St. Luke XVI:8

How do they "get around" the simple, direct, impenetrable Truth as stated by Pope Innocent III?

> Luckily for the advanced crew, however, they did
> have at their disposal the Thomistic love of making
> distinctions. Now these distinctions do have a certain
> utility. But unfortunately, they can be used to erode
> the plain meaning of any given phrase; as Leonard
> Wibberly observes in *The Mouse that Roared:* yes
> may be turned to no, or vice versa, provided sufficient
> verbiage be employed to do so. This has since degen-
> erated into the modern academic sort of criticism. It
> is a method of analysis which would take the sen-
> tence, "What do we mean by that?" and ask: "What do
> we mean by what? What do we mean by do? What
> do we mean by we?" and so on until one knows less
> than he did at birth. Applied to the present case,
> these distinctions allow one to adhere to the ancient
> dogmas, while avoiding their plain meaning. "Bap-
> tism is necessary for salvation? Of course! Natu-

> rally, the vast number of people, protected by invin-
> cible ignorance, are baptized by desire. No Salvation
> outside the Church? Certainly! But we need to un-
> derstand what is meant by Church ... or by Outside
> ... or by Salvation." In the end, the whole thing is
> pared down to meaninglessness, until one can hardly
> understand why the Church bothered with these things
> in the first place.
>
> —Thomas A. Hutchinson
> *Desire and Deception*

The degree to which he see our own attitudes mirrored in the above quotation, we have been poisoned. To the degree we are willing to admit the error of our thinking, we are on the road to recovery.

But there is more. Isn't there always, when we explore the Catholic Faith? That is part of Her delectable charm—She never ceases to tantalize us with more, for She beckons us to Infinity. Be that as it may, now might be a good moment to pause, if only to turn the page and begin a new chapter. Or perhaps to meditate on what we've covered thus far. Certainly a stop at the oasis of prayer is in order. A long draught of Our Blessed Mother inevitably calms the jitters.

Ah, much better. Now, my dear companions, we round the Cape of the Salutary Dogma, and behold the Great Sea which lays beyond ...

CHAPTER FORTY-SIX

... THEN:

I am the vine; you are the branches: he that abideth
in me, and I in him, the same beareth much fruit: for
without me you can do nothing.

—St. John XV:6

∞   ∞   ∞

ABOUT A HUNDRED YEARS after Pope Innocent III made his
ex cathedra declaration that Salvation was not possible outside
the Church, another pope made the following proclamation
(emphasis added):

> *Ex cathedra: "Urged by faith, we are obliged to be-
> lieve and to hold that the Church is one, holy, catho-
> lic, and also apostolic. We firmly believe in her, and
> we confess absolutely that outside of her there is nei-
> ther salvation nor the remission of sins,* as the
> Spouse in the Canticles (VI, 8) proclaims: "One is
> my dove, my perfect one. She is the only one of her
> mother, the chosen of her that bore her," who repre-
> sents one mystical body, whose head is Christ, and
> the head of Christ is God. In her there is one Lord,
> one faith, one baptism. There was indeed at the time
> of the deluge only one Ark, having been finished to a
> single cubit, had only one pilot and guide, i.e., Noah,
> outside of which we read, all that subsisted on the
> earth was destroyed ...
>
> "... *Furthermore, We declare, say, define and pro-
> nounce that it is absolutely necessary for the salva-*

tion of every human creature to be subject to the
Roman Pontiff."
—Pope Boniface VIII
in his Bull *Unam Sanctam,* 1302 AD
(Denzinger: 468, 469, emphasis mine)

Uh oh. What are we getting into here? Every human
creature must be subject to the Pope in order to be saved? But
what about Protestants? Aren't they our brothers in Christ?

There is no such thing as a religion called "Christianity"—there never has been such a religion.

There is and always has been the Church, and various heresies proceeding from a rejection of some of
the Church's doctrines by men who still desire to retain the rest of her teaching and morals. But there
never has been and never can be or will be a general
Christian religion professed by men who all accept
some central important doctrines, while agreeing to
differ about others. There has always been, from the
beginning, and will always be, the Church, and sun-
dry heresies either doomed to decay, or, like Mo-
hammedanism, to grow into a separate religion. Of a
common Christianity there has never been and never
can be a definition, for it has never existed.

There is no essential doctrine such that if we can
agree upon it we can differ about the rest: as for instance, to accept immortality but deny the Trinity. A
man will call himself a Christian though he denies
the unity of the Christian Church; he will call himself a Christian though he denies the presence of Jesus Christ in the Blessed Sacrament; he will cheer-
fully call himself a Christian though he denies the Incarnation.

No; the quarrel is between the Church and the anti-
Church—the Church of God and anti-God—the
Church of Christ and anti-Christ.
—Hilaire Belloc
The Great Heresies

Hard as it is, and even though we all have friends and relatives who are Protestants, we have to face certain facts. The first is that the fundamental premise of Protestantism is not that "man is saved by Faith alone and not by works," nor that "Scripture by itself contains all Revelation." No, the thing that gave the impetus, the "go ahead" for their split from Rome; the concept that provided the stimulus for Calvin and others to rewrite theology in their own image; the excuse that sparked, and continues to fuel the flames of the impulse to separate from the True Church, to "protest" and remain "Protest-ants"—is none other than the denial of the salutary Dogma:

EXTRA ECCLESIAM NULLA SALUS
OUTSIDE THE CHURCH THERE IS NO SALVATION

There was a time when Catholics stood firm on this Dogma, affirming that it was not mere theological speculation but the decision and command of Our Lord Jesus Christ. Over time, it appeared that the vast majority of Protestants who left the Church during the Reformation were never going to return to the fold, many of the Faithful began to lose heart. Living side by side with the enemy dulls the sense of danger, mitigates the great principles that separates one man from another, a noblewoman from her seamstress, the housewife from the local butcher. Their children play together, carry each other's books to school, and eventually intermarry. After a time, people begin to wonder what all the fuss was about.

But the *fuss* was about Jesus Christ, the Son of God; and His message was all too clear:

> Do not think that I came to send peace upon the earth: I came not to send peace, but the sword.
> For I came to set a man at variance against his father, and the daughter against her mother, and the daughter in law against her mother in law.
> And a man's enemies shall be they of his own household.
> He that loveth father or mother more than me, is not worthy of me; and he that loveth son or daughter more than me, is not worthy of me.

> And he that taketh not up his cross, and followeth
> me, is not worthy of me.
> He that findeth his life, shall lose it: and he that
> shall lose his life for me, shall find it.
>   — St. Luke X:34-39

"A man's enemies shall be they of his own household."
Wow. The message of Christ will turn families against each
other. Love for our own parents and children cannot displace
our love for Him. This in no way negates our filial responsibilities, our marriage vows, or our duty to raise our children to
the best of our ability; but rather places these things within a
larger structure, the framework of which is His call that we
follow Him. He insists that we get our priorities straight and
live by His Principles, no matter how hard, no matter the cost.
Complacency and Christianity are mutually exclusive tenets,
and once we believe in Him, we are called to live exclusively
for Him. All else is darkness, all else is insanity, all else is one
big beautiful, alluring invitation to Hell with gold-leaf twirls
around the singed edges.

In 1864, Pope Pius IX published his "Syllabus of the
Principal Errors of Our Time." Among the specific propositions which he condemned were the following—each statement should be preceded by the phrase, *"It is error to believe
that ....:"*

> 15. Every man is free to embrace and profess that
> religion which, guided by the light of reason, he shall
> consider true.
> 16. Man may, in observance of any religion what-
> ever, find the way of eternal salvation, and arrive at
> eternal salvation.
> 17. Good hope at least is to be entertained of the
> eternal salvation of all those who are not at all in the
> true Church of Christ.
> 18. Protestantism is nothing more than another
> form of the same Christian religion, in which form it
> is given to please God equally as in the Catholic
> Church.
>   — Pope Pius IX
>   *The Syllabus of Errors*

If the blood rushes to our faces as we read these words because we remember saying them ourselves, we must pause to
reflect that our primary concern is not to placate our feelings,
to cater to our likes and dislikes, to depend on our limited and
hampered reasoning, to look and sound "metaphysical," but
to adhere to the wishes of Our Lord and Savior Jesus Christ.
If we look at ourselves, if we concentrate on Man, we will fall
into the trap of seeing the Church as merely an institution of
influential men rather than as the Body of Christ guided by
the Holy Ghost. Truth does not change or adapt to fit the
growing store of Man's collective knowledge. What is True
today will be True tomorrow. The things Jesus said were
meant for all time, all places, and all circumstances. To say
that we need to create a "new understanding of what Jesus
meant" is to deny that He knew what He meant—to deny that
He was God.

> For the doctrine of faith which God has revealed has
> not been proposed, like a philosophical invention, to
> be perfected by human ingenuity; but has been deliv-
> ered as a divine deposit to the Spouse of Christ, to be
> faithfully kept and infallibly declared. Hence, also,
> that meaning of the sacred dogmas is perpetually to
> be retained which our holy Mother the Church has
> once declared; nor is that meaning ever to be departed
> from, under the pretense or pretext of a deeper com-
> prehension of them. Let then the intelligence, sci-
> ence and wisdom of each and all, of individuals and of
> the whole Church, in all ages and all times, increase
> and flourish in abundance and vigor; but simply in its
> own proper kind, that is to say, in one and the same
> doctrine, one and the same judgment.
>   —The First Vatican Council
>   *Dogmatic Constitution on the Catholic Faith*
>   Session III, Chapter 4

We would also do well to consider that we reside in a Protestant culture, and our thinking has been affected by living in
proximity to people who regard us as "throwbacks," or in
some cases, *enemies*. Indeed, amidst all the splintering of
Protestantism into literally thousands of sects, all professing

different beliefs and interpretations, there is only one thing upon which they agree: they are definitely *not* Catholics.

We also live in a democracy, a society in which "getting along" and "accepting one another" is emphasized at every turn. This kind of thinking percolates down into our psyche, sprouts roots, and takes on a familiar flavor, seeming to be our very own thoughts rather than seeds planted by our caretakers—proper, reasonable, and certainly conducive to "getting ahead" in the job market. But it is certainly not Catholic, nor can it be traced to the teachings of Christ. Catholics, as we discovered many chapters ago, are concerned with grasping and promoting the Truth, not with being "nice."

> ... St. Peter Julian Eymard has been here described as also rigorously unsentimental. Here is a passage from his writing to show it: "People often say, 'It is better to be a good Protestant than a bad Catholic.' That is not true! That would mean that one could be saved without the true faith. No. A bad Catholic remains a child of the family, although a prodigal, and however great a sinner he may be, he still has a right to mercy. Through his faith, a bad Catholic is nearer to God than a Protestant, for he is a member of the household, whereas the heretic is not. And how hard it is to make him become one!"[*]
>
> To be sure, competent Church authorities examined and approved the writings of these saints before they were canonized. That was before too many Catholics, including some Church authorities, fell into the habit of subordinating thought to emotion.
>
> —Gary Potter
> "Observations and Reflections"
> *The Angelus,* November 1993

What was Jesus telling us in the Parable of the Good Samaritan, if not that He came to save fallen Man, that He would leave behind the Sacraments as the Divine Medicines for his wounds, and that He left the Remedy in the care and keeping

---

[*] This quotation within Mr. Potter's article is from St. Eymard's book, *The Real Presence,* which is the *best* book I've ever read regarding devotion to the Blessed Sacrament.

of the Pope and the Catholic Church? What then can be said of anyone who rejects the Church or the pope? They are rejecting the wishes of Jesus Christ, and so place themselves outside the Inn:

> Here I may be allowed to say a few words in particular to sincere and well-meaning Protestants who are not careless about their salvation or indifferent with regard to truth. No matter how strictly you may consider your will bound by the commandments of God, no matter how much you feel bound to read the Bible and store your memory with its contents, your soul is still wounded and bleeding, and will remain so as long as you do not believe all and everything which Christ has taught, and which the Holy Catholic Church, established by Him to teach all nations, shall believe and teach to the end of time. But some will laugh at and scorn the ideas of binding their will to the firm belief of a certain creed; they prefer the fatal liberty to form their own opinion about divine truth, and to differ not only from the Catholic Church, but also from those of their own denomination. They admit that the word of God is infallible, or, in other words, that God is truth, and therefore cannot lie. Let them open their Bible and read from the sixteenth chapter of St. Matthew, verse 18: "I say to thee, that thou art Peter, and upon this rock I will build my Church; and the gates of hell shall not prevail against it." See here the infallibility of the Church; and again, from the concluding chapter and verse of the same Evangelist: "Behold I am with you all days, even to the consummation of the world." We also read from the same Gospel, at the seventeenth verse of the eighteenth chapter: "If he will not hear the Church, let him be to thee as the heathen and publican."
>
> Now, I ask, can any man of sense who admits the Bible to be the word of God read the sacred texts I have just quoted and not adhere to or embrace the Catholic religion? Here are the words of Christ; and will man, the child of dust, the being of nothingness,

whom He could crush with a mere glance—will he, I
repeat, have the audacity to contradict his Maker?
—Father Joseph Prachensky
Divine Parables Explained

Furthermore, the *ex cathedra* statement of Pope Boniface
VIII didn't just apply to Protestants. "It is absolutely necessary," he said, "for the salvation of *every human creature* to
be subject to the Roman Pontiff." Every human creature.
Even those in far-flung places, beyond the reach of Christianity?

"Certainly the pope couldn't have really meant that," say
the faithless modernists, "any more than Jesus meant that
Baptism of water was necessary for Salvation." So they resorted to two equivocations to make up for what was lacking
in the dim-witted proclamations of the Church and Her Founder: "baptism of desire" and "baptism of blood."

If a man or woman leads a "perfectly good life," but
isn't a Catholic, surely God will accept their "basic goodness" and "sincerity" as "enough to get them to Heaven."
If a native on a desert island has never heard of Jesus Christ,
but leads an "honest" and "upright" life within the culture
in which he was born, surely his "desire" to do "good" will
get him into Heaven. And certainly a man who dies for Christ,
even if he hasn't been formally Baptized, is purified by the
spilling of his own blood in the sight of God. Surely any enlightened man with an ounce of common sense would cherish
and understand these honorable concepts.

But are they honorable? Do they truly reflect a belief that
Jesus is indeed God? Are they not, rather, *exceptions* to His
express teachings? Are they not really *excuses* for the *loopholes* Jesus "apparently" left behind? Their proponents and
advocates call these obvious changes in Dogma "developments," but they should be regarded as what they really are:
departures, and ultimately outright denials. Students of
Logic—oh, right, we no longer study Logic—but if there *were*
students of Logic, they would tell us that the moment you find
an exception, you've just established a *rule*. In other words, if
the Church isn't absolutely necessary for each and every person to achieve Salvation, then it is necessary for no one. If
one person can bypass Her, then everyone can.

Tucked away within the comforting folds of "baptism of desire" and "baptism of blood," as the terms are commonly understood, is the denial of the reality of Original Sin and its consequences. It ignores the fact that a baby born in the state of Original Sin, as all babies are, is terminally ill—as terminally ill as a child born with a dysfunctional heart. The stain of Original Sin must be removed if the soul is to have life, just as the bad heart requires surgery.

Beneath another warm fold of "baptism of desire" is the flat denial of the need for the Sacraments. Its proponents say a person can lead a "perfectly good life" and die "free of mortal sin" without ever having been Baptized (which denies the mortal nature of Original Sin), never having gone to Confession (which denies the need for genuine Repentance or Absolution), nor ever receiving Holy Communion (which ignores the statement of Christ that we must eat His Flesh and drink His Blood in order to have life within us).

Where, we might ask, is this "person leading a perfectly good life"? While we Catholics struggle hour by hour, sometimes second by second, to avoid sin, to repent of the sins we commit in spite of our efforts, to grow spiritually by constant prayer and reception of the Sacraments which provide Grace which nourishes our souls; all the while reminding ourselves that our Salvation is not assured, that we may fail mortally tomorrow, that if we relax our diligence for but a moment we could very well wind up in Hell for all Eternity—while we put our "all" on the line for the Love of Christ, this "perfectly good person" somehow bypasses all that effort and skips joyfully into Heaven. Somehow his vague "desire" is worth more than the rest. Hard to believe. Very hard to believe. Especially when we remember that Jesus promised to supply water Baptism, the Sacraments, and lodging at the Inn to anyone with Good Will. If this "person" in question truly desired the Truth, he would have *found* it because it was readily available to him, or would have been provided for him.

> The belief in "Baptism of Desire" has never been held by the Catholic Church and cannot be found anywhere in the binding teachings of its Magisterium. No theology has ever been developed to define it or support it. It is true that speculation for and against its existence has been made by Saints, and

many catechisms today have erroneously included it, but if anyone ever tries to trace any authority for its existence back to Christ or His Church, they will be unable to do so.

—Tom Zola, President (now deceased)
Catholic Treasures Books
Quoted from a promotional blurb for the book
Desire and Deception by Thomas A. Hutchinson

"If anyone ever tries to trace any authority for the existence of 'baptism of desire' back to Christ or His Church, they will be unable to do so." Hmm. Interesting, isn't it, how quick some of us are to think we know better than Christ how men should get to Heaven, and how slow we are to suspect in our largess or apathy that He couldn't have been speaking to us when He said:

For there shall arise arise false Christs and false prophets, and shall show great signs and wonders, insomuch as to deceive (if possible) even the elect.
Behold I have told it to you , beforehand.
—St. Matthew XXIV:24-25

... and ...

For I testify to every one that heareth the words of the prophecy of this book: If any man shall add to these things, God shall add unto him the plagues written in this book.
And if any man shall take away from the words of the book of this prophecy, God shall take away his part out of the book of life, and out of the holy city, and from those things that are written in this book.
—The Apocalypse XXII:18-19

With this in mind, as well as both feet planted firmly on "square one," we must brace ourselves and look at one more *ex cathedra* statement. The "clincher," we might say:

Ex cathedra: "The most Holy Roman Church firmly believes, professes and preaches, that none of those existing outside the Catholic Church, not only pagans, but also Jews and heretics and schismatics, can have a share in life eternal; but that they will go into the eternal fire, which was prepared for the devil and his angels, unless before death they are joined with Her; and that so important is the unity of this ecclesiastical body that only those remaining within this unity can profit by the sacraments of the Church unto salvation, and they alone can receive an eternal recompense for their fasts, their almsgiving, their other works of Christian piety, and duties of a Christian soldier. No one, let his almsgiving be as great as it may, no one, even if he pour out his blood for the name of Christ, can be saved, unless he remain within the bosom and the unity of the Catholic Church."

—Pope Eugene IV
in his Bull *Cantate Domino*
at the Council of Florence,1441 AD
(Denzinger: 714)

Let us examine this statement in detail:

"The most Holy Roman Church firmly believes, professes and preaches ..." Okay, there can be no question that Pope Eugene IV was speaking as head of the Church, defining the teachings of the Church, to the entirety of the Church. *Ex cathedra* it is.

"... that none of those existing outside the Catholic Church ... can have a share in life eternal ..." Clearly nobody can be saved who is outside the Church. In the same infallible document, formulated by the Council of Florence and signed by Pope Eugene IV, we find the following statement about entry into the Church:

Holy baptism, which is the gateway to the spiritual life, holds the first place among the sacraments; through it we are made members of Christ and of the body of the Church ... The matter of the sacrament is real and natural water; it makes no difference whether cold or warm. The form is: *I baptize thee in the name of the Father, and of the Son, and of the Holy Ghost.*

(Denzinger: 696)

No other means of access to the Church is mentioned. Baptism with water is the only way. Those who are not baptized are not members. They are outside the Church. "Those existing outside" include pagans ...

"... but also Jews ..." —who are not Baptized, nor accept Jesus Christ as God;

"... heretics ..." —that is, those who reject part of the Catholic Faith while claiming to adhere to the rest, such as Arians, Jansenists, and all Protestants;

"... and schismatics ..." —anyone who is not subject to the pope, either by his explicit decree (as in, "I, the Pope, hereby declare that you are in schism") or by their denial of the validity of his papacy or his right to rule due to his inept handling of the office—those who in effect say, *"Sede vacantes*—the Seat is vacant."

"... but they will go into the eternal fire ... unless before death they are joined with her ..." They will go to Hell unless they embrace the Faith; and, once Baptized, submit to the authority of the pope (as per Pope Boniface VIII, *Unam Sanctam,* earlier this chapter).

" ... only those remaining within this unity can profit by the sacraments of the Church unto salvation ..." Only those within the Church are allowed to receive Her Sacraments; but even if a heretic or pagan should, perish the thought, receive Communion at Mass—the very Body and Blood of Christ—they derive no Grace from it.

"No one, let his almsgiving be as great as it may ..." It matters not the degree of our public charity, the apparent goodness of our deeds, nor the depth of our sincerity: if we are not within the Church, we are outside the veil of Salvation.

"... no one, even if he pour out his blood for the name of Christ, can be saved ..." Well, there goes "baptism of blood." And since "baptism of blood" is really just a dramatic extension of "desire"—which also reveals the lack of philosophical clarity and integrity in these speculations—both fall by the wayside. Even beyond that, what audacity we exhibit when we actually think that our own blood, the blood of a *mere creature,* can be equal in effect to Christ's own Precious Blood:

> Certainly, it is a notion which has no scriptural foundation: if one looks further, it would certainly have found no place among the Ultra-Realist early Church Fathers to whom one's own fallen blood, sprung from Adam, simply could not have the salvific effects of Christ's Precious Blood, which is applied to the individual soul through the waters of Baptism. If it did, why would Christ have come? Nor could a Platonist figure how something human would be able to perform such a task not in keeping with its nature.
>
> —Thomas A. Hutchinson
> *Desire and Deception*

If mere human blood could have opened the gates of Heaven to us, Adam or any of his descendants could have offered themselves—and some brave soul surely would have (every generation has its heroes)—as a sacrifice to God on behalf of the human race. But human blood, as with all things human, and all things created, is ultimately *nothing.* How can the shedding of nothing appease God for the sins of Mankind, or the sin of even one man?

As noble and lofty the idea of "baptism of blood" may at first seem to us, and as reasonable and magnanimous as it may sound when we expound about it over cocktails, it is absolutely contrary to the binding statement of Pope Eugene IV. It is also an obfuscation of the teaching which the Church has professed for twenty centuries. The Salvation Dogma today has become so repulsive to Catholics, due to bad teaching and faulty understanding, that when they're presented with it, say, casually over dinner, they are likely to turn beet red, pound the table, swallow their forks, question the ancestry or species of anyone who might accept such a thing, and get downright mean. Strange, isn't it, since this teaching was held as central to the Faith from the time of Christ to just shy of the present. The Salutary Dogma was formalized into Latin formula centuries ago, and in spite of all the protest and intellectual scrambling the modernists can muster, it still holds absolutely true:

If Jesus was God, then:

EXTRA ECCLESIAM NULLA SALUS
OUTSIDE THE CHURCH THERE IS NO SALVATION

CHAPTER FORTY-SEVEN

HERESY:
SON OF "YES, BUT ..."

> It is the essence of heresy that it leaves standing a
> great part of the structure it attacks. On this account
> it can appeal to believers and continues to affect their
> lives through deflecting them from their original
> characters. Wherefore, it is said of heresies that "they
> survive by the truths they retain."
>
> —Hilaire Belloc
> *The Great Heresies*

∞ ∞ ∞

WELL DO I REMEMBER the religion class back in high school
when Father C (you met him before in Chapter 25)—fresh out
of the Capuchin seminary determined to prove himself a harbinger of the "new theology"—ridiculed those people in bygone times who actually argued at great length over something as "inconsequential" as whether Jesus Christ was of the
"same" or of "similar" substance with God the Father. This
allegedly trivial matter was settled by the Council of Nicaea in
325 AD, which resulted in the drafting of the Creed which
stated in part (emphasis added):

CREDO IN UNUM DEUM,	I BELIEVE IN ONE GOD,
Patrem omnipotentem,	the Father almighty,
factorem cæli et terræ,	Maker of heaven and earth,
visibilium omnium,	and of all things visible
et invisibilium.	and invisible.
Et in unum Dominium	And in one Lord,
Jesum Christum,	Jesus Christ,

Filium Dei	the only-begotten
unigenitum.	Son of God.
Et ex Patre natum	Born of the Father
ante omnia sæcula.	before all ages.
Deum de Deo,	God of God,
lumen de lumine,	light of light,
Deum verum de Deo vero.	true God of true God.
Genitum, non factum,	Begotten, not made;
consubstantialem	*of the same substance*
Patri:	*as the Father:**
per quem omnia facta sunt.	by whom all things were made.

—The Nicene Creed of the Tridentine Mass

"Imagine," said Father C with marked academic exasperation, wiping chalk dust from his slender fingers, "they actually debated for days and days, arguing over a *word*. Now I ask you: how important—in the big scheme of things—can such a silly distinction really be?"   This, of course, was a question he did not answer. By leaving it hanging like that, he left us with the lasting—and I do mean lasting—impression that the theological arguments of the ancients were useless expenditures of super-heated air that could have been put to better use. Hot air balloons, for example, were huddled in the wings of possibility, just waiting for someone to come along and invent them.

But the fact is that all actions have consequences; and just as a single loose pebble can precipitate a massive landslide, the change of a mere word can have a devastating effect over historical time.

A large number of fourth-century bishops, for example, followed the lead of a Greek-speaking African cleric by the name of Arius (the Latinization of Areios), who had adopted the belief that Jesus, unlike the eternal Father, was created, was mutable and capable of development; that He had not come from Eternity, and was thus "similar" to God, but wasn't essentially the "same" as God. Over four fifths of the world's hierarchy became enchanted with this kind of modern—for them—and self-aggrandizing intellectualizing.

---

* Variously translated "consubstantial with the Father," "of one being with the Father," or "one in being with the Father."

Since it was very difficult to rationalize the union of the Infinite with the finite, since there is an apparent contradiction between the two terms, this final form into which the confusion or heresies settled down was a declaration that our Lord was as much of the Divine Essence as it was possible for a creature to be, but that He was none the less a creature. He was not the Infinite and Omnipotent God who must be of His nature one and indivisible, and could not (so they say) be at the same time a limited human moving and having his being in the temporal sphere ...

Essentially the movement sprang from exactly the same source as any other rationalistic movement from the beginning of our own time. It sprang from the desire to visualize clearly and simply something which is beyond the grasp of human vision and comprehension. Therefore, although it began by giving to our Lord every possible honor and glory short of the actual Godhead, it would inevitably have led in the long run into mere unitarianism and the treating of our Lord at last as a prophet and, however exalted, no more than a prophet ...

—Hilaire Belloc
The Great Heresies

The hero of orthodoxy in the face of Arianism was Saint Athanasius of Alexandria, who fought valiantly, and at great personal cost, for the Divinity of Christ, rather than His dis-deification. He was actually *excommunicated* for his trouble. Nonetheless, when sanity was restored, he was canonized. But that all seems so long ago. The fact that such erroneous thinking—"Jesus was just a good man, a tragic prophet," and so on—does not make us cringe today is a dire indicator that the same concepts, and the conditions in which they incubate, abound in our day. Typically, the modern Catholic couldn't care less.

But we cannot afford to be so nonchalant. Heresy is not just the smoke of too much theological thumb-twiddling; it is indeed serious business. One of the great beauties of Catholicism is its intricate, interwoven, interconnected and mutually-supporting complexity of Doctrines and Dogmas. No Catholic has the right to "pick and choose" that which they will and won't believe. To deny any one facet of the Faith is to deny it all, because it all hangs together. Snip one stitch, and the whole garment comes unraveled. Remove one line, one point, one angle, and the whole matrix begins to disintegrate. This is hard for us to understand in this modern day and age, unskilled as we are in Logic and Universals. It is nonetheless true.

For example, Catholicism teaches ...

> ... that the individual soul is immortal—that personal conscience survives physical death. Now if people believe that, they look at the world and themselves in a certain way and go on in a certain way and are people of a certain sort. If they except, that is cut out, this one doctrine, they may continue to hold all the others, but the scheme is changed, they type of life and character and the rest become quite another. The man who is certain that he is going to die for good and for all may believe that Jesus of Nazareth was Very God of Very God, that God is Triune, that bread and wine are transformed by a particular formula; he may recite a great number of Christian prayers and admire and copy chosen Christian exemplars, but he will be quite a different man from the man who takes immortality for granted.

> Because heresy, in this particular sense (the denial of an accepted Christian doctrine) thus affects the individual, if affects all society, and when you are examining a society formed by a particular religion you necessarily concern yourself to the utmost with the warping or diminishing of that religion. *That* is the historical interest of heresy ... The ecclesiastics who fought so furiously over the details of definition in the Eastern councils had far more historical sense and were far more in touch with reality than the French sceptics, familiar to English readers through their disciple Gibbon.

> A man who thinks, for instance, that Arianism is a mere discussion of words, does not see than an Arian world would have been more like a Mohammedan world than what the European world actually became. He is much less in touch with reality than Athanasius when he affirmed the point of doctrine to be all important. That

local council in Paris, which tipped the scale in favor of
the Trinitarian tradition, was of as much effect as a deci-
sive battle, and not to understand that is to be a poor historian.

—Hilaire Belloc
The Great Heresies

Bearing all this in mind, let us reflect for a moment on our
friend a few chapters back, the "certain lawyer" who sought
to justify himself by challenging Jesus Christ in public. We
noted that when Jesus answered his questions with questions of
His own, the lawyer became very selective about the Scriptural
passages he quoted, editing them to buttress his viewpoint.
While we all undoubtedly "cut to fit" some citations to support our arguments, this man got so caught up in justifying
himself that he missed completely the whole point of Jesus'
parable. He left with only a partial understanding—indeed,
with only a faint shadow of the mountain of knowledge he
could have acquired.

We must never follow suit. We must never confuse theology with personality. Dogmatic and doctrinal discussions
must never be reduced to mere battles of wits, attacks on character, or appeals to pathos. What is at stake is the Truth, not
egos. We are called by God not just to be right but to be
holy—not just to be the winners of debates, but to be the pro-
nouncers of the simple Truth. Make no mistake: the Truth,
with all its subtle ramifications which so titillate the alert and
discriminating cerebellum, is basically very simple. Those
who first proclaimed It were mere fishermen, not professors
and princes, not lecturers or actors skilled in the art of oratory.
And when the opportunity arises for us to speak It, we must
never assume that our own cleverness, cunning, or insight will
convince anyone of something they don't want to accept. It is
very possible to win an argument without convincing the other
person of anything except our superior verbal skills. Those of
Good Will are drawn to the Truth itself, not to acumen. It is
the Holy Ghost who touches hearts, not clever speeches. And
the tougher the going gets, the more true this becomes:

> But look to yourselves. For they shall deliver you
> up to councils, and in the synagogues you shall be

beaten, and you shall stand before governors and kings for my sake, for a testimony unto them ...

And when they shall lead you and deliver you up, be not thoughtful beforehand what you shall speak; but whatsoever shall be given you in that hour, that speak ye. For it is not you that speak, but the Holy Ghost.

—St. Mark XIII:9, 11

In a more perfect and sane century, I could have presented the infallible pronouncements of Popes Innocent III, Boniface VIII, and Eugene IV, eased back in my chair, lit my pipe, and sighed, "There you have it. 'Nuff said. Now we can get on with the business of living the Faith as Our Lord commands." Alas these are "exciting times," and nothing can be taken for granted. Nothing. The details of the Catholic Faith have become so obscure as to become one big blur to most people—clergy included. There's precious little time for blowing smoke rings. Explaining the Faith has become full-time work, and for the most part has fallen into the hands of the laity—the few who care. The battle is uphill all the way; and the hill is steep and the summit is lost in the distance.

I know from experience that some of my readers will categorically reject everything covered in the last seven chapters. They will clutter the air with intellectual objections, appeals to human reason, accusations of spiritual pride, allegations of judgmental thinking, and all manner of dodges and detours which obfuscate the Truth. They will not stand for anything that contradicts "baptism of desire" because they have a great personal stake in it.

Personal stake!? What personal stake?

The same one we all have when we confront the Salutary Dogma: EXTRA ECCLESIAM NULLA SALUS. If there is indeed no Salvation outside the Church, then everyone we pass on the street, encounter in our place of employment, greet in the supermarket, watch on television—everyone who is not a Baptized Roman Catholic will most assuredly go to Hell.* All

---

* The word "Hell," of course, requires some clarification, for the Church teaches that essentially it is the denial of the Beatific Vision. Eternal punishment is another matter, for there are degrees of culpability, and therefore corresponding degrees of punishment.

our friends and relatives, all the folks we know and love, all people who are not Catholics are headed for the same place.

Who do we think we are to say such things? Simple, we are scum like everybody else. We are first and foremost fallen Sons of Adam, born in the state of Original Sin. Second, we are struggling to be obedient followers of Jesus Christ, to keep the Catholic Faith. We make no maudlin claims of being in "higher tuned levels of spiritual awareness"—we'll leave such things to the children of newage. We make no claims of mental, emotional, intellectual or whateveral superiority to anyone else. We are simply reiterating what the Church has openly taught and defended for all but the last century of Her lifetime: there is absolutely no possibility of Salvation outside the Church. None. All our friends, relatives, co-workers, fellow K-Mart shoppers—everyone who is outside the Barque of Peter will surely drown in the Flood of Eternity.

What does that say about us? If we don't speak up, if we don't warn them of their peril, we become accomplices in their demise. On the other hand, if we do speak up, if we tell them the cold hard Truth, we risk committing the most dire sin imaginable in our modern American culture, an evil we have been systematically trained to avoid at all costs, something so sinister our municipal codes bristle with laws attempting to prevent it, a crime of such gross impropriety we can hardly bring ourselves to speak it:

We will *annoy* them.

So here we sit, poised between the defined Dogma of the Church and the derision of our fellow men. We would do well at this juncture to remember the words of Our Divine Savior:

> Therefore fear them not. For nothing is covered that shall not be revealed: nor hid, that shall not be known.
>
> That which I tell you in the dark, speak ye in the light: and that which you hear in the ear, preach ye upon the housetops.
>
> And fear ye not them that kill the body, and are not able to kill the soul: but rather fear him that can destroy both soul and body in hell.
>
> —St. Matthew X:26-28

The only One we need fear is God, for only He can cast us into Hell. The vilest and most violent of men, the ravenous minions of Hell, even Satan himself, cannot do that. And God commands that we speak the Truth, that we spread His message, that we warn our fellow men that they are doomed if they do not repent of their sins and enter the Church in which the Sacraments are preserved and practiced.

This is not being "judgmental"—it is being *obedient*.

Furthermore, when we allow fear, or intellectual pride, or anything at all to come between us and complete acceptance of the entirety of the Roman Catholic Faith, we enter the realm of heresy. Heresy is the denial of any part of the Faith, while maintaining the rest. Invariably it reeks of pride:

> We might put it vividly enough in modern slang by saying that Arianism, thus vigorously present in the new great discussions within the body of the Christian Church when first that Church achieved official support and became the official religion of the Empire, attracted all the "high brows," at least half the snobs and nearly all the sincere idealistic tories—the "diehards"—whether nominally Christian or not.
>
> —Hilaire Belloc
> *The Great Heresies*

Pride, after all, was the real catalyst for the Fall of our First Parents. They disobeyed, yes, but they did so because of their pride—they wanted to "be as Gods." Pride is also the key to our own demise. It starts with a simple "Yes, but ..." Left unchecked, it festers into a gangrenous sore.

With all its posturing concerning the abuse of indulgences, claims of *sola scriptura* and Salvation through Faith alone, the real bedrock of the Protestant Reformation was the denial of the Salutary Dogma. Before then, when people found blemishes and excesses in the Church, they set about correcting them, because there was no place else to go. But a century after Pope Eugene IV infallibly defined that ...

> The most Holy Roman Church firmly believes, professes and preaches, that none of those existing

> outside the Catholic Church, not only pagans, but
> also Jews and heretics and schismatics, can have a
> share in life eternal ...
>
> —Pope Eugene IV
> in his Bull *Cantate Domino*
> at the Council of Florence,1441 AD
> (Denzinger: 714)

... Luther, Calvin and the rest of the "reformers" decided on
their own that Salvation was indeed possible outside the Barque of Peter, and so jumped ship. Once freed from the
authority of the pope, they set themselves up as "arbiters" of
their own Faith—in other words, they decided for themselves
what "felt right," what was "too hard," and what was "true."
The problem was that they, being fallen to begin with, just
went right on falling. Cut off from the promise of the protection of the Holy Ghost, they were left to their own devices.
Hence each time someone got a new insight, they broke away
from their already broken-away sect to form yet another
splinter group, which was already building up to a mitosis of
its own before it began. Really now, it is stretching credulity
just a wee bit to postulate that when Saint Paul wrote ...

> I therefore, a prisoner in the Lord, beseech you that
> you walk worthy of the vocation in which you are
> called,
> With all humility and mildness, with patience,
> supporting one another in charity.
> Careful to keep the unity of the Spirit in the bond
> of peace.
> One body and one Spirit; as you are called in one
> hope of your calling.
> One Lord, one faith, one baptism
>
> —Ephesians IV:1-5

... he was envisioning the clamorous cacophony of over seventy thousand obstreperously disuniting Protestant groups,
disagreeing amongst themselves about every conceivable jot
and tiddle. They can't concur on the necessity of Baptism,
the reality of the Trinity, the Deity of Christ, the immortality
of the soul, the existence of Angels, the Blessedness of Mary,

or the time of day. The process of spiritual disintegration ignited by Luther continues to this day.

> We have before us now the ending experiment of the Reformation ... Such rationalistic efforts against the creed produce a gradual social degradation following on the loss of that direct link between human nature and God which is provided by the Incarnation. Human dignity is lessened. The authority of Our Lord is weakened. He appears more and more as a man—perhaps a myth. The substance of Christian life is diluted. It wanes. What began as Unitarianism ends as Paganism.
>
> —Hilaire Belloc
> *The Great Heresies*

The end, of course, is chaos. Yet somehow Protestant ministers—severed from all Sacramental powers and proud of it—call this rebellious cloud of heretical confusion "the Church." To justify this illusion, they conjure up a myth, a dramatic saga that begins in the first century with Christians who were apparently just like them in all things but television: Massless, priestless, popeless, and hopeless—naturally avoiding the fact that for the first four centuries Christians were also Bible-less. These spinners of remarkable tales go on to say that in the fourth or fifth century an evil faction called "Catholicism" appeared and somehow came to dominate the freewheelin' Christians, subjugating them with artificial ceremonies and contrived doctrines. This arduous slavery, they say, went on for a thousand years until—*bing!*—a savior arrived by the name of Martin Luther who, like a new Moses, freed the forlorn Christians from the snares of the Whore of Babylon, the false Church of Rome.

That none of this has any basis in historical fact is beside the point. They teach this kind of creative narration in their Bible colleges, preach it from their pulpits, and pump it out over the airwaves through their networks of television and radio stations. An afternoon listening to just about any "Christian" radio station—especially if they have professors of Patrology as special guests—can be quite entertaining in this respect. They tell their fabricated history with passionate inten-

sity and sincerity, all the while claiming profound love for the
Bible, the Word of God.

The one thing they omit is that they are all heretics.

They are heretics not because they fabricate history—that's a different sin—but because they deny the very
Words of God. They say Christ didn't mean what He said
about Baptism, establishing a Church under Peter, our need
for consuming His Flesh and Blood, and anything else that
doesn't "feel right" to them. And on and on.

The key, of course, is still "square one," and the degree
to which we place our trust in Jesus Christ. If we turn away the
moment He or His Vicar infallibly declares something, simply
because "we can't accept that"—placing as we do, such
grand importance on our awesome abilities of perception in
the matter—then we are just like the crowd who turned away
when He told them:

> Amen, amen I say unto you: Except you eat the
> flesh of the Son of man, and drink his blood, you
> shall not have life in you ...
> After this many of his disciples went back; and
> walked no more with him.
> —St. John VI:54, 67

Or worse, we become like those who ...

> ... passed by, blasphemed him, wagging their
> heads,
> And saying: Vah, thou that destroyest the temple of
> God, and in three days dost rebuild it: save thy own
> self; if thou be the Son of God, come down from the
> cross.
> In like manner also the chief priests, with the
> scribes and ancients, mocking said:
> He saved others; himself he cannot save. If he be
> the king of Israel, let him now come down from the
> cross, and we will believe him.
> —St. Matthew XXVII:39-42

"My flesh is meat indeed," He had told them, "and my
blood is drink indeed." (St. John VI:56) "Destroy this tem-

ple and in three days I will raise it up." (St. John II:19) They did not understand His sayings, so they balked. They "didn't get it," so they turned away or turned against Him—it amounts to the same thing.

What He did not do was cringe at their reaction and rush to placate them. He did not explain how He was going to do what He claimed—not immediately. He let His detractors stew in their confusion, boiling in their lack of Faith. Some people need to cook for a while before they tire of the struggle. Others, of course, leap from the kettle into the fire. In either case, He was patient. Unlike us, He didn't have to prove anything to save face, for He already knew how He would bring about the fulfillment of His pronouncements. "Transubstantiation" and "Resurrection" would come about, just as light was made in the beginning, by His mere utterance of the words.

Those of Good Will held their ground without full comprehension; while those without reviled that which they did not understand. Our modernist experts, who *still* don't understand, tell us that "we need to develop a new sense of what He meant." Hence they try to change His words into poetry or vague symbolism. But the Bible teaches us that what we need to develop is not a rewording of what He said, not a creative reinterpretation of what He meant, but the patience and trust to see how He will bring about exactly what He said He would accomplish.

The same applies to the Dogma: EXTRA ECCLESIAM NULLA SALUS. Three Vicars of Christ have so spoken *ex cathedra*. We can deal with them in one of two ways. If we choose to accept what they pronounced, trusting that Jesus meant what He said and that His Vicars are protected from defining error by the Holy Ghost, then we, like Peter, will discover that Jesus never lies. He will reward our Faith with a deeper realization and a much more profound appreciation for His power to do what He says He will do.

If, on the other hand, we refuse to believe them—if we deny their infallibility—we will find ourselves starting to justify our disbelief. We will explain away the pronouncements with intellectual arguments. We will hold up all manner of exceptions, excuses, and objections as to why they cannot possibly be so. We will seek to fill our spiritual gullet with words and more words, while our souls begin to wither and Jesus becomes less and less real.

It begins with "Yes, but ..."   But it ends, of course, with the inevitable chaos of heresy.

CHAPTER FORTY-EIGHT

BABEL II

> Come ye, therefore, let us go down, and there con-
> found their tongue, that they may not understand one
> another's speech.
>
> —Genesis XI:7

∞ ∞ ∞

AH YES, THE UPHILL BATTLE …

"But that's not the way I learned it," says a *certain Catholic person,* bristling. "I was never taught that." And then, after a moment's reflection: "And frankly, I cannot accept it."

The "that" in the above statement, refers to the Salutary Dogma of the Roman Catholic Church which has just been pointed out to the Catholic in question, a dogma with which the said Catholic is unfamiliar. Or rather, he is remarkably informed about "baptism of desire," but surprised and appalled by that which it denies, its inverse, namely EXTRA ECCLESIAM NULLA SALUS. We must carefully observe this person's reaction in light of the previous chapters.

"But that's not the way I learned it—I was never taught that." A curious basis on which to build a theological argument, is it not? This *certain Catholic person* assumes that they were somehow protected in their educational experience from exposure to error, by what invisible force or agent is not clear. Someone raised from childhood in Nazi Germany could have claimed as much. Generally, this kind of assertion from a Catholic's lips is a plea for the integrity and orthodoxy of the priests, nuns, and in some cases, parents who were responsible for their religious education. In effect: "Sister Celine taught me 'baptism of desire,' therefore it has to be true," or the weightier, "Father Fulbright said so, and he's a priest," or the mightiest fortress of sound American Catholic teaching of all: "It's in the *Baltimore Catechism.*"

One might, before pursuing the matter on more rigid rules of inquiry, examine the subsequent status of these hallowed people and institutions of sound Catholic pedagogy. Was this the same nun, one might ask, who subsequently traded in her traditional habit for the drab uniform of the modern femi-nun in knee-skirt, panty hose, drab blue sweater, and optional kitchen-towel veil? Is there now a quartz crystal dangling around her neck where once hung a Crucifix? Did she, along with so many of her brethreninas abandon her parish convent, leaving the instruction of Catholic children to the whims of ill-prepared and misinformed lay teachers? Did she leave her order to marry a priest, get a Ph. D. in psychology, adopt a neo-wiccan supra-feminist facili-philosophy, or all three?

Alas, an unbiased determination of nuns[*] and the strain of insanity peculiar to them we will leave to another book by another author, preferably in another language. But as for the critical assessment of priests:

Was this the same Father Fulbright who moved the Tabernacle from the center of the high altar to some dark alcove at the side or the Church, and who later told your daughter or son that it was perfectly all right for them to marry someone outside the Catholic Faith?—and they needn't worry about the religion of the children, if they decided to have any, which they also needn't? Is this the same priest who took all the statues of the Virgin Mary out of the classrooms in the parish school and then added "sex education" to the curriculum, since obviously the two contradicted each other? What became, in this "man of God's" mind and conscience, of the warnings of Saints Peter and Paul:

---

[*] Fairness requires that I mention that through the chaotic times following Vatican II there were many fine, holy nuns who found themselves caught in a vice between their vows and their superiors. Many sisters deserted or changed because they preferred social work to prayer, but other left because they could no longer reconcile the new theology with the old. I've yet to meet a nun who left for the right reasons who was not brutally scarred by the conundrum.

> Dearly beloved, I beseech you as strangers and pil-
> grims, to refrain yourselves from carnal desires which
> war against the soul ...
>
> —I St. Peter II:11

> But fornication and all uncleanness, or covetous-
> ness, let it not so much be as named among you, as
> it becometh saints:
> Nor obscenity, nor foolish talking, nor scurrility,
> which is to no purpose: but rather giving of thanks.
> For know ye this, and understand, that no fornica-
> tors, nor unclean, nor covetous person, which is the
> serving of idols, hath any inheritance in the kingdom
> of Christ, and of God.
> Let no man deceive you with vain words: for be-
> cause of these things cometh the anger of God upon
> the children of unbelief.
> Be ye not, therefore, partakers with them.
>
> —Ephesians V:3-7

What is sex education, if not the riveting of attention on
that which should "not so much be as named among you"?
For how many eons have men and women courted, married,
and procreated without the benefit of classroom instruction on
the matter? What moral or cultural advantage is derived from
focusing our children's minds on genitalia before they even
have the hormones to activate them? Well, let us not stray
down that jagged path. Let's stick to priests:

> I do not speak rashly, but as I feel and think. I do
> not think that many priests are saved, but that those
> that perish are far more numerous. The reason is that
> the office requires a great soul. For there are many
> things to make a priest swerve from rectitude, and he
> requires great vigilance on every side.
>
> —Saint John Chrysostom
> *Third Homily, Acts of the Apostles*

Sounds terribly anticlerical, I'll admit, but Saint John
Chrysostom was the Patriarch of Constantinople and a Doctor
of the Church. He died in 407 AD—how interesting that his

words are equally relevant today. As one of our contempo-
raries has written and for which he has been attacked by
newage Catholics for his trouble:

> One of the most difficult crises facing all Catholics
> today, including the upper clergy, is to see and to ad-
> mit, without hate or despair, that the existential
> church is rotten (to put it mildly) and needs to be
> saved from its awesome filth ...
> Reality is Truth. The truth is that the Church is
> rotten. One is either totally ignorant or demonically
> malicious if he denies the all too obvious.
>
> —Father Paul Trinchard
> *All About Salvation*

Surely, we want to respect our clergy. They are, after all,
the men who offer the Mass, hear our Confessions, marry us
and bury us. We wish to hold them up as examples to our
children. We'd like them to be like our ancestors remember
them. We want to feel towards them like our parents taught us
we were supposed to feel.

But the fact is that most have gone sour. Far too many
have degenerated into outright wickedness—embezzlement,
debauchery and pedophilia being only three examples of their
rampant deterioration—and oh so few are true defenders of
the Faith, if they know it at all. One can't help but grow
weary of making excuses for them, of resorting to phrases
like, "Surely he's a sincere man, even if he is thrashing the
parish." Any Catholic who has approached their pastor with a
request for the Tridentine Mass, or even just permission to receive Holy Communion while kneeling or the reinstitution of
Benediction and other time-honored devotions, soon learns
the true depth of the love and concern of the shepherd for his
flock. The boat, it would seem, has run aground.

We would do well to remember when soberly assessing
the current crisis in the Church that, historically, heresies usually originate amongst the clergy. This is, of course, a shock-
ing thing to say—but the Truth needs a hearing. Rest assured
that these "exciting times" in which we live will give rise to
far more upsetting problems, and far more unnerving revelations, than anything said thus far. Be advised: Courage is a
virtue well worth fostering *now*.

But let us say that Sister Celine and Father Fulbright* were not bad apples like most nuns and priests. Perhaps they were gems—devout, self-sacrificing, and inspiring influences in our lives. Even so, Saints have been wrong about extremely important things. Saint Thomas Aquinas, as we noted earlier, denied the Immaculate Conception—though long before it was infallibly defined. What makes us think that Sister and Father were incapable of error?—that having been taught error themselves, they would do anything other than teach error to their charges?

Chances are they were trained from the *Baltimore Catechism*—the same Catechism which formed most American Catholics for the last hundred plus years. This is where most people—your present author included—first read the phrases "baptism of desire" and "baptism of blood." But we must ask: since when is the *Baltimore Catechism* the sole and comprehensive depository of the Roman Catholic Faith? Since when did its contents assume infallibility?

"But everybody used it," says the *certain Catholic person,* eyes narrowing as if we were suggesting something slanderous about his kid sister. "All the bishops, all the priests, and for years."

Stop. Does the general use of something make it right? If the majority of Americans approve and practice abortion, does that make the thing morally sound? Hardly. Does something held by the majority of the world's bishops somehow become the Truth by virtue of applied democracy? Again: no. The Arian heresy was held by four-fifths of the world's bishops, but it was still heresy. Even Pope Liberius at the time signed—admittedly under pressure, but the example of thousands of martyrs under far more fierce persecution was certainly available to him—a creed of dubious orthodoxy. The Faithful found themselves with wolves for shepherds, and many were driven from their churches and cathedrals. Again, notice the heresy was promulgated by the clergy.

And so in the United States ...

---

* Incidentally, any resemblance of Sister Celine and Father Fulbright to any real characters, living or dead, is purely coincidental. I have never personally known a nun or priest with these names. I chose these names solely on the basis of their subtle suggestive sonic inference.

> ... the Americanists had already scored a victory
> which, unnoticed by their opponents, guaranteed them
> eventual control of the American Church. This was
> the insertion by Cardinal Gibbons into the *Baltimore
> Catechism* of certain questions regarding baptism in
> 1884. The child was asked how many kinds of Bap-
> tism there are, and was expected to reply that there are
> three: of water, of blood, and of desire. Thus was
> speculation erected into dogma. Generations of
> American Catholics were raised supposing that these
> ideas were as much a part of the Faith as the Trinity
> ... by this means the traditional teaching of the
> Church was made to seem quite alien to most of
> those raised with this catechism. After the collapse
> of catechetics in the wake of Vatican II, the compara-
> tive orthodoxy of the *Baltimore Catechism* seemed so
> much better than what was being taught in Catholic
> Schools, that every word of it was given by many
> faithful Catholics practically the status of Holy Writ.
> The idea that it could have been adulterated by earlier
> (and so more restrained) heterodoxy became unthink-
> able.
>
> —Thomas A. Hutchinson
> *Desire and Deception*

This was the same Cardinal Gibbons to which Pope Leo
XIII addressed his Encyclical in 1899, which condemned the
Americanist premise that:

> In order that those who dissent may more easily be
> brought over to Catholic wisdom, the Church should
> come closer to the civilization of this advanced age,
> and relaxing its old severity show indulgence to those
> opinions and theories of the people which have under-
> stood not only with regard to the standard of living,
> but even with regard to the doctrines in which the *de-
> posit of faith* is contained. For, they contend that it
> is opportune to win over those who are in disagree-
> ment, if certain topics of doctrine are passed over as
> of lesser importance, or are so softened that they do
> not retain the same sense as the Church has always
> held.—Now there is no need of a long discussion to

show with what a reprehensible purpose this has been
thought out, if only the character and origin of the
teaching which the Church hands down are considered
...

—Pope Leo XIII
Testem benevolentiae
(Denzinger: 1967)

"Those in disagreement," are of course, the Protestant
majority in the United States, which Cardinal Gibbons and his
fellow bishops were trying furiously to placate—to show them
that American Catholics could "get along" and "go with the
flow." In other words, American Catholics could be good,
cooperative, and docile *citizens*. The wish to relax the rigid
and seemingly harsh doctrines of the Catholic Church is
nothing new. Pope Gregory XVI had this to say about it in
1832:

Now we examine another prolific cause of evils by
which, we lament, the Church is at present afflicted,
namely indifferentism, or that base opinion which has
become prevalent everywhere through the deceit of
wicked men, that eternal salvation of the soul can be
acquired by any profession of faith whatsoever ... And
so from this most rotten source of indifferentism
flows that absurd and erroneous opinion, or rather insanity, that liberty of conscience must be claimed and
defended for everyone.

Indeed, to this most unhealthy error that full and
immoderate liberty of opinions which is spreading
widely to the destruction of the sacred and civil welfare opens the way, with some men repeatedly assert-
ing with supreme boldness that some advantage flows
therefrom to religion itself. But "what death of the
soul is worse than freedom for error?" Augustine used
to say ...

—Pope Gregory XVI
Mirari vos abritramur
(Denzinger: 1613, 1614)

In a country that flaunts phrases like "worship together in
the church of your choice," "we all worship the same God,

but not in the same way," and "you have your truth, and I have mine," the above Papal citations must give us pause. The cultural undertone of the United States, having been formed and fueled by Protestantism, has at its heart the rejection of papal authority, all Catholic practices, and most assuredly the Salutary Dogma. The United States is often described by her journalists and leaders as a "Christian country," so much so that it comes as a complete shock to most of us that:

> There is no such thing as a religion called "Christianity"—there never has been such a religion.
> There is and always has been the Church, and various heresies proceeding from a rejection of some of the Church's doctrines ...
> No; the quarrel is between the Church and the anti-Church—the Church of God and anti-God—the Church of Christ and anti-Christ.
>
> —Hilaire Belloc
> *The Great Heresies*

This is the hardest nut for many Catholics to crack: the fact that Christianity isn't what they thought it was. Dangling from the same cluster of unthinkable nuts is one that is almost impossible to swallow: the fact that the *Baltimore Catechism* contains dogmatic error, and this error was presented to them as official Church teaching. How mind-boggling it is to think that one has been lied to, and that one has lived the entirety of their lives believing, and even proclaiming the lie. The word "betrayal" is appropriate, for that is what happened; but the words "justifiable anger" do not come into play, because "denial" is what most often occurs. The Catholic says, "It cannot be that the *Baltimore Catechism* was wrong," or, in effect, "It cannot be that I have been misled."

This last is, of course, the heart of the matter: pride. The great and awesome "I" raises its insidious head yet again.

What the *certain Catholic* needs to remember is that all men are born in Original Sin, and all who grow to the age of reason commit actual sins of their own. All men are subject to error, and the only things which we can count on as being absolutely dependable are the revealed Truths in Sacred Scripture, the official teachings of the Catholic Faith, and the infallible statements of the popes.

So how did something which is patently not of the Faith come to be incorporated into a book which purports to be a presentation of the Catholic Faith? This is a long story, and one which has been handled better and at great length by others. Suffice it to say that the Catholic bishops in America as a whole have consistently shown a tendency to do everything they could to "blend in" to the cultural melting pot that is the United States. Historically they have demonstrated far more zeal in supporting "democratic principles" and "social issues" than determination to convert the Protestants and other religious groups into the True Faith. Essentially they have abandoned their calling and their duty as bishops, and they have rallied their subordinate priests and nuns to their new cause.

These are, of course, generalities. There have been good bishops among the bad. Cardinal McIntyre of Los Angeles was a remarkable example of a solid Catholic prelate who was a good shepherd to his flock in Los Angeles, all the while keeping a tight rein on the movie industry which was flickering licentiously in his backyard. But he was, alas, one of few exceptions.

The bishops of the United States got it into their heads long ago that if they got together and made verbose pronouncements, their decrees and decisions would carry some kind of weight. Instead of calling such events "usurpations of ecclesiastical power" or "quasi-cumenical councils of dubious intent or purpose," they call them "bishops' conferences." But whatever the handle, there is no provision in Tradition or the Code of Canon Law for such events, and their decisions are certainly not binding. The only councils that are protected by the Holy Ghost are those convoked and presided over by popes.

Cardinal Gibbons, not the pope, convened the Council of Baltimore in the last century. And it was at this august misassembly's direction that a new Catechism was drawn up. It was supposed to be a distillation of the pronouncements of the Council of Trent. This new Catechism for America, furthermore, contained some significant statements never defined or even discussed at Trent. The terms "baptism of desire" and "baptism of blood" among them.

What the Council of Trent *did* say was:

> Canon II. If anyone saith that true and natural water
> is not of necessity for baptism, and, on that account,
> wrests to some sort of metaphor those words of our
> Lord Jesus Christ: "Unless a man be born again of
> water and the Holy Ghost;" let him be anathema.
>
> —Countil of Trent
> "On Baptism"
> Session VII, Decree on the Sacraments

"But I know the Council of Trent said *something* about desire," says our *certain Catholic person.*

Yes, it most certainly did. So much, in fact, that we will leave it for the next chapter—

"But what about an ignorant native on a desert island?" interrupts a *second Catholic person,* a woman sitting next to the *certain one* with whom we've been conversing. This *second Catholic person* has a gleam in her eye, the knowing glow of the well-read. "What about invincible ignorance? Pope Pius IX said—ahem!—and I quote: *'it is certain that those who labor in ignorance of the true religion, if this ignorance is invincible, are not guilty in the eyes of God.'"*

Close. Very close. This line is often cited by modernists in support of "baptism of desire."* The problem here is threefold: 1) the matter was settled centuries ago by three infallible papal decrees and is therefore moot; 2) the allocution from which this is quoted was not an infallible statement; and 3) this quotation is taken completely out of context. In fact, when read within its original paragraph, we find that Pope Pius IX was actually *upholding* the Salutary Dogma:

> For, it must be held by faith that outside the Apos-
> tolic Roman Church, no one can be saved; that this is
> the only ark of salvation; that he who shall not have
> entered therein will perish in the flood; but on the
> other hand, it is necessary to hold for certain that
> those who labour in ignorance of the true religion, if

---

* Indeed, I have even found "invincible ignorance" referred to as Pope Pius IX's *Doctrine* on the internet. One can only imagine how His Holiness would react to such gross misrepresentation.

this ignorance is invincible, are not sustained by guilt in this matter in the eyes of God. Now, in truth, who would arrogate so much to himself as to mark the limits of such an ignorance, because of the nature and variety of peoples, regions, innate dispositions, and of so many other things? For in truth, when released from these corporeal chains "we shall see God as He is," we shall understand perfectly by how close a bond divine mercy and justice are united; but, as long as we are on earth, weighed down by this mortal mass which blunts the soul, let us hold most firmly, that, in accordance with Catholic teaching, there is "one God, one faith, one baptism;" it is unlawful to proceed further in inquiry.

—Pope Pius IX
Singulari quadem, December 9, 1854
(Denzinger: 1647)

Let us observe a few details:

"For, it must be held by faith that outside the Apostolic Roman Church, no one can be saved; that this is the only ark of salvation ..." Unless words don't mean what they mean, it would seem that Pope Pius IX was anything but a denigrator of the Salutary Dogma.

"... those who labor in ignorance of the true religion, if this ignorance is invincible ..." Okay, he did use the term "invincible" in connection with "ignorance." But before we jump to all kinds of conclusions, we should take notice:

> It should be readily apparent here that there is no question of "invincible" ignorance being *salvific;* merely that if it is truly "invincible" (and His Holiness confesses himself incapable of saying much beyond that) it absolves the individual from the guilt of the specific sin of refusing to join the Church. This is not the same thing as saying such a one will be saved thereby.
>
> —Thomas A. Hutchinson
> *Desire and Deception*

In other words, this invincibly ignorant person is not guilty *"in this matter"* — but he is still, nonetheless, outside the Church, outside of which *"no one can be saved."* Ignorance may be bliss, but it is not a virtue that makes one worthy of Heaven.

And in conclusion: *"... there is 'one God, one faith, one baptism;' it is unlawful to proceed further in inquiry."* Now this is an extremely important point, and one which seems to slip through the cracks ever so easily. The Dogma of the Church having been stated, it is *unlawful* to proceed with further inquiry. The word "unlawful" could also be translated "criminal." In other words, in spite of all these questions and details, the teachings of the Church are clear and are not to be questioned.

Or, to put it another way, when it comes to discussions of Defined Teachings of the Roman Catholic Church vs. the modernist case for "baptism of desire," the mathematics often boils down to something like this: on one side of the chalkboard we have the following column of addition:

>   *Ex cathedra* infallible Papal Statement
> \+   *Ex cathedra* infallible Papal Statement
> \+   *Ex cathedra* infallible Papal Statement
> =   Defined Dogma of the Church

And on the other side we have one simple subtraction:

>   Defined Dogma of the Church
> \-   Something said or written by a Pope or Saint in a
>   non-infallible letter or sermon taken entirely
>   out of context
> =   Aha! Proof of "baptism of desire"

Not only is this kind of thinking illogical, unreasonable, petty, and certainly contrived, it is also "unlawful" — (insert the word "sinful") — because it incorporates a flat denial of Papal Infallibility.

"And when were those papal statements made?" asks the *certain Catholic person,* leaning forward intently.
"Let's see ... 1215, 1302, and 1441 AD."

"Ah," he says, leaning back confidently. "There you have it."

"Have what?"

"Those pronouncements were made without full knowledge on the part of the popes."

"What do you mean, 'without full knowledge'?"

"They didn't yet know about the millions of people living here in the New World because it hadn't been discovered yet. If they had known, they never would have said such narrow-minded things."

"Hold on," we say, thumbing through our pocket edition of *Dogmatic Canons and Decrees of the Council of Trent*. "What year did Columbus discover America?"

"Is this a trick question?"

"No, what year?"

"1492."

"Well, in 1547 the Council of Trent declared:

> Canon III. If anyone saith that in the Roman Church, which is the mother and mistress of all churches, there is not the true doctrine concerning the sacrament of Baptism; let him be anathema ...
>
> Canon V. If anyone saith that baptism is free, that is, not necessary unto salvation; let him be anathema.
>
> —Council of Trent
> "On Baptism"
> Session VII, Decree on the Sacraments

Certainly the Council Fathers were aware of the pagan populations in the New World after it had been explored for half a century. Besides, the Church knew from the beginning that there were millions of people spread throughout the lands beyond their horizons. This never affected Her understanding of the need for them to be baptized in order to get to Heaven. Why else would Saint Francis Xavier, famous missionary to the Orient who Baptized some three million people, have composed this prayer:

> Eternal God, Creator of all things, remember that souls of unbelievers have been created by Thee and formed to Thy own image and likeness.

Behold, O Lord, how to Thy dishonor hell is being filled with these very souls.

Remember that Jesus Christ, Thy Son, for their salvation suffered a most cruel death.

Do not permit, O Lord, I beseech Thee, that Thy Divine Son be any longer despised by unbelievers, but rather, being appeased by the prayers of thy saints and of the Church, the most holy spouse of Thy Son, deign to be mindful of Thy mercy and forgetting their idolatry and unbelief, bring them to Him Whom Thou didst send, Jesus Christ, Thy Son, Our Lord, Who is our health, life, and resurrection, through Whom we have been redeemed and saved, to Whom be all glory forever. Amen.

"So what you're saying," says the *second Catholic person,* "is that only Catholics go to Heaven."

Yes, we are saying that, but not as a personal opinion, but rather as a statement of the defined dogma of the Church. But make no mistake: not all Catholics go to Heaven, either.

It looks very bad for God, they say, if five-sixths of the world are not going to Heaven, and only one-sixth of the world is. And then I have to explain that that one-sixth of the world does not necessarily go to Heaven, either, just because it is Catholic. A Catholic has a hard time to save his soul. It is not enough to be a Catholic to get to Heaven. One has to be a good Catholic.

Do I think *I* am going to be saved? I do not know for sure. I must measure up to the requirements of salvation. But I know for sure what those requirements are.

The first requirement is that I persevere in the Catholic Faith. This is the highest achievement a man can aspire to, and the highest favor God can bestow. No one can merit this great favor. One can only pray for it, while doing all in one's power to please God and to fulfill His commands.

It has been rumored that I have been telling those among whom I work that I, and possibly they, will go to Heaven, and that the rest of the world will go to

Hell. That is not true. We are Catholics, not Cal-
vinists. What I have been saying is that the majority
of the world will not save their souls, and we hope
and pray that we will not be part of that majority.
—Father Leonard Feeney MICM
Bread of Life

"By your way of thinking," says the *certain Catholic person,* "my Uncle Fred—who I'll have you know is a very intelligent, honest, hard-working Lutheran—will not go to
Heaven. I know for a fact he loves Jesus with all his heart and
soul. He can't help it if He can't accept the Catholic Faith."

Why can't he help it? What is it about him that makes it
impossible for him to accept the Catholic Faith—the Faith established by the very Jesus Christ he so claims to love?

"Invincible ignorance" in this case seems to have
come to mean: *hopelessly incapable of understanding.*
Since even little children can grasp the Faith, invincible ignorance must be a most dense form of stupid-
ity ... Liberal Catholics, at haste to protect the majority of Harvard faculty members and students from
our denunciation of them as atheistic, agnostic, and
heretical, have declared them to be, rather, simply
"invincibly ignorant." We do not think Harvard
would be happy about this designation, but might, on
the other hand, prefer our appraisal of them as "invincibly proud."
—Catherine Goddard Clarke
Gate of Heaven

By a remarkable flash of liberal double-think, modern
Catholics have been nurtured, coaxed and lulled into the accepting attitude that a man, even if he viciously rejects, denies,
and rails against the very thought that he might ever become a
Catholic, is somehow saved because he implicitly belongs to
the Church—the "Church" redefined as this vague idea of
the "people of God." That such a self-contradictory rationale is no rationale at all is lost to them—especially if the man
in question is Uncle Fred. But there is another point of view:

Hell is where Lutherans go.
—Saint Theresa of Avila
Quoted in *The Apostolic Digest*

"Who do you think you are," chimes the *certain Catholic person* and their new friend, the *second Catholic person,* in unison, "to decide who goes to Hell when they die?" Ah, when reason fails there is always personal attack, a clear indicator that frank discussion and genuine inquiry have just ceased.

The only reply to give, as we rise from the table to leave, is the honest answer: "I decide nothing. I am a wretched sinner who has just told you what the Holy Catholic Church teaches. No more, no less."

∞   ∞   ∞

And therefore the name thereof was called Babel, because there the language of the whole earth was confounded ...
—Genesis XI:9

CHAPTER FORTY-NINE

OF LAVERS AND LADLES

> Like most modern words, "Heresy" is used both vaguely and diversely. It is used vaguely because the modern mind is as averse to precision in ideas as it is enamored of precision in measurement. It is used diversely because, according to the man who uses it, it may represent one of fifty things.
>
> —Hilaire Belloc
> *The Great Heresies*

∞ ∞ ∞

THIS IS, ADMITTEDLY, A "HEADY" CHAPTER. Rather more academic than most. Perhaps our reader has prayed for Patience, and this it the answer to prayer. Hilaire Belloc, the historian, often referred to Catholicism as "the thinking man's religion." Whatever the case, let us proceed:

The other night I was having late-night under-the-stars kind of "deep" discussion with one of my students. A "former Catholic," he was big on expansive thoughts such as "there are many paths to God" and "God depends on *us* for His existence, since we are all God," but he was utterly clueless about such things as the Mass being a Solemn Sacrifice in which God is offered to God, or why there should be any religious definition of sin since "we should decide such thing for ourselves." I tried to show him, with admittedly abysmal success, that the "most wicked of organized religions," as he deemed Catholicism, is something outside his experience; something entirely other than the tasteless porridge fed to him by the lay teachers who replaced the nuns who fled the parish when they went insane. He did not know, because he had not been taught, anything about Original Sin, the Sacraments, or even the barest modicum of Revealed Truth. What he scorns is a sad, wispy parody of the Real Church.

He is not alone. Even the most Tradition-minded among us are groping their way through vast swamps of insidious misinformation. In no arena does this become more obvious than in discussions of the EXTRA ECCLESIAM NULLA SALUS vs. "baptism of desire and blood." It isn't just that sincere Catholics don't understand the finality of papal infallibility; they lack the basic grasp of foundational things without which they cannot make sound judgments about these matters.

> And every one that heareth these my words, and doth them not, shall be like a foolish man that built his house upon the sand,
> And the rain fell, and the floods came, and the winds blew, and they beat upon that house, and it fell, and great was the fall thereof.
> —St. Matthew VII:26-27

If, for example, the discussion enters the realm of Justification and Salvation, accusations of "you're splitting hairs" begin to fly. The fact is that Justification and Salvation are *not the same thing at all,* just as Salvation and Redemption *are not synonymous* (as we saw in Chapter 16). Oh, but there we go "getting technical again."

> We must begin by a definition, although definition involves a mental effort and therefore repels.
> —Hilaire Belloc
> *The Great Heresies*

Like it or not, the seeker of Truth must confront, understand, and absorb these things in order to comprehend clearly his own Faith, and then to explain it precisely to others. This is more true in today's world of "double-truths" and "non-specific disinformation" than ever. Furthermore, we need to perceive with what cleverness Satan through his modernist puppets has twisted the Truth into the imprecise swill which permeates the Church and from which we must somehow extract ourselves. This takes some degree of patient study. If precision of thought is against our nature, then perhaps life in a hermitage remote from the chaos of our day may just be our thing! Ah, but ...

> The wide world is all about you; you can fence yourselves in, but you cannot for ever fence it out.
> —J. R. R. Tolkien
> *The Lord of the Rings*

Be that as it may, let us start with Salvation, which is the *eternal* state of Happiness in Heaven. There, that wasn't so bad as definitions go, was it?

Justification: being in the *immediate* state of Sanctifying Grace, free from mortal sin. Again, not too hard.

The words *eternal* and *immediate* are italicized to emphasize their dissimilarity. Salvation, which is Eternal, is forever, and will only be experienced after death; whereas Justification, which is temporary, can be most fleeting, and has to do with the here and now. Mortal sin shatters it instantly. So completely distinct are Salvation and Justification that the Council of Trent treated them as entirely separate entities.

Now, let us deal with these two concepts in concrete fashion, drawing on premises we've covered throughout this book, observing carefully how the logic of the thing progresses:

We know from reading the Epistle of Saint Paul that Abraham was justified by his Faith:

> For we say that unto Abraham faith was reputed to justice* ...
> For not through the law was the promise to Abraham, or to his seed, that he should be heir of the world; but through the justice of faith.
> —Romans IV:9, 13

He was in the *immediate* state of Grace because he was justified by his Faith in God and His promises. But when he died, did Abraham go to the *eternal* state of Heaven?

The answer is *no*.

---

* The word *justice* in the Douay-Rheims translation is synonymous with *justification*.

If we were just taken aback because our answer was "yes," it shows that we've forgotten something very critical: the reality of Original Sin. Baptism by "water and the Holy Ghost" is the only means prescribed by Jesus Christ for entry into His Kingdom, for it is the only way to cleanse the immortal soul of the state of Original Sin into which it is born.

According to the Council of Trent, Justification is defined as being ...

> ... a translation from that state wherein man is born a child of the first Adam to the state of grace...
> —Council of Trent
> Session VI, Chapter IV

In the Old Testament, as with the case of Abraham, Justification could be achieved by Faith. But ...

> ... this translation, since the promulgation of the Gospel, cannot be effected without the laver of regeneration or the *votum* thereof, as it is written: "Unless a man be born again of water and the Holy Ghost, he cannot enter into the kingdom of God."
> —Council of Trent
> Session VI, Chapter IV

Since the "promulgation of the Gospel," the mandate of Jesus Christ takes all precedence. The "laver of regeneration," the Sacrament of Baptism, is required. (We will come back to the word *votum* in a moment.) Baptism is the only way to transcend the fate which would otherwise be ours. Baptism is the door by which we enter the Church, and it is within the Church that we find the *hope* of Salvation. The Church, by infallible papal declaration defines Herself as the Mystical Body of Christ (emphasis added):

> *Ex cathedra:* "Urged by faith, we are obliged to believe and to hold that the Church is one, holy, catholic, and also apostolic. We firmly believe in her, and we confess absolutely that outside of her there is neither salvation nor the remission of sins, as the Spouse in the Canticles (VI, 8) proclaims: "One is my dove, my perfect one. She is the only one of her

mother, the chosen of her that bore her," *who repre-*
sents one mystical body, whose head is Christ, and
the head of Christ is God ...

—Pope Boniface VIII
in his Bull *Unam Sanctam,* 1302 AD
(Denzinger: 468)

The words "Roman Catholic Church" and "Mystical
Body of Christ" are therefore synonymous. And, since ...

... no man hath ascended into heaven, but he that
descended from heaven, the Son of man who is in
heaven ...

—St. John III:13

... our only hope of entry into Heaven is to become One with
that Man Who Ascended, Jesus Christ and by extension His
Mystical Body, who descended from Heaven and ascends back
to Heaven.

Do you want to ascend to Heaven, too? Then become a member of Him Who alone ascends. For He
is one man with the other members! What do these
words mean if not that no one ascends into Heaven
who has not been made one with Him and, as a
member, becomes hidden within the Body of Him
Who has descended from Heaven? And what is that
Body if not the Church? ...
The Lord has determined that the kingdom of
Heaven should be conferred only on baptized persons.
If eternal life can accrue only to those who have been
baptized, if follows, of course, that they who die unbaptized incur everlasting death.

—Saint Augustine
Quoted in the *Apostolic Digest*

If there were "exceptions," surely Jesus would have stated
them. All His pronouncements in this regard were most force-
ful and specific. No man since Adam, no matter how righteous and faithful he was, no matter how much abuse he suffered at the hands of evildoers—*no man entered Heaven until*
Jesus' Ascension forty days after the Resurrection. All the

men and women who died before that grand event went to the
Limbo of the Just, which, being hidden from the Beatific Vision, is part of Hell. Those of us who recite the Rosary daily
are so used to saying the words of the Apostles' Creed that we
may have missed their significance:

> He descended into Hell; the third day he rose again
> from the dead.*
> > —The Apostles' Creed

We have been so jaded by fundamentalist ministers mis-
representing Hell that we refrain from using the word as much
as possible (except when we're angry), but the fact is that Jesus spoke more of Hell than Heaven in the New Testament—the reason being that the majority of souls go there.
When He died on the Cross, He went to that part of Hell called
the Limbo of the Just to teach all the souls who were awaiting
the Ascension since the dawn of time:

> Because Christ also died once for our sins, the just
> for the unjust; that he might offer us to God, being
> put to death indeed in the flesh, but enlivened in the
> spirit.
> In which also coming he preached to those spirits
> that were in prison:
> Which had been some time incredulous, when they
> waited for the patience of God in the days of Noe ...
> > —I St. Peter III:18-20

There they were taught by Jesus Christ Himself; there they
were prepared for entry into Heaven when Jesus ascended after His Resurrection. Thus did the men and women of the Old
Testament achieve their Salvation.

Since the "promulgation of the Gospel," however, and by
proclamation of Jesus Himself, Baptism became the fundamental requirement for the possibility of Salvation from that
time on. We cannot overemphasize the need for water Bap-

---

*If your missal or prayer book mistranlates this, "He descended among the
dead," it is clearly denying or circumventing this truth which has been
handed down to us from apostolic times.

tism, nor can we change the explicit words of Christ regarding it. As infallibly defined by the Council of Trent:

> Canon II. If anyone saith that true and natural water is not of necessity for baptism, and, on that account, wrests to some sort of metaphor those words of our Lord Jesus Christ: "Unless a man be born again of water and the Holy Ghost;" let him be anathema.
> —Council of Trent
> "On Baptism"
> Session VII, Decree on the Sacraments

What are "baptism of desire" and "baptism of blood" except attempts to "wrest to some sort of metaphor" the words of Jesus Christ, "unless a man be born again of water and the Holy Ghost, he cannot enter into the kingdom of God"? The same Council made it perfectly clear that just "believing" is not enough for Salvation; that participation in the Sacramental action of the Church is absolutely required:

> Canon IV: If anyone saith that the sacraments of the New Law are not necessary unto salvation, but superfluous; and that without them, or without the *votum* thereof men obtain of God through faith alone the grace of justification ... let him be anathema.
> —Council of Trent
> "On the Sacraments in General"

Furthermore, Faith alone will not absolve and justify a man. Sacraments are necessary for this, as well as active observance of the Commandments of God and of the Church:

> Canon XIV. If anyone saith that man is truly absolved from his sins and justified, because that he assuredly believed himself absolved and justified ... and that, by this faith alone, absolution and justification are effected; let him be anathema.

> Canon XX. If anyone saith that the man who is justified and how perfect soever is not bound to observe the Commandments of God and of the Church, but only to believe; as if indeed the Gospel were a

bare and absolute promise of eternal life, without the
condition of observing the Commandments; let him
be anathema.
                              —Council of Trent
                              "On Justification"
                              Session VI, Chapter XVI

If *explicitly believing* in the precepts of Christ and His
Church does not effect Salvation without the *actual physical
reception* of the Sacraments, then where does that leave people
who don't believe it at all?
    Most people, as they read the Trent Decrees, out of igno-
rance of these distinctions, mentally substitute "Salvation" for
"Justification" and *vice versa,* which leads to enormous confusion. The word "Salvation" only applies when we have
made it to Heaven. Baptism makes us members of the Church,
the Body of Christ, and therein lies the *only hope* of achieving
Salvation. Even so, being in the Church only makes Salvation
possible, not guaranteed.

No doubt, without Baptism no one can come to
God. But not everyone who receives Baptism comes
to God.
                              —Saint Augustine
                              Quoted in *The Apostolic Digest*

Most Protestants adhere to the belief that "faith alone"
assures, not only Justification, but Salvation; and that once
someone "believes," Salvation cannot be lost no matter what
sins one commits. They base this concept on one isolated
verse:

That if thou shalt confess with thy mouth the Lord
Jesus, and shalt believe in thine heart that God hath
raised him from the dead, thou shalt be saved.
                              —Romans 10:9
                              King James Version

Naturally, they rarely go on to the next verse, which di-
vides Justification as the result of a change of heart, from Salvation, the achievement of Sacramental action. (In the King

James Version we find the word "righteousness"* in place of Justice or Justification.)

> For with the heart man believeth unto righteousness; and with the mouth confession is made unto salvation.
> —Romans 10:10
> King James Version

Since the Council of Trent was called to clearly define Catholic Teaching in light of the Protestant Reformation, this basic Protestant tenet is exposed as error:

> Canon XVIII. If anyone saith that the commandments of God are, even for one that is justified and constituted in grace, impossible to keep; let him be anathema.
> Canon XIX. If anyone saith that nothing besides faith is commanded in the Gospel, that other things are indifferent, neither commanded nor prohibited, but free; or that the Ten Commandments no wise appertain to Christians; let him be anathema.
> —Council of Trent
> "On Justification"
> Session VI, Chapter XVI

We must struggle to keep our terms absolutely straight. "Believing," even explicitly, in the teachings of Christ will not bring about *eternal* Salvation, but only *immediate* Justification. One does indeed receive Grace by certain acts—such as Faith, Hope, Charity, Repentance, and Contrition, as well as the intention of receiving a Sacrament—but mere intention alone is not enough. Intention does not bring about the Reality of the Sacrament. Without actual water Baptism, Salvation is not possible.

---

* The Douay-Rheims translation is as follows: "For if thou confess with thy mouth the Lord Jesus, and believe in thy heart that God hath raised him up from the dead, thou shalt be saved. For, with the heart, we believe unto justice; but, with the mouth, confession is made unto salvation." *Justice*, remember, is the same as *Justification* in this translation.

> Canon V. If anyone saith that baptism is free, that
> is, not necessary unto salvation; let him be anathema.
> —Council of Trent
> "On the Sacraments in General"
> Session VII, Decree on the Sacraments

We don't tend to get into the same kind of turmoil with respect to the other Sacraments: If a devout woman "intends" to receive Holy Communion, but for whatever reason doesn't get to Mass, she doesn't somehow "receive" the actual Eucharist by virtue of her "desire" to do so. A man who attends the seminary because of his earnest wish to be a priest, but through some bizarre series of unfortunate circumstances while on leave to visit his parents gets stranded on a desert island, does not somehow receive Holy Orders—the power to confect the Blessed Sacrament and to forgive Sins—simply because that had been his sincere intention.

The "double standard" with respect to Baptism which kicks in with the introduction of "baptism of desire" suggests that we don't take Original Sin seriously; we don't see it as a real disease of the whole person. Similarly, we haven't been properly instructed in the need to incorporate ourselves into the Body of Christ—in essence, to "make us Jesus"—so that we can enter with Him into Heaven. Hence we don't take water Baptism seriously.

The Canons and Decrees of the Council of Trent are so clear on this issue—and the pronouncements of Trent, being ecumenical in the classic sense and ratified by the pope, are infallible—that one wonders how all the confusion got started. The decline in clear Catechetics has certainly played its part. For example, the *Catechism of the Council of Trent,* the summary of Catholic teaching ordered by the Council itself, says in the section on adult Baptism:

> ... should any unforeseen accident make it impossible for adults to be washed in the salutary waters, their intention and determination to receive Baptism and their repentance for past sins, will avail them to grace and righteousness.
> —*Catechism of the Council of Trent*

Though this sentence is often cited by modernists as proof that "intention" is enough to earn Salvation; the discerning reader will note that the specific return for "intention and determination" is "grace and righteousness" —Justification, not Salvation. We must realize that these words were written the way they were because the writers assumed their readers understood these basic differences. Little did they suspect that, several centuries hence, most Catholics would not know, or care to learn, the difference!

The *Catechism of Trent,* unlike the Council of Trent, is *not* infallible—which is why the term "unforeseen accident" appears at all. Since when do things "slip by" God? The suggestion that somehow God "blinks" and events go awry is absurd. If a catechumen dies before receiving Baptism, it cannot be a fluke—otherwise, God is not Omnipotent. It could well be that God perceives a lack of inner sincerity which we cannot detect; or it could be that God intends to work a greater miracle in the person's life by arranging for a Saint to raise him from the dead so that his Baptism may attract public attention.

> In the country of Neyll, a King Echu allowed St. Patrick to receive his beloved daughter Cynnia as a nun, though he bewailed the fact that his royal line would thereby end without issue. The king exacted a promise from Patrick not to insist that he be baptized, yet to promise him the heavenly kingdom. Patrick agreed, and left the matter in the hands of God.
>
> Sometime later King Echu lay dying. He sent a messenger to St. Patrick to tell him he desired Baptism and the heavenly kingdom. To those around him the King gave an order that he not be buried until Patrick came. Patrick, then in the monastery of Saballum, two days' journey away, knew of the situation through the Holy Spirit before the messenger even arrived. He left to go to the King, but arrived to find Echu dead.
>
> St. Patrick revived the King, instructed him, and baptized him. He asked Echu to relate what he had seen of the joys of the just and the pains of the wicked, so that his account could be used for the

proving of Patrick's preaching. Echu told of many
other-world wonders and of how, in the heavenly
country, he had seen the place Patrick had promised
him. But the King could not enter in because he was
unbaptized.

Then St. Patrick asked Echu if he would rather live
longer in this world, or go to the place prepared for
him in the heavenly kingdom. The King answered
that all the world had was emptiest smoke compared
to the celestial joys. Then having received the Eucharist, he fell asleep in the Lord.

—Father Albert J. Herbert, SM
Raised from the Dead *

So real is the need for water Baptism, that even unborn
and newborn infants who die without it, cannot enter the
Kingdom of Heaven. This is indeed hard to swallow; but so is
the dire fact of Original Sin.

On account of this rule of faith, even infants who
in themselves have not been able to commit any sin
are truly baptized unto the remission of sins, so that
the sin they contracted from generation may be
cleansed by regeneration ... Likewise, if anyone says
that it might be understood that, in the kingdom of
Heaven, there will be some middle place or some
place anywhere that infants live who departed this life
without Baptism, without which they cannot enter
into the kingdom of Heaven which is eternal life: let
him be anathema.

—Saint Pope Zosimus
Quoted in the *Apostolic Digest*

Here is where most people balk, and even the steel-
knuckled Traditionalists are tempted to embrace some kind of
escape clause for the sake of innocent babies. We must step
back and take stock of all that we've learned about God. First
and foremost, He cares for us with a Love beyond our imagination. Second, anyone dying in the state of Original Sin is

---

* Resurrection for the sake of Baptism is a common theme throughout this
remarkable book.

incapable of entering Heaven.   Third, "Hell" is the state of
being outside the Beatific Vision; while "eternal torment in
Hell" is reserved for the culpable, not the innocent—and the
amount of punishment is proportional to the degree of culpability.   To say that unbaptized infants go to Hell, or to a part
of thereof called "Limbo," is not to suggest they suffer torment; but rather they experience whatever natural happiness is
suited to their stage of development.   Fourth, it is not beyond
speculation or hope that on the Last Day many will be raised
to be Baptized à la Saint Patrick.*   And fifth, how Jesus plans
to work everything out has not been revealed to us, just as He
did not explain how He intended to rebuild the temple in three
days. The more we get to know God, and see Him working in
our lives, the more we grow to Trust Him. Here is where a life
of Faith really kicks in.

> Innocent III (patron of Ss. Dominic and Francis),
> was at great pains, however, to distinguish between
> the eternal fate of unbaptized infants and adults. "The
> penalty of original sin is the loss of the vision of
> God; the penalty for actual sin is the torment of ever-
> lasting hell" (Denzinger 410).   Lack of baptism
> leaves the individual merely a fallen man, incapable
> of ascending to Heaven and the beatific vision; actual
> and unforgiven sin is punished according to its kind.
> So the Just in the Old Law were confined in the
> Limbo of the Fathers until Christ freed them: without
> punishment, because their sins had been forgiven, but
> without viewing God, because of their very nature.
> The same was therefore held of unbaptized infants
> who had no actual sin because of their extreme youth,
> but were incapable of Heaven because of their human-
> ity.   To they too were said to be in a sort of
> Limbo—"of the Infants."   The rest of unbaptized
> adulthood obviously had greater or lesser sins on their
> souls, in addition to being part of Fallen Man.
> —Thomas A. Hutchinson
> *Desire and Deception*

---

* This is why obtaining and reading *Raised from the Dead* by Father Albert
J. Herbert, SM is a must, demonstrating as it does, the power and love of
Almighty God even in the face of death.

Now we must deal with the mystery word, *votum,* which has appeared in several Trent documents. Let us examine the following text, part of which we looked at before:

> By which words a description of the justification of the impious is indicated—as being a translation from that state wherein man is born as a child of the first Adam to the state of grace and of the adoption of the sons of God through the second Adam, Jesus Christ, our Savior. And this translation, since the promulgation of the Gospel, cannot be effected without the laver of regeneration or the *votum* thereof, as it is written: "Unless a man be born again of water and the Holy Ghost, he cannot enter into the kingdom of God."
>
> —Council of Trent
> Section VI, Chapter IV:
> Dogmatic Decree on Justification
> (Emphasis mine.)

In most English editions, *votum* is translated "desire." This is not only misleading, but flatly erroneous. A *votum* is a solemn oath, a serious promise to do something. It is normally translated "vow," and from it we derive our word "vote." It has nothing whatsoever to do with a "wish" or a "vague yearning," but is rather a word denoting a definite decision. The Latin word for "desire" is *cupidere,* which is certainly not in the original source text. Again we find evidence that the English language works against us, and that translators who speak it are influenced, albeit subliminally, by its anti-Catholic pro-Protestant undertones. Hence this kind of subtle obfuscation of the real meaning of the Trent decree.

The decree from which the above citation is taken is about Justification, not Salvation. What this passage is indicating is that in order to pass from the state of Sin into the state of Grace one must receive the Sacrament of water Baptism or its *votum,* i.e., formally-vowed intention. Taken out of context, this might be misunderstood as a loophole for "baptism of desire," but in light of the multitude of instances where Trent infallibly defines the various conscious acts which are necessary for making this vow—Perfect Contrition, True Repen-

tance, Acts of Faith, Hope and Charity, etc.—and the absolute
necessity for Salvation of actual water Baptism because as we
saw above, intention is not enough, the case for any kind of
vague "desire" being capable of achieving Salvation simply
dissolves.

How many people know what a "laver" is, anyway? Most
people assume it means a "ladle." In fact, a "laver" (pronounced lay´-ver) is a large basin used in ritual washing.
"Laver," as used by Trent, means a "bath." The person
seeking justification *vows* to be washed in that basin. He has
come to the mental and moral conclusion that this is what he
specifically wants to do: to be Baptized into the Catholic
Church. There is no hint here of the "not knowing that the
Catholic Church is the true Church" or the "loving God and
trying to do His will while not being officially attached to the
Church," errors which are propagated in the *Baltimore Catechism:*

**168.   How can persons who are not members of the
Catholic Church be saved?**

Persons who are not members of the Catholic Church can
be saved if, through no fault of their own they do not
know that the Catholic Church is the true Church, but
they love God and try to do His will, for in this way they
are connected with the Church by desire.

This I was taught in high school, as were many of my
readers—not to mention our parents. *It is a heresy, a gross
deviation from the defined teachings of the Catholic Church.*
It is a small jump from this kind of statement to one like ...

... a Protestant or Hindu or whatever, who doesn't
understand the Catholic Faith or never heard of it, is
of course united to the Church by their desire to
please God in their own way.
                        —Father Q back in Chapter 24.

... and but a lethargic skip and a jump to the logical conclusion:

*Their own way? If they can all get to heaven, why
should I go to Mass on Sunday and fast during Lent*

and all that hard stuff? Why should I be a Catholic?
Why don't I just become a something else? It'd be
easier.
— Mike, same chapter

How easy it is, indeed, to go from "Yes, but ..." to full-blown apostasy.

Just as someone can take verses of the Bible out of context and construct whole new religions from them, so too can modernists distort the decrees of Trent. Viewing the *votum* passage without any reference to the rest of the Council, its most liberal plausible interpretation might be that catechumens who die without Baptism could be saved through the *votum* to receive water Baptism if they die before reception of the sacrament, admittedly a view held by a miniscule number of venerable Saint and theologians. But when we study all of the documents carefully, we discover that "baptism of desire" is a denial, in word and intent, of the infallibly defines Teachings of the Roman Catholic Church.

We should also take note that the case for "baptism of desire," which so saturates Catholic thinking today, is not based on reason or logic anyway, but on the "desire" of the person holding this error to "play God."

> During most discussions concerning God's will for man's salvation, inevitably someone brings up the case of the classical native on an island who is wholly ignorant of God, the allegedly religiously ignorant "civilized man." What about this hypothetical person?
>
> Can he be saved? Must he be baptized? Must he believe in Jesus? Must *he* join the Catholic Church?
>
> All of these and similar questions become insignificant compared to *these* questions: *Why* does one bring up the question? What are the inquirer's goals? What pre-determined answers are acceptable to the questioner? Why? Why are other answers unacceptable? ...
>
> First, blinded by vanity, he tries to see evil as good. Then, he dares to create God in his own image and to his own likeness. He strives to be God—by "creating" God.

The inquirer fulfills God's curses on mankind—to be as god, and to decide good and evil. In doing so, *he,* in turn, is further "cursed by the Real God."

Worst of all, he is so cursed as to be convinced that he loves the classical native. He—*as God*—pardons the native from Hell.

In fact, our "loving inquirer" makes this native into a god, or, at least, a saint. *"Blessed* are the apparently ignorant, for they don't know any better," constitutes the ninth beatitude for the majority of people today.

—Father Paul Trinchard
All About Salvation

With this in mind we would do well to pray like we've never prayed before; asking God in His Mercy to enlighten us as to His Decisions on these matters.   No sincere Catholic wants to be a heretic, intentionally or unintentionally.   We must search all these documents and decrees, not to find obscure details and clever loopholes that bolster our self-asserting agendas, but clear and obvious statements that explain and define the Traditions of the Roman Catholic Church; so that during the Mass we will know exactly what we mean when we affirm (emphasis added):

[I believe] in one, holy, catholic
and apostolic Church.
I confess *one baptism* for the remission of sins.
And I look for the resurrection of the dead.
And the life of the world to come. Amen

—Nicene Creed of the Tridentine Mass

Chapter Fifty

The Mountains of Madness

*There are some forms of insanity which, driven to
an ultimate expression, can become the new modes of
sanity.*

—*BuSab Manual*
—Frank Herbert
The Dosadi Experiment

∞ ∞ ∞

RECENTLY A DEAR FRIEND flew into Los Angeles for the
Religious Education Conference held at one of this metropolis' humungous convention centers. She wanted to know what
was going on in the Catholic Church in the "big city." She
found out.

"Excuse me, Father," she said to a handsome young
priest who had just given a talk in one of the many workshops.
"I don't understand something. If Jesus said that we must eat
His Flesh and drink His Blood to have life within us, where
does that leave Protestants? They certainly don't do that."

"Sure they do," he replied offhandedly. "They eat His
Flesh and drink His Blood *in other ways.*" End of conversation.

If the subject of his workshop had been something practical, like "How to Make a Really Good Peanut Butter Sandwich," and the question posed to him in the lobby had been,
"What about the Ana-leguminites? They avoid any contact
with peanuts," would our reverend Father have made sense if
he had replied, "It's okay. You see, they consume peanuts *in
other ways*"???

Those who refuse to eat peanuts somehow do so by eating jelly instead? Is a peanut butter sandwich genuine if it contains no peanuts? No, this doesn't make sense.

What is so disheartening is that the Body and Blood of Christ, as well as Jesus' assertions on the subject of the necessity of consuming them, are treated exactly like this by modernists. Spiritual matters are relegated to some kind of vague, imprecise, and non-substantive metaphor. In other words, they don't mean a thing, so nothing said about them does, either.

> The bottom line is the salvation of souls. How are souls saved? There's only one true Church, the Roman Catholic Church. Period.
> "But, but ..."
> No, the "buts" come from the devil.
> —Father Paul Trinchard
> "What If Anything Can Be Done with Rome?"
> VNI Conference, Monrovia, CA August 1993

Small wonder people are leaving the Church in droves. When the tenets of the Roman Catholic Faith become perceived as poetry, as mere fluff, just so many nice-sounding words without weight, mass, fiber, substance, and any real pertinence—what's to keep them? When real people are in the midst of real crises in their very real lives, they don't want fog, they want concrete answers. When you're laying on the asphalt, your life's blood dripping from gashes all over your body, you don't want a soft-spoken troubadour to come along and hum you a lullaby rich in symbolic, rainbowed imagery—you want a sharp-eyed, strong-bodied paramedic with a satchel of clamps, sutures, and whatever it takes to put you back together again. You want help, not euphemisms.

We are the fallen Sons and Daughters of Adam and Eve. We are sprawled by the side of the road that descends from Jerusalem to Jericho. In these later years of the twentieth century, who is it that walks by? First comes the priest at the Religious Education Conference. What is to be said of the spiritual aid he offers, if his understanding of the Sacraments is so dim?—if he, in effect, doesn't really see them as substantive and necessary?

Second comes *his* boss, the bishop.   Surely he will set matters straight.   But rather than fall on his knees beside us, ready to pour the *oil* and *wine* into our wounds, anxious to feed us the Body of Christ which we so desperately need and which has been left in his keeping for our explicit benefit, he climbs to the top of a nearby outcrop and proclaims (emphasis added):

> Therefore, at the Sunday Eucharist *Christ's presence is to be recognized, first of all, in the assembly itself* which is the coming together of the members of the Body of Christ.   The *primacy of the assembly* calls for a genuine concern on the part of all to be attentive to our brothers and sisters joined in worship, and for participation in the complete celebration of the Sunday Eucharist.   *Christ is also present in the Word proclaimed, and in ministry, the service rendered to one another in Christ's name,* particularly the ministry of the ordained.   *And Christ is uniquely present in the central sacramental action of sharing the Body and Blood of Christ...*
>
> Of particular importance is the ministry of the ordained.   *The role of the Priest-Presider is to lead the Eucharistic community at prayer and to call forth the great variety of gifts and services which are found in the Body by relating these to the praise of God.*   This is most effectively done when the priest is a person of deep prayer and rich interior life who understands himself to be first and foremost a part of the community that God calls, sharing in its life, struggles and concerns...
>
> The Eucharistic action is the very heartbeat of the Catholic community ... *In the simple acts of presenting, blessing and breaking bread and sharing the cup, Christ is present in memory and in hope.*
>
> —Archbishop Roger Mahoney
> *The Day on Which We Gather:*
> *A Pastoral Letter on Sunday Eucharist*
> Holy Thursday, March 31, 1988

Notice that nowhere in this apparent celebration of the English Language, is there any specific mention of what the Holy Eucharist actually, concretely *is:*

> And this faith has ever been in the Church of God, that immediately after the consecration the Veritable Body of our Lord and His veritable Blood, together with His soul and divinity, are under the species of bread and wine ...
>
> —The Council of Trent
> Session XIII, Chapter III
> *Decree Concerning the Most Holy Sacrament*
> *of the Eucharist*

Where in this so-called pastoral letter, do we read that the Blessed Sacrament is the Body, Blood, Soul and Divinity of Christ? When did we last hear those words from any pulpit? Faith is a *fragile* thing, and it is the duty of our priests and bishops to remind us constantly about the specific details of that Faith, lest we stray. But what do we get from them?

"Christ's presence is to be recognized, first of all, in the assembly itself ..."   ???? What is this supposed to mean? Is Christ more fundamentally present in the congregation than in the Sacrament? While it is certainly true that Jesus said ...

> For where there are two or three gathered in my name, there I am in the midst of them.
> —St. Matthew XVIII:20

... He was describing His immanence when we pray as a group. But that is a *different mystery* than His Real Presence in the Holy Eucharist. If we truly look for Him *first* in the *primacy of the assembly,* are we not in danger of worshipping Man rather than God? Has this not, when we get down to brass tacks, been the whole point of the turned-around altar in the "new liturgy"—the celebration of Man?

"Christ is also present in the Word proclaimed ..." Again, true as far as it goes. We do encounter Him in Sacred Scripture, but not in the same sense that we receive Him in the Blessed Sacrament. Hearing someone talk about a person you want to meet is not the same as meeting that person yourself. You can learn about Him from a third party; but you *experi-*

ence Him only in direct contact.   Clock-watchers (like your
author) have noticed how much longer the "Liturgy of the
Word" is compared to the "Liturgy of the Eucharist."   If
time is any indicator, the Word takes precedence over the
Flesh.

   *"... and in the ministry, the service rendered to one an-
other in Christ's name."* Again, true —

> Amen I say to you, as long as you did it to one of
> these my least brethren, you did it to me.
>   — St. Matthew XXV:40

— but hardly what the Mass is really all about.   We go to Mass
to offer Solemn Sacrifice to God, to Worship Him as He
wishes us to do.   Service to one another is also required, but in
addition to and apart from, not instead of Worship.

   Notice the next bit of clever wording: *"Christ is uniquely
present in the central sacramental action of sharing the Body
and Blood of Christ ..."*   Christ's Presence is traditionally defined as being in the Sacrament Itself, not in the *action* of
"sharing" it.   It all sounds "nice" (never forget the original
meaning of that word! — See Chapter 5.) but on closer examination, *it means nothing.* That is the trouble: it really doesn't
mean anything.   A person is present in fact, not in an action.
This confusion is further drummed home by this noble shepherd's profound conclusion:

   *"In the simple acts of presenting, blessing, and breaking
bread and sharing the cup, Christ is present in memory and in
hope."*

> Memory and hope, you say?   Fine.   That's how my
> money will be present in the collection plate from
> now on.
>   — Charles A. Coulombe
>   Breakfast conversation at Mimi's Café
>   Monrovia, California

   To suggest that something is present in "memory and in
hope" — in the past and in the future — is to declare that it is
not present at all.

The same archbishop who wrote *The Day on Which We Blather...* ahem, um *...Gather* also had this to say in an interview with a reporter from a major newspaper:

> A: ... There was Pope John XXIII who first started dealing with the question: "Where is salvation?" We used to say unless you were a Catholic there was no salvation. We don't say that anymore. We say salvation is from God.
>
> Q: You can be a Jew or a Muslim or an agnostic and have salvation?
>
> A: Sure, we aren't the ones that provide the salvation; fortunately it is God that provides salvation.
>
> —Robert Scheer's Interview
> *The Lost Angeles Times*
> December 26, 1993

One wonders if our shepherds ever stop to think about what they're saying. Do they not see the logical end to the chain of events they set in motion when they utter such drivel?

> What's that, Father? The Church is not necessary for Salvation? Then let's abolish it, and you go find a *real job.*
>
> —Charles A. Coulombe
> Same breakfast conversation
> Monrovia, California

Drivel, nothing—it's outright heresy. Saint Athanasius once wrote in the fourth century that as a result of the shenanigans of the bishops, "We awoke to find ourselves Arians." We Catholics of the late twentieth century have awakened to find ourselves Protestants.

> Do you not perceive how many qualities a bishop must have that he may be apt to teach; patient towards the wicked, *firm and faithful in teaching the Word?* How many difficulties herein.
>
> Moreover the loss of others is imputed to him. I need say no more. If but *one* dies without baptism, does it not entirely endanger his salvation? For the loss of one soul is so great an evil as no man can un-

derstand. If the salvation of one soul is of such importance that, for its sake, the Son of God became man and suffered so much, think of the penalty the loss of one soul will entail ...

If then one were to approach to the chief priesthood as an office full of solicitude and anxiety, no one would undertake it. On the contrary, nowadays, we aspire to this dignity as if it were a secular office, for the sake of glory and honour before men ...
> —Saint John Chrysostom, Doctor of the Church
> *Third Homily, Acts of the Apostles*

In their haste to get to Jericho, the priest and the bishop have passed us by on the steep downhill road, leaving us to shiver and shudder in the inexorably growing pool of our own blood. So who comes along next? Would that it could be that "certain Samaritan on his journey" who approaches as the shadows lengthen and the air chills; but alas, instead comes His Vicar, the bishop's boss:

> Amen I say to thee, that in this night before the cock crow, thou wilt deny me thrice.
> —St. Matthew XXVI:34

This is such a touchy subject, and we are all tempted to avoid it, or sugarcoat it, remembering the solemn warning of the historical Church:

> QUI MANGE LE PAPE, MORT.
> He who eats the Pope, dies.

So we will not eat him, or gnaw on his bones, or scandalize him in any way. He is Peter—of this we must never lose sight. But we also must remember that Peter himself denied Jesus three times. He regretted it bitterly until the end of his days; but in a crunch, he learned—and we along with him—that even Peter and his descendents can stumble.

In light of all that has been said in the last half-dozen chapters, what can we say about a Pontiff who ...

> ... on February 2, 1986, in a public ceremony ...
> was religiously signed*, "blessed," and publicly ac-
> knowledged to be a worshipper of the pagan god,
> Shiva. This Tilac blessing was received by the Pope
> at Delhi's Indira Gandhi Stadium.
> —Father Paul Trinchard
> *All About Salvation*

While we all hope that the Holy Father's intention was to show some kind of "ecumenical openness" to the Hindus—we certainly don't think for a minute that in his mind he was being initiated into a pagan cult (even though that's precisely the purpose of the ceremony in which he participated)—we do not exceed the bounds of propriety if we simply ask, "Did this promote the message of Jesus Christ to go and teach all nations? Did this bring anyone into the Roman Catholic Church outside of which there is absolutely no Salvation? Or rather, did his example—unaccompanied by any explanation to the Faithful—suggest to Catholics the world over that it is perfectly okay for them to embrace Hinduism?"

> Let me just give you one question: have you ever
> heard the Pope write or say, and speak in such a way,
> that brought people to the Catholic Church? Ask
> yourself that. Ask yourself that.
> —Father Paul Trinchard
> "What If Anything Can Be Done with Rome"
> VNI Conference, Monrovia, CA; August 1993

If the answer is in the negative, then we indeed have a crisis on our hands.**

Four Popes have ascended the Chair of Peter since 1950, when Pope Pius XII defined the Assumption of Our Lady into Heaven. None of them have made any *ex cathedra* pro-

---

* *i.e,* cow dung was smeared on Pope John Paul II's forehead.

** On May 14, 1999, Pope John Paul II kissed a copy of the Koran in public. When we consider that historically millions of Catholics chose death rather than commit such an act, the breadth and depth of this crisis becomes increasingly apparent.

nouncements in the interim[†], though all of them have been masters of prolix indistinctness and verbose indirectness. With the possible exception of Pope Paul VI's *Humanae Vitae*—which was never enforced so what good was it?—papal documents have become exercises in liberal double-talk. As the Church crumbles into ruin all around us, we wait and wait for our Pontiffs to do something, *anything* about the dire situation.

When Pope John Paul II finally released a long-awaited encyclical, we all welcomed it with open arms ... until we sat down and tried to read the thing (emphasis his):

> The Church knows that the issue of morality is one which deeply touches every person, it involves all people, even those who do not know Christ and his Gospel or God himself. She knows that it is precisely *on the path of the moral life that the way of salvation is open to all.* The Second Vatican Council clearly recalled this when it stated that "those who without any fault do not know anything about Christ of his Church, yet who search for God with a sincere heart and under the influence of grace, try to put into effect the will of God as known to them through the dictate of conscience ... can obtain eternal salvation."
>
> —Pope John Paul II
> *Veritatis Splendor*

One can't help but wonder at the conversation that would ensue if Popes Innocent III, Boniface VIII, and Eugene IV were in the same room with John Paul II comparing their *ex cathedra* statements with his published opinions. It is hard to reconcile the present Holy Father's religious principles with those of his predecessors. They officially declared that mem-

---

[†] Since the time of this writing—ironically considering the topic of this chapter, but demonstrating that even the most questionable popes are guided by the Holy Ghost when they do their job—Pope John Paul II did make two infallible statements. In *Ordinatio Sacerdotalis* (May 22, 1994) he formally denounced the notion that women can be ordained priests; and in *Dominus Iesus* (August 6, 2000) he formally declared that that the Church is one, there are not many churches. No doubt both statements will be ignored by most, but at least they are on the record for future generations.

bership in the Catholic Church was essential for the hope of Salvation, whereas he believes otherwise.

It is important to distinguish the difference between an *infallible pronouncement* and the *personal opinion* of a pope. The first is binding on the faithful, the second is not. Catholics are not bound by a pope's conclusions as a private theologian, and *Veritatis Splendor* is clearly that.

Excuses were made by some that *Veritatis Splendor* was some kind of fluke, a mistake, or the result of mistranslation, but sadly we know this is not the case. John Paul II went on to widen his departure from the traditional teachings of the Church in his best-selling book in which he again relied on Vatican II for support (emphasis his):

> The Council speaks of *membership in the Church* for Christians and of *being related to the Church* for non-Christian believers in God ... Both these dimensions are important for salvation, and each one possesses varying levels. People are saved *through* the Church, they are saved *in* the Church, but they are always saved *by the grace of Christ*. Besides formal membership in the Church, the *sphere of salvation* can also include *other forms of relation to the Church*. Paul VI expressed this same teaching ... when he spoke of the various *circles of the dialogue of salvation* ... which are the same as those indicated by the Council as the spheres of membership in and of relation to the Church. This is the authentic meaning of the well-known statement "Outside the Church there is no salvation."
>
> It would be difficult to deny that this doctrine is extremely *open*. It cannot be accused of an *ecclesiological exclusivism*. Those who rebel against claims allegedly made by the Catholic Church probably do not have an adequate understanding of this teaching.
>
> —Pope John Paul II
> *Crossing the Threshold of Hope*

Excuse me, but with all due respect: It would be difficult to deny that the doctrine, Outside the Church there is no Salvation, is extremely *open????* This doctrine cannot be ac-

cused of *exclusivism????* Those who rebel against this dogma
do not adequately understand it?????

On the contrary, it is precisely because *words mean what
they say* that so many have rebelled against the Church over
the centuries! If Salvation had always been understood to be
open to everyone, whether they embraced the Catholic Faith
or not, there never would have been any missionaries or martyrs. Clearly they selflessly expended their lives precisely because *the Dogma was not open, was exclusive, and was easy
to understand.*

But the Holy Father goes on and on in his book, shifting
the meaning of words to suit his purpose. By the time we
wade through all his back-peddling subjunctives and overac-
tive bifurcations which are mere preliminary to full-blown do-
ceca-furcations, we are left with nothing concrete on which to
stand. Liberal thinking requires a liberal language with liberal
doses of words with meanings that can be applied ever so lib-
erally. Thank Heaven the Gospels were not so written!

The pope continues to promote and quote the pronouncements of Vatican II, which was indeed a legally-
convened ecumenical council, and which under normal circumstances would have as such been considered infallible.
However, that same council declared its mission to be "pastoral" rather than "dogmatic," therefore nothing it promulgated was to be considered infallible unless it reiterated dogmas already defined by previous councils and popes. One
almost wonders why they bothered.

Judging from the Holy Father's own citations, in light of
so much that has been quoted in this book, Vatican II presented a *radical departure* from traditional teachings of the
Catholic Church. The very quotations above clearly defy the
pronouncements of the Council of Trent.

Vatican II was not an infallible council, yet its champions
have done more to overturn every vestige of Traditional Catholicism than any previous heresy, schism, political upheaval,
or plague in the history of the Church. The Vatican II Documents were among the most ponderously wordy and inacces-
sible mountains of verbiage ever conceived under the sun,
which is precisely why dishonest pastors get away with virtually anything they want by invoking to "the spirit of Vatican
II." Who's going to contradict them? Who's got the bloody
time to read those awful documents? Hence the Church has

been turned completely inside out with respect to everything She has ever held, taught, or expected of the Faithful. And the Pope himself continues to promote it.

How did this happen?

Restrictions of space and time prohibit a thorough exploration of this question in the present volume, but suffice it to say that over the last century liberal modernism has infiltrated the Church like a virus, and the symptoms of the illness have finally erupted in blasphemous boils with a vengeance. The sacrilegious disease was stewing for a long time before it revealed itself openly, tracing its origins back to the Protestant Reformation.

> Now the Spirit manifestly saith, that in the last times some shall depart from the faith, giving heed to spirits of error, and doctrines of devils ...
> —I St. Timothy IV:1

Pope Pius IX tried to combat the modernist infiltration with his *Syllabus of Errors* in 1864, as did his successor, Pius X in his Encyclical Letter *Pascendi Dominici Gregis,* "On the Doctrine of the Modernists" in 1907, but the mercurial modernists were not eradicated, only forced to keep their mouths shut and penetrate further into the organism of the Church, awaiting the day when they could unveil themselves with impunity. That day has arrived.

Unlike the diseases of cells and microbes which can be treated with unguents and serums; pestilence of the heart, mind, and soul requires another form of elixir, and it cannot be administered without the patient's full consent. Humble acceptance of the Truth is the cure, and the Will is free to refuse it.

Modernism—an applicable name for this insidious disease—is a curious affliction. Those under its influence seem completely unaware of the consequences of their philosophy. Essentially, they are worshippers of Man. That they are sincere is without question, but sincerity alone doesn't get anyone to Heaven. They usually begin by idolizing some liberal teacher whose books they read or whose lectures they attended in college. Their appreciation for themselves becomes greatly enhanced because they are ingenious enough to understand their mentor's revolutionary ideas. Their self-appreciation grows into adoration, which spreads to include Mankind in general as an extension of themselves. Finally, they end up worshipping Man as the be-all and end-all of everything. But, as with all things Man sets in motion without proper reflection, Frankenstein Monsters are often the result which come back to punish their unwitting creators:

> ... I looked sternly at my offspring and saw him chewing away. His cheeks were colored with embarrassment and the muscles of his jaws stood rigidly out.
> "You know the rule," I said coldly.
> To my amazement tears came into his eyes and while his jaws continued to masticate hugely, his blubbery voice forced its way past the huge lump of bubble gum in his mouth.
> "I didn't do it," he cried.
> "What do you mean, you didn't do it?" I demanded in a rage. "I distinctly heard and now I distinctly see."
> "Oh sir!" he moaned, "I really didn't. I'm not chewing it, sir. It's chewing me."
> —John Steinbeck
> "The Affair at 7, Rue de M—"

Yes, the gum—sticky thinking—they thought they were chewing suddenly takes over and begins chewing *them*. With Mass attendance dropping, seminary enrollment plummeting, parish schools closing, nuns and priests deserting, and revenues diminishing, the modernists will be left with empty churches and emptier pockets. Their pitiful pleas of "I sincerely didn't know" will not fall on deaf ears, but rather on no ears at all.

Modernism is inherently self-destructive, for by its nature it undermines the power base of those who profess it. A predilection for suicide is not the mark of sane thinking.

Meanwhile, here we are bleeding beside the road ...

∞ ∞ ∞

Something that has played a big part in all of this sacerdotal insanity was the example made of Father Leonard

Feeney by the increasingly modernist hierarchy. Father Feeney, in his heyday, was a nationally popular priest. During the thirties he edited the Jesuit magazine, *America*. His prose and poetry lined the bookshelves of most Catholic homes, schools, and hospitals. In 1942 he became the spiritual director of Saint Benedict Center for Catholic students across the street from Harvard in Boston. The story of his shameful persecution is too long and involved to be adequately covered here,* but suffice it to say that he made a very grave mistake: he showed incredibly bad judgment by actually converting Protestant and Jewish students to the Roman Catholic Faith, some of whom resigned from the college as a result. Their influential families brought pressure upon the bishop, who naturally preferred God's animosity to theirs.

In a series of incredible circumventions of the Code of Canon Law, Archbishop Cushing took away Father Feeney's priestly faculties in 1949 (thus depriving him of the right to say public Mass, hear Confessions, or perform any normal priestly duties); Father Feeney was then dismissed from the Society of Jesus for the "crime of serious and permanent disobedience" (the one crime that can always be pinned on someone who doesn't cooperate with the nefarious religious establishment); and after a bureaucratic run-around with the Holy Office in Rome that would send most American Congressmen running for the Bromo-Seltzer, he was finally excommunicated in 1953 and remained so for two decades. The validity or invalidity of all these interdictions which were summarily issued without due process will be the subject of unresolved canonical scrutiny for generations to come.

> [The decree of excommunication] was signed only by a notary, one Marius Crovini, not by either Cardinal Pizzardo or the Pope himself, whose signatures alone could make such a decree valid; nor did it carry the seal of the Holy Office.

---

* Excellent and reliable sources of information on the "Boston Heresy Case" include *The Loyolas and The Cabots* and *Gate of Heaven* by Catherine Goddard Clarke, *Desire and Deception* by Thomas A. Hutchinson, *They Fought the Good Fight* by Thomas Sennott, and *Father Feeney and the Truth about Salvation* by Br. Robert Mary, MICM Tert.

Even so, Fr. Feeney and his followers were treated
as excommunicates for almost twenty years after this
... Yet in 1972 all censures were lifted from Fr.
Feeney, and he was not asked to make a retraction of
his beliefs.* This implied (much to the annoyance of
Liberal Catholic papers at the time who vociferously
denounced this) that Fr. Feeney had been right, and
his opponents heretical. But of course, in true cleri-
cal fashion, rather than making any kind of real decision, the whole thing was merely considered closed,
and the authorities in the case merrily slithered along.
Indeed, from the 1950s to the present, "Feeneyism"
and "Feeneyite" have been used as buzzwords to dismiss both the traditional teaching and one rash
enough to hold it in this age of freedom and libera-
tion. If your author had not conducted an extensive
research into American Church history on this whole
subject, he might fear being tarred with the "Feeneyite" brush himself for not having included a ritual denunciation of the man in this chapter. But he knows
no scholarly person who would be so foolish in his
regard.

—Thomas A. Hutchinson
Desire and Deception

The word "Feeneyite," which today has come to denote
anyone who holds the Dogma, OUTSIDE THE CHURCH THERE
IS NO SALVATION, is well-known to seminarians the world
over. They may not have a clue about the Sacrificial Nature
of the Mass, nor grasp the first thing about Moral Theology,
or Original Sin, or anything useful in the practical work of
saving souls, but one thing they all know for sure is that if
they ever want to be assigned to "nice parishes," or hope to
be promoted to "pastor," or look forward to having a "secure pension" in those declining years when all the work they
should have been doing still isn't done, then they had better
not do or say anything that might be construed as acceptance
of the Dogma EXTRA ECCLESIAM NULLA SALUS. No matter what the Popes of the Roman Catholic Church have de-

---

* Ironically, his excommunication was lifted by none other than Pope Paul
VI.

clared infallibly, they have been taught a more important truth
...

> *What happened to Father Feeney*
> *can happen to you.*

... and that settles that.

So, freed from the Truth, the priests, bishops, and hierar-chy have been going about the business of rebuilding the Church of Jesus Christ into the Church of Modern Man. Where once God was worshipped in awe, Man is celebrated in frivolity. Where the Church once ennobled Man by uplifting his soul and imagination, Man now guts the Church of all art and beauty, and fills the void with the excesses of his own vul-garity. The result of course, is the widespread loss of Faith.

> But yet the Son of man, when he cometh, shall he
> find, think you, faith on earth?
>   —St. Luke XVIII:8

Many centuries before Christ walked among us, God the Father warned that there must never be false gods before Him. This wasn't just for His sake, but for ours. When Man bows to idols of his own making, he knows in his heart of hearts that the thing to which he pays homage is a sham. Realizing this, it is the height of hubris to continue polishing the unholy mir-ror; the pinnacle of futility to keep the image in good repair; and the depth of depravity to go on worshipping the ugly thing. When Man controls his god, insanity reigns:

AZATHOTH

Out in mindless void the daemon bore me,
Past the bright clusters of dimensioned space,
Till neither time nor matter stretched before me,
But only Chaos, without form or place.
Here the vast Lord of All in darkness muttered
Things he had dreamed but could not understand
While near him shapeless bat-things flopped and fluttered
In idiot vortices that ray-streams fanned.

They danced insanely to the high, thin whining

Of a cracked flute clutched in a monstrous paw,
Whence flow the aimless waves whose chance combining
Gives each frail cosmos its eternal law,
"I am His Messenger," the daemon said,
As in contempt he struck his Master's head.

—H. P. Lovecraft
Fungi from Yuggoth

CHAPTER FIFTY-ONE

ELSEWHERE

Blessed are the clean of heart:
for they shall see God.
— St. Matthew V:8

∞ ∞ ∞

IF THIS IS A WEEKDAY, he's out there.

If this is a weekend, he's doing his laundry and preparing to go back out there.

He calls out there "the beat."

It's what he does.

He would not be pleased if his name appeared here, so it won't. I'll just call him Brother FX. He has written no lengthy books in defense of the Faith. He doesn't have a regular column in one of the Traditionalist magazines, nor is he a regular on the Catholic Activist's lecture circuit. You can't buy cassette tapes or videos of his profundities, and the idea of making such things would never occur to him. His exploits are not covered by the *LA Times* or the *Tidings*, nor has he ever appeared on *Sixty Minutes*. It is doubtful he'll be officially canonized when he dies because no one of ecclesial import will have ever heard of him (and they wouldn't agree with him if they had).

While the eyes of the great are looking far and wide and the wings of evil are seeking dominion over the earth, while the fledgling knights of intrepid crusades apprehensively sharpen their swords and the rings of power are flashing bolts of power illuminating the churning sky, Brother FX is busy elsewhere. He is out on the beat.

Every weekday he marks out a small section of the vast grid of the city map, takes up a small satchel swollen with books and pamphlets, catches a bus to his target destination, and starts going door-to-door in the business districts.

"Ohio," he says, entering a tiny sushi bar. This is not his favorite football team, but Japanese for "Good morning." He isn't fluent in Japanese, but in Los Angeles most Oriental proprietors who don't speak English do speak Spanish, the language of their bus boys. He isn't fluent in Spanish, either, but he knows enough to get his message across.

"Yo soy un missionario Catolico," he tells them in whatever pidgin dialect works. "I am a Catholic missionary."

Once, moved by an impulse I hadn't really thought through, I asked Brother FX if I might accompany him one day, just to see what he does—in the parlance of the newage church, "to share in the experience."

"I'll have to ask the boss," he said, meaning his religious superior.

Brother Boss said it was permissible, provided I wore a black suit like the other brothers in their tiny monastery. Not owning one at the time, I had to borrow one—Brother Boss' as it turned out, sharing as we do, the same noble girth.

It was decided that since I was new at this kind of thing and the Los Angeles Public Transportation system was a mystery to me, we would take my car rather than the bus. That way if I had to bail for any reason—panic attack, acute persecution complex, blisters or fatigue—I could find my own way home.

Brother Boss, much to my surprise, decided to come along. "I haven't been out there for years," he said wistfully. "My health, you know. I do so miss it." Since the rigors of door-to-door were beyond him, he sat in the car doing paperwork while Brother FX and I went up and down the block. I trust he was enjoying himself, though I wondered at the time if he was just keeping an eye on me. Hard to say.

Since my only language is that peculiar megalopolitan dialect of English known as Angeleno, all I had to do was stand slightly behind Brother FX and look sagacious while he did all the talking.

"If they're of Good Will they'll listen," he explained to me as we approached the first store. "If they're not, they won't."*

It all sounded so easy.

But after only ten minutes on the beat, I wanted out. I realized I had committed myself to something that was anything but easy. Whatever mask of wise serenity I assembled with my facial muscles, my inner wish was to drop the satchel and run. An hour later I felt like crawling into a gutter—it would have been more comfortable than the looks we got from most proprietors:

"Good morning, Madam, I am a Catholic mis—"
"Don't want any."
"Good day."

"Good morning, Sir, I am a Ca—"
"No soliciting."
"Thank-you for your time."

"Good m—"
"Out."
"Thank—"
"I said *out.*"

After three hours we hadn't had a polite conversation or sold a single pamphlet. Since the Brothers depend on book sales for income, it was discouraging on a financial as well as a personal level. By noon I would have given just about anything for a kind word or a warm look.

Instead, it was time for lunch.

"I made us some sandwiches," said Brother FX eagerly, producing a brown bag from the back of my car.

"I'm famished," I admitted. "What've you got there?"

---

* This was, of course, an oversimplification since God gives us a lifetime to find the Truth. We all vacillate between various degrees of Good and Bad Will as we go about our tasks. I have found, though, that those who work "out there" amidst the masses, and especially among the poor, tend to develop simple and uncluttered notions regarding their missionary work.

He handed me a small bundle wrapped in wax paper.
"Peanut butter, bologna and mustard."

"   …?"

I now understand the secret of Brother FX's patience and
courage: peanut butter, bologna and mustard sandwiches. It
wouldn't surprise me in the least if the recipe was discovered
in the memoirs of Saint Francis Xavier. I hope I'm not revealing some well-guarded missionary secret, but …

They're actually very good.

I know, I know, it's hard to believe. I didn't believe it
myself until, after politely taking a bite, I started to dutifully
chew. The kinetic tang of the French's mixed with the subtle
spice of Oscar Meyer, glued together by the cement of
Skippy's, it all produced an unexpectedly non-unpalatable
taste. Not bad, not bad at all. (Or so I told myself.)

"It's not a matter of what we'd *like* to eat," explained
Brother Boss as he indulged along beside us. "It's cheap, it
fills you up, and it keeps you going."

Back on the beat.

One matronly Japanese woman simply turned her back to
us and proceeded to talk on the phone. We left. Fifteen minutes later, however, she came up to us on the street. Ashamed
of her impoliteness, she sought us out, silently handed us a
sealed envelope, and wordlessly returned to her shop. When
we opened it we found five dollars.

The one real gem of the day was a woman from South
America who ran an Italian restaurant near the beach. Once
she understood we were Catholics and not Jehovah Witnesses,
there wasn't enough she could do for us. She bought a copy
of *Saints to Remember* so she could look up her namesake,
Saint Margaret Mary. She made us a couple of meatball
sandwiches—oh yes, salad, too!—to take with us. She kept
calling us "Fathers," and we kept explaining to her that we
were not priests. Her blessed enthusiasm made our day.

"You see," said Brother FX as we carried our "loot" to
the car. "There *are* people of Good Will."

I had begun to think otherwise.

Some months later, I invited Brother FX to have dinner
with me at one of those Japanese restaurants where you sit at

the grill and the chef cooks your food in front of you, hacking it deftly into bite-size pieces with the showy clatter and clang of oversized knives. I thought it would be a nice break from the rigors of his usual Top Ramen dinner routine.

"*Ko-neechee-wah,*" he greeted as the chef arrived with his cart of raw meats and cooking implements. "Where in Japan are you from?"

"I not Japanese," said the chef as he nimbly ladled oil from a clay pot, making a smoking "happy face" in the center of the grill. "I was born in Bangkok."

"Ah, Thai," nodded Brother FX.

"No, Vietnamese."

Undaunted, Brother FX made the Sign of the Cross: "*Non Dun Chah, Vacon, Vah Tan Tan. Amen.*"

The chef began whittling a pound of shrimp into tiny, sizzling chunks. "You speak Vietnamese?"

"No," said Brother FX, crossing himself again. "*Au nom du Père, et du Fils, et du Saint Esprit. Ainsi-soit-il.*"

I looked at him blankly.

"Most of the Vietnamese from older families speak French," he confided to me, accepting a cup of tea from the waitress gratefully. "That's one language I do know."

The chef's face was imponderable.

A little later, when the Mexican bus boy came by to take away some of the dishes, Brother FX took out a small plastic bag from his pocket. "Miraculous Medals," he told the lad. "*Benditos*—blessed by a priest."

In fact, by the end of dinner, the waitresses and the chefs all had little pamphlets or prayer cards in their own tongues protruding from their pockets, all the Mexican help had medals or scapulars, and just about everyone who had come in contact with Brother FX was aware that he was a *missionario Catolico.*

"*Arigato,*" said the waitress as we left. "Thank-you."

∞   ∞   ∞

Someone recently asked me, "How do you stand it, the state the Church is in? I get so darn mad—"

"Don't just get mad," I interrupted. "Get *excited.*"

"But sometimes I just want to explode, or cry. There's nothing I can do. I feel such ... despair."

Despair certainly is a temptation.   But nothing?   Did someone say there's *nothing* we can do?

Hogwash. There's plenty for the Faithful Catholic to do. In fact, there's so much to do, a lifetime is hardly long enough to fit it all in.   But first, before we go off just doing things for the sake of doing them, there's one paramount thing we absolutely have to do first:

> Be still and see that I am God ...
> —Psalm XLV:11

Before anything else, we need to get right with Him.   All else is frills and excitement, banter and excess.   Courageous action is well and good, noble deeds are certainly commendable, and bravery in the sight of the overpowering enemy is worthy of fanfare. *But ...*

> If I speak with the tongues of men, and of angels, and have not charity, I am become as sounding brass, or a tinkling cymbal.
> And if I should have prophecy and should know all mysteries, and all knowledge, and if I should have all faith, so that I could remove mountains, and have not charity, I am nothing.
> And if I should distribute all my goods to feed the poor, and if I should deliver my body to be burned, and have not charity, it profiteth me nothing.
> —I Corinthians XIII:1-3

The word *Charity* is often translated *Love*.   Whichever word we prefer, we must never lose sight of the centrality it must hold in our hearts and in our lives.   All that we do we must do with Charity.   All that we proclaim to others we must proclaim in Love.   Not gooey sweet syrup—LOVE! Has God ever been gooey with us?   Hardly.   His Love cost Him His Son:

> And we have seen, and do testify, that the Father hath sent his Son to be the Saviour of the world.
> Whosoever shall confess that Jesus is the Son of God, God abideth in him, and he in God.

> And we have known, and have believed the charity,
> which God hath to us. God is charity: and he that
> abideth in charity, abideth in God, and God in him.
> —I St. John IV:14-16

If I can recognize the terrible things my bishop is insti-gating in my diocese, good for my head. It shows I'm think-ing. But if I forget to pray fervently that God will have mercy on the man, bad for my soul. I have missed the point entirely. I have not loved as I am commanded to love.

We must never lose our joy, our confidence, our trust, and our all-consuming hunger for God. Through His guidance, we will learn how to foster Love for our fellow men and women. Devotion to the Blessed Virgin is particularly helpful in this regard, being as She is the Help of Christians and the Seat of Mercy. The Angels and Saints are also pulling for us. With this clearly in mind, nothing can truly harm us. No matter to what levels of debauchery our bishop may descend, no matter what atrocities are fostered on us by our pastors, no matter what anyone does that wounds our body or soul, we will pray for them and forgive them. No matter what: pray and forgive.

> Then came Peter unto him and said: Lord, how of-
> ten shall my brother offend against me, and I forgive
> him? till seven times?
> Jesus saith to him: I say not to thee, till seven
> times; but till seventy times seven times.
> —St. Matthew XVIII:21-22

No matter the offense, we must learn to forgive. If we can't bring ourselves to forgive, then we must pray for the Grace to do so. This is not a suggestion, it is an Order from the Top. To forgive does not mean to ignore the damage they do, or to somehow enter a fantasyland where the world is rosy and our clergy are all sweet as honey. It means to adopt an internal attitude which recognizes their humanity as well as our own, to realize that we might well be in their shoes if we had experienced the same things. More than anything, it means to accept our own fundamental wickedness and our need for God's mercy first, for in His Eyes we are probably just as vile if not worse than they are.

> Or how canst thou say to thy brother: Brother, let
> me pull the mote out of thy eye, when thou thyself
> seest not the beam in they own eye? Hypocrite, cast
> first the beam out of thy own eye; and then shalt thou
> see clearly to take out the mote from thy brother's
> eye.
>
> —St. Luke VI:42

We look at the Saints and think, "Oh, how pure they were." But by their own writings they saw themselves as vile, corrupt, and atrocious. Why? Because the closer a man or woman comes to God, the more they see themselves in the His light, which is Perfection. Likewise, the closer we draw to His Perfection, the clearer will our imperfections become. The stains that seemed so tiny become gnarly and grotesque when compared to Infinite Perfection. How great is God's Love and Patience, that He endures us as He does.

We would do well to remember, too, that the step from holiness to sinfulness is all too brief, and though it is an old cliché to say, "The way to Hell is paved with good intentions," it is nonetheless true. Often the vilest of sins begins with the sincerest of motives. Often what we think is centeredness on God is actually self-centeredness disguised.

In this regard, allow me to draw again upon the pen of H. G. Wells, and with the same justification as before. In his short story, "The Pearl of Love," there was a prince in northern India who fell madly in love with a beautiful princess.

> Love was theirs, full of joys and sweetness, full of
> hope, exquisite, brave and marvelous love, beyond
> anything you have ever dreamt of love.

Alas, she died suddenly, and the prince was heartbroken. Her body was laid in a coffin of fine scented woods and gold, and that was placed within an ornate sarcophagus of alabaster inlaid with precious stones. After several days of deep grief, the prince rose up with a sense of new purpose. He resolved to build a monument to his beloved.

> A building it should be of perfect grace and beauty,
> more marvelous than any other building had ever been

or could ever be, so that to the end of time it should
be a wonder, and men would treasure it and speak of it
and desire to see it and come from all the lands of the
earth to visit and recall the name and the memory of
his queen. And this building he said was to be called
the Pearl of Love.

Builders and craftsmen were summoned from all over the
land. A great foundation was hewn out of living rock and the
sarcophagus placed in its center. Around this rose pillars and
arches and domes and spires of magnificent artistry.

With awe and amazement people saw the Pearl of
Love sweeping up from its beginnings to a superhu-
man breadth and height and magnificence. They did
not know clearly what they had expected, but never
had they expected so sublime a thing as this. "Wonderful are the miracles," they whispered, "that love
can do," and all the women in the world, whatever
loves they had, loved the prince for the splendour of
his devotion.

The work went on for many years, the prince constantly
on hand, dreaming up newer and better ideas. As he grew
older, the prince's artistry matured, and so parts of the original structure were removed to make way for more refined ar-
chitecture. Earlier decorations were taken away so as not to
interfere with the newer, grander motif. And so the work blossomed and continued.

Finally, the work was complete—or so everyone thought.
The prince came again to view his masterpiece.

Only one thing there was to mar the absolute harmony. There was a certain disproportion about the
sarcophagus. It had never been enlarged, and indeed
how could it have been enlarged since the early days?
It challenged the eye; it nicked the streaming lines.
In that sarcophagus ... was the queen, the dear immortal cause of all this beauty. But now that sarcophagus seemed no more than a little dark oblong
that lay incongruously in the great vista of the Pearl

of Love. It was as if someone had dropped a small
valise upon the crystal sea of heaven.

The prince had the solution:

"Take that thing away," he said.

How easy it is to forget the reason why we started out
along the road once we encounter the scenery along the way.
Many families have suffered when the focus of activity became fixing up the house at the expense of the home. How
many apostolates go aground because the focus turns from
promoting the Faith to making money to sustain the business?

As I arrive at the end of this book, I must admit that there
have been moments when I got too wrapped up in the writing
itself rather than the purpose for the writing. There were
nights I neglected my prayers to complete a chapter, only to
awaken the following morning to the realization that I had not
done the better part. At times I was impatient with others because their conversation intruded on my creative thoughts. In
these things I sometimes failed, momentarily losing sight of
the whole point, vacillating between what seemed important
and what was truly important. It is an endless struggle.

The modernists who have wrought their destruction in the
Church doubtless began with sincere intentions. Surely our
clergy and hierarchy answered their call to the religious life
out of some sense of devotion to God. Perhaps they really
believed the liturgical reforms and revised morality were good
things, but they got so caught up in the frenzy of innovation
that they forgot the message they were trying to promote in
the first place.

We are not exempt from the same fate.

One of the saddest things these days is the friction between
the various Traditionalist Catholic factions. The bickering and
suspicion that goes on between this group and that—between
Trad and Trad—is shameful. Our intensity of emotion is un-
derstandable because we are in many respects the only ones
left who care. And we care deeply. While our concern is
commendable, our uncharitable attitudes are often not. It
would seem that, to some of us, the measure of a man's fervor
is the speed with which he will cancel his subscription to a

conservative magazine the moment he reads an article with which he disagrees.

> Indeed in nothing is the power of the Dark Lord
> more clearly shown than in the estrangement that di-
> vides all those who still oppose him.
> —J.R.R. Tolkein
> *The Lord of the Rings*

We must pray unceasingly that our fervor for Jesus Christ does not go the way of the prince's Pearl of Love.

∞ ∞ ∞

This is, of course, why there are people around like Brother FX—to remind of what we're really about:

"Well, I'm off," says the good Brother, crushing his napkin. He rises from the table at Mimi's Café and gathers his satchel thick with books. "I am a Roaming Catholic, and I best be roaming."

"How do you do it?" asks another person at breakfast—me—digging around in my wallet for the tip. "I mean, how do you keep going the way you do?"

"Extra Ecclesiam Nulla Salus," Brother FX shrugs as he puts on his hat. "In the 'Spirit of Vatican I,' somebody has to tell them."

"God bless you, Brother."

"And Mary keep you."

It's good to know he's out there on the beat.

Exeunt.

AUTHOR'S AFTERWORD

STILL SANE AFTER
ALL THESE YEARS

> I want to live life while I'm living it. We hear a
> lot about the people who are afraid to die, but we
> don't hear so much about the people who are afraid to
> live; yet it's a common failing.
>
> —Perry Mason in
> Erle Stanley Gardner's
> *The Case of the Caretaker's Cat*

∞ ∞ ∞

IT SEEMS SO LONG AGO. This book was my first after my
return to the Catholic Faith. It was also the first to which I af-
fixed what has since become my signature statement:

	Nihil Obstat:	Huh?
✛	*Imprimatur:*	Are you kidding!?!?

I so remember giving Mike Malone a copy of the manuscript for review as he and his wife, Jane, headed for their hotel
during one of their visits to Los Angeles. He later sent me a
photocopy of the page across which he had scribbled:

We laughed so hard they called security!

That was back in 1994. Mike succumbed to multiple can-
cers in 2000 shortly after the publication of his magnum opus,
The Only-Begotten. I miss him terribly.

At the time I wrote *While the Eyes of the Great are Else-where* I was freshly returned to the Catholic fold. Writing a book is an arduous and lengthy task, as anyone who has made the effort can surely tell you. By the time the author writes "The End" on the final page (or as in this case, *Exeunt*) he finds himself, after months of concentrated labor amidst the concurrent conundrums that life inevitably dishes forth, a different man than he was at the outset. In rereading his manuscript he discovers that much of what he wrote months ago he would write differently now because experience has given him new insights as well as more scintillating anecdotes with which to illustrate his points. He may also find that his interests have expanded, and now wishes he could start the project all over. Hence, in a certain sense, a book is never really done. There simply comes a point when the author must leave it alone and move on to other things.

Though a number of people took interest in this tome, it remained unpublished for eleven years. Well, actually, the chapters dealing with Our Blessed Mother were extrapolated from the manuscript and published in 1995 by Catholic Treasures under the title *Of Mary There Is Never Enough*. I am pleased to say that this little booklet was well received by many Tradition-minded Catholics, enjoyed brisk sales, and underwent a second printing in hardcover in 2002. (Some of these chapters are edited slightly differently in this version.)

Meanwhile I began writing my novels featuring Fr. John Baptist, a late vocation and former homicide detective, and Martin Feeney, his arthritic and curmudgeonly gardener. To tell you the truth, I didn't think *Elsewhere* would ever see the light of day. Imagine my surprise, just a few days ago, when Stephen Frankini at Tumblar House asked me to prepare my forgotten opus for publication!

In blowing the dust off the manuscript, I have come face to face with the man I was eleven years ago, a man who had only recently come to grips with the Realities of life and who had instigated a host of changes in said life to accommodate those Realities. Some of the topics with which I struggled at the time have become part and parcel of the man I am today; but in the mean time so many other events have taken place that have propelled me into deeper areas of inquiry that I must stifle the urge to rewrite the whole book. No, this opus must stand as it did when I wrote *Exeunt*, because it addresses so

many issues that are important to the seeker who now stands
on that same threshold where I myself stood.   Perhaps, if all
goes well, a sequel will be in order *(While the Eyes of the
Great BLINKED ... ?)*—but I must not get ahead of myself.

I wrote this book, in the first place, in hopes of reaching
others of my generation who were, for various reasons, finding
their roads leading inexorably toward Rome.   Secondly, by
quoting copiously from sound sources, I hoped to point my
readers toward those books which say all this better than I ever
could.   Lastly, I wrote because I had a story to tell—mine.
The story still stands, and is indeed the foundation upon which
I continue to base my life and attempt to grow in the Faith.

To the seeker, I wish I could shout, "Here in the bosom of
the Catholic Church you will find peace and happiness!" but
alas, the Eternal City has been sacked and the smoke of confusion billows from every shattered Sanctuary.   I wish I could
say, "Here you will find good and faithful shepherds—listen
to them!" but unfortunately the clergy, with the exception of
a mere handful, have abandoned us to the winds of modernism.   The best I can do is to profess, "Here, despite the camouflage of confusion, you will find the Truth, and rest assured,
there will be Consequences!"

No, the picture isn't pretty—and it's been undergoing
considerable uglification with every passing year.   So why
would anyone in their right mind jump aboard a sinking ship?
Therein lies the tale.   Why, indeed?

As in times past, the Faith must be carried on the backs of
the laity while the shepherds are out to lunch.   Some day, we
hope, the clergy will be shamed back to holiness by the example of their flock.   That day is a long way off, considering the
condition of the sheep currently wandering around the countryside.   Some day, we pray, we'll prove ourselves worthy of a
holy and competent clergy.   Until then, we must discover the
Faith of our Fathers, educate ourselves regarding the Truths of
Catholicism, and live our Religion as though our lives depend
on it.

One aside I would like to address in this curious afterword:
my refusal to ignore the evils brought about and sustained by
the clergy.   While some try to hide certain negative facts from
the seeker lest they become disheartened or repulsed, I insist
on calling a spade a spade, and if the tool in question is a
priest, then call him I will.   The usual objection to this kind of
assertion goes something like this: "Surely all priests aren't

bad—you can't make blanket statements." To which I respond:

"In the hills above my home live many rattlesnakes. I encounter them sometimes when I go hiking. They are a 'protected species,' so it is a crime to kill them. Now it is important to bear in mind that when a rattlesnake kills its prey, its fangs often break off. For a few days, while the new fangs are growing into place, the rattlesnake is completely benign. It is therefore quite possible that any rattlesnake I may encounter on the trail is harmless ... but I never make that assumption. It is far safer to give all rattlesnakes a wide berth rather than find out the hard way. And so it is with clergy. Surely there are some who are good ... but I certainly don't assume that the one currently in the pulpit is one of them. Whether he's celebrating a Tridentine Mass or the Novus Ordo, every priest is suspect. As a group they have behaved deplorably, and as individuals they must now prove themselves. I will not carelessly risk my eternal destiny on any of them until I'm certain of their agendas. This is not unwarranted or mean-spirited anticlericalism—it is simply common sense."

By the way, I no longer work at that book store, Catholic Treasures by name. This is but one of many things that has changed in my life over the years. I do, however, with the help of my good friend, Charles A. Coulombe, lecture there once a month, discussing many important facets of the Catholic Faith to a small but loyal audience. Consider this an invitation—all are welcome!

More than ever—if my reader is curious about my spiritual status today—I am still clinging to sanity, continuing to work out my Salvation in fear and trembling. That is an effort that never ends this side of the grave. I hope this book will convince others to do likewise.

As before, I beg the prayers of anyone who derives anything worthwhile from the pages of this book.

Through Christ the King
and Mary, Queen of Heaven

—William L. Biersach
Rock Haven
August 11, 2005
The Feast of St. Clare (1253 AD)